Reading against Culture

READING *AGAINST* CULTURE

*Ideology and Narrative
in the Japanese Novel*

David Pollack

Cornell University Press

Ithaca and London

And although there may be perhaps as sensible people among the Persians or the Chinese as among ourselves, it seemed to me that the most useful would be to adapt my behavior to that of those with whom I would have to live, and that, to know which were truly their opinions, I should take notice rather of what they practiced than of what they said.

—René Descartes, *Discourse on Method*

Goa to iu
　　machi no matsuri o
shiritakeredo
　　koko wa soramitsu
　　Yamato no kuni zo.

[Sometimes I think it might be nice
　　to know more about the festivals
of someplace like faraway Goa . . .
　　But this is, after all, Japan—
　　The Land of The Rising Sun.]

—Machi Tawara, *Sarada kinenbi*

Contents

Preface

This book is addressed to the general reader of the novel in its many international guises. My hope is that it will prove useful to those interested in the relationship between literature and culture and its reflection in Japanese practice. My major concern throughout, therefore, has been to bring close readings of particular Japanese novels to bear on Western and Japanese ideas concerning that relationship. The book discusses Japanese novels already widely available in English translation, those that friends in other fields of literature have found of interest and have wanted to know more about.

I have also taken an unusual step for a specialist—one bound to incur the criticism of specialists and purists—by putting the names of the Japanese authors treated here in Western order. The names of most of these authors are already best known in that order to readers of their works in English translation (e.g., Yukio Mishima), and it is in that order that their names invariably appear on their translated works. Only Natsumé Sōseki's name is left in Japanese order, since he wrote at a time when authors were still customarily identified by pen-name (Sōseki) rather than by family name (Natsumé).

I decided on this strategy with not a few misgivings, since it can easily be construed as the sort of distortion of another culture's own practice that might undermine the credibility of my own critical position. What made Western name-order in a work such as this seem useful was finding that Chinua Achebe, having read the work of a Japan specialist, cited the important folklorist Yanagita Kunio as "Kunio," clearly believing that to be his family name.[1] I simply hoped to avoid confusion, and this seemed the most certain way to achieve that end. I inflict this perversion only on the names I think may for one reason or another turn out to be of interest to the reader of English, so that the names can be easily found elsewhere and discussed with

1. Chinua Achebe, "What Has Literature Got to Do with It?," in *Hopes and Impediments: Selected Essays* (New York: Doubleday, 1989), p. 156. After quoting a passage from Marion J. Levy of Princeton University, Achebe adds, "If Kunio was right the point made by Professor Levy is very instructive." (The folklorist's family name can be pronounced either Yanagita or, as Achebe quotes Levy, Yanagida.)

confidence. In annotated references to those authors whose work is found only in Japanese (and so I presume will be of interest only to those who read Japanese), I have left the names in Japanese order. My hope is that even if some readers are put off by this practice, more will find it helpful.

I have also resorted to one small modification in the customary system used for romanizing Japanese names, strictly for the purposes of indicating proper pronunciation where it might prove to be a problem: since I have found that the value of final *-e* is frequently misjudged, I have added an acute accent to make its pronunciation clearer, (e.g., Abé, Kanamé, Natsumé). I have retained the customary macron or long mark used to distinguish short from long vowels.

This book spans the twentieth century, which includes the Meiji (1868–1912), Taishō (1912–26), Shōwa (1926–89), and Heisei (1989–) eras. Such "reign-titles" (*nengō*)—a Chinese system used since the dawn of Japanese historiography—have been employed since the Taishō era to indicate the entire reign of a preceding emperor. Thus, after 1912 one speaks of "the Meiji emperor," meaning the emperor who reigned during the Meiji period. Before the Meiji period, however, an emperor might have used several reign-titles in succession, so that a single reign-title was not necessarily coterminous with his reign; the Kōmei emperor (1847–66) who preceded Meiji, for example, used six. A currently reigning emperor, however, is always referred to in Japan only as His Imperial Majesty (*tennō heika*), never by a name or reign-title. Although emperors do have given names (that of the Shōwa emperor, Hirohito, was used only before his accession to the throne; the royal family has no family name), their use is a purely Western practice, and after the emperor's accession to the throne his given name is never used in Japan. More detailed discussion of this rather arcane issue can be found in Chapter 10.

Some of the material in this book draws on previously published articles: "Action as Fitting Match to Knowledge: Language and Symbol in Mishima's *Kinkakuji,*" *Monumenta Nipponica* 40 (Winter 1985); "Wang Wei in Kamakura: The Structural Poetics of Mishima's *Spring Snow,*" *Harvard Journal of Asiatic Studies* 48 (December 1988); "Framing the Self: The Philosophical Dimensions of Human Nature in *Kokoro,*" *Monumenta Nipponica* 43 (Winter 1988); and "Modernism Minceur; or, Is Japan Postmodern?" *Monumenta Nipponica* 44 (Spring 1989). I thank the editors for permission to make use of them.

I am grateful to the Social Science Research Council and the U.S. and Japan Fulbright Commissions for their generous support during the writing of this book. The comments of anonymous readers for Cornell University Press were very helpful to me in revising the manuscript for publication.

DAVID POLLACK

Rochester, New York

Introduction
Reading against Culture

I was curious to see whether this man, who had come out equipped with moral ideas of some sort, would climb to the top after all and how he would set about his work when there.

—Joseph Conrad, *Heart of Darkness*

This book is about "reading against culture" in at least two senses of that ambiguous phrase. In the first and more ordinary sense, it means that we read (or write) not in a vacuum but rather against the background of what we already know and believe, both as lived and as learned experience, about our own and other cultures. Our every Africa, before it learned to shout back loudly enough to make us hear its own voices, first had its Rider Haggard, our every Orient its Gérard de Nerval, our every India its Rudyard Kipling, and later their Hemingways, Durrells, and Scotts. Eventually we learned to balance the exoticizing claims of the Westerner, claims already inherent in that suggestive word "novel," against a prosaic indigenous demand to be *ordinary*. Such a balancing, which began to happen only within the last century, is now the subject of various so-called postcolonial and subaltern studies. But the indigenous voice has had and will continue to have to contend for a long time against the enthusiastic Western chorus that persists in trying to transmogrify all of Egypt into Verdi's *Aïda*, all of India into Bizet's *Pearl Fishers*. Our picture of Japan too is in large part a pastiche of (among many other things) colorful and exotic dramas, bloody revenges, delicate emotions, inscrutable suicides: a whole confusing realm of the senses that has little coherence at all until caught against the backdrop of, say, *Madama Butterfly* or *The Mikado*. It is *there*, against these exotic backdrops, for better or for worse, that we have ended up making sense of it. The many vectors of interpretation this study will have to account for, then, include those polarities of culture which Homi Bhabha summarizes as "the *heimlich* pleasures of the hearth, the *unheimlich* terror of the space or race of the Other; the comfort of social belonging, the hidden injuries of class; the customs of taste, the powers of political affiliation; the sense of social order, the sensibility of sexuality; the blindness of bureaucracy, the strait insight of institutions; the quality of justice, the common sense of injustice; the *langue* of the law and the *parole* of the people.[1]

What these polarities affirm is that culture (assuming for the moment that such a concept can be defined) deploys both a transitive and an intransitive voice: constructed in part of literary and other aesthetic productions, it simultaneously serves as the shaping environment within which further production is carried on. The idea of culture may thus fairly be called a *mise-en-abîme*, an endless series of self-reflecting regressions (I treat it later in this sense as a hall of mirrors), attempting to naturalize itself to those within and without as something that, as Clifford Geertz puts it, is "turtles all the way down."[2] It is this mythologizing function of the idea of culture that I propose to read *against*, to resist, and this is the second sense of what I mean by "reading against culture." While it is only human to enjoy magic tricks, it is equally human to want to know just where all those rabbits (or turtles) are coming from.

In his public lecture upon accepting the Nobel Prize for Literature in 1968, the novelist Yasunari Kawabata admirably posited the Japanese version of culture in a narrative we might call "cherry blossoms all the way down": "Saigyō frequently came and talked of poetry. His own view of poetry, he said, was far from the ordinary. Cherry blossoms, the cuckoo, the moon, snow: confronted with all the varied forms of nature, his eyes and ears were filled with emptiness."[3] This passage captures as well as any other the tone of his oddly rambling essay, everywhere full of "cherry blossoms, the cuckoo, the moon, snow"—and of course of "emptiness." I do not put it like this because I dislike Kawabata's work; to the contrary, I find it profoundly beautiful, viewed from either side of the cultural abyss. But what seem the most important questions are what Kawabata thinks he is doing when he retails this narrative, and what the Japanese think they are doing when they buy into it.

One indicator of the retailed nature of the narrative is the mercantile value it immediately came to possess. With the help of Dentsū, the world's largest advertising agency, the then Japan National Railways (since privatized) adopted the title of Kawabata's published Nobel Prize acceptance speech,

1. Homi Bhabha, ed. *Nation and Narration* (London: Routledge, 1990), p. 2.
2. Clifford Geertz, "Thick Description: Toward an Interpretive Theory of Culture," in *The Interpretation of Cultures* (New York: Basic Books, 1973), pp. 28–29.
3. Yasunari Kawabata, *Utsukushii Nihon no watakushi; Japan the Beautiful and Myself* (bilingual ed.), trans. Edward Seidensticker (Tokyo: Kodansha International, 1969), p. 42; Kawabata is quoting here from the biography of the monk-poet Myōe written by his disciple Kikai.

"Japan the Beautiful and Myself," as the central image and slogan for a 1970 campaign urging the public to "Discover Japan."[4] For several years this command was to be seen everywhere on gorgeous posters of photogenic locales which, if one knew them, were clearly as much parts of the myth as the phrase, the idea, the speech, the language. "Somewhere out there," beguiled one ad, "there are still earth-walled villages." Perhaps there were, but they were more states of mind than fact, the imaginary "hometowns" (*furusato*) of an imagined past promised to travelers on the Japanese National Railways as their natural destinations in life's journey. It never seemed the least bit incongruous that the lyrical "journey of wandering" (*hyōhaku no tabi*), a part of the national mythology at least since the poet Bashō's *Narrow Roads to the Far North* three hundred years earlier, was now assumed to be best achieved by means of rail transport; by the time of the Bashō tricentennial in 1989, literal locomotion was simply taken for granted.

One is significantly pulled back into the first or *constructive* sense of "reading against (the background of) culture," however, when one realizes that in Japan, travel has *always* been understood to be more a state of mind than a fact.[5] It was one's own fault if one arrived at the tranquil seaside fishing village picturesquely advertised in the National Railways poster only to find tour buses disgorging hordes of tourists, cement factories howling day and night, a dreary landscape of asphalt parking lots, and noisy inns filled with drunken mah-jongg players and serving bad food. After all, who in his right mind would really want to isolate himself in a lonely village?[6] Most of the villagers themselves had long since deserted such miserable places to take up modern lives in the big city. It is true: there are whole villages, looking exactly

4. The Japanese title of Kawabata's speech, *Utsukushii Nihon no watakushi*, a poetically ambiguous and untranslatable phrase whose syntax indicates something like "The I of a Beautiful Japan" or even "The Beautiful Japanese Self," was changed for the purposes of the Dentsū Corporation's public relations campaign (and Seidensticker's translation) to *Utsukushii Nihon no watakushi*, "Beautiful Japan and Myself." The campaign is examined in detail by Marilyn Ivy in "Discourses of the Vanishing in Contemporary Japan" (Ph.D. diss., Cornell University, 1988), pp. 33–86; see esp. p. 54.

5. The great Japanese paradigm is Matsuo Bashō's *Narrow Roads to the Far North* (*Oku no hosomichi*, 1698; see Earl Miner, *Japanese Poetic Diaries* [Berkeley: University of California Press, 1976], pp. 39–47), in which topography figures almost entirely as a literary and religious *topos*, and every notion we have of "fact" is abandoned.

6. See Yukio Mishima's untranslated 1960 essay "Puraibashii" (Privacy; significantly, there exists no native word for the idea), in *Mishima Yukio zenshū* (hereafter *MZ*), vol. 30 (Tokyo: Shinchōsha, 1975), pp. 19–22. The word, Mishima says, indicates a *foreign* concept that conceals within itself "the terrible loneliness of the 'private room.'" We alienated modern Japanese urbanites must go back to these noisy little villages, he writes,—he knows from his own experiences, hilariously recounted, that they are not quiet—to relearn the joys of living *publicly* and so communally again. Not a little ironically, Mishima places the blame for the destruction of what he calls "Japan's old-fashioned communal life between paper walls" squarely on the advent of "that foreign monstrosity, the transistor radio."

as they must have looked two hundred years ago, still lying deserted in inaccessible mountain reaches.

Another example of this sort of willful mystification of culture can be seen in a recent discussion between the Japanese-Anglo novelist Kazuo Ishiguro and Kenzaburō Ōe (whose work I treat later in this book). After venting his customary spleen against Yukio Mishima, who he knows is much better known than himself in the West, as someone who was not "authentically Japanese" (and leaving the reader with little doubt as to who *is*), Ōe proceeds to hail Ishiguro's work as affording foreigners a magnificent opportunity to see "us Japanese" as we *really* are—not, that is, as "military and economic invaders" but as "a quiet and peaceful people who produce lovely ink-paintings of blossoms."[7] Even the Westerner whose familiarity with Japan is limited to Ruth Benedict's problematic work *The Chrysanthemum and the Sword* (1946) knows enough by now to look for the warrior when confronted with an insistence on the peaceful artist alone. There is no doubt a hard kernel of truth in the cultural perception the Japanese hold of themselves as a people shaped, as the seventeenth-century phrase already had it, by "both the literary *and* the military arts" (*bunbu ryōdō*). Relentless emphasis on the first only generates a strong suspicion that there must be a sword in there somewhere. For all Ōe's political awareness and active opposition to belligerence, he sometimes seems, in his resolve to be recognized as an authentic victim, to wish simply to forget the sword out of existence.[8]

It is part of my purpose, then, on the one hand, to explore some of the particular ways in which Japanese authors have attempted to weave themselves into seamless constructions of culture and, on the other, to point out how these constructions have served as the ready-made "con-text," that "weaving together" within which their work has both taken and been given form. Certainly the National Railways campaign was not Kawabata's doing,

7. Kenzaburō Ōe, "Nijusseiki e mukete: Sakka no yakuwari" (Toward the twentieth century: The role of the writer"), *Kokusai Kōryū* 14 (June 1990): 103. It is interesting that this passage is deleted in the Japan Foundation's official English transcription of the discussion ("The Novelist in Today's World: A Conversation between Kazuo Ishiguro and Ōe Kenzaburō," *Japan Foundation Newsletter* 17 (March 1990): 10.

8. Throughout this study I attempt to compensate for the persistent Japanese view of themselves since World War II as victims (a view known in Japan as *higaisha ishiki*) with their neighbors' equally persistent view of the Japanese as victimizers (*kagaisha ishiki*)—a view that has no part in Japan's modern ideology. Yukio Mishima wrote in his "Bunka bōei ron" (On the defense of culture), *MZ*, 33:367, that wishing the sword out of existence was not merely the heartfelt wish of a war-weary people but rather an act of official ideology: "After the war, the bureaucrats of the Ministry of Culture and the Foreign Ministry gave us a clear answer to the question 'What is Japanese culture?' This answer, following the policies of the Occupation, was to sever the vicious circle of *The Chrysanthemum and the Sword*. The gentle culture of a peace-loving, flower-arranging, tea-ceremony-performing people could not be a menacing one."

but his participation was required to breathe life into it (to use the literal meaning of "conspire"), and the fact that he was still alive at the time only makes his complicity more explicit (he committed suicide two years later). It was entirely in character for Kawabata to want the Japanese to know more about the "beautiful Japanese selves" he believed they had lost sight of since the war.

Inherent in my second purpose, as the reader can see, is a desire to resist the blandishments of the smooth reading that context is always so helpfully eager to provide, to try to read *against* the allurements, persuasions, entice-ments, wheedlings, coaxings, beguilements, and seductions of a culture that would have us accept it blindly and unquestioningly as human, as natural, as the only reality. At the same time, therefore, that we must and can accept certain cultural essentializations (dream versus reality, spiritual presence versus material illusion, travel as a state of mind, the moral purity of the defeated) as others' useful, necessary, often attractive, and even captivatingly mysterious ways of locating themselves in the world, we must also learn to resist the roles these cultural discourses play as self-serving and deceptive. I say this not to be perverse but for what I consider a very important reason: as soon as we situate ourselves in the world by means of essentialized ideas of culture, we also situate the Other in relation to those essentializations. This situating, furthermore, is never simply a neutral process of differentiation or individuation: it always has as well a partisan agenda of *invidiation*—of prej-udice, of denial, of withholding—and so has obvious and profound implica-tions for the way we relate to others and they to us. This book takes as a moral principle the necessity of always standing simultaneously inside and outside culture, both one's own and that of the Other, of being able to *accept* and simultaneously to *resist* culture's distinctive maneuver of including the one always at the price of excluding the other.

These two aspects together, then, are what I mean by "reading against culture." The most obvious weakness of this inherently ambiguous dialecti-cal approach is that in the process I may appear to be essentializing not only Japanese culture but my own as well, perhaps even gratuitously denigrating both. Such an approach, however, seems to me the only way neither to exalt nor to deprecate *either* cultural position. It represents an attempt to indicate something of the complex nature of those arrangements by which we go about trying to account for ourselves in a world full of others who are not only unreceptive to our particular project but are also trying to do exactly the same thing. I have tried, however, always to bear in mind the cautionary example of Kurtz's report, in *Heart of Darkness*, to the International Society for the Suppression of Savage Customs, which begins with the benevolent desire to "'exert a power for good practically unbounded' etc. etc.," but ends in what is probably literature's most horrifying postscript: "Exterminate all the brutes!"[9]

I set the stage with an account of how two very different Western writers, Rudyard Kipling and Roland Barthes, have engaged in "reading" Japan, an account that is in many respects paradigmatic for the chapters that follow. I then turn to the successive exploration of four major problems involved in "reading against culture," arranged in a progression that reflects the chronology of an evolving problematic with regard to Japan in particular (though the same problems seem important to the process of reading against any culture): problems of (1) the individual self, (2) ideology and its particular articulations, (3) the novel as a mode of representation, and (4) the concept of culture. Inasmuch as each of these problems has both positive or constructive as well as negative or confining heuristic value, each can be regarded as generative precisely in the way in which it imposes significant restrictions on the acts of writing and reading. Such concepts are of course so intricately intertwined that they can only artificially be prised apart for the purpose of analysis, and they must eventually be resynthesized, for example by the tracing of some of their many interconnections. One way of reintegrating them here is to treat them as different aspects of the larger problem that constitutes the purpose of this book: reading against culture.

Part I concerns the idea of the individual self that played such an important part in the process of Japan's modernization—not because that process has arrived or ever will arrive at an endpoint (any more than it has elsewhere), but because it occasioned significant and even traumatic changes that were to have important consequences. The works especially of Natsumé Sōseki and Jun'ichirō Tanizaki explore the problematic psychopathologies of a new kind of social being, drawing together new problems of a tentative individual identity and those of the nation as a whole within that aspect of emergent literatures that Fredric Jameson has termed "national allegory."

Part II focuses on the question of ideology, especially on the way it is both essentialized and articulated by means of two particular discourses, aesthetics and science. Aesthetics is concerned with those forms by means of which the web of culture (which I elaborate *as* ideology) is expressed and made knowable. I have therefore chosen to examine as twin aspects of this proposition the ideology of expression (that is, aesthetics) in the work of Yasunari Kawabata, and the ideology of knowledge (that is, science) in that of Kōbō Abé. These mediating structures by means of which we understand our world are the most in need of interrogation precisely because they propose

9. Joseph Conrad, *Heart of Darkness*, in *Great Short Works of Joseph Conrad*, ed. Jerry Allen, (New York: Harper & Row, 1967), p. 262.

themselves as the least problematic: they are after all our very *means* of feeling and knowing.

Part III is concerned with Yukio Mishima's unique endeavor to overcome what he took to be the central and fatal paradox of the very idea of the "modern Japanese novel." Both for himself and for Japan, that paradox is inherent in the representational adequacy of that narrative form we know as the novel. Along with Western technology in general, the novel was adopted early in Japan's period of modernization as an essential tool for the representation of the authentically modern native story. The problem lay in its intrinsic inability to represent that story in any terms but those of fundamentally alien narrative. This problem is so central to the work of Mishima, and so self-contained there, that I have felt it possible to limit my illustration of it to the study of his final tetralogy.

Part IV examines the idea of culture as a concept of confinement, in specific contrast to the idea of culture as expressive essentialism. The novels of Kenzaburō Ōe and Takeshi Kaikō, particularly involved with problems of culture and reading, are characterized in large part by their attempts to write against culture. This they do not only in the sense of explicitly recognizing that those before them wrote more unselfconsciously within it, or even for it, but also in the sense of clearly coming to a point, never before reached, where their fictional horizons can no longer continue to be limited by that culture alone, into which they have long been entirely inscribed, as a confining concept either of inclusion or exclusion. In these authors' respective attempts to write themselves out of culture, I contrast what I perceive to be Ōe's sometimes pretentious failures and Kaikō's more unassuming successes in writing not only against Western culture (which is of course relatively easy to do) but, more important, against and even out of their own (which is exceedingly difficult).

It is altogether too easy to try to interpret another culture by expecting it to conform or, more likely, to fail to conform to our own ambitions and fears. Since on an everyday individual basis we undeniably relegate even familiar others to the role of mere correlatives of our own problematic selves, it is little wonder that we should do exactly the same to those who seem truly different. And although Japanese seem more truly different to many Americans than we do to one another, this assumption may turn out to be useless as anything more than a point of entry into the convoluted problems of identity that are examined here.

Paul Theroux's *Mosquito Coast* parodies the inevitability of cultural misunderstanding in a "first encounter" scene lampooning the stereotyped anthropological cliché of the white man's confrontation with what he wants to believe is an uncorrupted native innocence which will justify his own existence but which, sadly, always turns out to be merely a projection onto the Other of his own particular brand of insanity. Father and children have spent days dragging an enormous and improbable block of ice (which we can understand as literally representing the white man's burden) through the mountains and jungles of central Honduras for the express purpose of finding some natives to edify and astound with it. After many grueling days of this they finally encounter a few natives, and the meeting is staged as a burlesque of the anthropologist's ritual of cultural first encounter. Hacking a piece of ice from the rapidly melting block, Father hands it to the "Gowdy" (chief):

> Father was still winking at us as he spoke to the old man, the Gowdy. "What's the verdict?"
>
> "Good morning to you, sah. I am well, thank you. Where are you garng. I am garng to the bushes." The Gowdy's wire glasses had been knocked crooked by the pushing people. "Today is Monday, Tuesday, Wednesday. Thank you, that is a good lesson."
>
> He bobbled the ice as he spoke.
>
> "Hasn't the slightest idea," Father said to us.
>
> The ice was melting in the old man's hand. Water ran down his arm, leaving dirt streaks on his skin. It dripped from the knob at his elbow.
>
> "Completely in the dark," Father said. He put his arm around the old man's shoulders and gave him a wide smile.
>
> The Gowdy shivered.
>
> "What's that?" Father said, and pointed.
>
> "Hice," the Gowdy said.
>
> "*Jesus Christ Almighty!*" Father roared, and gave the Gowdy a shove, nearly knocking the old man over.
>
> But no sooner had he spoken than every one of the people, including the Gowdy, dropped to his knees. . . . "*Ah Fadder wart neven hello bead name—*"[10]

The missionaries, as always, have gotten there first; and native innocence, as ever, turns out to have been already corrupted. The Theroux episode is reminiscent of Claude Lévi-Strauss's famous "Writing Lesson" among the Nambikwara Indians recorded in *Tristes Tropiques*, a scene whose author, Jacques Derrida discovers, is up to something quite different from what Lévi-Strauss himself supposed: "The critique of ethnocentrism," reports Derrida, " . . . has most often the sole function of constituting the other as a model of original and natural goodness, of accusing and humiliating oneself,

10. Paul Theroux, *The Mosquito Coast* (Boston: Houghton Mifflin, 1982), pp. 187–88. Quoted by permission of the publisher.

of exhibiting its being-unacceptable in an anti-ethnocentric mirror."[11] Lévi-Strauss himself wrote that he had been nostalgically "looking for a society reduced to its simplest expression"; what he found instead was what James Clifford has called "ethnography's disappearing object"—that phantom construction which, exactly like the impossible block of ice dragged through the jungle, always seems to melt away whenever the cultural investigator arrives in hot pursuit of the Other.[12]

Other scholarship has gone on to call into question the nature of the suspiciously uniform "I" that presumes to be asking such nosy questions about Others. According to Vincent Crapanzano, for example, in Clifford Geertz's celebrated essay "Deep Play: Notes on a Balinese Cockfight" it is possible to isolate a sequence of four distinct chronological narrative viewpoints, each of which depends on what the cultural investigator is trying to accomplish.[13] The first "I" of Geertz's essay comprises the well-funded white anthropologist and his wife and is intended to win over the reader to the anthropologist's side; the next, consisting of the anthropologist and the Balinese but no wife, now has pretensions to scientific objectivity; the third, the anthropologist alone (now with neither wife *nor* Balinese), spotlights the brilliant solo interpreter of culture; and by the end, the anthropologist has tactfully withdrawn from the picture entirely to leave the reader ("you") to commune alone with High Culture. In the end, Geertz and we appear to have stepped out together for a chat, leaving the "disappearing object," now entirely known and accounted for, to be absorbed completely into the higher cultural realm of such superior works as *King Lear* and *Crime and Punishment*.

In a work such as this one, such groupings and disappearances are probably inevitable. Once forewarned, the reader ("you") should have no trouble deciding when the author has stepped out for a theoretical beer, leaving the Japanese (and perhaps "you" as well) to fend for themselves; or, conversely, when he is proposing that "we" gang up against "them"; or again, when he and you have gotten together in a huddle and seem to have forgotten "them" completely. After all, these virtual combinations are inherent in the very nature of the hall of mirrors that is proposed in Chapter 9 as a metaphor for

11. Jacques Derrida, *Of Grammatology*, trans. Gayatri Chakravorty Spivak (Baltimore: Johns Hopkins University Press, 1976), p. 114.

12. James Clifford, "On Ethnographic Allegory," in *Writing Culture: The Poetics and Politics of Ethnography*, ed. James Clifford and George E. Marcus, (Berkeley: University of California Press, 1986), p. 112; Claude Lévi-Strauss, *Tristes Tropiques*, trans. John and Doreen Weightman (New York: Pocket Books, 1977), pp. 331–43.

13. Vincent Crapanzano, "Hermes' Dilemma: The Masking of Subversion in Ethnographic Description," in Clifford and Marcus, *Writing Culture*, pp. 68–76. It is also clear that all during his brilliant performance Geertz understands that the reader is aware of his much-praised writing style as another master voice hovering transcendentally over all the rest; see Geertz, *The Interpretation of Cultures* (New York: Basic Books, 1973), pp. 412–53.

culture; and since there are nothing but reflections everywhere and no obviously privileged point of view, we shall just have to take notice of the inevitable collisions and false leads as we examine what Michel Foucault has called "the exotic charm of another system of thought" which always involves "the limitation of our own, the stark impossibility of thinking *that*."[14]

To read against culture, especially to attempt to be both privileged insider and critical outsider—and from two points of view at once—is no easy trick. I cannot pretend to have always succeeded, any more than have the authors examined here. Perhaps the task is impossible. As Christopher Miller has written of his approach to the European construction of Africa:

> The goal of breaking through the nets of Western criticism, of reading African literature in a nonethnocentric, nonprojective fashion, will remain both indisputably desirable and ultimately unattainable. No matter how many languages I learn or ethnologies I study, I cannot make myself into an African. The Western scholar's claim to mastery of things African, albeit motivated by xenophilia rather than xenophobia, risks subjugation of the object to a new set of Western models.[15]

On the other hand, notes Miller (who is neither African nor African-American), neither does the fact of being biologically or culturally African necessarily guarantee or permit any sort of purely authentic "African" reading.

Perhaps the most meaningful ethical framework for my book is provided by Catharine R. Stimpson's call for the feminist theoretical stance she terms "heterogeneity." Among other issues this stance emphasizes the examination of the *actualities* of power, in contrast to the false assumption of universal powerlessness, and a "fidelity to the complexity" of women's lives and attention to the real points of difference among them that are blurred by the "falsely universal." Only gestures such as these, she writes, have the possibility of dismantling the "monolithic thinking" that thrives on a simplistic recourse to the facile antinomy of woman/man dualisms: "Heterogeneity is the marking of differences among women, for themselves and as a way of recognizing and living generously with all but homicidal difference/s—

14. Michel Foucault, *The Order of Things* (New York: Vintage Books, 1973), p. xv.
15. Christopher Miller, "Theories of Africans: The Question of Literary Anthropology," *Critical Inquiry* 13 (Autumn 1986): p. 121. I am not sure that we can or should even try to be "nonprojective"; it may be that we can only try to take our projected biases into account before, during, and after reading. My own position is one neither of xenophobia nor of xenophilia: there are probably just as many things I like and dislike about my own culture as about Japan's, though I know I would not like to live in Japan permanently, for reasons that will become clear in the Conclusion. I live *here* largely for the same reasons that most of us do, but that is no excuse not to examine the fact.

among tongues and texts; tribes and territories; totems and taboos."[16] "Recognizing and living generously" with difference is perhaps the hardest thing we shall ever be asked to do. I believe it is among the most powerful promises of such a critique to suggest a way back from the brink of the automatic assumption that all difference *is* in the final analysis necessarily "homicidal," and to propose that only by careful attention to and appreciation of modes of difference will we be able to deterritorialize the contentious ground that we all, ourselves and our others, stand on and must finally learn to share.

16. Catharine R. Stimpson, "Woolf's Room, Our Project: The Building of Feminist Criticism," in *The Future of Literary Theory*, ed. Ralph Cohen (New York: Routledge, 1990), p. 143.

A Paradigm
Kipling and Barthes in the
Empire of Signs

The dawn was once in the Orient, and its light marched southward, and now issues from the Occident. France, it is true, by her central position in the civilized world, seems called to gather all the notions and all the poetries around her and to give them back to other people marvelously worked and fashioned.

—Baudelaire, "De l'idée moderne du progrès appliquée aux beaux-arts"

"The whole of Japan is a pure invention. There is no such country, there are no such people. . . . The Japanese people are . . . simply a mode of style, an exquisite fancy of art," writes Oscar Wilde in his 1889 essay "The Decay of Lying."[1] "Mister Oscar Wilde of *The Nineteenth Century* is a long-toothed liar!" retorts Rudyard Kipling in a letter of the same year, written from Japan and published in the Allahabad *Pioneer*.[2] Kipling has only just landed in Nagasaki, but already he knows that there *is* a Japan, which he too declares to be a place of exotic beauty and exquisite art. Unfortunately, however, as he continues at some length, Japan is ruining her exquisiteness by learning to tinker with Western politics, manners, and dress. This is where the views of the two observers part company. Wilde, having had the cleverness (or good fortune) to stay at home in England, can insist humorously on the sole reality of the Englishman's vision of "Japan" as an artistic representation; Kipling, who is traveling around the world on doctor's orders for his health and would "rather be smelling the blossoms and pinching the pretty girls," finds himself instead forced to ride on irritatingly well-run Japanese trains.

Everywhere in Kipling's record of his "conversations" with a fictional

1. From "The Decay of Lying," *Nineteenth Century*, January 1889, in *The Complete Works of Oscar Wilde* (London: Collins, 1966), p. 988.
2. Published July 30, 1889, reproduced in *Kipling's Japan: Collected Writings*, ed. Hugh Cortazzi and George Webb (London: Athlone Press, 1988), p. 35. Further references to Kipling on Japan cite page numbers from this edition.

traveling companion whom he calls "the Professor," there surfaces an ironic awareness of his own uncomfortable relation to this new-found Eden:

> "It would pay us to establish an international suzerainty over Japan to take away any fear of invasion or annexation, and pay the country as much as ever it chose, on condition that it simply sat still and went on making beautiful things while our men learned. It would pay us to put the whole Empire in a glass case and mark it, *Hors Concours*, Exhibit A."
> "Hmmm," said I. "Who's us?"
> "Oh, we generally—the *sahibs* all the world over." [P. 56]

Having lived in India all of his adult life—he was only twenty-six when he wrote this—Kipling knows well enough that Japan is a European invention no more "merely" than (or perhaps just as much as) is India. But he is apparently discomfited to find that Japan, unaccountably, is not willing to permit itself to be thought of as a European responsibility; for some incomprehensible reason it refuses to play the White Man's Game Kipling so admirably portrayed in *Kim*. Kipling's letters from Japan are informed with both nostalgic regret and a present and palpable unease over his discovery that it is already too late to put this delicate, problematic country safely *hors concours* under Europe's benevolent, protective bell jar.

Kipling admires everything about Japan's idyllic and imaginary past. But the modern Japanese character he does not like at all, and it occurs to him that what he does not like about it is precisely the way the Japanese have somehow managed to turn the tables on the sahib:

> Chance had brought me opposite the office of a newspaper, and I ran in demanding an editor. He came—the editor of the *Tokyo Public Opinion*, a young man in a black frock-coat. There are not many editors in other parts of the world who would offer you tea and a cigarette ere beginning a conversation. My friend had but little English. His paper, though the name was printed in English, was Japanese. But he knew his business. Almost before I had explained my errand, which was the pursuit of miscellaneous information, he began: "You are English? How you think now the American Revision Treaty?" Out came a note-book and I sweated cold. It was not in the bargain that he should interview *me*. [P. 170]

This brief encounter, rife with contradiction, unfolds like the account of a one-sided judo match. The Englishman superciliously runs in "demanding" an editor, only to be confronted by someone whose Western dress does not seem to admit of demands. Caught off balance, Kipling is then disarmed by unexpected (for which we should no doubt read "devious Oriental") courtesies; noblesse oblige is, after all, supposed to be the role of the superior! Despite a weak thrust of scorn at his interlocutor's "little English" (there is nothing that so undermines a sense of superiority as having to converse with the inferior foreigner in one's own language), Kipling finds himself pinned by an unexpectedly direct assault upon the most politically sensitive issue of the day: the long-proposed revision, led by the United States, of the infamous Unequal Treaties giving foreigners extraterritorial rights in Japan. Floored now, all he can do is squirm, temporizing with the only weapon left to him, his native ability to equivocate in his own language: "I Gladstoned about the matter with the longest words I could," he ends, more than a little pathetically.

This is neither the first nor the last time that something in Japan has gone awry—has, as Kipling phrases it, "taken a distinctly Oriental turn" (p. 213). Even as he sneers at some amateurishly unimposing army maneuvers, he admits presciently that with a little training these people "ought to be first-class enemies" (p. 166). His gallant attempts at scorn and ridicule finally ring hollow: "Good gracious!" he exclaims. "Here is Japan going to run its own civilization without learning a language in which you can say Damn satisfactorily. I must inquire into this" (p. 169). With a bit more perseverance he might even discover that the Japanese language has managed to compensate nicely for its deficiency in English expletives.

His every jab at the silliness of Japanese politics only succeeds in bringing home to him all too clearly the silliness of Britain's. Having utterly failed to convey his derision toward Japan's new Constitution of 1889 or to impress the Japanese newspaperman with the brilliance of Britain's successes in India, Kipling finds himself without the energy to parry the editor's final laconic but telling thrust:

"But you have a Constitution in India?"
"I am afraid we have not."
"Ah!" [P. 172]

On another occasion, a representative of the Japanese Ministry of Education undertakes to grill Kipling about British educational policies in India, "and in a quarter of an hour got from me the very little that I knew about primary schools, higher education, and the value of an M.A. degree. He knew exactly what he wanted to ask, and only dropped me when the tooth of Desire had picked clean the bone of Ignorance" (p. 192).

Considering Kipling's lack of success among the Japanese intelligentsia, perhaps it was just as well that he was not yet famous, as he would be on his next visit to Japan in 1892—though even then, only among his fellow Westerners. Unlike Roland Barthes nearly a century later, Kipling is never lionized, feted, scheduled, or otherwise insulated from direct contact with *otherness*, that special "smell" of the Orient he identifies as compounded of part mystery and part human dung. Even when he is dined by the Tokyo Club on his return trip of 1892, every one of the Japanese guests invited turns out to have had more pressing business elsewhere.

Unlike Barthes, too, Kipling knows that he comes to Japan not as a blank slate, a *tabula rasa*, but with the profoundly ironic awareness of the colonial sahib whose most cherished principles the all-too-intelligent native insists on misinterpreting as the obvious source of so much European bloodshed (p. 171). Whatever Japan does with Western things may seem in Kipling's eyes a parody, but he is aware that nothing points up quite so viciously as a good parody the absurdity of the original. Even when he is traveling outside India, it is easy to agree with V. S. Naipaul's summary evaluation of him: "No writer was more honest or accurate; no writer was more revealing of himself and his society."[3]

Kipling gets close to the heart of the issue in a passage in which the mysterious difference between the "unsmiling Chinamen" in Nagasaki and their Japanese brethren seems to boil down to a particular sort of "look." "I do not like Chinamen," he writes:

They stand high above the crowd and they swagger, unconsciously parting the crowd before them as an Englishman parts the crowd in a native city. There was something familiar in their faces which I could not understand, though it was familiar enough.

"The Chinaman's a native, 'Fessor," I said. "That's the look on a native's face, *but the Japanese isn't a native, and he isn't a sahib either. What is it?*" The Professor considered the surging street for a while.

"The Chinaman's an old man when he's young, just as a native is; but the Japanese is a child all his life. Think how grown-up people look upon children. That's the look that's puzzling you."

I dare not say that the Professor is right, but to my eyes it seemed he spoke sooth. As the knowledge of good and evil sets its mark upon the face of a grown man of our people, so something I did not understand had marked the faces of the Chinamen. They had no kinship with the crowd beyond that which a man has to children.

"They [the Chinese] are the superior race," said the Professor ethnologically.

"They can't be. They don't know how to enjoy life," I answered immorally.

"And anyway, their art isn't human."

"What does it matter?" said the Professor. "Here's a shop full of the wrecks of

3. V. S. Naipaul, *An Area of Darkness* (New York: Vintage Books, 1964), p. 201.

old Japan. Let's go in and look." We went in, but I want somebody to solve the Chinese question for me. It's too large to handle alone. [Pp. 54–55; emphasis added][4]

Kipling's letters make much of the delicately "human" arts of the Japanese, which he contrasts with the monumental "inhuman" arts of the Chinese. And although the Japanese seem always to be playing and picnicking, they also seem at the same time to be "running eternally for ten cents an hour" in front of his rickshaw while he leisurely "studies Japan," or delicately weeding their already immaculate rice paddies before dawn apparently just for the aesthetic joy of it. It is the irony of his discomfort with the Chinese, "unconsciously parting the crowd before them *as an Englishman parts the crowd in a native city*," that brings him to the most perplexing problem of all: it has been long settled to the satisfaction of the British in their Chinese concessions that the Chinaman is definitely a "native," and here he is merely mimicking his betters. But what then is one to make of the Japanese, who seems neither native nor sahib—or perhaps somehow both? It is revealing that Kipling should identify this in the end as his "Chinese problem" when his perplexity is clearly with the Japanese. There seems to be something too uncomfortable to be faced squarely here, a discomfort easily displaced onto that other problem which the British had long since managed to resolve to their own satisfaction.[5]

The preceding observations have taken us in the direction of the post-colonialist analysis in which the artistic products of Europe and America—primarily art and literature and their supporting critical practices—are considered aspects of a much larger complex that continues older hegemonic

4. For a complementary view from the "Chinese" side of the issue (and note the problem of who is speaking for whom here), the reader might consider the following snatch of dialogue from one of Earl Derr Biggers's Charlie Chan novels, *The House without a Key* (New York: Grosset & Dunlap, 1925), p. 59:

"Waiter," [Chan] said, "Be kind enough to summon the proprietor of this establishment." The proprietor, a suave little Japanese man, came gliding. He bowed from the waist.
"Is it that you serve here insanitary food?" inquired Chan.
"Please deign to state your complaint," said the Jap.
"This piece of pie is covered with finger-marks," rebuked Chan. "The sight is most disgusting. Kindly remove it and bring me a more hygienic sector."
The Japanese man picked up the offending pastry and carried it away.
"Japanese," remarked Chan, spreading his hands in an eloquent gesture.

5. An entry in Natsumé Sōseki's diary dated Friday, March 15, 1901, written during his two-year stay in England, bears on the same problem from the other side: "We Japanese hate being called Chinese, but the Chinese are by far the more honorable race, even though at present they have fallen upon hard times. I would think it more honorable to be called a Chinese than a Japanese" (*Sōseki bungaku senshū*) ed., Ara Masatō, [Tokyo: Shūeisha, 1974], 11:174).

and imperialistic practices of expropriation. In this view, European civilization is understood as practicing a sort of cannibalistic patriarchalism that feeds and swells on its own images of others.

In response to such reproaches, the academy now tries (not without resistance) to include at least some examples of the work of underrepresented, minority, and otherwise marginalized peoples (collectively termed "subalterns" by some) in its institutionalized canon of "world literature"—though when this is done programmatically and unreflectively, it perhaps only ensures their more secure marginalization. To read a light and seductive work such as Roland Barthes's *Empire of Signs* is in a sense to be able to congratulate ourselves on the correctness of our cosmopolitan outlook.[6] Barthes is after all theoretically chic; and Japan, if not exactly the Third World culture Kenzaburō Ōe appears to consider it, is also much in vogue. As an exotic still beyond the purview of most literature courses,[7] the new Japanese version of "Orientalness" can now be updated as compounded in equal parts of great wealth, malign mystery, and grimy factory smoke, exactly the atmosphere evoked in Ridley Scott's film *Black Rain*.[8] And it is quite possible that some are prepared, on the strength of the validation of Barthes's prestigious pronouncements, to countenance Japan as a valid subject for critical scrutiny, if only briefly—fond of Japanese brevity, Barthes writes a brief book about Japan. If Japan has lately announced itself to be the very paradigm of the postmodern, alternating dizzyingly between utopia and dystopia, this only demonstrates, as Barthes understands, how little real it really is.

Far from the utopia that Kipling had hoped to find, what Barthes was apparently expecting to discover was something like the "heterotopia" Michel Foucault had described four years earlier in an allusion to Jorge Luis Borges's "Chinese encyclopedia." "Heterotopias are disturbing," writes Foucault, "probably because they secretly undermine language, because they make it impossible to name this *and* that, because they shatter or tangle common names, because they destroy 'syntax' in advance."[9] Within the heterotopic function, however, lies a profound problem. For Barthes, Japan

6. Roland Barthes, *The Empire of Signs* (*L'empire des signes*, 1970), trans. Richard Howard (New York: Hill & Wang, 1982). Page references cite this edition.

7. However, the famous eleventh-century Japanese work *The Tale of Genji* may become the Modern Language Association's first non-Western title in its Approaches to Teaching series.

8. Two films with this title appeared in 1989; the other is Imamura Shōhei's cinematic version of Masuji Ibuse's novel *Black Rain*, advertised in Japan as "the *real Black Rain*." Scott's film was universally panned in Japan as yet another unwelcome addition to the "Japan-bashing" trend, thus sadly reducing the scope of Scott's brilliant "Blade-runner" dystopias to a kind of malign cultural chauvinism. But in Japan, *any* foreign view of the country that is not positive has come to be immediately excoriated as "Japan-bashing."

9. Foucault, *The Order of Things*, p. xviii.

is to be treated not in some rigid, commonsense fashion as a "real" place but rather as a very special sort of *condition* that necessitates the deconstruction of his own Western thought. We are concerned not with Japan at all, we are told, but rather with "Japan"—a "fictive nation" in which Barthes locates a "fissure of the symbolic" which "has afforded him a situation of writing" (pp. 3–4). "Japan" is thus much like the "China" of which Foucault wrote, "that picture that lacks all spatial coherence . . . a precise region whose name alone constitutes for the West a vast reservoir of utopias. In our dreamworld, is not China precisely this privileged *site* of *space?*"[10] Just as Wilde nearly a century before had found in Japan a site of rhetorical discovery, an "invention" that was "simply a mode of style, an exquisite fancy of art," Barthes is concerned with the opportunity provided him by Japan's historical reputation for strangeness to indulge in a revolutionary rhetoric of contrariety about the bourgeois commonsensical. Barthes's anticipation of finding just such a utopia of liberation inevitably collides, however, as did Kipling's, with the unfortunate problem that the emperor *does* in fact have clothes, and not just fairyland kimonos but solid Western business suits. Since they stubbornly refuse to go away, it seems we shall have to account for them.

We can understand Barthes's position here as one of being not on the inside looking out but rather on the outside looking in, a stance and a vision altogether different from, and perhaps even more important than, the one he desires to take toward this condition he terms (following Wilde's "pure invention") a "fictive nation." As Christopher Miller has observed of the European invention of "Africa," however, the dichotomy of this sort of discourse is always suspended in "the unresolvable tension between a pseudo-object projected onto the void *and a real object that bears the same name.*"[11] We ignore either pseudo-object *or* object only at the peril of having it return, as the repressed always will, to haunt us. Even Barthes, in his influential 1957 essay "Myth Today," noted the crucial distinction between imaginary signifier and real signified which is inherent in such spaces: "China is one thing, the idea which a French petit-bourgeois could have of it not so long ago is another: for this peculiar mixture of bells, rickshaws and opium-dens, no other word possible but *Sininess.*"[12] And there, I think, lies the giveaway, in "the idea which *a French petit-bourgeois* could have of it"—that silly, contemptible class from whose ideological stupidities the French academic is so careful to exclude himself, though he will have forgotten, in his pretensions of chic revolutionary gestures, to take his attitudes along with him. In *Empire*

10. Ibid., p. xix.

11. Christopher L. Miller, *Blank Darkness: Africanist Discourse in French* (Chicago: University of Chicago Press, 1985), p. xi (emphasis added).

12. Roland Barthes, *Mythologies* (*Mythologies*, 1957), trans. Annette Lavers (New York: Hill & Wang, 1972), p. 121. The word Barthes uses is *Sinité*.

of Signs Barthes sets out to do for Japan what he had earlier done in *Mythologies* (p. 11) for French culture—that is, "to track down in the decorative display of *what-goes-without-saying* the ideological abuse of what, in my view, is hidden there." But, oddly enough, he seems to have discovered no ideological manipulation at all of signs that reveal "the mystification which transforms petit-bourgeois culture into a universal nature" (p. 9). All the signs turn out, remarkably enough, to be quite empty, and since he is by his own admission unencumbered by any signified that might serve as a brake to the free play of signs, how could the signs have been otherwise?

When we place Barthes and Kipling side by side and ask which of the two has better managed the difficult balancing act of simultaneous objectivity and subjectivity in reading culture, we find that Barthes does not stack up very well. For one thing, he begins, as Kipling does not, by disingenuously expecting us to believe that he comes to his fantasy land as *tabula rasa*, a notion no one could possibly take seriously. Kipling knew exactly what he expected Japan to be, and when it turned out not to be that at all, he vented his spleen as much at his own failure as at Japan's. Barthes, by contrast, is full of disingenuous disclaimers to any prior knowledge at all about the place; he even asserts that his "lack" of knowledge about Japan is precisely what will constitute his strength.

Simply to make such a claim, however, is to reveal the absurdity of such a position. Every French intellectual, after all, is already crammed to the bursting point with received knowledge of Japan, and even Barthes must acknowledge "the Orient of Voltaire, of the *Revue Asiatique*, of Pierre Loti, or of [the magazine] *Air France*" (p. 4)—to which we can add films ranging from Marguerite Duras and Alain Resnais's brutal *Hiroshima mon amour* to François Truffaut's equally brutal *Domicile conjugal*, and move on to everything from art to antiques, food to fashion, scooters to stereos, rockets to real estate. Barthes died just a little too soon to have seen the Japan that has most recently reconquered France. "Someday," he declares with a self-satisfied prescience—not now, to be sure, but someday—"we must write the history of our own obscurity—manifest the destiny of our narcissism" in such projects, the delay of which "can only be the result of an ideological occultation" (p. 4). Since someday may be too late, however, I shall have to make a modest start on such a project here—perhaps where Barthes himself would most have appreciated it.

Although our intended goal is "the Empire of Signs," we find we have to approach it by way of a detour. Even to utter the word "Japan" is inevitably to feel the shadow of Edward Said hovering preemptively over our shoulder to accuse us of practicing "Orientalism," which is to say of constructing ourselves as a subject at the expense and to the detriment of a land and a people of whom we are not and can never be a part, of making ourselves familiar only in the act of making others strange. It is Said's name for that practice by which we first "produce" and then "manage" our alien culture.[13]

And of course, in all the solemn and serious ways that we can imagine, Said is absolutely correct. Certainly in the minds of the Japanese the West appears forever to repeat the forced entry of Commodore Perry into Tokyo Bay in 1853, ready to destroy the object of what he cleverly called (foreshadowing the usages of modern American diplomacy) his innocent and "pacific overtures" if refused unwelcome entry. A sovereign and blameless people are once again to be treated as mere extensions of the brutal European and American lust for empire and colony, materials and markets, as well as of a more recent, unreasonable American desire for their hearts and minds as well.

The noticeable thickening of irony here only serves to indicate a sense that, at least in the case of Japan, something has gone awry with the "Orientalism" model. And it is simply that one cannot these days fail to be aware of an aspect of the problem to which Said never even alludes: Japan and we are actually *in complicity*, locked in the embrace of mutual self-definition, just as are Europeans and Arab peoples, the Israelis and Palestinians, the English and the Irish, and so on in terrible twos all around the globe. Few today can remain oblivious to the fact that at the moment we "Orientalize" Japan, we too, exactly as Kipling discovered, are being "Orientalized" from the other side. Even as we shamelessly manipulate that Other to validate of our own identity, it is quickly brought home to us in that very act that the Other has somehow contrived (perhaps by the same sort of mysterious and unfair jujitsu used by Kipling's Japanese newspaper editor) to construct itself as a subject—*our* subject, and at *our* expense.

For one thing, we find that we are not sahibs but rather *gaijin*, the common if somewhat derogatory term for "foreigners": literally "persons outside," implicitly outside the pale of civilization and culture.[14] The word has something of the etymological range of the Latin *idiota*: "uneducated man, ignorant person, outsider," with the unfortunate overtones of its narrower English derivative, "idiot." If we follow this etymology back into the Greek, however, we arrive at the paradox that *idiotai* meant "one's countrymen," in contrast to *barbaroi* or "barbarians." This suggests that what is one's own (*idios*) always refers to that which is "peculiar" to one, in both senses of the

---

13. Edward W. Said, *Orientalism* (New York: Vintage Books, 1978), pp. 3, 43. I use the words "we" and "they" here with full knowledge of the presumption of unity they represent.

14. *Gaijin* as a general term is reserved for Caucasian Europeans and Americans and as such automatically conjures up the conventional image of a "blue-eyed blond" (*aome kimpatsu*). The increasing numbers of others recently arriving in Japan as illegal workers, willing or unwilling, are generally referred to as *nanmin*, "refugees," and specified by country. Like any other language, Japanese also has far nastier words for foreigners.

word: that is, unique, separate, distinct, as well as strange, words that indicate different aspects of the same thing. Freud, writing on the nature of wit, was interested in the double nature of words that contain their own opposites, a phenomenon he termed "representation through the opposite." He also realized that what we perceive as Other is actually a radical displacement elsewhere of those parts of ourselves we find unacceptable.

All foreigners resident in Japan eventually come to understand that it is their common destiny to be that unacceptable Other against which Japaneseness is continually defined and tested. And gaijin are all familiar with at least some of the unnerving results of this process. It is often remarked, for example, that invariably one of the first questions asked us upon our arrival in Japan is just when we are planning to return home. Scarcely a disinterested inquiry, this is often proffered with enough anxiety to imply that the interlocutor would be relieved to find our departure scheduled for the next flight. We are complimented on our ability to speak Japanese in inverse proportion to our actual ability; real fluency seems actually to evoke mistrust and apprehension. It does not take long for Caucasian foreigners to realize they have been placed on a pedestal, with the same results that Western women have long experienced in their own cultural milieu. If anyone could justifiably be felt to be the victim of "Orientalism" (or perhaps Occidentalism), it is surely the foreigner in Japan.

What Said seems to take to be a matter of simple racism, then, turns out to be more like a hall of mirrors in which we stare at others, some more like ourselves and some less, all of whom are staring back at us. Recall Kipling's uncomfortable perplexity over the ambiguous Oriental "look": as brutally or anxiously as we glower at them in this hall of mirrors, our gaze is returned from every angle to brutalize and express anxiety about us in turn. Writing about Velazquez's painting *Las Meninas*, Foucault locates in the ambiguous function of the mirror the central condition of representation itself: "The mirror, by making visible, beyond even the walls of the studio itself, what is happening in front of the picture, creates, in its sagittal dimension, an oscillation between the interior and the exterior."[15] Mediating between two worlds and reflecting each back toward the other, the mirror "restores, as if by magic, what is lacking in every gaze," even while it conceals "as much as and even more than it reveals"—which is to say that it represents a central and problematic aspect of narrative itself.[16]

The image of the mirror will also recall Jacques Lacan's famous "mirror function" in which the infant, "fixing his attitude in a slightly leaning-forward position, in order to hold it in his gaze, brings back an instantaneous

15. Foucault, *The Order of Things*, p. 11.
16. Ibid., p. 15.

aspect of the image" in what Lacan calls a "jubilant assumption of his specular image."[17] This condition can be extended to the naive foreigner who is immersed for the first time in another culture and who also, in his similarly infantile "nursling dependence," seems "to exhibit in an exemplary situation the symbolic matrix in which the *I* is precipitated in a primordial form, before it is objectified in a dialectic of identification with the other, and before *language restores to it, in the universal, its function as subject.*"[18]

This may seem somewhat remote from the experience of the mature adult thrust for the first time into a foreign social matrix. And yet perhaps it is only a matter of ontogeny recapitulating phylogeny, as it were: the development of self-identification in the infant repeated, like a self-embedded fractal, at the level of the already mature social being. As Lacan notes, "This development is experienced as a temporal dialectic that decisively projects the formation of the individual into history," representing a "breaking out of the circle of the *Innenwelt* into the *Umwelt*," thus extending the range of Foucault's mirror function beyond the scope of either the merely human individual at one extreme or, at the other, some vaguely impersonal universal.[19]

A further complexity of this hall of mirrors is suggested by what Fredric Jameson proposes in *Marxism and Form* as that "look" which forces us to "see ourselves from the outside, defining ourselves against the Other, by interiorizing the other's look, and transforming what initially was experienced in shame into a sense of pride or identity."[20] This is much the same dialectic which, I have proposed elsewhere, was at play in the construction of a Japanese concept of a historical "self" as such a self evolved in relation to the otherness of China.[21] There can be no question that as early as the third century A.D.—that is, as early as records exist on the subject—China was practicing a ruthless economic, political, and cultural "Orientalism" on Japan, as well as on every other people within its cultural sphere; nor can there be any doubt that Japan quickly found ways to return China's "look," not only constructing itself thereby as a subject but, as Jameson says, also coming to experience what had at first been a sense of cultural inferiority as a new sense of national pride and identity. And just as Japan's military defeat of China in 1895 and its adventures there in the 1930s and 1940s show that there is nothing historically permanent in the valorization of subject and object as it pertains to Asia, so the events of the 1970s and 1980s have shown

17. Jacques Lacan, "The Mirror Stage as Formative of the Function of the I" (1949), in *Ecrits: A Selection* (*Ecrits*, 1966), trans. Alan Sheridan (New York: Norton, 1977), p. 2.

18. Ibid. (emphasis added).

19. Ibid., p. 4.

20. Fredric Jameson, *Marxism and Form: Twentieth-Century Dialectical Theories of Literature* (Princeton: Princeton University Press, 1971), p. 301.

21. See David Pollack, *The Fracture of Meaning: Japan's Synthesis of China from the Eighth through the Eighteenth Centuries* (Princeton: Princeton University Press, 1986).

that "Orientalism" in all its global ramifications is also, not surprisingly, a two-edged sword.

Jameson was referring specifically, in this essay on Sartre, to the development of class consciousness in Europe, especially of a proletarian consciousness as it came to define itself against its bourgeois antithesis. His analysis has the advantage of providing with a dimension of political dialectic what in Said's view is otherwise merely a lowest common denominator of racism, with its manifold cultural implications of European inhumanity to Arab. While no one can deny the achievement of Said's eloquent and pioneering study, I am finally troubled by his argument, not because it is true but because it is true only as far as it goes.[22] Certainly, Japan has been brutalized by my regard; but I have always been aware of being made exactly the same sort of debased object in return. *Each* of the parties involved in that "look," as Jameson notes, "comes to gain a new consciousness of its oppressor, as a look in its turn, fascinating for the oppressors, attractive or terrifying by turns, in any case exercising a profound ontological magnetism: that which puts me into question in my very being, and with which, in one way or another, I must come to terms."[23] Whether we profess attraction or terror, or—as in Jameson's example and in Foucault's word "sagittal"—oscillate between the two (which seems most likely), we still confront a problem with which we too must somehow finally "come to terms."

Jacques Derrida has shrewdly observed that "the ethnologist accepts into his discourse the premises of ethnocentrism at the very moment when he denounces them."[24] Said, in what we might call the ecstasy (in the literal meaning of *ekstasis*) of being morally "beside himself," seems unaware of the paradox that if one cannot study culture as something outside oneself, it is just as true that one cannot *but* study culture as something outside oneself. It is because of this principled refusal to admit to the dialectical necessity of a

---

22. Said's approach has been criticized for leaving a great many questions unasked as well as unanswered. For a thorough critique of his work, see James Clifford, "On Orientalism," in *The Predicament of Culture: Twentieth-Century Ethnography, Literature, and Art* (Cambridge, Mass.: Harvard University Press, 1988), pp. 255–76. In "Representing the Colonized: Anthropology's Interlocutors," *Critical Inquiry* 15 (Winter 1989): 205–25, Said continues to insist on the victim's monological view rather than a truly dialogical one: "It therefore behooves us as intellectuals, humanists, and secular critics to grasp the role of the United States in the world of nations and of power, from *within* the actuality, and as participants in it, not as detached outside observers" (p. 217). One would prefer to see an attempt to grapple not merely with the "role of the United States" but with *both* realities simultaneously, yet that is exactly the ability that Palestinian partisanship denies Said. One wonders whether he is finally willing to extend to both sides of the Israeli-Palestinian conflict the necessity "to see Others not as ontologically given but as historically constituted" (p. 225).

23. Jameson, *Marxism and Form*, p. 304.

24. Jacques Derrida, "Structure, Sign, and Play in the Discourse of the Human Sciences" (1966), in *Writing and Difference* (*L'écriture et la différence*, 1967), trans. Alan Bass (Chicago: University of Chicago Press, 1978), p. 282.

stance outside one's "self"[25] that his theoretical position is ultimately merely pathetic, in the literal meaning of that word as "intended to excite pity or sympathy."

The trick in speaking of "inside" and "outside," of course, is that one must define where the center lies. As it is understood by Derrida, the "center" is not a fixed locus to one or the other side of which we can locate our discourse; it is rather a *function* that refuses to prioritize any particular claim to moral centrality: "a sort of non-locus," as he conceives it, "in which an infinite number of sign-substitutions come into play."[26] And it is clearly from this same point of view that Barthes is claiming to construct his own non-locus of "Japan." But the paradox involved is almost too sublime: how does one go about constructing a non-place without substituting it for the very place one had hoped not to build in the first instance?

To be sure, Derrida has only been warming up to his own agenda, which is the deconstruction of the archstructuralist Lévi-Strauss, just as Said and Jameson each has his: respectively, the cultural implications of the European's abuse of the Arab, and the development of a dialectical criticism valid for our time. Derrida's radical insistence on decentering may be unnerving, but it is only by means of such a rigorous and dialectical deconstruction of the notion of "center" that we are able to participate in the full and unlimited *jouissance* of the structure—a point to which I return in analyzing Barthes's particular "enjoyment" of Japan.

Here, however, at the risk of seeming to "Orientalize" Japan myself by participating in one of its own cultural essentializations (which I do often, though I hope always at least to note the fact), I want to pursue this notion of a rigorously dialectical deconstruction of the center. The insistence on a paradoxical and self-consciously playful and decentering mode of discourse is clearly sympathetic to the Buddhist mode of discourse—may even, in fact, have been facilitated by it as part of that long history of complex (though often unarticulated and invisible) engagements between European and Asian cultures. To examine this dimension of a Euro-Asian interplay of ideas is, after all, to step beyond the confines of that implicit Judeo-Christian world view that Jonathan Culler has called the last sacrosanct bastion of Eurocentric discourse.[27]

Derrida's decentering dialectic closely resembles the mode of discourse of the Zen sect of Buddhism, with its firm and paradoxical refusal to locate itself in anything other than the most rigorous dialectic. I am speaking of Zen not as it has become nativized in America in terms of motorcycle mainte-

---

25. This is a refusal Said reiterates and passionately defends rather than reconsiders in "Orientalism Reconsidered," *Cultural Critique* 1 (Fall 1985): 89–107.

26. Derrida, "Structure, Sign, and Play," p. 280.

27. Jonathan Culler, "Comparative Literature and the Pieties," *MLA Profession 86*, pp. 30–

nance (we could neutralize it by calling it by its Chinese name, *Chan*) but rather as it appears in its earliest records: a living practice as yet almost entirely untouched by concerns of social or political approbation—something, in other words, in many ways as alien to the Japanese of today as it is to ourselves.

Consider, for example, a koan, or "case study," from the great thirteenth-century casebook of Chinese Chan Buddhism known most widely in the West by its Japanese title *Mumonkan* or "Gateless Pass" (perhaps the ancient Chinese equivalent of the Greek word *aporia* as it is used in Western critical theory today):

> [There was a monk who] called to himself every day, "Master!" and answered, "Yes, sir!" Then he would say, "Be alert!" and answer, "Yes, sir!" "Henceforward, never be deceived by others!" "No, I won't!"[28]

Today we would simply say the poor monk was obviously suffering from a split personality—and of course in terms of an Aristotelian (or for that matter a Confucian) world outlook, we would be right.[29] But in the context of Zen thought, such apparently "insane" language and action is the only real indication of sanity in a world already mad. Mumon, the compiler of this text (the title puns on the literal meaning of "Mumon's Barrier-gate"), says by way of commentary on this koan: "This old monk buys and sells himself. He takes out a lot of god-masks and devil-masks and puts them on to play with them. What for, eh? One calling and the other answering; one wide awake, the other saying he will never be deceived. If you stick to any of them, you will be a failure."[30] Once dialectical free play has been destroyed by the valorization of one thing over another, in other words, once the possibility of one center has been given priority over another, then the play of meaning is closed off, forever short-circuited. In this sense, a koan represents what Lévi-Strauss termed a *scandale*: something, as Derrida notes, that is central

---

32. Said's own perception of a new mindless and zealous fundamentalism in the "high-pitched monologue in narrow corridors" (*The World, the Text, and the Critic* [Cambridge, Mass.: Harvard University Press, 1983], p. 292) carried on between academic conservatives and radicals is clearly intended to counter a rising tide of media portrayals of a rabid Islam. Said's brief bout of worry over trends that would locate the ultimate sources of authority, critical or otherwise, in *either* the Bible or the Koran, and that would accept the idea of essential cultural difference on the basis of these as sacred writ, develops further and in unexpected ways the sorts of dangers that Culler warns of.

28. *Two Zen Classics: "Mumonkan" and "Hekiganroku,"* ed. and trans. Katsuki Sekida (New York: Weatherhill, 1977), p. 53.

29. It should be noted that thinkers in the long Confucian and neo-Confucian traditions in China and Japan were no less antagonistic to what they perceived as the dangerous and destructive nature of Chan (Zen) thought in their own time than are descendants of the British-American philosophical traditions suspicious of deconstructionist theory today.

30. *Two Zen Classics: "Mumonkan,"* p. 53.

to the creation of structure and yet simultaneously deconstructs it.[31] Any device that can accomplish this absurd task cannot but be absurd on the face of it, and everyone knows how absurd *koans* are.

In *The Empire of Signs* (which, published the same year as the more famous *S/Z*, perhaps thereby skirted critical notice), Roland Barthes sets out to make Japan itself his personal *scandale*, a text that will create a center for his playfulness while simultaneously decentering both itself and its author. Japan is to become for him "a certain disturbance of the person, . . . a subversion of earlier readings, a shock of meaning lacerated, extenuated to the point of its irreplaceable void, without the object's ever ceasing to be significant, desirable" (p. 4).

Perhaps the first question one wants to ask is just how seriously this work was intended to be taken. It was, after all, published originally by Skira as a sort of coffee-table book, and not by Seuil or Minuit as a work of serious import. If we consider the context of Barthes's writing as a whole, however, we may allow that neither is the book by any means a mere *hors d'oeuvre*, literally something standing outside the main body of his work. Its overt and covert agendas are no more paradoxical than those of his other imaginative texts, published in the spirit of *épater la bourgeoisie* while simultaneously intended to appeal to an audience comprising a particular segment of haut-bourgeois French academic culture. Like many of his writings and those of the *Tel Quel* group in general, *The Empire of Signs* amounts to an attractive stick with which to belabor institutional culture, a private act of anti-authoritarian fantasy to hurl in the face of authoritarian "fact." As such, it is quite an attractive work, a work of the imagination, a suggestive and even seminal project; it also has—intentionally, I think—the look of an innocent trifle that begs to be carried onto the airplane, where it has been timed to explode.

That this work must be regarded as something of a *scandale* for ourselves as well is suggested by the following passage from Barthes's *Mythologies*:

> If I am a woodcutter and I am led to name the tree I am felling, whatever the form of the sentence, I "speak the tree," I do not speak about it. This means that my language is operational, transitively linked to its object. . . . But if I am not a woodcutter, I can no longer "speak the tree," I can only speak *about* it, *on* it . . . I no longer have anything but an intransitive relationship with the tree; this tree is no longer the meaning of reality as a human action, it is an *image-at-one's-disposal*.[32]

31. Derrida, "Structure, Sign, and Play," p. 283.
32. Barthes, *Mythologies*, pp. 145–46 (original emphasis).

Fellow nonwoodcutters who live within the world of theory are asked to admire Barthes's persistent acts of deconstruction and desire. Inevitably, however, there are going to be other "woodcutters" who will feel that he has been barking up the wrong tree and who will take umbrage at his cavalier treatment of a language and culture—even the *signs* of a language and culture—which he clearly knows nothing about. I sometimes feel this sort of irritation at those who, viewing all culture as mere grist for the deconstructionist mill, adopt the international terrorist style and set about blowing up lovely things that others have devoted a lifetime to peacefully and intelligently constructing; and who, having deconstructed, move on to their next target— much as Barthes, proceeding to ignore Japan entirely after the éclat of this one slim volume has subsided, moves on to explore the more (one might say) virginal joys of other texts.

Gayatri Spivak has leveled similar criticism at Julia Kristeva's *About Chinese Women*, displaying a massive scorn for the uneducated and illiterate "reading" of a speechless people for whom the clever educated European proposes to provide a voice. "Even as the Western-trained Third World feminist deplores the absence of the usual kind of textual analysis and demonstration," writes Spivak, "she is treated to the most stupendous generalizations about Chinese writing, a topos of that very eighteenth-century [Chinese mentality] Kristeva scorns." And in this manner, Spivak says, "always with no encroachment of archival evidence, speculation has become fact."[33] The equally ignorant (though not blank) Barthes succeeds in the same way in substituting, in the same sort of terms, the absence and emptiness of a desirable non-place for the presence and fullness of an undesirable place and, in so doing, succeeds in recreating the very topos he scorns.

In some natural and entropic manner, however, there finally must, and indeed always does, arrive an end to the free play of *jouissance*. Regarding this problem, Norman Bryson has thought to ask, "How free is such 'free play of the signifier?'"

Only in a state of euphoric utopia, or dysphoric atopia, are the signifiers capable of *cancelling* each other out. If the signifiers are theorised at the level of *langue*, then indeed they may collide, disperse, form temporary groupings and nonce collectives, they may enjoy all the random motion of a cloud chamber, without

33. Gayatri Chakravorty Spivak, "French Feminism in an International Frame," in *In Other Worlds: Essays in Cultural Politics* (New York: Methuen, 1987), pp. 138–39. Spivak's response to Julia Kristeva, *About Chinese Women* (trans. Anita Barrows [London: Marian Boyars, 1977]; reviewed critically in Philippe Sollers, "On n'a encore rien vu" [Once again they saw nothing], *Tel Quel* 85 [Autumn 1988]: 9–31 is aimed precisely at the French intellectual who presumes to speak for people she knows nothing about, and who assumes that to know everything requires only the keen intelligence of the theorist and her portable feminist sympathies. Spivak is especially concerned to point out the lack of any genuinely political dimension in such work.

constraint on their powers of free association; mobility of the signifier is the-oretically endless—*outside* the social formation, and outside history.[34]

When the sadomasochistic thrills of Barthes's "subversion," "shock," and "laceration" are done with, the object does in fact cease to be "significant" and "desirable"; it becomes *vieux jeu*, yesterday's papers, incapable of stimu-lating the subject to further *jouissance*.[35] The Orientalism in each of us might be usefully redefined in the language of this "professor of desire" (to use Steven Ungar's adaptation to Barthes of Philip Roth's title) as the phallo-centric search in the Other for the self, for which no single Other can suffice to stimulate continually the incessant demand for yet more *jouissance*.[36] Just as Marxist analysis does not permit us to forget the reification of social relations and fetishization of culture which characterize the capitalist con-struct, it seems only fair to illuminate the phallocentric nature of Barthes's own project in light of Lacan's injunction not to forget that "the organ that assumes this signifying function [the phallus, that is to say, the signifier of the desire of the Other] takes on the value of a fetish."[37] And, as Lacan goes on to note, it is precisely such a phallic demand for satisfaction by the Other that motivates the subject toward infidelity, turning each therefore necessarily unsatisfying Other into both virgin and whore. Barthes has his virginal fan-tasy of Japan perform a sensual Dance of the Seven Veils in order to stimu-late his pleasure, and he comes away from the experience every bit as en-tranced as Flaubert had been with his Kuchuk Hanem and her "voice as she sang songs that for me were without meaning and even without distinguish-able words."[38] Of course the voice, empty, free of troublesome signification, has no meaning in it; and Japanese is not a *real* language for Barthes any

34. Norman Bryson, *Vision and Painting: The Logic of the Gaze* (New Haven: Yale University Press, 1983), p. 142.

35. Terry Eagleton offers a biting critique of Barthes's overall project: "Caught up in this exuberant dance of language, delighting in the textures of words themselves, the reader knows less the purposive pleasures of building a coherent system, binding textual elements masterfully together to shore up a unitary self, than the masochistic thrills of feeling that self shattered and dispersed through the tangled webs of the work itself. Reading is less like a laboratory than a boudoir. Far from returning the reader to himself, in some final recuperation of the selfhood which the act of reading has thrown into question, the modernist text explodes his or her secure cultural identity, in a *jouissance* which for Barthes is both readerly bliss and sexual orgasm" (*Literary Theory: An Introduction* [Minneapolis: University of Minnesota Press, 1983], pp. 82–83, discussing Roland Barthes, *The Pleasure of the Text*). As Eagleton (ever the good Marxist) goes on to observe, "There is something a little disturbing about this self-indulgent avant-garde hedo-nism in a world where others lack not only books but food."

36. Philip Roth, *The Professor of Desire* (New York: Farrar, Straus and Giroux, 1977); Steven Ungar, *Roland Barthes: The Professor of Desire* (Lincoln: University of Nebraska Press, 1983).

37. Lacan, "The Signification of the Phallus", in *Ecrits*, p. 290.

38. Quoted in Said, *Orientalism*, p. 187.

more than Ottoman Turkish was for Flaubert.[39] The purpose of Oriental courtesan "tongues," after all, is the stimulation of Western male phallic fantasies, not the utterance of difficult and problematic meanings.

Here, I think, lies much of the problem with Barthes's insertion of himself into what he calls that "fissure of the symbolic" of Japan. He is having so much fun with his desire, his deconstruction, his *jouissance*, is so appreciative of the passing spectacle, that he forgets (admirably, of course, but still forgets) the spectacle he is making of himself in the inevitable and equally demanding "look" of the Other—which is, of course, just as intent on getting its fair measure of enjoyment out of Barthes. As Lacan suggests, there is a particular danger that comes of this constant leading with the indexical phallus of desire, a danger that can be illustrated by another famous koan known, appropriately enough, as "Gutei's finger":

> Whenever the monk Gutei was asked about Zen, he simply raised his finger. Once a visitor asked Gutei's boy attendant, "What does your master teach?" The boy, too, raised his finger. Hearing of this, Gutei cut off the boy's finger with a knife. The boy, screaming with pain, began to run away. Gutei called to him, and when he turned around, Gutei raised his finger. The boy suddenly became enlightened.[40]

As to the meaning of this koan, the compiler Mumon tells us only, though magnificently, that "the enlightenment of Gutei and the boy *does not depend on the finger.*" Our reaction to what I have called "the indexical phallus of desire" is precisely that of a dog to a pointing finger: the dog's attention, that is, is focused entirely on the finger rather than on what it points to. Only by cutting it off could Gutei show the boy that it was in the way. Similarly, for all its fun, Barthes's—finger?—stands in the way of his search for enlightenment, as well as of our own; only by a figurative amputation can this phallocentric vision of Japan be relieved of its intrusive self-presence.

Perhaps something of the sort might have been achieved if someone had translated for him the article about his visit to his "fictive nation" which appeared in the *Kobe News*. Only a small bit of it is reproduced in his book (p. 90), just the fragment of text surrounding the photograph of himself (which he considered to be "Japanned" about the eyes, an effect I fear must have

39. One is also reminded of Gérard de Nerval's chapter "The Language Lesson" in his *Journey to the Orient* (London: Michael Haag, 1984): though the European expects his newly purchased slave woman to teach him Arabic, the language quickly proves too difficult for him, and he finds it an easier matter to teach her French—a language whose purpose is not in the least bit enigmatic to *her*; it is the language of luxurious shopping (pp. 51–60).

40. *Two Zen Classics: "Mumonkan,"* p. 34.

been apparent only to him): after a brief rehearsal of his lecture itinerary, the fragment states merely that "the name Barthes is practically unknown in Japan." But perhaps he would only have been all the more ecstatic to know that he, as well as Japan, was to be "exempt from meaning," that he in his turn had become an "image-at-someone-else's-disposal."

One can read Barthes with much pleasure. His approach to the interplay of culture, language, writing, and sign is of intrinsic interest, and his methodology assumes an increased seminal power in a field that sometimes seems entirely given over to the traditional pedantic tasks of translation, collation, and annotation. But for all our pleasure, surely it does not require the promptings of an Edward Said to make us wince at such a statement as this: "What the Japanese carry, *with a formicant energy*, are actually empty signs" (p. 46; emphasis added). What is one to make of the critical observer of cultural signs who, apparently quite consciously, blithely reduces an entire (and unitary) people to ants? Such old European clichés about Asians make one blush, and in spite of our pleasure and admiration, we find ourselves blushing entirely too often in *The Empire of Signs*.

But I would argue further that nested deep within the labyrinthine ant-tunnels of this work lies a problem much more intractable than the trivial "Orientalist" giveaways that merely reveal Barthes's proper stance to be irretrievably outside the culture he is looking at. This persistent problem is his failure to locate himself at the same time *within* the symbolic text he has created to provide him with a sense of his own otherness. Because he is ignorant of his subject—and the book reveals everywhere his ignorance even of its particular system of signs—his attempts to decenter himself implode halfway, ultimately dooming to inevitable collapse the project of creating a new and meaningful text. That Barthes was aware of the necessity of what Mumon calls "putting on god-masks and devil-masks" might be inferred from his famous essay in *Mythologies* concerning the spectacle of professional wrestling. He writes, as Philip Thody notes, from the point of view of the Roman actor's conventional attitude toward the fiction being enacted on stage as it is disclosed in the phrase *larvatus prodeo*: "I come forward pointing at my mask."[41] The problem is that Barthes is unable to take one mask off and put on the other, to call to himself and then answer himself. In other words, he is unable to stand simultaneously outside his text and inside it—let alone, as Spivak would further require, to "support a way of reading that would continue to break down these distinctions, never once and for all, and *actively* interpret 'inside' and 'outside' as texts for involvement as well as for change."[42]

41. Philip Thody, *Roland Barthes: A Conservative Estimate* (London: Macmillan, 1977), pp. 9–10.

42. Spivak, *In Other Worlds*, p. 102.

To illustrate this problem I turn to a passage in the last chapter of *The Empire of Signs*, "The Cabinet of Signs," describing what Barthes calls a "Shikidai gallery" (just where he gets his names for things is often a mystery), which he characterizes as "tapestried with openings, framed with emptiness and framing nothing"; in it,

> there is no site which designates the slightest propriety in the strict sense of the word—ownership: neither seat nor bed nor table out of which the body might constitute itself as the subject (or master) of a space: the center is rejected (painful frustration for Western man, everywhere "furnished" with his armchair, his bed, proprietor of a domestic location). [P. 108]

This is in fact an evocation of the architecture that was the height of the medieval Zen temple–inspired style known as the *sukiya-zukuri*, or "connoisseur style," favored by the wealthy and cultivated upper samurai class and apotheosized in the luminously beautiful seventeenth-century Katsura Detached Palace (Katsura Rikyū), a short drive southwest of Kyoto.[43] Of course few Japanese actually live within the context of such a spacious and elegantly empty aesthetic anymore. In fact, the appropriate government ministry felt it necessary not many years ago to issue new construction guidelines (since ignored) governing the minimum amount of space per resident, after a horrified Belgian diplomat in Tokyo declared to the world in 1982 that the Japanese lived in overcrowded "rabbit hutches" (*usagigoya*), a term that still rankles in Japan.[44]

The real force of Barthes's description lies precisely in its contrast to the Western sense of what ought properly to constitute a room (he appears to be thinking of something like Versailles), noting especially the irony of the "immobilizing vocation" of what are called in French *meubles* or "movables." However, when we examine the accompanying photograph in the book more closely (pp. 50–51), we find that it represents not a room in a building like the Katsura Detached Palace, but rather a *corridor* of the Nijō Palace in Kyoto, a very different sort of space and quite unlikely to have been "fur-

43. This compound has probably had a more profound influence than any other in Japan on Western ideas of building and landscape architecture, most notably in the work of Frank Lloyd Wright.

44. To get the full flavor of such language, we might substitute for the term "rabbit hutch" (by which the diplomat may have intended only "crowded" but carries has the connotation of overly procreative animals) the word "warren" (i.e., where rodents live) or even "sty" (where pigs live). Still, the Japanese appear to be sensitive to any foreign statements about them which involve animal metaphors. Thus the (perhaps backhanded) compliment made two decades ago, in light of the resurgent Japanese economy, that the Japanese were indeed "economic animals" was widely interpreted in Japan not in the Keynesian sense that "man is an economic animal" but rather to mean that, as distinct from Western economic *men*, the Japanese are economic *animals*.

nished" with anything at all other than its famous "nightingale" floorboards, built by distrustful samurai to squeak loudly at the slightest footstep in a dangerous age when it was vital to know who might be lurking in one's hallways. The rooms this corridor circumnavigates were in fact intended to be "furnished" with highly movable objects appropriate to the particular occasion for which the rooms were to serve, whether sleeping or eating or diplomatic receptions. These objects were not left permanently in place, to be sure, but kept in storage areas and brought out as needed.

The problem of the putative "emptiness" of the rooms returns us to the most interesting part of the passage in question:

> Uncentered, space is also reversible: you can turn the Shikidai gallery upside down and nothing would happen, except an inconsequential inversion of top and bottom, of right and left: the content is irretrievably dismissed: whether we pass by, cross it, or sit down on the floor (or the ceiling, if you reverse the image), there is nothing to grasp. [P. 110]

As if to offer a practical test of Barthes's observation, a book company's advertisement arrived in my mail shortly after I read this passage, with a photograph inside of a somewhat similar structure *but reproduced upside down*. Once one realizes what has gone wrong, the effect of such a simple error is at once trivial and serious, comic and electrifying: this upside-down view of Japan is irremediably Western, at the very least *foreign* (the book company is located in the United States but has an Asian name), and it nicely illustrates just what is wrong with Barthes's clever observations: the view is his own, and it is comically wrong. A close look at this photograph shows that the ceiling slants at such a severe angle that it would serve very poorly as a floor; that there are immovable transoms blocking doorways through which one must pass; that a stone step hangs perilously from the ceiling; that one would have to leap from the slanting floor perhaps two feet up into the rooms; that the doorpulls are at face level; and finally, that it might be—disorienting?—to find trees growing down from the sky. If we could see inside the supposedly reversible rooms, the problems would become even more acute to the gaze that (both literally and figuratively) *reads* rather than merely gazes desirously: built-in writing surfaces, for example, doorways, windows, shelves, tatami mats . . . It is a nice idea, complete invertibility, but it simply doesn't work when one knows what things are actually *for*.

This is only one of many instances in which Barthes finally fails to understand, to "see" and not just "look," and so can only remain stuck inside his "fissure of the symbolic," fluently engaging himself in unseminal fantasies of desire. Here I defer to Philip Thody's admittedly rather unreceptive recitation of Barthes's Japanese itinerary of pleasure, almost every station of which he finds booby-trapped with elementary and fatal misunderstandings about that country:

> He likes everything about Japan: the food, so much lighter than European food, never covered with a thick coating of sauce or shovelled into the mouth in great spoonfuls, always served almost raw and in a way that enables the diner to compose his menu in the order that he prefers; the elaborate politeness of the Japanese, which seems aimed not at flattering the self-esteem of a particular person but at sketching out an abstract concept of good manners; the literary conventions of the haiku, in which nothing is said and where the delicacy of the form is everything, the content nothing; Japanese religion, where "the signs are empty and the ritual without a God," and where no systematic theology offers a fallacious explanation in terms of intellectual concepts such as the Trinity, the Incarnation or the Real Presence; the Japanese face, in which everything is on the surface and there is no hint of a mysterious and ineffable personality lying behind the beauty of the eyes; the militant students, whom he presents with slightly disquieting enthusiasm as about to fight for the sheer delight of pure combat, unalienated and uninspired by any actual belief in the political validity of what they are doing; and, perhaps more surprisingly, the sprawling, un-planned, and unmapped Japanese towns, where the absence of a centre nev-ertheless fits in with his permanent aesthetic preference for experiences organised around an emptiness rather than around a kernel of solid truth.[45]

In short, Thody, though he may finally understand as little about Japan as does Barthes, finally tires of watching him trying to precipitate his I in primordial form before language restores to him his function as subject, to paraphrase Lacan. Thody quotes with entirely justifiable exasperation one enthusiastic interviewer's declaration that Barthes "was clearly able to write in Japanese without actually understanding the language."[46] Barthes, in his own words, finds himself in exactly the position he seeks to escape, in the *scandale* of trying to have his cake and eat it too or, as he puts it, "trying to kill the wolf by lodging comfortably in its jaws" (p. 8). There is undoubtedly a koan in here somewhere. Such misprisals of signs as misreading the lan-guage that he is so proud of not knowing, should, more than anything else in the lesson he would have *us* learn from Japan, "[cast] suspicion on the very ideology of our speech" (p. 8).

While we must admit that in a perverse sort of way Barthes's work "gives us permission" to consider Japanese semiotics, I have also been at pains to

45. Thody, *Roland Barthes*, pp. 121–22.
46. Ibid., p. 123.

raise, by questioning his project in particular, the more general question of what is sometimes referred to as the seamy side of semiotics. How can the study of sign systems, which claims to be a universal science, account for the problem of local particularity? How are signs to be read *across* cultural boundaries? Can the student of signs simply assume that a general theory is valid across all cultures, or are sign systems—the ways signs function to signify, to generate meaning—in fact culture-specific? Since "language" and its relationship to cultural forms lies at the heart of semiotics, there may in fact be any number of equally valid semiotic systems, and every attempt to create a metasystem to describe them must end in a rubble of particularity. Finally, we must ask whether the inimitable Gallic "style" of writers such as Barthes translates into a universally valid methodology.[47] Or is Barthes in the end guilty of practicing what Edward Said might have called a "semiotic Orientalism" on Japan? Said certainly makes us think he would say so when he rails against "the invasion of literary discourse by the *outré* jargons of semiotics, post-structuralism, and Lacanian psychoanalysis [which] has distended the literary critical universe almost beyond recognition."[48]

What I have tried to suggest here, and continue to suggest throughout this book, is that such an accusation is valid—but, as before, valid only as far as it goes. Once again, the real problems appear to be more profound. My own tentative response to these questions is to stress that a particular semiotic analysis is valid *only* so long as the dialectical movement between culture and signification remains alive and vital. Context in relation to sign systems is not a given set of "facts" but rather a process whereby and within which sign systems operate. To ignore this is, in the terms of the dialectical approach I have discussed, to prefer one thing to another, to choose "god-masks" over "devil-masks"; and to become entranced with sign systems without reference to their defining contexts is to mistake the pointing finger for Truth. In this sense, Barthes can write only a valid French—perhaps only a valid Barthesian—theory of "Japanese semiotics," one that allows itself to be stimulated by the presence of the Other. But to do so would require making this limitation explicit, which is precisely what Barthes does not do.

In the end, this line of reasoning begins to resemble the modern-sounding scientific principle that one cannot observe an event without changing its

47. I do not know whether it can be considered in support of or in opposition to Barthes when Kipling writes that in describing Japan, "only a Frenchman could succeed in spirit, but he would be inaccurate" (*Kipling's Japan*, p. 154). Kipling also observed that "if there is one thing that the Oriental detests more than another, it is the damnable Western vice of accuracy" (p. 201). So far as the Englishman is concerned, at least, the Gallic and Japanese "styles" appear to coincide at the point of a shared cavalier attitude toward the more properly Anglo-Saxon concern for accuracy. When one considers the permanent love affair between Japan and France, one is tempted to think that Kipling may have been on to something.

48. Said, *The World, the Text, and the Critic*, p. 228.

very nature. While humanists no doubt take liberties with the language of scientific inquiry in constructing their fanciful and suspicious metaphors, it seems clear that something of this same problem of fundamentally altering the nature of the event must occur when Self tries to think about Other. By positing a dialectical stance, by simultaneously thinking ourselves into and out of culture, we can at least strive to retain the awareness of the problematic nature of that dialectical oscillation between context and signification. We may look more than a little odd, calling to ourselves and then answering ourselves like the monk in the koan. But we can take some satisfaction in knowing that if we seem to be selling ourselves out with the one, we have also managed to buy ourselves back—that is, to redeem ourselves—with the Other.

Part I

Constructions of the Self

Chapter 1

The Idea of the Individual Self

I also considered how very different the self-same man, identical in mind and spirit, may become, according as he is brought up from childhood amongst the French or Germans, or has passed his whole life amongst Chinese or cannibals.
—René Descartes, *Discourse on Method*

It was during the Meiji period (1868–1912) that the Japanese encountered for the first time, as part and parcel of all the other sorts of "modern" ideas suddenly being imported from Europe and America, the notion of an autonomous individual "self" and realized, not without misgivings, that they were going to have to have one of these, too. The urgency of this realization has returned especially in periods of conflict or crisis (a condition which, during the past century, might well be regarded as endemic) to take the form of a question only the terms of which have changed in succeeding historical periods: what does it mean to be Japanese *with respect to what is foreign?* One might imagine that Japan's long and formative history of having asked this same question with regard to China might provide some clue as to how it would be answered with regard to the sorts of problems later posed by the West. This is true, however, only to the extent that the answers forthcoming were considered to be pragmatically useful in effecting the intimately related twin projects of discovering the self and building the nation, or what Yukichi Fukuzawa, arguably the greatest political thinker of the Meiji period, called "national independence through personal independence."[1] Before its "independence" could be achieved, however, the all-important "person" first had to be located.

1. *Fukuzawa Yukichi's "An Encouragement of Learning,"* trans. and ed. David A. Dilworth and Umeyo Hirano, (Tokyo: Sophia University Press, 1969); Fukuzawa Yukichi (1835–1901), *Gakumon no susume* in *Fukuzawa Yukichi zenshū,* (Tokyo: Iwanami Shoten, 1960), 3:39. See also Carmen Blacker, *The Japanese Enlightenment: A Study of the Writings of Fukuzawa Yukichi* (Cambridge: Cambridge University Press, 1964); and Janet A. Walker, *The Japanese Novel of the Meiji Period and the Ideal of Individualism* (Princeton: Princeton University Press, 1979), p. 26.

This recurring "problem of a self" has never been resolved, of course, nor could it be, since it is finally a false one. All peoples have managed to live quite satisfactorily, variously functional or dysfunctional, regardless of whether or not they have claimed for themselves the idea of an individual self. To propose that Japan required an alien notion of self to survive and compete in the world seems very much the counterpart of a modern Western inclination to fret that our own various national problems with respect to Japan might be attributable to our lack of an equally foreign notion of *wa* or "harmony." This is only to say that people tend to attribute what they perceive as wrong with themselves to a lack of whatever seems unique in those they perceive as being successful.

To one degree or another, such perceived differences are real enough, and the racist attitude is characterized as much by the refusal to admit that real difference exists at all as by the exaggeration of its importance. To use perceived differences as the sole explanation of our own or others' problems, however, is inevitably to make invidious comparisons of right and wrong, good and bad, which can have little validity. No people lacks some sense of individuality, just as none lacks a corresponding sense of social cooperation; a people may elevate one or the other extreme to the level of a social ideal, but the range exists as a potential in every society. Both "team spirit" and "rugged individualism" are valued in the United States, but it is the latter quality that has been elevated to the level of cultural myth; in practice, however, this quality is often shunned by corporate psychologists as characteristic of the whistle-blower or the loose cannon. There is no question, however, that Americans persist in seeing themselves as more individualistic and less conformist than Japanese, regardless of whether or not these very relative positions mean anything in real terms.

During the the Meiji period the notion that Japanese lacked a concept of an individual self was frequently called upon, both at home and abroad, to explain a lack of power in a dangerous world that seemed predicated on the idea of possessing and projecting such a concept. From the start, the Japanese took for granted the European understanding that an individual self lay at the very heart of the modern Western nation-state's economic and political organization and strength, as well as of its ability to project that strength economically and militarily in the world. At the end of the nineteenth century the troubling example of China, whose long-held notions of the relationship between the individual and society were the basis for Japan's own, made it appear exceedingly urgent that the Japanese quickly learn to acquire whatever was needed to allow them to project themselves back against the West if their country was not to suffer a similar fate. China was of great historic concern to Japan, and the Japanese felt that they ought to strive to keep it their concern, that it would not do to stand idly by while others carved

China up for their own less "legitimate" interests. The powerful writings of the modern Chinese writer Lu Xun concerning the perils of tradition and the desperate need for modernization were widely read in Japan and taken to heart there possibly even more than they were in China.

Nor is it likely, as I suggest later in discussing the problem of the novel, that the Japanese failed to grasp the significance of the role played by the individual in that literary form by which Western imperialism and colonialism represented itself to itself and others. Like the strange new imported foreign perspective in art that enabled all vision to originate from and be referred back to a single authoritative but always vanishing point, the individual self could be seen as an integral and central part of the orchestration and representation of the technology of power. A socially sanctioned self, freed from the age-old restraints of traditional Confucian-based social philosophy, was clearly something both inherently powerful and disturbing. At the start of the Meiji period this new quality was still felt to be so pernicious to the social order that the old pre-Restoration (that is, pre-Meiji) insistence on the subordination of the individual to the state—lively public debate over the issue during the 1870s and 1880s notwithstanding—was to persist as the keystone of official state ideology. Such being the paradoxical environment within which the fictional representation of the self had to establish a place for itself, it is little wonder that the process should have been so difficult and problematic.

Over the past half-century and more, the question of what it means to be Japanese has taken the form of a persistent discourse known as *nihonjinron*, or "theories of Japaneseness," involving explanations of national character expressed in social-scientific, quasi-scientific, and pseudoscientific terms. This development was probably inevitable in view of an Allied success in World War II that was in part supported and explained by Ruth Benedict's analysis of Japanese behavior (commissioned by the U.S. government) with its famous distinction between Western "guilt culture" informed by moral ethical absolutes, and what could be interpreted in the light of Japan's defeat only as the inferior and amoral ethical relativity of Japanese "shame culture." As the shortcomings of Benedict's work became increasingly apparent, and partly in reaction against it, other theories of "national character" began to be expounded in Japan and abroad, each involving the similar shortcoming of attempting to account for an entire people's behavior by means of a single set of sweeping explanatory terms, usually framed as sets of binary oppositions. Some of these theories contain at least a kernel of insight that helps make real cultural difference visible, and so they remain to some degree viable, despite their inevitable tendency toward distortion for the purpose of invidious comparison.

A number of such theories have become popular both in Japan and in the

West as ways of explaining respective differences in concepts of the self. Among the best known of these theories are Takeo Doi's concept of *amae*, or healthy emotional "dependence" conceived in opposition to a Western sense of healthy independence, each of course holding the opposite quality to be unhealthy; Chie Nakane's theory of *tate no shakai*, or the significance of "vertical social relationships" as opposed to a Western emphasis on horizontal social relationships, both terms inflated far out of proportion to what they actually explain; and Shumpei Kumon and Eshun Hamaguchi's concept of an Asian *kanjinshugi* or socially harmonizing "interpersonalism" in contrast to a Western rugged and socially antagonistic *kojinshugi* or "individualism," a theory that ignores the degree to which both qualities operate complementarily in any society, whatever their different values, emphases, and expressions.

To the extent that such theories of identity are mobilized to explain and account for absolute difference, or serve to support myths of absolute opposition and mutual antagonism, they are of course useless and even harmful. To the extent that they are actually bought into by a culture to explain itself to itself and to others, however, they serve to point up different emphases or claims operating within a wide range of behaviors, usefully reminding us that human beings, as Descartes observed, do seem to have quite a lot in common, even if we can already see in his casual distinction (in the passage that heads this chapter) between French and Germans on the one hand and "Chinese and cannibals" on the other the inevitably invidious character of the seventeenth-century European project of founding a rational society on the bedrock of a rational, skeptical self and projecting elsewhere the qualities of primitive unreason and belief.

While it is impossible to talk about cultural values in terms of absolute dichotomies, then, it should still be possible, within limits, to discuss the expression of different acceptable ranges of behavior and especially what people appear to *believe* distinguishes them from others. For example, both Westerners and Japanese tend to believe that Europeans and Americans place rather more importance on the virtues of the individual and Japanese on those of the group (again, I emphasize that this is merely an observation of what people seem to believe about themselves in contrast to others, not an attempt to state these beliefs as objective fact). One noteworthy Japanese attempt to develop such (perhaps mythical) perceptions as fact in the direction of a uniquely Japanese social trait—always the sure sign of a problem— is the theory proposed by Shumpei Kumon and Eshun Hamaguchi expounding what they term "Japanese collectivism."[2] It would serve little pur-

2. Hamaguchi Eshun [*sic*] and Kumon Shumpei, eds., *Nihonteki shūdan-shugi* (Japanese collectivism) (Tokyo: Yūhikaku, 1982), parts of which are summarized in Shumpei Kumon, "Some Principles Governing the Thought and Behavior of Japanists (Contextualists)," *Journal of Japanese Studies* 8, no. 1 (1982): 5–28.

pose to elaborate this theory here, except to note the possible usefulness of contrasting a value they call "the intersubjective" (*kanjin*) with the one we already know as "the individual" (*kojin*).[3] In indicating the extremes of a continuum of behavior and thought rather than absolute values, these terms permit us to consider the possibility that a Japanese (more than a Euro-American) sense of self requires that one take others into account in determining one's own actions. The insistence that one's actions be determined by those of others (*seken*) is developed in Tanizaki's novel *Some Prefer Nettles* (see Chapter 3 below), and the idea that people's lives can be related in extremely complex and unforeseen ways (*en*) is central to Kawabata's *Thousand Cranes* (Chapter 5).[4]

Perhaps the most useful effect of a concept of "intersubjectivity" is that it allows us to consider narrativity as something dispersed or scattered among people who are talking among themselves, rather than as something focused on a single "I" who is talking to others among whom is embedded a "you." This seems very similar to the sort of difference involved in the multiple or floating perspective employed in traditional Japanese and Chinese art in contrast to the novel Western one governed by a single vanishing point, a perspective that was imported into Japan at about the same time as the notion of an irreducible individual "I." A concept of "intersubjectivity" thus allows us to consider the possibility of a Japanese mode of narrativity, undergoing its own development over time, in works ranging from the eleventh-century *Tale of Genji* to the nineteenth-century *Shank's Mare* (*Tōkaidōchō hizakurige*), permitting us to think of narrative in terms of conversation (talk, gossip, chat, etc.) rather than "lecture"—something based, that is, in a sense of the primacy of a social orality that obtains between narrator and listener over the private asocial literacy between writer and reader.

Other aspects of a possible Japanese understanding of what constitutes a "self" may also bear on our interpretation of the Japanese novel. Takeo Doi's concept of *amae* or mutual dependence, for example, grows out of and is

3. This terminological opposition is proposed in Esyun Hamaguchi, "A Contextual Model of the Japanese: Toward a Methodological Innovation in Japan Studies," *Journal of Japanese Studies* 11, no. 2 (1985): esp. 299–301 (Hamaguchi, however, translates *kanjin* as "the contextual"). Although the article is riddled with the sweeping universal-particular assertions typical of *nihonjinron* writing, it also has the usual kernel of ideas useful so long as they are not deployed in the service of demonstrating the absolute uniqueness (and superiority) of one group or another. The author summarizes three different social systems that we might characterize in Goldilocks fashion as exhibiting too little, too much, and just enough control: the Western capitalist model of "independent decentralized control"; the Communist totalitarian model of "centralized control"; and, as one might expect, the Japanese model of "holonic decentralized control," "in which individuals cooperate spontaneously in the control of their behavior so that the whole is properly ordered" (p. 321). In effect, this makes Japanese society a model for the entire Third World. For the ideological implications of an otherwise unexplained "spontaneous cooperation," see Chapter 4 below.

4. Hamaguchi ("Contextual Model," p. 310) calls *en* "correlative causality," by which he means "the extremely large system of human causal chains."

meant to explain the observable fact that Japanese children are brought up to anticipate a great deal more from their mothers, both emotionally and physically, and a less intrusive relationship with their fathers than is typically the case in Western cultures.[5] This is considered not only right and proper but necessary if the child is to become a healthily functioning adult. Far from being put as early as possible into a room of its own and left to cry once hunger and physical discomfort have been taken care of, a Japanese child is typically allowed to sleep with its mother for several years, sometimes to the extent of supplanting the father in the bedroom.[6]

To the extent that these observations are valid, such child-rearing practices would appear to diminish the likelihood that the Japanese would place as much weight as did Europeans on the notion of an Oedipus complex—that unique family story with which Westerners have frightened themselves since Freud's time and expressed their particular abhorrence of incest.[7] As Doi suggests, however deeply this story may have worked its way into the Western sense of who we are and how we have come to be that way, this and much more of the Western model of the dynamics of inter- and intrapersonal relationships proves inadequate or even useless as a way of explaining, predicting, or treating the psychological behavior of Japanese. Far from being a theory purporting to explain not only the development of the individual but all of "civilization and its discontents" besides, the Oedipus complex, seen from a more relativistic point of view, turns out to be just one more social myth among all the others.[8]

Even a cursory examination of the Confucian model of the development of a psychosocial self, common throughout much of East Asia, reveals expecta-

5. Takeo Doi, *The Anatomy of Dependence*, trans. John Bester (New York: Kodansha International, 1973); *Amae no kōzō* (Tokyo: Kōbundō, 1971). Although this comparative study contains several plausible notions, it has properly been criticized as an example of *nihonjinron* thought for its view of an absolute Japaneseness in contrast to an absolute Westernness. For a critique of Doi and others, see Hamaguchi, "Contextual Model," pp. 294–95.

6. See, e.g., William Caudill and David W. Plath, "Who Sleeps by Whom? Parent-Child Involvement in Urban Japanese Families," in *Japanese Culture and Behavior*, ed. Takie Sugiyama Lebra and William Lebra (Honolulu: University of Hawaii Press, 1974), pp. 277–312.

7. Recent historical work has been revising a century's reverence for Freud, focusing on what Jeffrey Masson has called his "abandonment of the seduction theory," as well as on significant misrepresentations in his most famous case studies. Pragmatic fields of psychology and psychiatry have managed to get along quite well without much of Freud, and it is humanists who continue to find his (and Karl Marx's) ideas most useful in the interpretation of culture, even if they also often find them to be wrong.

8. Robert Graves, pondering the origins of the Oedipus story in *The Greek Myths* (Baltimore: Pelican Books, 1966), 2:13, could not resist mocking the notion of its universality: "Under the old system, the new king, although a foreigner, had theoretically been a son of the old king whom he had killed and whose widow he married; a custom that the patriarchal invaders misrepresented as parricide and incest. The Freudian theory that the 'Oedipus complex' is an instinct common to all men was suggested by this perverted anecdote; and while Plutarch records (*On Isis and Osiris* 32) that the hippopotamus 'murdered his sire and forced his dam,' he would never have suggested that every man has a hippopotamus complex."

tions sufficiently different from those of Europeans and North Americans to render preposterous any claim for the latter as universally applicable. As the sociologist Francis Hsu has suggested, although there are significant differences between the Japanese and Chinese versions of this model, as well as between their encounters with and adaptations to their Western counterparts, the two models resemble each other much more closely than either does the Euro-American.[9]

The Confucian idea of the self originates and is imbricated within a particular vision of the social continuum. This continuum is expressed historically (or diachronically) in terms of a generational continuum, the existence of the present generation validated only as one link in a chain of antecedent and subsequent generations stretching into distant clan horizons. In the Confucian scheme, the individual exists only as a link in the social chain that recognizes its own ancestors and is in turn recognized as an ancestor by succeeding generations. In structural (or synchronic) terms, the social continuum is expressed in roles comprising the five pair-oppositions (ruler/minister, father/son, husband/wife, elder brother/younger brother, and friend/friend) first propounded in the writings of the post-Confucian philosophers and later adapted to syncretic theories of a family-state homology. Over a lifetime, social man (this idealized discourse concerns itself only with males, and then only insofar as they are ultimately socialized into the service of the state) is located entirely within each of these paired oppositions as son, brother, husband, father, official, and colleague. As well as evolving from one set of terms to the next, some of these roles by their very nature also evolve diachronically from one term of a pair to the other; some obviously cannot. This continuum, which accounts for every recognized relational situation within the family, within the state, and among colleagues, is elaborated specifically for the purpose of a establishing a family-state homology (what Tu Wei-ming, following Mircea Eliade, has called the "anthropocosmic vision")[10] in bureaucratic terms, since the primary principle of the Chinese system of education is that the individual matures within the family to emerge as a functioning part of the larger concerns of the greater social entity of the state. The family thus acts as the primary locus for socialization, which consists of the inculcation of those principles—primarily filiality (*hsiao*) and civility (*li*)[11]—which will properly be turned eventually toward the higher good of the state, whose largest goals are in turn the

---

9. Francis L. K. Hsu, *Iemoto: The Heart of Japan* (New York: Wiley, 1975), p. 25. The particular *iemoto* system of kinship relations that Hsu is examining is specific to Japan; for contrasting elements between China and Japan, see his chapter "Sino-Japanese Contrasts in Perspective," pp. 218–35.

10. Tu Wei-ming, *Centrality and Commonality: An Essay on Confucian Religiousness* (Albany: State University of New York Press, 1989), p. 9.

11. These are more commonly though misleadingly translated as "filial piety" and "ritual."

orderly continuity of the group and effective distribution of roles within it over time.

Within this scheme, the individual can best be defined as a quantity fulfilling a set of well-defined roles in the interest of ensuring group continuity. The individual clearly cannot fulfill that role by abstracting itself from society, as Descartes did, for the purpose of engaging in radical doubt and skepticism. There *is* a skeptical tradition in Chinese philosophy, to be sure, but its goal is to support the rational humanist order by questioning the irrational and positing it as either inhuman or of unconcern to humans. The paradigmatic East Asian example of the fate of the would-be Cartesian thinker is the well-known attempt in 1492 by the neo-Confucian Chinese philosopher Wang Yang-ming to intuit reality (in this case the essential nature of bamboo) by meditating intensely and exclusively upon it in a popular philosophical exercise known as "the investigation of things" (*ko-wu*). After a week of such intense cogitation, however, Wang succeeded only in making himself ill, and he judiciously abandoned the rash attempt as not only a waste of time but a positive injury to the health—"the result of thinking too hard," he wrote, which seems an eminently rational conclusion.[12]

This is certainly not to suggest that there is no room for individual difference within what might appear to some to be a very confining model of socialization. There is every reason to believe that the East Asian model provides at least as much room for eccentricity, which is always socially defined, as does the Western scheme, in which relatively less compulsion to conform (but in exactly which communities?) may as a consequence entail less freedom to be truly different. The Western word "character," originating in the Greek word for "inscription" or "stamp," has the telling ambiguity of both something set in stone and someone unconventional or eccentric. The Japanese word for "character," *katagi*, belonging to a complex of words meaning "pattern" or "model," evolved from the great character-shaping types of traditional Chinese historiographical biography which (much like its parody in Borges's famous "Chinese Enyclopedia) appear to provide a conventional place for nearly everything and everyone. They even include the eccentric genius, typically portrayed as a person unusually tall, thin, pale, and absentminded, with long bushy eyebrows and long hair and nails, a prodigy of superhuman abilities who dies while still young. Art and poetry were

---

12. See Wing-tsit Chan, *A Source Book in Chinese Philosophy* (Princeton: Princeton University Press, 1963), p. 689. Because of its insistence on the inseparability of knowledge and action, the Wang Yang-ming (or Yōmei) school became regarded both in China and Japan as a socially threatening heterodoxy. Wang's perception of the effects of "thinking too hard" seems to be the basis on which Morita Shōma (1874–1938) based his form of psychoanalysis early in this century.

traditionally exercised as part of the cultivation of the social man, and the eccentric genius in these arts was typically a case of prodigious excess, the normal "portion" of talent unregulated and out of balance with the rest of what was held to constitute the normally socialized human being.[13]

If man in this scheme is always *social* man, idealized as the scholar-poet-bureaucrat in state service, there is also a place for what can be called "man out of office" with his trappings of the reclusive Taoist hermit. These complementary roles have equal importance in such great classic novels as Lo Kuan-chung's *San-kuo chih yen-i* (Romance of the chronicle of the three kingdoms), a book avidly read in Japan and nativized in Japanese culture during the seventeenth and eighteenth centuries, first through translation and later as themes running throughout Japanese literature, drama, and art.

We must note that while this system of psychosocial identity firmly subordinates females to male authority (in Confucian terms, the lives of women are expressed only as sequential states of vassalage to males: the daughter subordinate to her father, the wife to her husband, the widow to her son), it does at least manage to provide them with a legitimate place in the social scheme. This is something with which the Freudian account of Western psychosocial development never really manages to come to terms, so that Kaja Silverman has had to conceive of her task in *The Subject of Semiotics* in part as an attempt "to create a space for the female subject . . . even if that space is only a negative one—one, that is, which reflects the marginality to which she has been subject for centuries."[14]

In the Chinese model, the familiar opposition of male/female (in the complementary opposition of *yin/yang*, a much more inclusive and dynamic concept than the Western terms suggest) is developed not as confrontation but rather as a process of mutual interaction and balance, "normal" referring to a range of behavior within which health is maintained and outside of which behavior becomes pathological. The seventeenth-century Chinese novel *Chin Ping Mei* (Golden lotus) offers a good example of this model's operation in the social realm, depicting the particular psychological problems of women not as a manifestation of something simply innate in all females (as "hysteria" was represented in the West) but more complexly and realistically as the direct result of the male-dominated harem politics of the upper-class polygamous household. The libidinally depraved and fallen females who populate the works of the eighteenth-century Japanese novelist Ihara Saikaku—*The life of an Amorous Woman* (*Kōshoku ichidai onna*), for example—are likewise products not only of the failure of a rigidly Confucian-oriented

13. See Hans Frankel, "T'ang Literati: A Composite Biography," in ed. Arthur F. Wright, *Confucianism and Chinese Civilization* (New York: Atheneum, 1959). The T'ang poet Li Ho is probably the best-known Chinese example of the *kuei-ts'ai* or "demonic genius."

14. Kaja Silverman, *The Subject of Semiotics* (Oxford: Oxford University Press, 1983), p. 131.

society to account satisfactorily for women's legitimate physical and psychological needs but of its failure as well to relate those needs to anything but those of men.

Jun'ichirō Tanizaki's novel *The Makioka Sisters* (*Sasameyuki*, 1943, 1947–48), a work concerned almost exclusively with the lives and problems of women (the male characters are virtually incidental to their story), provides an excellent modern Japanese example of the operation of *yin-yang* theory as it is embedded within a general Confucian cultural ethos.[15] We can propose for the sake of illustration (although it is admittedly a schematic formulation) that the absence of the male principle in the Makioka family (by death and other means) and the resulting overabundance of females has left the *yin*, or female principle, unnaturally dominant. Problems associated with excessive *yin* are manifested in this exclusively female world in the form of a family decline that leads to difficulty in marrying off daughters expeditiously and in proper sequence, which further leads to such problems as immoral liaisons, miscarriages, stillbirths, illegitimate children, and even such macrocosmic meteorological phenomena as unusually inclement weather, destructive flooding, and (for all its conspicuous absence) perhaps even the war that has removed so many males from the social realm. The patriarch of the family has died before the story begins, and the male (*yang*) principle has been transferred from Osaka to Tokyo (the head of the major branch of the family is the eldest son-in-law by adoptive marriage—another problem of *yin*). This has left the female-dominated cadet branch of the family behind in the Osaka region, itself "female" (dark, cold, subtle) in contrast to "male" Tokyo (bright, warm, brash).

It is not so much that women "cause" such problems as that, in the absence of a balancing *yang* force, the unalloyed female principle is capable of great destruction (as indeed in opposite circumstances the male should be but rarely is). The story's structure reflects the operation of "complementary bipolarity" (that is, *yin-yang* theory) analyzed by Andrew Plaks in Ts'ao Hsüeh-ch'in's Qing dynasty novel *Hung-lou Meng* (Dream of the red chamber, 1791), especially as regards the great variety of problems inside and outside the home caused by excessive *yin* in all its various mundane guises.[16]

This general technical framework also provides the social context for

15. Chinese Confucian, Buddhist, and Taoist ideas and practices have been synthesized over the centuries into a complex of cultural traits which, with variations of particular emphasis, is common throughout East Asia. Westerners are generally more familiar with the Buddhist elements, clearly visible in art and architecture, than with the less conspicuous Confucian and Taoist elements that define what are for outsiders the less visible realms of social relationships, medical practices, divination, fortunetelling, geomancy, the widespread use of agricultural and social almanacs based on the lunar calendar, and so forth.

16. See Andrew Plaks, *Archetype and Allegory in "The Dream of the Red Chamber"* (Princeton: Princeton University Press, 1979).

Tanizaki's chronic demonizing of women in his early and late works. In such stories as "The Tattoo" (*Shisei*, 1910) and "Aguri" (*Aoi hana*, 1922), it is precisely the weakened male that permits the female to grow to grotesquely excessive strength (though her perverse strength may also be interpreted as the cause of his progressive weakness). The once well-fleshed Okada of "Aguri," for example, wastes away to skin and bone, while his feline young paramour Aguri ("ugly") grows more and more powerful as she dons her new "skin" of exotic Western clothing.

Such problems on the level of the individual can be further understood as a reflection of the problems within the larger context, beginning with the start of the Meiji period in 1868, of Japan's new relationship to the West. The narrator of Tanizaki's *Naomi* (*Chijin no ai*, 1924–25), speaking of his disastrous "modern" marriage, feels that "as Japan grows increasingly cosmopolitan [*kokusaiteki*], Japanese and foreigners are eagerly mingling [*kōsai suru*] with one another; all sorts of new doctrines and philosophies are being introduced; and both men and women are adopting up-to-date Western fashions. No doubt, the times being what they are, the sort of marital relationship that we've had, unheard of until now, will begin to turn up on all sides."[17] The problems of the social breakdown caused by the new indiscriminate relationships between male and female are thus framed within the larger problem of the damage caused by the indiscriminate mingling (*kōsai*, "intercourse") of Japanese and foreigners. By the end of the story the entirely Westernized Naomi ("Now Me"), supported by her submissive Japanese husband Jōji ("George"), who is permitted to worship her only from the background, carries on her own independent "intercourse," sexual and otherwise, exclusively with foreign men who have names like McConnell, Dugan, and Eustace.

In the writings of Tanizaki and others, the foreign is often represented as an almost paralyzing threat to the Japanese. A more contemporary, horrifyingly comical expression of just how paralyzing that threat can be is found in Akiyuki Nosaka's 1967 story "American Hijiki [Seaweed]," in which the mere attendance at a live sex show in Tokyo of the former occupation GI Higgins, an overpowering, randy old goat, is enough to prevent the Japanese male performer from achieving an erection—a failure that swiftly escalates to become "a matter of pecker nationalism."[18] Nosaka attributes the man's

17. Jun'ichirō Tanizaki, *Naomi*, trans. Anthony Chambers (New York: Alfred A. Knopf, 1985), p. 3; *Chijin no ai*, in *Tanizaki Jun'ichirō zenshū* (hereafter *TZ*), vol. 10 (Tokyo: Chūōkōronsha, 1961), p. 3.

18. Akiyuki Nosaka, "American Hijiki" ("Amerika hijiki"), trans. Jay Rubin in *Contemporary Japanese Literature*, ed. Howard Hibbett, (New York: Knopf, 1977), p. 466. What the starving residents of a ravaged Tokyo at the end of the war mistake for nutritious seaweed dropped in tins from American planes turns out to be unfamiliar tobacco.

terrifying failure to the same source to which Takeshi Kaikō attributes his own impotence in *Into a Black Sun*: the trauma of Japan's inability to "rise to the occasion" of the American bombing of Japan in World War II and the country's subsequent occupation (see Chapter 11 below).

I have tried here to give some idea of the importance of East Asian Confucianism in shaping the Japanese notion of a self. When we inquire about the possibility of a Buddhist concept of the self, however, we run up against a contradiction in terms, because Buddhism regards the self as mere illusion, a temporary and fugacious aggregation of symptoms glued together by sticky attachments and fueled by volatile desires, something ideally to be attenuated, ultimately to be extinguished altogether. Yukio Mishima does construct a complex Buddhist metaphysics to account for his characters and their interactions, but that comes later in our chronology (see Chapter 8), and in any case provides little insight into the question of what a Buddhist concept of self might properly be. What matters here is that in either the Confucian or the Buddhist interpretive scheme, the idea of a "self" is something to be viewed with mistrust, if not actual alarm.

In fact, the only significant subject that seems to have been located specifically by Buddhist discourse (and really only in Japanese Buddhism at that) is the female one, and this is mainly because she presents such a terrible problem.[19] Her inherently jealous nature has her haunting others to their deaths in works as early as *The Tale of Genji*, and she appears in the medieval Nō drama in a variety of forms that resemble Tanizaki's own personal vision of females: pleasant, ordinary young women who turn out to be terrifying monsters. The moment in the Nō drama when the awful *hannya* demon mask is donned—or, even more impressively, when the Bunraku theater puppet's internal mechanism is triggered to convert a sweet young female face into a horned, fanged, fright-wigged, red-eyed visage—is one of the truly chilling moments of art. Perhaps because of the Shinto abhorrence of the pollution of blood and thus of female biological processes in general, and building on the masculine presumption that such unpleasant emotions as jealous rage and madness-inducing grief are experienced most powerfully, indeed incapacitatingly, by women (one can just as easily point to Shakespeare's ambition-crazed Lady Macbeth, shrewish Kate, and mad, melancholy Ophelia), the female "self" is viewed with alarm in Japanese Buddhism as having far greater potential for destruction than the male—this, to be sure, in the face of centuries of exclusively male civil carnage. Similarly,

19. For other views on the question of the Buddhist idea of the self in Meiji literature, see Walker, *The Japanese Novel of the Meiji Period*, pp. 96, 98; and Edward Fowler, *The Rhetoric of Confession: Shishōsetsu in Early Twentieth-Century Japanese Fiction* (Berkeley: University of California Press, 1988), pp. 14, 82.

although the *yin-yang* system is theoretically value-free when applied to such constructs as medicine and climate in which either *yin* or *yang* may be out of balance, it is difficult to think of an equally detailed investigation of excessive *yang* in fiction—unless that affliction should be considered simply the every-day state of affairs, accounting like some overabundance of testosterone for such ordinary and therefore unremarkable miseries as oppression, corruption, and warfare, whose effects (if not causes) are more easily attributed to the male realm of government than to the domestic domain of the female. However she is thought of, Japanese woman is definitely the weaker vessel, although we should at least acknowledge that, in exchange, she is neither honored nor cursed by being placed on a pedestal and patronized as "the fair sex."

In fact, it is taken for granted that *man* is the fairer sex, and his right to dominance and to solicitous female regard is presumed as well. In Natsumé Sōseki's works, however (see Chapter 2), modern man has forfeited his right to this regard because of a profound moral disease of the soul. Yet far from positing a corresponding ascendancy of woman, Sōseki gives every indication that, in Confucian terms, his badly treated women are ready enough to be womanly if only their wretched men will pull themselves together and get on with being manly. Tanizaki's males, by contrast, having perversely abdicated their manliness, are obsessed with an equally perverse desire for a corresponding female dominance. Thus, the old pervert of his *Diary of a Mad Old Man* (*Fūten rōjin nikki*, 1961) lives only to lick his daughter-in-law's toes in the shower and spends his remaining days on earth scheming to have an image of her foot engraved on his tombstone as a sign of his utter subjection (that only he knows it is not merely the conventional funerary emblem of the Buddha's footprint is his sole and secret source of joy).[20]

The official premodern and early modern Japanese state ideology was based on the premise, debated and affirmed in China and Japan over the centuries, that human nature is essentially good and thus worthy of being encouraged to perfection through moral education, rather than unregenerately evil and amenable only to harsh police-state repression. In literature, however, this optimistic premise seems never to have been taken very seriously, perhaps because it tended to make for rather dull, exhortatory prose. In its least harmful, most positive aspects, the conventional Edo-period (1603–1867) self was viewed as comprising a clutch of more or less tolerable personal quirks, idiosyncrasies, eccentricities, and aberrations. At its modern worst, its unsocial or even antisocial nature meant that it was

---

20. Jun'ichirō Tanizaki, *Diary of a Mad Old Man* (*Fūten rōjin nikki*, 1961), trans. Howard Hibbett (New York: Knopf, 1965). "Depraved" seems a better translation for the *fūten* of the title than "mad."

criminally pathological and perverse to the point of deviancy. The next two chapters show how this problematic emerging modern self is given shape in the work of Natsumé Sōseki and Jun'ichirō Tanizaki, two authors who were even more concerned with its terrors than they were engaged by its possibilities.

Chapter 2

The Psychopathic Self: Natsumé Sōseki's *Kokoro*

> In the sudden change that had come over her heart she wildly looked for her former self, but all knowledge of that self had gone, and she remained overwhelmed by a brutal invasion of thoughts of vengeance that drove away all the goodness in her life.
>
> —Emile Zola, *Thérèse Raquin*

The genius of Japan's Meiji period is often located in Natsumé Sōseki's identification of his own severe physical and spiritual problems with those that obsessed Japan in that confused early period of Westernization: Who am I? What is my place in the world? The span of Sōseki's life (1867–1916) is very nearly that of the Meiji period itself, during which Japan embarked on a dizzyingly rapid and wholesale adoption of the Western world's values and institutions.

If Sōseki has always represented one aspect of the quintessential "Meiji man" for the Japanese, however, it is certainly not because his fictional characters embody its heroic quest for "civilization and enlightenment" (*bunmei kaika*), the publicly declared official ideology of the period. Rather, it is because his characters explore so thoroughly the dark side of that quest: the problematic nature of real human beings, in contrast to the unproblematic proclaimed ideal. Beginning with the lightly ironic and picaresque humor of *I Am a Cat* (1905) and *Botchan* (1906), his novelistic career tended steadily through an increasingly modernist problematic toward the stark and unrelieved alienation of such later works as *Kokoro* (The Heart). Studies of this later Sōseki are generally dominated by the shadow of what has been called the "dark side" of the author, a phrase that echoes through the literature about him as though the public imagination read these works as explorations of the wrong side of Japan's new modern moon.

Sōseki's *Kokoro* (1914) is set within the historical framework of the death of the Meiji emperor in July 1912 and the subsequent ritual suicide (*junshi*) of General Maresuke Nogi and his wife on the morning of the imperial funeral in September. By Sōseki's time the ancient feudal ideal of following one's lord in death was already so antiquated as to seem entirely outlandish, a fact that is often forgotten in discussions of the event. Sōseki's character Sensei says of *junshi* only that "I had nearly forgotten the word, having no use for it in everyday life" (245/248).[1] And it is only natural that it should have been forgotten: the Tokugawa authorities some 250 years earlier had outlawed the act as the manifestation of an obsolete notion of feudal loyalty entirely unsuited to the needs of a centralized bureaucratic state.

Few modern Japanese authors have been the object of such intense psychoanalytic scrutiny as Sōseki. He suffered several severe nervous breakdowns, and the psychopathological states depicted by his characters, as well as his frequent reports in letters to friends of his own mental and physical problems, have made him fair game for this sort of inquiry. One incident in particular, the so-called "Shuzenji crisis" of 1910 (named after the popular spa where Sōseki suffered a devastating breakdown), has become the focus of special attention. A Sōseki disciple and hagiographer, Toyotaka Komiya, designated this brush with death a major turning-point in the master's thought.

As in the case of Yukio Mishima, the messy story of Sōseki's early childhood proposes itself as a simple and satisfying answer to many pressing questions about the adult man. Several of his novels repeat the theme of a family fortune stolen by a treacherous uncle, an act that induces a severe case of misanthropy in the young protagonist. It is just such an act of treachery in *Kokoro* that sets the scene for Sensei's betrayal of his friend K and leads to his final conclusion about mankind: given the slightest opportunity, says Sensei, a man will inevitably betray every trust. Like Mishima too, Sōseki apparently saw this breakdown in human relations in large part as the inevitable result of a society whose traditional values had been replaced by a modern esteem for only one thing: money. In Sensei's opinion, money invariably turns a gentleman into a scoundrel: "What turns a good man turn bad? . . . I replied with a single word: money" (141/70). (The word Sensei uses for "good man" here is the antique *kunshi*, fraught with significant Confucian overtones.)

The central problem of Sōseki's most famous novels is the Meiji problem of the nature of the individual self. Even before he and Japan could ask "Who *am* I?" they had first to ask an even more fundamental question: "What *is* an 'I'?" His unrelenting search for the meaning of the self is

---

1. Natsumé Sōseki, *Kokoro*, trans. Edwin McClellan (Chicago: Henry Regnery, 1957); *Kokoro* (The heart), in *Sōseki zenshū* (hereafter *SZ*), vol. 9 (Tokyo: Iwanami Shoten, 1928–29). Combined references to the English and Japanese versions respectively are cited in the text; unless otherwise noted, however, the translations are mine.

generally framed in the psychosocial terms of Meiji Japan's quest for a viable sense of its own identity in the face of the West and, in particular, within the sociopolitical terms of the need to invent, for the sake of modernization, an analogue to the Western "self" as the necessary precursor to the political concepts of "liberty," "freedom," and "rights" which are founded upon it. Especially relevant to this discourse is Thomas Hobbes's vision in *Leviathan* of the essentially antisocial nature of man in that pre–social contract "state of nature" understood since Rousseau to be his given primordial condition. These problems were (and sometimes still are) also interpreted in the light of Christian thought, the arguments couched in the eschatological and soteriological terms of originally sinful nature, the meaning of death, and the final possibility of atonement, forgiveness, redemption, and salvation.

In the end, however, analyses expressed in Christian terms seem as forced and unnatural as what Sōseki calls in *Kokoro* "introducing the smell of a Christian into the home of a Confucianist" (50/56). When we consider that Sōseki's own life has a distinctly "Confucianist" smell about it, this phrase acquires special significance. It is usually only briefly mentioned, and quickly forgotten, that his earliest education was in Chinese letters, and it was always to Chinese literature that he returned for solace in moments of spiritual crisis. Although he was known as Japan's preeminent scholar of English literature, his reception of and reaction to English culture was predicated on and formulated in terms of a lifelong love for Chinese philosophy, literature, poetry, and art. He wrote that when he was still a student, he had foolishly believed that because Chinese literature was good, English must be even better.[2] It is often assumed, therefore, that he must have conceived of Sensei's suicide in *Kokoro* in Western and even Romantic terms, a native Japanese vision of the ultimate meaning of death as an act of positive social import—that is, as an authentic reinterpretation of the act of *junshi*.[3] Sōseki seems to have found his ultimate refuge from the inevitability of suicide in such desperate circumstances, however (as a writer such as Ryūnosuke Akutagawa could not), in the cold consolation of a reasoned position which held that a principled "individualism" necessarily entailed an almost unbearable sense of alienation, under which the principled man had no other alternative than to bear up stoically.

2. Beongcheon Yu, *Natsume Sōseki* (New York: Twayne, 1969), p. 24.

3. English marginal comments in Sôseki's copy of Nietzsche's *Thus Spake Zarathustra* are often cited in discussions of his view of suicide: "Our saying is 'it is dishonour not to die at the right time.' The question is to find out the right time. Moralists say that it is not one's life and therefore it is immoral to take away one's life by oneself. . . . Consider whether it is the right time or not and decide for yourselves" (quoted in Yu, *Natsume Sōseki*, p. 131). In a letter of November 14, 1914, to Hayashibara Kōzō, Sōseki states that though he would never suggest suicide as appropriate for anyone else, he would be content if others happened to agree with his own feeling that "death is man's concluding and most fortunate state" (*SZ*, 19:376–77).

This view is further complicated by the problem that we must distinguish Sōseki on the one hand from a writer such as Mori Ōgai, who after Nogi's suicide turned to writing stories in praise of such noble acts of *junshi*, and on the other from an Akutagawa, whose 1922 story entitled "The General" (*Shōgun*) actually ridiculed it. Critics have sometimes pondered the extent to which Sōseki's identification with the "spirit of Meiji" should be considered a reflection of patriotic or even nationalistic feeling on his part, a widely accepted interpretation suggested by Sensei's words in *Kokoro*: "I felt as though the spirit of the Meiji era had begun with the Emperor and had ended with him" (245/248).[4] Press opinion in Japan at Nogi's suicide was divided between nationalistic pride and a sense of shame in the eyes of the world for such a barbarous action.[5] For his own part, Sōseki meticulously recorded in his diary the various newspaper accounts of the testimonials to the emperor written by those in power, and he himself wrote a proper eulogy to Meiji. Nogi's suicide, however, clearly left a less than favorable impression on him, and he was especially annoyed at the government's action closing down popular amusements at the news of Nogi's death.[6]

On balance, Sōseki can justifiably be seen as having shared in the ambivalence of his times. Perhaps the best clue to his real feelings about Nogi's anachronistic death comes from a letter he wrote almost immediately after the event to Toyotaka Komiya in September 1912, reporting in an entirely deadpan manner that his recent surgery for hemorrhoids had left him with a certain sympathetic reverence for the suffering that General Nogi's suicide must certainly have entailed.[7]

Sōseki's eulogy to the late emperor conspicuously refers to a single imperial act, Meiji's promulgation of the Imperial Rescript on Education of 1890; he sees the monarch as a teacher who brought education to enlighten the benighted heart of man.[8] This central Confucian tenet of the ruler as the teacher of his people was developed especially in the work of the post-Confucian philosopher Hsün Tzu (fl. B.C. 298–238). It seems entirely logi-

---

4. Jay Rubin, *Injurious to Public Morals: Writers and the Meiji State* (Seattle: University of Washington Press, 1984), p. 9, notes: "The emotional upheavals surrounding the grandly orchestrated funeral of the Meiji emperor . . . symbolized the psychological struggle that most sophisticated Japanese would continue to experience as the government sought to preserve the aura of a united national family against the influx of cosmopolitan culture."

5. Carol Gluck, *Japan's Modern Myths: Ideology in the Late Meiji Period* (Princeton: Princeton University Press, 1985), p. 225.

6. Ibid., 219. Much the same controversy erupted over the government's ineffectual proclamation of national "self-restraint" (*jishuku*) following the death of Hirohito (the Shōwa emperor) in 1989, when many popular entertainments felt constrained to close briefly in reponse.

7. *SZ*, 19:165. Sōseki's diary during this period reports almost exclusively on his problems with hemorrhoids, and the protagonist of his unfinished final novel *Meian* (Light and darkness) also suffers from an agonizing case of "anal fistula."

8. *SZ*, 10:165.

cal, then, to read *Kokoro* as an exploration of human nature developed precisely in terms of the famous historical dispute between Hsün Tzu and his older contemporary, the post-Confucian Chinese philosopher Meng Tzu (Mencius, B.C. 371–?289), over whether human nature is essentially good or evil. The neo-Confucian orthodoxy in China (and later in Japan) eventually upheld Mencius's view that human nature is essentially good. Hsün Tzu's heterodox pessimism has subsequently been regarded (along with his interest in the nature of rhetorical logic) as the crack in the Chinese armor that allowed the far more radically pessimistic Buddhist view of human nature to enter Chinese and Japanese thought.

The cover of the original edition of *Kokoro*, designed by Sōseki himself, consists of the character for "heart," followed by a passage from Hsün Tzu: "[The heart is] that which governs the material being and rules the spiritual faculty." In the original Chinese text this passage is preceded by the statement: "All human misery arises from the fact that [the heart] is covered over with warped ideas that conceal its capacity for reason. . . . By what means does man know of the Way? By means of the heart."

Hsün Tzu's pessimistic view of man is revealed from the very opening words of his chapter "Man's Nature":

> Man's nature is evil; goodness is the result of "artifice" [*wei*, "that which is man-made," generally interpreted as ritual and law]. The nature of man is such that he is born with a fondness for profit. If he indulges this fondness it will lead him into wrangling and strife, and all sense of courtesy and humility will disappear. He is born with feelings of envy and hate, and if he indulges these, they will lead him into injury and destruction, and all sense of loyalty and faithfulness will disappear. Man is born with desires of the eyes and ears, with a fondness for sounds and beauty. If he indulges these, they will lead him into lewdness and licentiousness, and all the pattern and order of propriety and righteousness will be lost. Hence, any man who follows his nature and indulges his emotions will inevitably become involved in wrangling and strife, will violate the forms and rules of society, and will end in violence. *Therefore, man must first be transformed by the instructions of a teacher* and guided by ritual principles, and only then will he be able to observe the dictates of courtesy and humility, obey the forms and rules of society, and achieve order. It is obvious from this, then, that man's nature is evil, and that his goodness is the result of artifice.[9]

Sōseki's casting of the Meiji emperor in the role of the sage-teacher reflects, more than two millennia later, this ancient Chinese notion of the importance

9. *Basic Writings of Mo Tzu, Hsün Tzu, and Han Fei Tzu*, trans. Burton Watson (New York: Columbia University Press, 1967), p. 166, slightly amended following Chan, *Source Book*, p. 128 (emphasis added).

of the teacher in socializing the evil of man's untutored original nature. Before Japan could look to the West for new institutions, it had first to reexamine the nature and utility of those it had earlier so thoroughly adopted from China. *Kokoro* is perhaps the best-known piece of soul-searching in all of Meiji literature.

In his chapter "A Discussion of Heaven" Hsün Tzu further develops the idea of what he means by "the heart":

> When the work of heaven has been established and its accomplishments have been brought to completion, the form of man is whole and his spirit is born. Then love and hate, delight and anger, sorrow and joy find lodging in him: these are called his heavenly emotions. His ears, eyes, mouth, nose, and body all come into contact with the world, though their sensory functions are separate: these are called his heavenly faculties. *The heart* dwells in the center and governs the five faculties, and hence is called the heavenly lord. Provisions are not of the same species as man, and yet they serve to nourish him and are called heavenly nourishment. He who accords with what is proper to his species will be blessed; he who turns against it will suffer misfortune. These are called the heavenly dictates. To darken the heavenly lord [the heart], disorder the heavenly faculties, reject the heavenly nourishment, defy the heavenly dictates, turn against the heavenly emotions, and thereby destroy the heavenly accomplishment, is called dire disaster.[10]

If Sōseki's character Sensei (whose name means "teacher") is somewhat paradoxically a living demonstration of what Hsün Tzu refers to as "disorder of the heart," it is because Sensei himself lives in an age of evil when teachers are, unfortunately, necessary, and because he too has inevitably been touched by that evil. Sensei is a man without any interest in the joys of life, one whom "disorder of the heart" has led to destructive acts that will inevitably end in the "dire disaster" predicted by the ancient philosopher. *Kokoro* is a quite practical demonstration of what happens when, in response to new Western ideas, one strips away the positive Confucian "artifice" that society has so painstakingly created for the purpose of concealing and tempering man's original nature. For what is thus revealed is his essential evil, now disastrously unseasoned by any of the attributes of a social being.

George DeVos and Hiroshi Wagatsuma, following a major line in Sōseki studies, note that Sōseki's works are "pervaded with background leitmotifs derived from Confucian ethical values" and suggest that "there is an underlying fear in Sōseki that people, freed from these values, would become

---

10. Hsün Tzu, "T'ien-lun," translation based on Watson's in *Basic Writings*, pp. 80–81 (emphasis added).

egocentric, untrustworthy, cold, and even cruel—and, most importantly, somehow incapable of structuring relations with others."[11] This central problem of "structuring relations with others" in a degenerate age is reflected in the very organization of Sōseki's novel. Both the characters and plot of *Kokoro* can be understood as expressly and systematically stripping away the orthodox Mencian framework of the social order, one constituent element at a time, to reveal the true nature of the egotistical, presocial "self" postulated by the pessimistic Hsün Tzu.

Apart from his more optimistic view of human nature, Mencius is also the *locus classicus* of an understanding of the social order based on what Hsün Tzu called the "artifice" of rules and ritual action. Confucius had merely suggested this understanding in his well-known if somewhat mysterious dictum "If the ruler acts as a ruler, then the minister will act as a minister; if the father acts as a father, then the son will act as a son" (*Lun Yü* 12:11). Mencius elaborates this homology of interdependent feudal obligations based on familial relationships in a passage concerning the centrality of the teacher:

> It is the Way of the common people that, when full and warm, if allowed to live idly without education, they will degenerate to the level of animals. Being concerned about this, [Shun] had Hsieh become Minister of Education and instruct the people in human relations.

There follows a list of the primary "five social relationships," each characterized by its proper human attributes: (1) between father and child there is "affection" or "love"; (2) between ruler and minister, "righteousness" or "duty"; (3) between husband and wife, "distinction" or "attention to separate functions"; (4) between elder and younger brother, "proper order" or "precedence"; (5) between friends, "fidelity" or "faith" or "trust."[12] The list begins with the family, the locus of filiality, and ends in the only recognized nonhierarchical and nonfamilial relationship.

By the time the order of the five social relationships appears in a significantly revised later formulation in *The Doctrine of the Mean* (*Chung Yung*, a systematized codification of earlier Confucian ideas) as the five "modes of the Way" (*ta-tao*), it has become the hierarchical basis for the family-state with the primary relationship of ruler/minister now at the top, having taken

11. George DeVos and Hiroshi Wagatsuma, "Alienation and the Author: A Triptych on Social Conformity and Deviancy in Japanese Intellectuals," in *Socialization for Achievement*, ed. George DeVos (Berkeley: University of California Press, 1973), pp. 546–47.

12. *Mencius*, III.A.8, cited in Chan, *Source Book*, pp. 69–70; D. C. Lau, *Mencius* (London: Penguin Books, 1970), p. 102.

precedence over that of father/child.[13] These relationships are also paired with their proper corresponding social ideals, beginning with the basic attribute of "sincerity": if one is sincere to oneself, he will be obedient to his parents; if he is obedient to his parents, he will have the trust of his friends; and if he has the trust of his friends, he will have the confidence of his superiors.[14]

It may seem strange that these antique Confucian values could have held any significance for the concerns of a modernizing Meiji Japan in the face of direct intellectual competition from Western ideologies. Yet Enomoto Takeaki, who was minister of education when the Imperial Rescript on Education was promulgated in 1890, stressed in an interview given on the occasion that the principles of Mencius and Hsün Tzu were in fact the *only* proper basis of a modern Japanese concept of education and emphasized in particular the importance of these ancient cardinal relationships.[15] The ideological significance of this stance is borne out quite literally in the brief text of the Rescript (which we recall is the single act of the Meiji emperor that Sōseki singled out for praise), at the heart of which lie the old Mencian precepts: "Be filial to your parents, affectionate to your brothers and sisters; as husbands and wives be harmonious; as friends, true."[16] This ideology formed the mainstay of the Ministry of Education's policies, which during the 1880s were enacted in edicts forbiding the use of foreign morals texts in Japan and substituting more traditional ones, and enforced by an active police censorship of books that did not conform to this ethic.[17]

Kokoro presents social situations embodying each of the five cardinal social relationships, only to strip them away in turn until at the end of the novel nothing remains but the isolated "self," like some tiny newborn rat, defenseless and unattractive, to face alone the empty bleakness of its newly atomized universe.

The first of the novel's three sections ("Sensei and I") opens with a description of the budding friendship between the young narrator and the somewhat older man he calls Sensei, then turns in the second section ("My Parents and I") to an examination of the relationship between the narrator and his parents. The narrator has dutifully returned home to attend his

13. *Chung Yung*, 20:8, cited in Chan, *Source Book*, p. 105.
14. Ibid., 20:17, cited in Chan, *Source Book*, p. 107.
15. Gluck, *Japan's Modern Myths*, pp. 119–20.
16. As translated from the Imperial Rescript in Herbert Passin, *Society and Education in Japan* (New York: Teachers College, Columbia University, East Asia Institute, 1965), p. 151.
17. See Kenneth Pyle, *The New Generation in Meiji Japan: Problems of Cultural Identity, 1885–1895* (Palo Alto, Calif.: Stanford University Press, 1965), p. 121. The issue is also discussed in Jay Rubin, "Sōseki on Individualism: *Watakushi no kojinshugi*," *Monumenta Nipponica* 34, no. 1 (1979): esp. 25.

dying father who provides, together with the devoted wife who looks after him, the very model of the proper relationship between husband and wife. This traditional old couple's easy and comfortable rapport forms a stark contrast to the strained and unhappy marriage of Sensei and his young wife. A visit home by the narrator's elder brother reveals that there has never been much brotherly affection lost between the two. During the father's last days, news arrives of the Meiji emperor's demise, which the father takes to be an intimation of his own. Before he expires, however, the narrator receives a long letter disclosing Sensei's intended suicide; he abandons his dying father and rushes off to Tokyo to find Sensei.

This letter, which the narrator rereads on the train, forms the third part of the novel ("Sensei and His Testament"). In it Sensei explains that his own wretched state of soul (to this point amply depicted but its cause left a mystery) must be traced to his youth: after his father died, Sensei's uncle had betrayed him by usurping his patrimony. Sensei is aware that he himself must share the blame, since he had selfishly refused to return home from college to marry and take up his family duties as his father's heir. Nevertheless, the uncle's usurpation of his inheritance had turned Sensei into a misanthrope who feels that human nature is fundamentally evil and that all human relationships inevitably end in betrayal. This feeling was subsequently borne out by Sensei's own betrayal of his college friend K in an attempt to win the woman they both loved. Hence, Sensei informs the narrator that he avoids all friendships now because he knows they will only mean betrayal later. While Sensei contemplates the ruin of his life—his betrayal of his dead father's trust by his refusal to return home to marry, the elder brother's betrayal of the younger, his own betrayal of his best friend's trust, his near-abandonment of his wife—news of General Nogi's suicide is announced, and Sensei resolves that only by a similar act can he atone for his own wretched life.

The relationship between ruler and minister, according to Mencius, is one properly governed by "duty" or "right conduct," and General Nogi's self-immolation following a life of waiting to atone for the shame he felt he had incurred during the Seinan Uprising thirty-six years earlier (1877) is a model of such conduct—though in the world of the distant past where gestures of this sort still counted, not in a modern world that sneers at them as acts of barbarism. This is the only one of the five traditional social relationships that the characters in the novel succeed in upholding—though of course these are not really characters in the novel, the story of Meiji and Nogi lying entirely outside the novel's fictional framework. Or rather, it is more accurate to say that their story stands as the solid, permanent frame within which the more mutable fiction of modern life takes place. Their passing marks the end of the old order of things, a time when the old values still held. Sōseki himself, like many Japanese, was no longer able to believe wholeheartedly in such an outdated notion of feudal loyalty; but he leaves it intact, like the charred but still-standing frame of a house destroyed by fire, to remind his readers of the now ruined strength and security it had once implied. Kenneth Pyle nicely summarizes this human inability to shake off an outdated frame of reference: "When the introduction of Western science broke up the Confucian world-view and undermined belief in a natural social order, trust in the old values began to weaken. The former assuredness was no longer possible. Many Japanese, . . . though still emotionally tied to old values, were nevertheless intellectually alienated."[18]

The qualities of obedience and affection that should characterize the relationship between father and child are betrayed by the young Sensei's refusal to return home to take up his patrimony and likewise by the young narrator's failure to remain at the side of his dying father. The relationship between husband and wife is depicted in its ideal traditional form in touching scenes of the narrator's mother caring for her dying husband, as well as in its alienated modern form in the terrible distance and coldness that separate Sensei and his wife. In the subplot of Sensei's uncle and father, elder brother betrays younger; in that of Sensei and K, friend betrays friend. We are left with a series of deaths, absences that characterize the emptiness and alienation of the modern "self": no ruler, no minister, no fathers, no brothers, no husbands, no friends. Such is the lesson in human relations that this teacher has arranged for his young pupil. *Kokoro* is a lesson delivered by a teacher about the human "heart," and Sōseki leaves us in no doubt as to exactly what sort of heart it really is.

In the end, then, it is difficult to accept Jay Rubin's conclusion that in his later novels "Sōseki's increasingly dark view of man and the world never lacks for despair, but it stops short of condemning human nature as inherently evil."[19] A practical demonstration of Hsün Tzu's vision of man's inherently evil nature in the face of the opposing Mencian ideal supported by Meiji ideology, the novel ends with precisely this despairing vision of human nature. *Kokoro* is Sōseki's response to what he saw as the vile hypocrisy of the state's ideological blindness to the terrifying truth of the modern human condition.

A few days following the publication of *Kokoro* in 1914, Sōseki delivered his famous lecture "My Individualism" to students at the Gakushūin, or Peers' School, where Nogi had been president from 1907 until his death in 1912. In his rambling talk the novelist is appropriately ambivalent about the

18. Pyle, *The New Generation in Meiji Japan*, p. 128.
19. Jay Rubin, "The Evil and the Ordinary in Sōseki's Fiction," *Harvard Journal of Asiatic Studies*, 46, no. 2 (1986): 337.

recently imported concept of "individualism": it is good because it is modern and necessary, but it is bad because it is un-Japanese and destructive; one should be an individual and have a *self*, but one should not be egotistical, *selfish*.[20]

The "selfless self" implicit in the Japanese script is even more problematic than the English oxymoron suggests. The ordinary Japanese word for "I" (*watakushi*) used in the novel is written with a character that has almost universally negative connotations in combination with other words (Sino-Japanese *shi*; Chinese *ssu*), regularly denoting "selfish, illegitimate, irregular, misappropriated, unfair, ill-gotten, pretended, secret, counterfeit," among other meanings. In the philosophical writing of the Edo period the long-accepted counterpart of this term was *ōyake* (*kō*; Chinese *kung*), denoting "public, communal, for the common good, out in the open, fair, self-evident, civic, official."[21] During the Meiji period the time-tested Chinese model of how man properly functions as a social being was, in response to the assimilation of Western ideas, beginning to change gradually to something new that was still struggling toward definition, and its opposite quality was also in the process of redefinition. Though it is unlikely that the Japanese have ever consciously found anything particularly negative about the use of the character that denotes "I," it is striking that the word most commonly used for the modern "self" should have come to be represented by such an unpleasant and even antisocial character.[22]

Sensei's recognition of *junshi* as a proper response to the problem of the evil of the human heart may have been prompted, consciously or unconsciously, by the fact that the Japanese reading of the Chinese characters used to write the name "Hsün Tzu" happens to be "junshi." This punning equation (punning has always been a more common, serious, and acceptable discursive mode in Japan than in the West) sheds some light on the problem of what Jay Rubin calls a persistent inability on the part of critics to explain "exactly how the suicide of General Nogi is related to the suicide of Sōseki's protagonist in *Kokoro*."[23] The answer can only be that the death of the traditional philosophical concept of the self literally entails the death of the self. It is perhaps ironic, and reveals the tentative nature of Sōseki's own

20. Natsumé Sōseki, "My Individualism," trans. in Rubin, "Sōseki on Individualism"; "Watakushi no kojinshugi," *SZ*, 11:431–63.

21. The two words thus have something of the oppositional sense of "subject/object" and "subjective/objective." The important *ōyake/watakushi* polarity has been examined by H. D. Harootunian in "Between Politics and Culture: Authority and the Ambiguities of Intellectual Life in Imperial Japan," in *Japan in Crisis: Essays on Taishō Democracy*, ed. Bernard S. Silverman and H. D. Harootunian (Princeton: Princeton University Press, 1974), esp. pp. 119–20.

22. See Pollack, *The Fracture of Meaning*, p. 217.

23. Rubin, "Sōseki on Individualism," pp. 22–23.

philosophical position, that this equation could hold true only within the traditional family-state homology, for it certainly has no meaning outside it.

Sōseki's adaptation of Chinese ideas is revealed even in the appearance of the book jacket he designed for *Kokoro*. On the front cover is the Chinese character for "heart"—which can be read in both Chinese and Sino-Japanese (the reading usually followed for sounding out passages of Chinese and for single characters out of context) as *shin*[24]—followed by the Chinese text from Hsün Tzu; on the spine, however, the Japanese reading of that character, *kokoro*, is spelled out in the native syllabic script. Thus, just as Japanese involves a complex voicing of Chinese script with entirely Japanese readings that are no longer felt to be at all alien, Sōseki's novel can be understood as a Japanese voicing that translates a set of age-old Chinese philosophical concepts into a modern and entirely Japanese world of meaning. This complex translation does not need to be spelled out for the reader point for point; rather, it hovers, invisible but all-pervasive, as a mediating construct that both creates and occupies the space between the generative but no longer familiar Chinese philosophical abstraction deep in the background and the familiar modern Japanese figures who populate the surface of the novel.[25] In so doing, it creates a sense of depth of which the modern reader—Japanese or otherwise—is unlikely to be aware.

The self in *Kokoro* is plotted along the axes of traditional pair-oppositions by which the Confucian social scheme defines the (male) individual in society. A vertical hierarchical axis distinguishing greater from lesser authority (senior from junior, male from female) is intersected by a horizontal axis that joins the macrocosm of the state to the microcosm of the family in what Mircea Eliade has called the "anthropocosmic vision." At any point in the traditional pattern of a life, a man might be precisely located along these axes in his chronological progress within the family from younger to elder brother, to husband, and to paterfamilias; and within the state from junior and subordinate private person to senior and superordinate public man.

The "individual" in such a scheme is deemed worthy only of thorough suppression as posing a threat to the social order. The concept of "the private" cannot entail *privacy* in our sense of the word; Mishima, as I noted in the introduction, tells us that the borrowed foreign word *puraibashii* expresses in Japanese an antisocial and even pathological foreign condition involving all the negative connotations catalogued above: illicit, selfish, biased, and so on. It follows that a "self" can be located only in a set of

24. Although the current official romanization in China is *xin*, the pronunciation is much the same in Sino-Japanese and in Chinese, with the difference that Japanese lacks the Chinese tone.

25. I have treated this same technique of the "translation" of Chinese into Japanese in earlier periods in *The Fracture of Meaning*, especially pp. 74–76.

discourses very different from our own. In the Sino-Japanese cognitive world, fiction, long considered part of the illicit "private" (*watakushi/shi*) realm, becomes something literally "unauthorized"; what can be "authorized," to the contrary, pertains only to the realm of the public (*ōyake/kō*).

The Chinese understanding of these parameters is reflected in the titles of such novels as Wu Ching-tzu's mid-eighteenth-century *An Unauthorized History of the Scholar-Bureaucrats* (*Julin waishih*) and Lu Xun's early twentieth-century *An Authorized Biography of Ah Q* (*A Q Cheng Chuan*), works in which the relationship of the unauthorized writer of "private fiction" to the authorized facts of "public history" is at issue. This problematic relationship might usefully be contrasted with the very different cognitive world presupposed by the congruent senses in English of such complexes of words as author/authority/authorize, and create/creator/creative, which seem to point explicitly to the writer of fiction as someone fully authorized to be creative. Confucius was traditionally held to have circumscribed the proper limits of writing when he said that he "transmitted but did not create," and the traditional evaluation of his role as editor of the "Spring and Autumn Annals" limits his contribution to the suggestion of oblique moral judgments on the facts of history by careful selection of words alone. Authors in China and Japan ever since have had to transgress these restrictive traditional and officially sanctioned boundaries to one degree or another whenever they have done more than "transmit" the facts of history or pass implicit moral judgment upon them—that is, whenever they have written fiction.

In *Kokoro* the self is understood as something essentially parasitic, antisocial, and frighteningly destructive of both the social fabric and its human host. Stripped of its traditional social definition it clearly resembles Meiji man in that, in its new undefined and dangerously chaotic state, it has lost its traditional sense of what it is, where it is going, or what its purpose may be. Sitting alone in his study, Sensei comes to a conclusion that will haunt later Japanese writers: self-conscious thought, far from Descartes's reassuring *cogito*, is itself a kind of evil and an act of betrayal of all that it means to be human.

While Sōseki's negative view of the self is something new in Japanese thought, Sensei will certainly not be the last wretched man to agonize over the horror of human nature. In the broad range of Sōseki's characters are adumbrated the very types of modern man that populate twentieth-century Japanese fiction, spanning the gamut from Botchan, the cheerfully hapless Mr. Chips of Sōseki's popular early work, to Sensei at its later limits. Indeed, the problem that there seems so little middle ground between the bumbling but witty picaro and the gloomily self-absorbed modern character might be attributed to the possibility that Sōseki's thorough and compelling explorations of the possibilities of modern character left little choice in the matter for later generations of writers. If the natural urge to respond to traditional conventions of character inevitably resulted in the former type, anything else could only fall into the new categorical abyss of the "I-novel" character's relentless absorption with the problems of his miserable self, which is discovered, somewhat like Descartes's *cogito*, to be the only solid ground left to stand on. Later writers continued to probe the viability of the equivocal middle ground, but as we shall see in subsequent chapters, it is surprising how faithfully the male characters of later generations—Tanizaki's Kaname, Kawabata's Kikuji and Shimamura, Abé's two-bit private eyes, Ōe's feckless Bird and Mitsu, even Kaikō's modern alienated narrative selves—seem to reflect the problems of their common ancestral mentor, Sensei. It is as if they were unable, exactly as Sensei had planned they should be, ever to free themselves of his terrible paralyzing burden, the "testament" (*isho*) that constitutes the last third of *Kokoro*. It is hardly surprising that they should so often end up tied to women who resemble Sensei's intelligent, nurturing, and self-effacing wife, as if that doomed and barren coupling could be the only model for the transmission to future generations of such a doomed and barren literary paternity.

In exploring the possibilities of a Japanese "self" that might correspond to a presumed Western one, Sōseki discovered at its "heart" (*kokoro*) much the same darkness that Joseph Conrad did in *Heart of Darkness*, published in 1902, near the end of Sōseki's two-year stay in London.[26] This early process of self-definition may be deemed a constructive one to the degree that Sōseki's early works continue to be read, along with Kawabata's *Izu Dancer*, Mishima's *Sound of Waves*, and Ōe's *Seiteki ningen* (Sexual man), as young adult novels of self-discovery. But the destructive nature of that exploration in the later works was to have a much more powerful and enduring effect. It is as if, having constructed a mirror, Sōseki's problem turned out to be like that of the vampire: he was fearful not so much of what he would find in that mirror as of the horror of finding nothing there at all. Yet even if the result is only to frighten himself to death, the author perversely continues to long, more than anything else, to find himself in that mirror, to gain recognition for his work, to be authorized. Literature in Japan, as anywhere else in the world, remains the special mirror in which such hopes are invested; but the fear of what is to be found seems to have continued to exert a special force in Japan.

26. See Chapter 10 below.

Chapter 3

The Deviant Self:
Jun'ichirō Tanizaki's *Some Prefer Nettles*

That women are spiteful is quite true,
For after death they'll follow you,
Tormenting demons in hell they'll be
To use their whips on you and me.
—Jippensha Ikku, *Tōkaidōchū hizakurige*

When you go to visit a woman, don't forget to take your whip.
—Friedrich Nietzsche, *Thus Spake Zarathustra*

In his 1924 novel *Naomi*, Jun'ichirō Tanizaki (1886–1965) carries the consequences of modern man's abdication of his reponsibilities to his own and the opposite sex well beyond the point of no return. And as young Jōji is torn apart by those consequences, like both Sensei and the young narrator of *Kokoro* he inevitably rends the fabric of society at large.

In need of ever larger sums to support Naomi, his beautiful but increasingly demanding young mistress, Jōji writes to his widowed mother in the countryside to ask for money. To ensure that she will send it, however, he resorts to lies rather than confess the truth that he knows will only confirm his own despicableness to both her and himself. He finally returns home only when his mother dies, and the realization that he would never have returned otherwise awakens him to the worthlessness of his deceitful life. Wretched and repentant, Jōji resolves briefly to stay on the farm and reform but soon acquiesces in an uncle's suggestion that he return to Tokyo. A modern electrical engineer, the uncle observes, has little future in the countryside. Torn between the traditional but stifling world of his rural hometown and the excitement of the modern metropolis, Jōji frames his dilemma in terms of a quandary of self:

Until yesterday I'd been crazed, body and soul, with Naomi's charms. Today I was kneeling before the deceased and offering incense. There seemed to be no connection between these two worlds of mine. "Which is the real 'I'?" asked the voice that I heard when I examined myself, lost in tears of grief, sadness, and surprise. And from another direction I heard a whisper: "It's no surprise that your mother died now. She's warning you; she's leaving you a lesson."[1]

A literal translation, though awkward in English, reveals more clearly the syntactical mechanisms by means of which the narrator structures his dilemma:

The "I" which until just yesterday was crazed body and soul with Naomi's scent of lust, the "I" which now knelt by the deceased, offering up the scent of incense—these two worlds of "I" seemed to have no connection. "Is the 'I' of yesterday or the 'I' of today the real 'I'?" I seemed to hear a voice ask from nowhere as, amidst sighs, grief, and shock, my self thus reflected upon itself.

The ironic morpho-syntactic parallelism of the deliberately overtranslated "scent of lust" (*iroka*, "beauty") and "scent of incense" (*senkō*, "incense"), which juxtaposes the depraved lust of the world of the living to its fatal results in that of the dead, is inaccessible in English, but clearly intentional and immediately obvious in the Japanese. An English translation also necessarily calms somewhat the overwrought nature of "my self reflected upon itself" (*jibun de jibun o kaerimiru*). The disjointedness of the language in the original reveals the narrator's agitated state of mind as it alternates jerkily between this "I" and that, no longer even certain of what an "I" may be. The effect is not unlike that of the passage in Zola's *Thérèse Raquin* in which Thérèse's mind is finally rent into its constituent warring parts, the barbaric passion that has overwhelmed her and the civilizing reason it has driven away: "In the sudden change that had come over her heart she wildly looked for her former self, but all knowledge of that self had gone, and she remained overwhelmed by a brutal invasion of thoughts of vengeance that drove away all the goodness in her life."[2]

The repetition in *Naomi* of the word "I" (*watakushi*; its problematic nature is discussed in the preceding chapter) has the effect of depriving it of any meaning, and it must therefore be replaced by a clumsy gloss: the "I" now becomes "a self that reflects upon a self," clearly the by-product of that sickness of introspection begun by Sensei in *Kokoro*. Likewise, the "lesson"

1. Tanizaki, *Naomi*, p. 202; *Chijin no ai*, pp. 218–19.
2. Emile Zola, *Thérèse Raquin* (New York: Penguin Viking, 1986), p. 207.

(*kyōkun*) Jōji's mother has left him is very much the same as the "testament" Sensei left his young friend, concerning the evil of the human heart when it abandons those values by which it has traditionally been socialized. Beginning to feel himself polluted by the ever more-demanding Naomi, whom he now reviles as "a filthy slut" (*kegarawashii impu*), Jōji fantasizes that he can purify himself of the city only by returning to the pure soil of the country and becoming a farmer. Tanizaki, intent on continuing his exploration of human depravity in the big city, does not follow through on this brief resolve here, but a few years later, in *Some Prefer Nettles*, he considers more thoroughly the option of returning to the soil.

Tanizaki began *Some Prefer Nettles* (*Tade kuu mushi*, 1928) when he was forty-two, following his move to Osaka after the Great Kantō Earthquake, which leveled much of Tokyo in 1923. The work's themes presage its author's increasingly complicated domestic life, marked by a divorce in 1930, remarriage in 1931, a second divorce in 1933, and a third marriage in 1935. If the physical, spiritual, and domestic problems of Natsumé Sōseki and his fictional characters seem so accurately to manifest those of the body and psyche politic of Meiji Japan, the marital and domestic passages of Tanizaki and his characters seem suitably to express the problems posed by this somewhat later period in Japan's ongoing and fitful relationship with the West. Like *Naomi*, *Some Prefer Nettles* explores the homology between a problematic personal sexual identity and an equally problematic national one. And, perhaps in part responding to a rising *Zeitgeist* of nationalist enthusiasm (itself a response to the challenge of "modern"—that is, Western—values), the novel explores the possible solution of a return to tradition.

Some Prefer Nettles continues to develop Tanizaki's fetishization and demonization of woman, extending to the West in general his obsessive fascination and repulsion. The work thus elaborates another of his major psychological themes: a perverse fascination with the Whore of the West, the other side of a "natural" obsession with Mother Japan. The theme is inscribed in Tanizaki's work as early as "Longing for Mother" ("Haha o kouru ki," 1919). This loose, intensely poetic evocation of the author's mother emerges in translation, unfortunately, less as a powerful outpouring of poeticized emotion than as trite sentimentality. The essay is what the Japanese would term a "mother-piece" (*hahamono*), the term usually applied to a play or film that evokes and celebrates with copious tears all the tender-hearted sentiments proper to that great and primal passion, mother love. In it Tanizaki recreates a fantastic topography of Mother, embodied in the vitality of the old downtown merchant Tokyo of his childhood, its most powerful emotions invested in place names used as poetic evocation (a technique known as *makurakotoba*) and contrasted with the nameless bleak and lifeless countryside through which the adult male is doomed to wander.

Strolling dejectedly through a dreary autumnal landscape, the author sees a light in the distance that comes progressively into focus in a dramatic cinematic closeup as a montage of metonyms: a farmhouse, a kitchen, a fire, food—mother! Starved for those culturally interchangeable quantities mother and food, he rushes in, only to be rebuffed by an old crone who declares sharply that she is most certainly *not* his mother.

As he leaves, frustrated, the warm light of these always unattainable home fires is translated poetically into the moon shining over Japan's most sacred spots—the groves at Miho, the Bay of Tago—in a second remove of the idealized topography of poeticized emotion whereby Mother simply *becomes* Japan. The message of this translation is that, no longer a child, a grown man cannot expect to find solace in Mother and must transfer that eternally unfulfillable longing to the greater and more proper entity that will always welcome him with open arms, Mother Japan herself (the modern corporation will later take over a large part of this role). Conventional poetic images of Japaneseness, invoked in turn and suffused with the power of Mother, finally coalesce in the memory of a wandering female musician walking the streets, the narrator-child's wet nurse humming an imitation of the samisen's plunk (conjured in the nurse's repeated nonsense phrase, "*I* want-some *tem*-pu-ra" (*tem*-pura *ku*-i-tai). The musician is a young woman fetishized in yet another metonymic sequence only as a white neck, a black hairdo, an ear, a nose, powder, tears. Her tears become the narrator's own, and as they cry together, she is finally revealed to be—Mother: "She kneels down and embraces me. I hug her with all my might, and smell her warm, sweet breasts through the folds of her kimono."[3]

For Tanizaki, memory is invariably something that begins in music and ends in Mother. Thus, when in *Some Prefer Nettles* Kanamé enters a puppet theater for the first time since his childhood, the old familiar sound of the samisens immediately conjures up the inevitable flood of powerful memories: "As he stepped from his sandals and felt the smooth, cold wood against his stockinged feet, he thought for an instant of a time, long ago—he could have been no more than four or five—when he had gone to a play in Tokyo with his mother. He remembered how he had sat on her lap" (22/16).[4]

3. Jun'ichiro Tanizaki, "Longing for Mother," trans. Edward Fowler, *Monumenta Nipponica* 35, no. 4 (1980): 478; "Haha o kouru ki," in *TZ*, vol. 7 (Tokyo: Chūōkōronsha, 1958), p. 205.

4. Jun'ichiro Tanizaki, *Some Prefer Nettles*, trans. Edward Seidensticker (New York: Knopf, 1955); *Tade kuu mushi*, in *TZ*, vol. 12 (Tokyo: Chūōkōronsha, 1973). Combined page numbers in the text cite the English and Japanese respectively. The connection is even more powerful and direct in Tanizaki's story "The Floating Bridge of Dreams" ("Yume no ukihashi," 1959) in which Tadasu both as infant and grown boy cannot sleep without suckling first his mother's and later stepmother's breast while she sings lullabies to him.

Exactly the same associations are stirred later when O-hisa, the young mistress of Kanamé's father-in-law, sings the old Osaka song "Snow" (*yuki*), accompanying herself on the samisen: "As Kanamé listened to the music, a memory came back from his childhood" (86/108–9). Again Tanizaki's narrative deploys a cinematic zoom inward from the bright world of consciousness to the darkened world of subconscious images: a broad shot of the old merchants' quarter narrows to traditional latticed shop fronts, moves inside to pass through rooms receding into dark interiors, emerges into a tiny garden courtyard and the hushed interior recesses of the family quarters, and finally ascends to an upstairs window from which the pretty young neighbor girl, Fu-chan, is seen sitting on the veranda opposite, quietly singing the song "Snow." In this dreamlike environment Kanamé feels the forbidden thrill of sexual portent as each metonymic sight and sound is fetishized in his obsessively recalled "first sprouting of woman-worship." Even Fu-chan's manner of sitting reminds him of Mother, from whom he has learned that "'Snow' was a song the girl [Fu-chan] seemed especially to like." He has since sometimes heard the song again, once sung in the heavy voice of an old geisha in Kyoto. Now, listening to O-hisa, he feels that her singing is "indeed too pretty, too lacking in this throaty suggestiveness. But Fu-chan those years before had had the same bell-like voice as O-hisa. The latter's singing was therefore a still more powerful inciter of memories" (88/110–11). The stimulation of memory becomes a significant part of a woman in its unique ability to evoke and replace the always displaced Mother.

O-hisa, a young woman fancifully outfitted and trained by her elderly lover as a sort of antique Japanese doll, is the exact opposite of her earlier counterpart, Naomi. Jōji had dreamed of training Naomi to become his fantasy of a Western woman, but in carrying out this dream he had made her entirely foreign, his "canary in a gilded cage." O-hisa, however, is an entirely Japanese warbler in an almost comically Japanesque bamboo cage. The all-important difference is that the foreign bird could only make Jōji's life miserable, whereas the native warbler makes life sweet for the old man. Observing them together, Kanamé begins to suspect that his father-in-law may just be on to something.

Some Prefer Nettles is defined by the intersection of two major axes, as shown in the accompanying figure. The vertical axis delimits a traditional opposition between the Kantō (Eastern) and Kansai (Western) regions of Japan. This axis begins in the brash, modern Kantō culture of the Tokyo that Tanizaki has abandoned, where a "vulgarity and preoccupation with the material" (35/33) have replaced everything that might once have been authentic (that is, memory). It continues through the older traditional Kansai merchant culture of Osaka, in which Kanamé senses both a "depressing

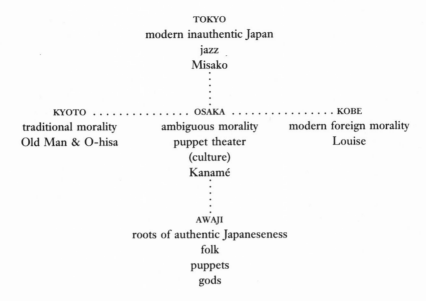

TOKYO
modern inauthentic Japan
jazz
Misako

KYOTO . . . . OSAKA . . . . KOBE
traditional morality   ambiguous morality   modern foreign morality
Old Man & O-hisa   puppet theater   Louise
                              (culture)
                              Kanamé

AWAJI
roots of authentic Japaneseness
folk
puppets
gods

mouldy darkness" and a "quiet mysterious radiance" (36/34). The other pole of this topographical axis lies deep in the "primitiveness" of Awaji Island, just off the port city of Kobe, where Kanamé will have his epiphanic encounter with the "deepest roots of the race."

The second axis, cutting across the first, is framed entirely by the culture of the Kansai region. It begins in the traditional culture and morality of Kyoto, the ancient capital where the old man lives with O-hisa, continues through the half-traditional and half-modern morality of Osaka, and ends in the modern and entirely amoral "foreign" culture of Kobe, where the Eurasian prostitute Louise lives.

The diachronic first axis marks the past, present, and future of both Kanamé and Japan, while the synchronic second axis signifies the structure of the present-time Japan of the novel. They intersect in the present and ambiguous world of the Osaka region, where Kanamé and his wife Misako (and Tanizaki himself) live. Long alienated in spirit from the modern world of Tokyo, Kanamé is headed in the direction of the ancient folk traditions of Awaji, though of course as a modern man he would never actually be able to live there. By the end of the novel, however, grounded and brought to life again by the epiphanic experience on Awaji, he seems ready to renounce the new amorality of Kobe for the old morality of Kyoto. On either axis, Tanizaki is clearly moving toward rejecting a confusing and upsetting sense of a meaningless foreign "modernity" for the more comforting experience of a meaningful native antiquity. This corresponds well with the Japanese studies in the roots of Japan's own folk culture (stimulated by German scholarship in the idea of the *Volk*) being undertaken by two of Tanizaki's contemporaries, the ethnologist and folklorist Kunio Yanagita (1875–1962) and his student Shinobu Origuchi.[5]

Joining and mediating between the two axes is the traditional *jōruri* puppet theater and the continuities and differences between its urbane Osaka and rustic Awaji forms. The story itself can be read as a *jōruri* drama acted out as a play within a play against the work that lies at its heart: Monzaemon Chikamatsu's famous domestic tragedy *The Love Suicides at Amijima* (*Shinjū ten no amijima*, c. 1720), a performance of which Kanamé and Misako attend at the old Bentenza Theater in Osaka, together with Misako's father and his young mistress, at the start of the novel. The play, concerning the tragic love of the married Osaka merchant Jihei for the prostitute Koharu, is traditionally classified as both a love suicide play (*shinjūmono*) and a domestic tragedy (*sewamono*). Crucial to these genres is the traditional concept of *seken* (reputation, honor), which constitutes the absolute and immutable social boundary of the only possible Japanese context for happiness. The novel sets this quality in opposition to such Western notions as "freedom" (*jiyū*) and "individuality" (*kojin*), meaningless abstractions that guarantee only atomization and alienation: for all his daughter's proclaimed preference for the newfangled foreign ways such words imply, says the old man, Misako is a profoundly unhappy woman. Furthermore, *seken* provides the background against which are played out the tensions of the traditional dramatic conflict between *giri* (the claims of social responsibility) and *ninjō* (the claims of human emotion), a conflict that lies at the heart of all such plays and so at the heart of any truly Japanese life. These are the terms that inform the entire novel.

The action of the play is both amplified and parodied by Tanizaki's couples: the socially sanctioned but passionless relationship of husband and wife by Kanamé and his wife Misako; the illicit but socially accepted and passionate relationship of man and mistress by the old man and O-hisa; the relationship of physical lust between Kanamé and Louise; and finally, in a very "modern" twist, the "new" relationship—of a kind heretofore untreated in Japanese fiction because entirely socially unacceptable (and here all but invisible)—of Misako and Aso, the married woman and her lover. The only viable choice in Tanizaki's story is the traditional one of man and mistress, the old man and O-hisa; the traditional institution of marriage, as apparently became the case in Tanizaki's own life, offers very little real choice at all.

---

5. For an evaluation of the nativist direction of this folklore scholarship, see H. D. Harootunian, *Things Seen and Unseen: Discourse and Ideology in Tokugawa Nativism* (Chicago: University of Chicago Press, 1988), pp. 401–40.

We might notice how different these thematic couplings are from those permitted in the traditional Confucian scheme of society examined by Sōseki in *Kokoro* (though marriage in Sōseki's novels is every bit as problematic as it is in Tanizaki's). Aside from the significantly undeveloped relationship between Kanamé and his confused small son, the only relationship in the work sanctioned in traditional philosophy is the problematic one of husband and wife. One might make a case for the frank and open bond between Kanamé's son and Takanatsu (the boy's uncle and Misako's cousin) as a variant on the elder brother/younger brother theme; and though Kanamé is only a son-in-law, his rapport with the old man is clearly an important variant of the father-son relationship. But what the old man is in fact is Kanamé's *sensei* or mentor, for it is from him alone that Kanamé learns something about the real choices he has in life.

The "modern" couples in *Kokoro* and *Nettles* are estranged in very different ways, but their estrangement in both cases is complete and terminal. Sensei's incapacitating perception of his own fatally flawed nature dooms him and his wife to a misery which he believes only his suicide can end. Kanamé and his wife are not so much unhappy as vaguely dissatisfied (perhaps stylishly recreating the novelist Akutagawa's famous contemporary mood of a fatal "vague anxiety"). Not at all inclined to philosophical *angst*, however, Kanamé does not feel himself or anyone else to be actually *evil*, and suicide is certainly never in question. Kanamé seems plagued less by existential terror than by existential ennui.

The average Japanese of this period probably had little sense of what Western notions of society and politics, so avidly being adopted, were actually supposed to mean to them. Much like the uneasy and ill-defined new relationship between Japan and the West, Kanamé and his wife have simply "drifted" into some new undefined and uncomfortable "arrangement," for no better reason than the lack of any particularly compelling reason to do otherwise. Joined in an arranged marriage of neither's volition, husband and wife—East and West—are somehow felt to be "incompatible"—whatever that might mean. As no good reason presents itself to do anything to the contrary, however, they hope simply to continue drifting apart until they find themselves, somehow, finally divorced and therefore—by some uncertain logic—happy.

For Kanamé, the dialogue in the *jōruri* play between the merchant Jihei and his wife O-san uncomfortably evokes the misery of his own marriage: "'Why am I left so alone? Do I nourish in my breast a serpent, a demon?' the narrator chanted for O-san, and for Kanamé the line expressed, with grace and circumspection but with an acuteness that tightened his chest, the innermost secret of a marriage from which sexual passion had disappeared" (32/30). But the truth the line expresses, as Kanamé knows, is that marriage in traditional terms is the socially sanctioned arrangement between families for the bearing and raising of children, those building blocks of continuity for the society at large. It is the last place to expect sexual passion, and to look for it there is to do an injustice to the institution itself. Even the play's O-san, who loves her husband deeply with a properly domestic affection, realizes that his reputation (*seken*) as a merchant takes precedence over all else, and tells him he must honor the pledge he made to redeem Koharu's indenture contract, even though it will cost them everything they have and more.[6]

The conflict between married love and sexual passion is central to the domestic drama precisely because it is the weakest point in the neat Confucian social scheme, which recognizes the realities of human passion only in terms of pathological human failure. As the old man tells Kanamé with the traditional wisdom of his years, "If you think you're not compatible, don't worry too much about it. Time will pass and you'll find you're very much suited for each other after all. O-hisa's far younger than I, and we aren't what you could call well matched, but when two people live together an affection does develop and somehow they get by while they're waiting for it to. *Can't you say after all that that's what a marriage is?*" (135/173; emphasis added).

Kanamé, however, has no particular opinion as to "what a marriage is." The problem, as he perceives it, is that he, who "preferred to live quietly, unobtrusively, casting no dishonor on his ancestors" (19/12), must at the same time worry that Misako's actions might force her father to "feel himself compelled for the sake of public opinion [*seken*] to disown her" (19/13).[7] In other words, they have managed to substitute in place of any truly compelling problem with their marriage one that consists entirely of a concern for appearances (Tanizaki's masterly descriptions of the quiet harmony of their ostensibly unhappy domestic life contradict entirely the likelihood of any *real* misery). The solution that Kanamé and Misako have proposed to this more manageable problem is "to work quietly toward an understanding that would alienate no one" (20/13), carefully monitoring their daily lives to ensure that there will be no possibility of scandal. In this sense they are typical Tokyoites, in contrast to the open, brash Osakans: "The sense of how to comport oneself is no doubt better developed in Tokyo than in Osaka," notes Tan-

6. See Chikamatsu Monzaemon, *The Love Suicides at Amijima*, trans. Donald Keene, in *Four Major Plays of Chikamatsu* (New York: Columbia University Press, 1964), p. 193.

7. It is interesting to note that the common theme in Edo-period fiction of disinheritance (*kandō*), invariably applied to profligate young men, is applied here to a woman instead. Female adultery was traditionally regarded far more harshly (at least by men): in Tsuruya Namboku's very popular play *Tōkaidō Yotsuya kaidan* (1825), for example—one of the stories on which the popular film *Kwaidan* was based—an adulteress and her lover are bound to a door back to back and flung into a river to drown.

izaki. "Sometimes, indeed, it is so well developed that it leads to an excessive concern with appearances and a timid unwillingness to act" (33/31).

Just how narrowly constrained these Tokyoites are by their problems is demonstrated in the novel's complex opening scene with its almost comical lack of decisiveness and "timid unwillingness to act" on the part of either husband or wife. Each waits, carefully watching for the other to make the first move: "Whenever they had to decide whether or not to go out together, each of them became passive, watchful, hoping to take a position according to the other's manner" (13/4). This unwillingness to act is not only more typical of Tokyo than of Osaka but characteristic as well of Japan's paralyzed relationship with the West. To be sure, Kanamé (and Japan) clearly have a preference: he most certainly expects Misako to go with him to the theater and not to Suma to visit her lover. But they waltz carefully around this issue for the space of an entire chapter before it is satisfactorily settled: "All in all," Kanamé finally ventures at chapter's end, "maybe you ought to wait till tomorrow" (18/10). Even so, having made this much progress, they can only repeat the same game as soon as they enter the theater: "'What do you want to do?' Misako turned to Kanamé. 'It makes no difference to me.' His answer was as vague as ever." As soon as she can decently arrange to leave, Misako departs for Suma—in "a new American cab," specifies Tanizaki, deliberately emphasizing the very foreign nature of her quite literal departure from tradition.

But Kanamé is not really interested in *testing* the old morality; he is in fact quite concerned about it and generally upholds it. Nor does he really have more than a passing concern for the new immorality, in which he dabbles secretly if somewhat uncomfortably with Louise. (His occasional nagging feeling that he "shouldn't" keep doing these things is the nearest he comes to acquiring one of those newfangled Western consciences; Misako, however, like all of Tanizaki's women, is portrayed as quite comfortably and naturally amoral.) At any rate, a principled adherence to either one or the other is out of the question.

What does interest him is the unformalized *sub rosa* and universally accepted sort of "arrangement" between man and woman which, like that between his father-in-law and O-hisa, have long been sanctioned by social convention and which have nothing at all to do with such terms as "morality" and "human nature" on the one hand, or "freedom" and "individuality" on the other. As the old man says of his daughter's perilous situation, "Talk of 'free choice' [*jiyū no sentaku*, an uncomfortable translation of the uncongenial foreign idea] all you like, there's no free choice whatsoever in the matter" (134/172). They may choose to think that she is "free" to do as she pleases, but the old man knows that is not the way "the world" (*seken*) works.

Kanamé is as ambivalent as modern man can be, and for Tanizaki it is his ambivalence, rather than the despair or the alienation or the agonizing moral dilemmas of Sōseki's characters, that epitomizes the modern condition. Ever cautious about his and his wife's good names (*seken*), Kanamé finds himself initially opposed even to accepting his father-in-law's invitation to attend the puppet theater with Misako—not because, like her, he is averse to going but precisely out of respect for the ancient Confucian virtue of "filial piety" (*oyakōkō*):

> Surely there was no reason for him to go on cultivating her father. It would have been another matter, of course, if it had seemed that the old man was to go on being "father" to Kanamé indefinitely, but with the end of the relationship so near, were there not indeed reasons why it might be better to be more aloof? It would only upset the old man the more to hear of the divorce after this careless display of filial piety. [20/14]

But Kanamé is anxious to have "one last chance to demonstrate his sense of filial duty" (14/5) to the old man, and when his wife objects to going, he asks that she too "think of it as filial piety" (16/7). It even occurs to him that he would in fact be far unhappier to give up his father-in-law than to give up his wife.

In Japanese, *kanamé* denotes the crucial rivet holding together the ribs of a fan. The very epitome of modern man, Kanamé is the point joining Japan's past, present, and future, and like that central pivot he is caught at and at the same time defines the crux of the demands of native tradition (*seken, giri*) and those of foreign modernity (*jiyū, kojin, ninjō*). Misako's name, on the other hand, is written with characters that mean only "pretty helpmeet," and except for the fact that she likes Western jazz and has (albeit rather lack-adaisically) taken a lover, there is not much to her: "This modernness of hers is a pretty thin veneer," her father tells Kanamé, and that about accounts for her character. She is so little traditionally Japanese that even the thought of going to the unfamiliar, old-fashioned puppet theater only makes her worry about her own comfort: "That means we sit on the floor? I can't stand it, really I can't. My knees will be agony afterwards" (15/7). The artist Yasui Sōtarō caught her visual counterpart in a wonderful 1939 portrait of just such a *modan* (modern) Japanese woman sitting in a chair, attired in Western garments and looking as if she would truly be as unable as any Westerner to sit with her legs tucked under her in the traditional feminine Japanese posture.

Kanamé's interest focuses increasingly on the relationship between Misako's father and his mistress O-hisa, whose name means literally "Eternal Woman." She is specifically equated with the character Koharu in *The Love Suicides at Amijima*, whom Tanizaki also specifies in Sino-Japanese as "the eternal woman" (*eien josei,* 28/23). She and the old man, while entirely believable eccentrics and two of the most interesting characters in Japanese fiction, are in fact only caricatures, more puppet-theater types than real humans. As appealing as the pathetic O-hisa may seem, the human aspect of her character is almost entirely submerged in the old man's demand that she *act* a role to complement his own. Doing so requires enormous labor and discomfort on her part, for to keep him happy she must dress uncomfortably, speak oddly, prepare bizarre meals, take all manner of useless lessons, blacken her teeth, and even whiten her skin with the traditional nightingale dung. For himself he has chosen the traditional part of the aging dilettante—the "Old Man"—and their dress and even their actions are very like those of *jōruri* puppets in a traditional play. Old age is not for him a condition to be mourned; it is just another role to be played like all the rest, and he intends to play it with zest and enthusiasm. As Kanamé ironically but perceptively comments to Misako, "Being old is another of your father's hobbies" (24/18).[8]

Two of the best lines in the work describe what we might call literally this "stage" of life in terms that positively exalt the old man's present condition. In one, Kanamé, wistfully observing his father-in-law's immense contentment at the puppet theater, reflects that there is "much to be said for seeing a puppet play with a bottle of saké at one's side and a mistress to wait on one" (26/21).[9] And much later, when parting from the old man and O-hisa in Kobe after their trip to Awaji, Kanamé muses on the man's enviable life: "Off to Awaji appointed like a doll on the stage, accompanied by a doll, in search of an old doll to buy" (110–11/140). To Kanamé these roles represent more than the pleasures of old age; they have come to seem the very essence of a life worth living. The conclusion that the highest enjoyment in life is to fulfill the *roles* that determine one's character seems extremely Japanese. Much as the aging Shingo in Kawabata's *The Sound of the Mountain* discovers that sadness and happiness, far from being absolutes, are actually inherent in the subtle and manipulable nuances innate to the fixed persona

8. When Kanamé later writes to Misako's father explaining their marital situation, he receives in return a letter written in the dreadful antique epistolary style known as *sōrōbun* (123–24/157–58). Kanamé's comment to his wife about her father's letter is exactly true: "When you write an old-fashioned letter you pretty well have to say old-fashioned things. Probably he did it just for the fun of being old-fashioned" (125/159). The single English word "old-fashioned" serves in the translation to render three very distinct expressions in the original: *mukashifū* (old-fashioned), *kyūshiki* (the antique style), and *shūmi de* (just for the fun of [being old-fashioned]), the same term as that used for "as a hobby."

9. The Japanese here has a rhythm and flavor that entirely eludes translation: *"Naruhodo ningyō jōruri to iū mono wa mekake no soba de sake o nominagara miru mon da na,"* literally, "Yes, a puppet play is something one watches while drinking saké with a mistress by one's side." The particular grammar of this sentence, perfectly normal in Japanese but unavailable to English, turns the puppet theater into something whose very essence is defined by these apparently trivial but actually synecdochically significant attributes of its *audience.*

of each Nō mask, Kanamé finds that meaning in life does not lie in grand Western abstractions like "freedom of choice" but rather inheres in the very roles in terms of which one's life is acted out.

We also cannot help noticing that the old man's happy contentment in his particular role is entirely dependent on his creation of still another one, that of a woman to wait on him hand and foot. O-hisa as "Eternal Woman" is, after all, Mother and expected as such to cater to the male whim—and the old man is as whimsical a male as was ever invented. Tanizaki assigns to O-hisa all the intensity of his Tokyoite woman-worship; for him the locus of this "Occidental" fetishism was Tokyo, where he could see the films in which "Hollywood was forever dancing attendance upon women" (35/34).[10]

By the story's end, as Kanamé is bathing in the old man's antique wooden bathtub and fantasizing that he has left his wife to live this sort of new life, he seems clearly to be moving toward what he calls "the type O-hisa." But, as he has earlier told his wife's cousin Takanatsu, he has always found the "whore type" easier to leave than the "mother type" (49/54).[11] Torn between the two, he is hopelessly confused. O-hisa is rather more the "whore" than the "mother," and Kanamé's wife is the reverse, but neither is as clearly one *or* the other as is the Eurasian Kobe prostitute Louise. Such words, abstract role-types, were simply never intended to apply to the psychosocial complexities of *real* people. Because Louise is in fact a whore, he finds it easiest to leave her, if only inevitably to be drawn back again to the physical charms of this very likable woman. But to leave Misako, who is after all his wife and the mother of his son, is entirely another matter. As he confides to Takanatsu,

"I wouldn't consider marrying a woman who's actually been a professional. I've never taken to geisha. What I have in mind is a smart, intelligent modern woman with something of the whore in her [*haikara na chiteki na shōfugata*]."

"And would you like it then if she played the whore after you were married?"

"She would be intelligent, I said. She would have some self-restraint."

"You are being very demanding indeed. Where, I wonder, will you find the woman to satisfy you? You really should have stayed single—all woman-worshippers [*feminisuto*] should be single. They never find the woman who answers all the requirements." [50/56][12]

10. "Hollywood" is the translator's more satisfactory rendering of the Japanese text's "Los Angeles movies" and "the American movie world."

11. The contrast is intensified by Tanizaki's coinage of the word *bofugata* (mother type) as an antonym for the common *shōfugata* (whore type).

12. Where Seidensticker prefers the more euphemistic "courtesan" for *shōfu*, I have substituted the perfectly accurate "whore." The odd usage here of the English word "feminist" to mean a man who worships women, while absent from the *Oxford English Dictionary*, is attested in its Japanese equivalent, the twenty-volume *Nihon kokugo daijiten*. But the entry for this usage of the word "feminism" (*feminizumu*) cites as its authority this same passage from *Some Prefer Nettles* (the authority cited for *feminisuto* is a work by Satomi Ton).

The central and pivotal episode of *Some Prefer Nettles* is Kanamé's epiphanic return to the soil and the folk roots of his race. Chapters nine through eleven recount a trip taken by the old man and O-hisa, with Kanamé tagging along, to see the traditional folk puppet plays performed on the island of Awaji, a short ferry ride from Kobe. This journey is understood by the characters (and intentionally described by Tanizaki) as an imitation of both the traditional pilgrimage (*junrei*) to the Buddhist holy sites of Awaji and the equally conventionalized lovers' journey (*michiyuki*) in the *jōruri* drama, narrating the lovers' passage through a highly poeticized landscape. In order to travel properly through a landscape made famous in poetry and song, O-hisa and the old man dress as pilgrims, learn the appropriate pilgrim chants, and naively and touchingly (if rather comically) pattern their itinerary on those narrated in the old songs and poems.

The descriptions of the dark old village where the puppet plays are held seem taken straight from Tanizaki's essay *In Praise of Shadows* (*In'ei raisan*), a work in which the author adumbrated his personal interpretation of traditional Japanese aesthetics.[13] At an inn where the trio stops for the night, Kanamé listens to the low voices of this odd couple in the next room as they lie talking together in bed, compares the unaffected warmth of their relationship with his own affectionless marriage, and realizes with even deeper envy what he has been missing.

The center of this episode is the day's performance at the Gennojō theater on Awaji, really only a large tent, of puppet plays traditionally put on by the peasant farmers of the island. In stark contrast to the highly subtilized and aestheticized view of art expressed earlier—things are best left only hinted at, old songs can't be analyzed grammatically, old villages should reflect reserve and soft austerity, and so on—the reader is confronted here with the full brunt of the power of "the folk": its noise, its stink, its rowdiness, its crudeness, its raw vitality. Here are none of the etherialized vaporings about art or the exaggerated reverence for it evinced by urbane city people. Instead there is a transcendent *passion* by means of which categories of time, space, and social distinction are made to collapse: "While one was thus taken back to the far past, one had at the same time the feeling that the action was extremely near at hand, popular, plebian" (105–6/133). The delicately cultivated O-hisa finds to her horror that the only available "sanitary facilities" are slop buckets placed out in the open and used indiscriminately by all adults, while the children simply relieve themselves in the aisles. Nor is this a refined, big-city audience that sits sedately through an entire performance without a sound; the crowd treats the day's performance as a sports event,

13. Jun'ichiro Tanizaki, *In Praise of Shadows* (*In'ei raisan*), trans. T. J. Harper and E. G. Seidensticker (New Haven: Leete's Island Books, 1977).

drinking too much, cheering its local favorites, and booing the competition. By the end of the day, partisans in the audience are brawling outright while the performer they are fighting over goes on singing, completely unnoticed in the pandemonium.

Like the ethnologist Kunio Yanagita, Tanizaki is at pains here to recreate a "real folk," celebrating this "peasant art born from the pure soil of village tradition" as "the work of the race" (*minshūteki*) (98/124). The power of this concept to override distinctions of time, space, and social class permits it to transcend *all* such analytic categories, so that its most powerful effect is to induce a kind of hypnotic state which obliterates all the debilitating oppositions that plague and paralyze modern man—exactly what "modernity" means to Tanizaki. Under its spell are forgotten the troubling differences that have separated what was once an authentic, ancient, Japanese, rustic, popular, and communal *folk* from what has degenerated into the inauthentic, modern, Western, urbane, elite, and civic *individual*. Under the enchantment produced by the warmth, the crowd, and the music, Kanamé falls into a drowsy reverie in which the present blends imperceptibly with memories of the past and youth to create a warm public bath of eternal unity: "Kanamé would find himself drifting off to sleep and pull himself awake; twice, three times, the drowsing off and the quick awakening . . . and again and then again. . . . It was as if a hundred formless and uncollected dreams were passing through his mind, the dreaming and the waking fused one into the other" (100/126). In Japanese the language becomes hypnotically beautiful here, reproducing in its very rhythms the experience of dozing off and coming to with a start ("torotoro toshite wa *hat*to me o samasu"), of dreaming and waking over and over ("yume mi*te* wa same yume mi*te* wa same").

Tanizaki somehow manages to amass a host of small details to achieve an effect whose power—compounded of sunlight, music, crowd noises, children, candy, smells—is entirely sensual. In this blurring and melting (*tokete iru*), the most important distinction obliterated is that between particular details and overall effect, and so between individuals and the communal whole. The means by which this is achieved is the replacement of the troublesome entity of the individual with conventionalized types, or *kata*.[14] As each puppet is a type whose features and movements conform to a pattern established centuries ago, exactly the same can be said about the human beings who come to participate as performers and observers at this rustic gathering; even the distinction between "performer" and "audience" is obliterated in this welter of participant actor-farmers. The old man and O-hisa,

14. The word *kata*, widespread throughout Japanese culture, indicates the conventionalized fixed patterns that form the basis of the martial arts, dance, flower arranging, calligraphy, and so on. These can be transcended only by being learned to the point of unconscious perfection.

too, "appointed like a doll on the stage, accompanied by a doll, in search of an old doll to buy," are just as clearly types. Authenticity, far from involving any notion of "free choice" or "individuality," here implies the ability to fulfill one's role; "to conform to a type, to be the captive of a form [*kata ni hamaru toka kata ni torawareru*]" (104/132), requires a necessary and entirely positive abandonment of self.

In capturing the essence of what it means to be Japanese, such passages also capture the particular appeal of what it might have meant to think like a fascist in the Japan of the 1920s and 1930s. The nostalgia for *Blut und Boden*, the search for an authentic Volk, the refusal to cope with a troubling modernity, coupled with a return to a delirium of happy antiquity, all lie at the heart of the sort of racist fantasies that led both Japan and Germany into World War II. It is hard to condemn Tanizaki, one of the least offensive of Japanese writers of the wartime period,[15] as one might condemn such a writer as the Norwegian Knut Hamsun, whose spellbinding *Growth of the Soil* offers itself as a natural counterpart to his own anti-Semitic sentiments. And yet if we are to condemn either, we shall for exactly the same reasons be unable to read not only the rabidly anti-Semitic Ferdinand Céline but more appealing racists such as Ezra Pound and T. S. Eliot. The complex relationship between ideology and art, unfortunately, cannot simply be reduced to a gratifying act of moral or political judgment. As usual, for the same reasons, literary criticism seems to serve better as analysis than as instrumentality.

Having found, explored, and celebrated the folk roots of the Japanese experience, Tanizaki is rescued from the cheap and disastrous failure of the fascist solution to the trying dilemmas of modernity precisely by virtue of his personal weaknesses (which might make us wonder about the unsuspected importance of these in our everyday lives). On the return ferry to Kobe, Kanamé has booked a room in the Japanese-style part of the boat in deliberate preference to the Western; on a sudden impulse, however, he changes quickly from a kimono into a Western suit (interestingly, the former is a choice no longer available to Japanese males), signaling his preparation for a visit to the Eurasian prostitute Louise in modern, foreign Kobe.

In spite of the world of difference between the two performances, Kanamé enjoys the "aggressive, noisy vitality" (121/155) of Louise and her madame, the alcoholic and maudlin Mrs. Brent, in exactly the same way he enjoyed that of the Awaji puppet theater. As he promises Louise he will return soon (all the while swearing to himself he will never come back again), we understand that he is hopelessly drawn to the charms of "this woman of a different nation and a different race" (123/157). The past few days' orgy of racial

15. See Donald Keene, "Japanese Writers and the Greater East Asia War," in *Appreciations of Japanese Culture* (Tokyo: Kodansha International, 1981), pp. 300–321.

purity seems to have had this particular backlash effect on the all-too-human Kanamé. We can be charitable and believe that he is searching for some sort of balance, but in the context of Tanizaki's *oeuvre* it is clear that what he is really looking for is the unique thrill of degradation he feels whenever he subjects himself to impurity. It is really "the dark glow of her skin, with its faint suggestion of impurity" (116/148) that attracts Kanamé, and it is only the fact of Louise's exotic foreignness that absolves him of what he feels to be his otherwise inexcusable "animal behavior." Having purged that impure side of himself with a properly impure woman and then bathed, he can, like any good Victorian or Edwardian husband, return home to his wife with a clean conscience.

The remarkable presence of these varied and often interesting foreigners in Tanizaki's work is worth some elaboration. In *The Makioka Sisters*, for example, the interplay of the Makioka family with the Russian Kyrilenko and German Stolz families seems quite unique in the Japanese fiction of the time, and perhaps of any time. The Stoltzes leave Japan to return to Germany at the start of World War II, thus fulfilling the destiny of all "good" foreigners in Japan, which is precisely to return home. The White Russians, however, are much more problematic: as stateless emigrés from the Russian revolution, they have no "home" to return to and are considered every bit as exotic as Louise, who is presumed to be of mixed Russian and Manchurian parentage. The terrible ambiguity of the Kyrilenkos' situation is symbolized perfectly by the furnishings of their house, where one room boasts a portrait of the Russian czar and czarina, another a portrait of the Japanese emperor and empress. While the young son of the family (named Vronsky!) appears to be quite wealthy, there is never the slightest suggestion that he could ever be considered a match for the always urgently eligible Yukiko, third of the four sisters: it is after all equally urgent that foreigners marry their own.

It is little wonder that the military censors halted publication of *The Makioka Sisters* shortly after it began. The novel is often understood as having reflected too feminine a world, in too unpatriotic a state of decline, to be acceptable to an era of optimistic militarism and imperialist expansion.[16] Its theme is the loss of masculine and patriarchal authority with its corre-

16. The book's publisher was called before a military censorship board in March 1943 and belabored for publishing a work about "the soft, effeminate, and grossly individualistic lives of women" (Rubin, *Injurious to Public Morals*, p. 264). It is interesting to speculate that Tanizaki may have been indebted to the censors for his ever having written about anything but sadomasochistic erotic obsession: his work was banned so frequently (once in two separate literary magazines in the same month of 1916) that he was forced to consider seriously how else he might pursue a literary career. For the unpredictable results of censorship in the Edo period, see Donald Shively, "Bakufu *vs* Kabuki," *Harvard Journal of Asiatic Studies* 18 (December 1955), reprinted in Robert Hall and Marius Jansen, eds., *Studies in the Institutional History of Early Modern Japan* (Princeton: Princeton University Press, 1968).

sponding increase in female and matriarchal power and all the problems
associated with them (see Chapter 1 above). But even beyond these pressing
matters is the work's subversive suggestion of a disturbingly permanent alien
presence concealed within Japan itself, and not just the usual one looming
threateningly as always beyond the watchful vigilance of Japan's physical and
cultural borders. The problematics of the novel associates two very different
things with the dominant theme of decline, whether of family or of Japan,
suggesting an equation between an excess of femaleness and an excess of
foreignness. China, Manchuria, Taiwan, Korea are all within Japan's "proper" sphere of influence and, like India for the British, are regarded enthusiastically as environments where energetic, ambitious, and otherwise superfluous young sons (like Takanatsu of *Nettles*) might acceptably be sent to
make a new sort of extended Japanese life for themselves. But Japan is
certainly never to be regarded as being within any foreigner's proper sphere,
and by 1936 Japan had long rid itself of its *o-yatoi-sama*, the Western "honorable hired gentlemen" who had temporarily been so urgently necessary to
Meiji Japan's rapid modernization. Most of these foreigners will return
home; those who, like Mrs. Brent and the imposingly large female American
dancing teacher in *Naomi* who so completely and comically overpowers Jōji,
die in Japan, being regarded as essentially homeless, will be buried in the
famous "foreigners' cemeteries" (*gaijin bochi*) in Tokyo and Yokohama and
Kobe, ghastly embassies of a sort of honorary foreign land of the dead, the
strange inscriptions engraved on their foreign tombstones seen as monu-
ments to the curious separateness of foreigners.

Some Prefer Nettles concludes with every bit as much ambiguity as it begins.
Kanamé and Misako are invited to spend the night at the home of her father
and O-hisa in Kyoto, and the old man takes his daughter out to dinner to try
and talk some sense into her. He leaves O-hisa to serve Kanamé dinner at
home "in the old-fashioned way," clearly hoping that this will suggest to his
son-in-law the proper and acceptable way out of his dilemma: he too should
take a mistress in the traditional way. Relaxing in the traditional hospitality of
an old-fashioned wooden bath steeped in cloves in a darkened bathroom
straight out of *In Praise of Shadows*, Kanamé inevitably muses on the possibility of a life like this with his own "type O-hisa" doll.

Having eaten, about to fall asleep in the bed O-hisa has prepared for him,
he is startled by what he takes to be O-hisa herself rising up through the
gloom, only to realize with some regret that this vision is nothing but the
coveted puppet the old man has brought back from Awaji. The real O-hisa
then makes an appearance with some books for Kanamé to browse through
before falling sleep, and comments in her Kyoto lilt that "it's finally started to
rain [*iyoiyo futte kimashita naa*] (143/185). The translation of her comment at

this point, "It's finally begun," seems unwarrantedly suggestive of a new beginning for Kanamé, perhaps even one that will somehow involve O-hisa herself.[17] But our final view in the last sentence of the novel is merely of "a faintly white un-doll-like face sitting across from him in the light shadow"— the real O-hisa, exactly where the doll had been a moment before. The final ambiguity of O-hisa and the puppet returns us to the ambiguity of the beginning of the novel. But this ambiguity, resting within its new and entirely Japanese framework of choice, seems empowering, whereas the earlier ambiguity of a problematic Japanese relationship with the West had been merely debilitating. Nothing has been resolved in the end, but Kanamé, like Japan, is beginning to learn to ask very different questions.

Hsün Tzu's pessimistic view of man as inherently evil and barbaric, so difficult for actual *man* to sustain for long, was quickly transposed in the early 1900s onto *woman* (and, by much the same equation, foreigners), where, after long centuries of Buddhist, Shinto, and Confucian moralizing, it seemed properly to belong. The notion of woman as an equal of man was an imported Western one, certainly not Japanese. One Meiji novelist, Tayama Katai, perceived sex much as Zola had in *Thérèse Raquin*: "an uncontrollable force," he called it, "a primitive irrational threat to modern rationality." And in 1908 the popular novelist Kunikida Doppo had used his dying breath to revile her: "Woman," he gasped, "is a beast."[18]

While the relationship between men and women in Tanizaki's novels is set within the traditional paradigm of superior and inferior, it is most fully explored in its darker aspect of master and slave. The attempt to make that relationship modern results only in a new perversion of traditional roles, with dominant woman on the top in both sexual and political terms. What we might call Japan's fear of being screwed over by foreigners in this period becomes in Tanizaki's work a sexual inversion of the social order in which men cooperate in an unnatural elevation of women that can only signal trouble in the world.

In a period that also produced the seminal folklore studies of Yanagita, Tanizaki succeeded in imagining the life and thought of a Japanese folk, if only by means of a narrator for whom such an idea can be merely a kind of nostalgia. This recurring nostalgia includes Yukio Mishima's delight in discovering in Yanagita's *Tales of Tōno* (*Tōno monogatari*, 1910) a truly Japanese technique of the novel which Mishima praised as evoking through the au-

17. The closest that American English might come to the effect of her speech would be a soft, cultivated southern accent.
18. Quoted in Rubin, *Injurious to Public Morals*, pp. 61–62.

thentically supernatural the sense of a native reality far more profound than any that could be achieved by mere foreign naturalism.[19] Tanizaki succeeded in turning Nagai Kafū's nostalgic project of elegiacal memory toward the modern nation's demand for useful mythical memories. If these could no longer be the traditional male/native–dominated ones, they would have to be dominated by the female/foreign whose locus is that mythical "Hollywood," the embodiment of Tanizaki's equally mythically potent woman-worship.

19. "Shōsetsu towa nanika" (What is 'the novel'?), pt. 9, *MZ*, 33:262. On this important subject, see also Ivy, "Discourses of the Vanishing in Contemporary Japan," pp. 87–137.

Part II
Ideology and Its Articulation

Chapter 4

Ideology, Aesthetics, Science

I ventured to hint that the company was run for profit.
—Joseph Conrad, *Heart of Darkness*

By speaking of aesthetics and science as entirely self-contained discourses, we might easily avoid having to use the uncomfortable term "ideology" at all. If we believe with Conrad's Marlow that the company *is* "run for profit," however, then it follows that we must also understand that discourses are *not* self-contained but rather deployed in the interest of supporting privileged relations of power. In what follows, I first offer a provisional definition of ideology that should be useful for understanding the context of power relations within which reading and writing are carried on. I then turn to an examination of some of the ways in which ideology is articulated through two important discourses, aesthetics and science, terms I take to indicate respectively our primary modes of representation and knowledge.

Rather than resume here the difficult history of the term,[1] I would like to propose the following perhaps overly simplistic definition:

Ideology comprises the contending webs of economic, political, social, religious, and cultural relations through which power is distributed and exercised, and within which our lives are lived.

From this axiom follows a corollary:

Since our lives are played out entirely within these webs of relations, ideology is characterized primarily by the fact that its relations appear always to have already been present and thus to constitute an entirely natural given "reality."

1. See Terry Eagleton, *Ideology: An Introduction* (London: Verso, 1991).

That this "reality" is constructed, and how it is constructed, are things of which we are necessarily usually unaware in our daily lives.[2]

As a technical idea rather than merely a derogatory word, "ideology" is usually reserved for Marxist theory, where it is generally treated as a monadic concept within which the competition of power interests assumes the form of a class struggle. Fredric Jameson, while generally adhering to this conception, offers a rather more complex formulation in his commentary on Jean-François Lyotard's competing European "master narratives" of legitimation, summarized on the one hand in a French myth of the "liberation of humanity" (the *paralogic*, represented by Lyotard), and on the other in a German one of the "speculative unity of all knowledge" (the *homologic*, represented by Jürgen Habermas).[3] We should use the plural "ideologies," then, to acknowledge that, far from monadic, this concept has varying modalities which—like Communism and Catholicism, capitalism and socialism, or feudalism and modernism—are not necessarily either mutually exclusive or inclusive, naturally antagonistic or supportive, but simply *different* and thus in competition.

"Ideology" first and foremost concerns power and how lives are lived within and through it—concerns, as Terry Eagleton puts it, "the ways in which what we say and believe connects with the power-structure and power-relations of the society we live in."[4]

It is when we ask how such a concept of ideology might be developed within a specifically Japanese context that we run into a problem that has

2. This definition somewhat resembles Dominick LaCapra's treatment of ideology as (1) involving mystification; (2) illegitimately serving the interest of part of society by generalizing that interest to the good of the whole; (3) presenting what is historically variable as if it were universal; (4) related to the hegemony of one formation over others; and (5) assuming the attempt to see "meaningful" order in chaos. See LaCapra, *Soundings in Critical Theory* (Ithaca: Cornell University Press, 1989), pp. 147 ff. However, Eagleton (*The Ideology of the Aesthetic* [London: Blackwell, 1990], p. 379) has recently rejected the idea that ideology involves concealment of its own motives: "There is no reason . . . to assume that all dominant social ideologies involve a persuasive, systematic naturalization of history, as a whole lineage of thinkers, from Georg Lukács to Roland Barthes and Paul de Man, have apparently presupposed."

3. Fredric Jameson, Foreword to Jean-François Lyotard, *The Postmodern Condition: A Report on Knowledge*, trans. Geoff Bennington and Brian Massumi (Minneapolis: University of Minnesota Press, 1984), p. ix. Jameson's own preference, of course, is for that "great single collective story," the only one that counts "for Marxism, the collective struggle to wrest a realm of freedom from a realm of Necessity." See Jameson, *The Political Unconscious: Narrative as a Socially Symbolic Act* (Ithaca: Cornell University Press, 1979), p. 19.

4. Eagleton, *Literary Theory*, p. 14. This relatively laconic and restrained definition can be contrasted with the less moderate version that characterizes his earlier *Criticism and Ideology* (London: New Left Books, 1985), p. 54: "A dominant ideological formation is constituted by a relatively coherent set of 'discourses' of values, representation, and beliefs which, realised in certain material apparatuses and related to the structures of material production, so reflect the experiential relations of individual subjects to their social conditions as to guarantee those misperceptions of the 'real' world which contribute to the reproduction of the dominant social relations."

made matters somewhat difficult for Japanese Marxism: from the seventeenth century on in Japan, one is confronted with a discourse not of essential conflict but rather of essential concord (*wa*). Against Marx's quaintly Eurocentric, nineteenth-century notions of a primitive and static "Asiatic mode" of communism and its politics of "Oriental despotism," some recent contributions to the discussion have even proposed that modern Japan is in fact the only truly successful "communist" society, which is clearly to confuse a form of social communalism for communism. Still, considered from the point of view of a utopian Marxist *telos*, there might be grounds for making such an assertion about a society whose laboring masses have been educated—successfully, to all appearances—to believe that their lives contribute in meaningful ways to the collective welfare, that they are not alienated from their labor, and that neither their lives nor their labor have been appropriated by a class of oppressors with whom they are locked in mortal combat.

Of course, such a discourse ignores the very real history of social conflict in Japan, including the realities of class structure and conflict, the historic oppression of various minority groups and of women, and the appalling environmental pollution and severe degradation of social life in contemporary Japan (as elsewhere). Such a discourse even serves, it may legitimately be argued, precisely as a means of obscuring such problems. Japan is sometimes portrayed by outsiders not as a utopia at all but rather as a dystopia, as for example in Karel van Wolferen's recent rather apocalyptic vision (based largely on Chalmers Johnson's more temperate study) of Japan as a malignly oppressive capitalist-development state run amok in every facet of culture, a sort of runaway freight train careening dangerously out of control through the international countryside.[5] Western thinking about Japan has always tended to one or the other extreme of the utopia-dystopia dyad, just as it has to the universalist-particularist one, and most typically to both at once, as we have seen in Kipling's alternating delight and disillusionment.

Edward Said has remarked with considerable justification that modern critical theory is often "practiced as if Western culture were being dismantled" when Western culture is the *last* thing that concerns it.[6] Such theory does appear remarkably blind to the problem that it itself operates within a closed Eurocentric world of assumptions not necessarily or even remotely shared by other cultures. Developed for the purpose of rendering visible certain central assumptions underlying the Western construction of a

5. Karel van Wolferen, *The Enigma of Japanese Power: People and Politics in a Stateless Nation* (London: Macmillan, 1989); Chalmers Johnson, *MITI and the Japanese Miracle* (Stanford, Calif.: Stanford University Press, 1982).

6. Edward W. Said, "American 'Left' Literary Criticism," in *The World, the Text, and the Critic*, pp. 159–60.

transparent "reality," poststructuralist and especially deconstructionist thought is itself entirely contained within a world governed by Greek and Judeo-Christian assumptions about the unquestionable primacy of such matters as presence, origins, ends, and speech (*ousia, ontos, telos, logos*), matters that entirely define its discursive horizons. As even Paul de Man has remarked in "The Rhetoric of Blindness," a "critical reading of Derrida's critical reading of Rousseau shows blindness to be the necessary correlative of the rhetorical nature of literary language."[7] The "postmodern" too seems less important for what Jean Baudrillard considers the purportedly exhilarating and liberating effect of telematic postindustrial technology on human lives than for Lyotard's view of Modernism as constituting an enormous and highly integrated system of knowledge constructed for the purpose of confirming and supporting the closed circle of Euro-American economic, political, social, and cultural discourse. The ideology of Modernism found its most fearful images of the other reflected in that very mirror it held to nature, and the phenomenology of that mirror is marked by its peculiar blindness to anything but the narcissistic gaze which it entirely contains. As the West's dominant mode of representing "reality" to itself, Modernism has characteristically been able to account for everything *except* its own blindnesses about itself: that is, about the way it has appeared to its own others, and the effects it has had on them.

But along with the discovery that the mirror reflects only a particular sort of vision has come the recognition that "knowledge" too has long ceased to be regarded as a shining instrumentality with which to illuminate the world, a beam of light piercing the darkness in order to clarify an already given "reality." It is now more often conceived of in terms of the beam of light emanating from a movie projector as it blinks its images out upon a blank screen at twenty-four frames per second, not revealing but rather *creating* by means of an acknowledged and well-studied illusion (some would say deception) the world we perceive. Far from simply revealing preexisting universal truths, such a knowledge itself comprises the scripts of stories, the scenarios that we tell about ourselves and others in order to explain—or even better, in the useful psychoanalytic sense, to explain *away*—the world that impinges on us. It is in this sense that our knowledge of others can quite literally be called a "projection." Those stories by which we authorize ourselves always de-authorize others; only after we have succeeded in creating a place for ourselves do we attempt to fit in around the periphery all those whom we have projected outward and marginalized in the service of explaining (away) all that is wrong with "our" world.

Such an analysis of ourselves and others suggests that "fiction," in every

7. See Paul de Man, *Blindness and Insight: Essays in the Rhetoric of Contemporary Criticism* (Minneapolis: University of Minnesota Press, 1983), p. 141.

sense of the word, is in fact the appropriately ambiguous designation for the site where ideology is manufactured, comes into play, and begins to operate in our lives. We are inserted at birth into an already entirely constructed world by means of the roles which our accepted knowledge of that world (which is to say, our learned constructions of it) permits us to play.

As part and parcel of that "profit" for which Conrad tells us the company is run, we must thus include the novel stories its directors and beneficiaries have learned to tell themselves about their relationship to those whose exploitation allows them to exist. The tale of Kurtz is of course superbly ambiguous, so entertaining in its horror. We find a rather less ambiguous example in T. Coraghessan Boyle's recent *East Is East* (1990). Hiro (whose name not coincidentally sounds like the English word "hero") is a mistreated half-Japanese sailor who jumps ship off the Georgia coast, only to suffer the horrors of cultural misunderstanding at the hands of Americans.

Hiro amounts to little more than an exotic plot device that provides tragic relief to the antics of a zany crew of residents at an artist colony; while their reality is heightened by means of rich satire, however, Hiro is too desperately pathetic to be either satirical or real. The tormented Asian is fun for a while, and when he stops being fun he commits suicide, in imitation of a character out of one of the novels of his personal hero, Mishima. Since the author has no idea what to do at the end with this sad caricature once he has wrung all the laughs he can get from him, his narrator seems like a boy having fun tormenting a bug until the bug surprises him by dying. As the rest of the novel isn't prepared for such tragedy, Hiro's death becomes a senseless anomaly. The novel scores its laughs by playing off a cheap caricature of an exotic Oriental whom the author seems certain his audience will enjoy seeing tormented.

Terry Eagleton has recently suggested that in the United States the idea of ideology is always involved in "the conflict between high-sounding metaphysical claptrap and having your fingers in the till." *East Is East*, though more fun than metaphysical claptrap, seems to share in that rather less high-sounding enterprise, the great American interest in those profits for which Conrad has told us the company is after all run. In this case, the profits are derived at least as much from a troubling exploitation of the torment and humiliation of one of America's favorite historical Others as they are from healthy laughter at ourselves.[8]

An important characteristic of our formal models of representation is that they are not merely constructed; like any convincing construction, they are constructed *aesthetically*. The aesthetic can be defined as anything that serves

8. T. Coraghessan Boyle, *East Is East* (New York: Viking, 1990); Eagleton, *Ideology of the Aesthetic*, p. 375.

as an emblem of the shared ethical norms of the social group privileged to create, possess, use, and interpret it. At first glance this may appear to apply only to something like sacred writ such as the Bible or a body of laws such as the Constitution, something that literally requires "interpretation." To confine the definition to such artifacts, however, would be to circumscribe too narrowly the heuristic power of the idea. We can indeed argue that the Bible or the Constitution is "aesthetic" insofar as it expresses the highest truths we know *and* is written in a manner historically valorized as "artful," a word that means no end of things: beautiful, allusive, gorgeous, awe-inspiring, moving, pithy, elegant, compact, exciting, impressive, convincing—and also, it will be noted, crafty, deceptive, sly, sneaky, wily. Even or perhaps especially the strictest fundamentalist interpretation justifiably holds that it is the very Word of scripture itself (as opposed to a pietà, altarpiece, cantata, or sermon) which defines "the beautiful." In much the same way that a particularly economical (or impressive, or convincing) mathematical or scientific narrative can be called "elegant" or "beautiful," so may a bowl, a painting, a piece of music, a novel, a dancer's movement, a mode of dress. These things are understood by conventional agreement (and maintained by education) to embody the truth of a particular group's proprietary construction of reality in tangible, sensual, and even ideational form.

The aesthetic is one of the metadiscourses by means of which ideology is articulated at the human level and made knowable, speakable, palpable. To give expression to one's knowledge, speech, or feeling is therefore inevitably to express one's ideological affiliations and commitments. The aesthetic artifact is an emblem of a group's sense of itself in the world which summarizes the story of its relations with those others against whom the group defines itself. As Fredric Jameson puts it: "The aesthetic act is itself ideological, and the production of aesthetic and narrative form is to be seen as an ideological act in its own right"; such an act is performed for the purpose of "inventing imaginary or formal 'solutions' to unresolvable social contradictions." In Jameson's treatment, this model is merely "a first specification of the relationship between ideology and cultural texts or artifacts," one that we soon leave behind as we proceed to "pass over into the second horizon" of the *social*, from which vantage point the more important considerations of "class conflict and its antagonistic discourses" begin to emerge into proper focus, as prophesied by the phrase "unresolvable social contradictions." Focusing more sharply brings us to a "third horizon" comprising "a field of force in which the dynamics of sign systems of several distinct modes of production can be registered and apprehended": in other words, the site at which the concerns of semiotics (the way artifacts are arranged ideologically into systems of meaning) encounter the "production" of these artifacts themselves (production considered as the form any labor takes under specific social conditions) to emerge as what Jameson usefully terms "the ideology of forms." At this point, the restless critic is already on the move again toward a still farther horizon in which narrative and time intersect to form a "history-effect"—a phrase, modeled on Roland Barthes's "reality-effect," which permits us to bracket the word "history" as construction rather than as essence.[9]

Little confirms Jameson's statement that "the aesthetic act is itself ideological" so well as Yasunari Kawabata's little delirium "Japan the Beautiful and Myself" (see my Introduction). This text of this speech resembles nothing so much as a forced march through a blizzard of cherry blossoms that has the effect of blinding us to any other aspect of the scenery. Rarely has the aesthetic been made to *feel* so palpably ideological. Kawabata stuns his audience with Zen emptiness and dazzles them with cherry blossoms until they are thrilled quite into a numbness in which the only possible thought is, "Ah, the very mysterious and ineffable Orient itself!" It was in large part his appeal to a foreign yen for Japanese exoticism that made him such a perfect choice for the Nobel Prize.[10]

Kawabata's acceptance speech flaunts the same monumental smugness as the famous last lines of John Keats's "Ode on a Grecian Urn," is in exactly the same haste to equate Beauty and Truth—an equation which (despite the messages of speech and urn) novels and poems are invariably at some pains to defer. But what we especially want to ask is why "Beauty is truth, truth beauty" is "*all* we need to know": why this unseemly haste to segue so smoothly from one to the other? This was the problem that raised Theodor Adorno's suspicions when he wrote that "modern artistic consciousness mistrusts an aesthetics which, thematically and stylistically, has all the trappings of an ideology."[11] To ask such a question is to be wary of claims about the innocence of culture, perhaps merely a more sophisticated and less crude and contentious way of rephrasing Hermann Goering's famous remark, "When I hear the word culture, I reach for my revolver."

What I am calling "the aesthetic" thus covers a much broader spectrum than our customary restriction of the term to such phenomena as music, art,

9. Jameson, *The Political Unconscious*, pp. 79, 83, 88, 98.

10. See Kjell Espmark, *The Nobel Prize in Literature: A Study of the Criteria behind the Choices* (Boston: G. K. Hall, 1986), p. 157: "In the Japanese perspective on this period [1967–87], as viewed by Yoshio Iwamoto, Junichiro Tanizaki was 'by far the most deserving of Nobel recognition.' He died, however, in 1965; the prize going to Kawabata instead in 1968 must 'be judged a felicitous choice.' Iwamoto also gave an account of the questions raised by the Japanese in the midst of their rejoicing: 'Why Kawabata, without a doubt the most "Japanese" in his artistry, when there were in their estimation other writers more international in their appeal?' He supposed that 'exoticism' was a decisive factor." See also Yoshio Iwamoto, "The Nobel Prize in Literature, 1967–87: A Japanese View," *World Literature Today*, special issue (Spring 1988), "The Nobel Prizes in Literature, 1967–87: A Symposium."

11. T. W. Adorno, *Aesthetic Theory*, trans. C. Lenhardt (London: Routledge & Kegan Paul, 1984), p. 464.

poetry, crafts, and the like. Beyond artifacts themselves and their manipulation exists the world of *style*, which encompasses local systems within which all artifacts exist and are assigned meaning (to claim to have no style or interest in it is itself entirely a matter of style). Roland Barthes saw style as a coherent sign system for conferring meaning upon things and relating them to others, and illustrated its operation in such contexts as cuisine, fashion, cars, and furniture. When we move to such complex systems as merchandising and advertising, medical education and health-care delivery, and the relationship of the phenomenon known as "the news" to the media that propagate it, what we know as style merges perceptibly with the world at large to the degree that style can be defined as the site at which artifacts are inserted into ideology, the arena in which aesthetics begins to take on the meanings of the power relations that constitute our lives.

What we call reality, then, comprises ideological assumptions articulated and occulted through particular aesthetic constructions. These same assumptions are articulated by particular constructions of the "scientific," in exactly the same way and toward the same end of creating both a world and a mode of knowing and speaking about it. Both aesthetics (the way in which we *represent* the world) and science (the way in which we *know* it) can be understood as discourses, metalanguages which, in Foucault's sense, are not spoken by us as subjects but rather "speak" us as their objects instead.

The Marxist structuralist Louis Althusser introduces the concept of "science" as a third term into the more usual discussion of the relationship between ideology and aesthetics. Since ideology involves in his view a kind of false knowledge of the world insofar as it involves not only a "recognition" but also a "misrecognition," Althusser notes that Marxism then requires an opposing true knowledge to which it applies the term "science." He uses the word, in a sense very different from the usual understanding of it, to mean the "correct" application of dialectical materialist thought. Althusser places aesthetics between the other two terms and conceives of it as a unique and independent form of knowledge of the world, implying by this positioning its mediating role.[12]

Both Georg Lukács and Roland Barthes understand ideology, like myth, as functioning to produce a "false imaginary," or Barthes's "reality-effect," characterized by its ability to naturalize the world it produces as a seamless, given presence. To oppose this essentially deceitful and false form of knowledge—understood in Marxist terms as part and parcel of the bourgeois world-view's profound need to conceal, as much from itself as from

12. Louis Althusser, "Ideology and Ideological State Apparatuses," in *Lenin and Philosophy, and Other Essays* (London: New Left Books, 1971), pp. 204ff. My discussion follows in part the analysis of Tony Bennett in *Formalism and Marxism* (New York: Methuen, 1979).

others, the unsavory nature of its oppressive power relations—Marxist theory requires a true knowledge, a "science" that will allow it to account for the real, producing not an ontological "reality-effect" but an epistemological "knowledge-effect." If ideology is thus a kind of malevolent delusion calculated to pacify, tranquilize, and enslave by conjuring an unchangeable world that simply is, always was, and always will be, "science" is to the contrary the expression of a consciousness incapable of delusion, one that is instead positively enabling, activating, and liberating. "Science" in this sense is much the same shining instrumentality that Enlightenment positivism conceived it to be.

In this view, "science" indicates the truly Marxist epistemology and stands in clear contradistinction to other forms of knowledge of the world, all of which amount to false consciousness. Rather than deceitfully "limiting inquiry by advancing false claims of knowledge," as Tony Bennett notes in *Formalism and Marxism*, such a science frankly "opens up a new conceptual space . . . of which a knowledge is to be produced." Knowledge being material and thus requiring a material mode of access, however, this scheme further posits a realm of "art" as that which "enables us to 'see,' 'perceive' or 'feel' something that alludes to reality."[13] As that by which we experience and through which we express our own and others' realities, art serves to render them inhabitable by representation.

The inherent limitations of such a proposal are clear enough, as are its heuristic abilities to stimulate further thought, and I shall not engage here in a defense or elaboration of it. Rather, I shall simply presume that *all* ways of knowing the world are equally capable of falsification, and that *all* constructions of reality are as inherently useful for our own purposes as they are inherently pernicious for the assumptions they make about others, founded as they are on distinctions that, in the ideological realm, are always *invidious* distinctions. It is for this reason that it was necessary to begin by subsuming the idea of knowledge of the world within a broader and more neutral definition of ideology.

The assumption that there exists a truly scientific knowledge of the world is only one of the features Marxism shares with European Enlightenment thought in general—a commonality apparent as well in its mode of analytical inquiry, which posits an incremental and optimistic movement of steady material progress toward a utopian *telos*: that is, positivism. The Marxist analysis also shares much of the vision and methodology of what we commonly think of today as science, although it takes as its subject the relationships that pertain in the realm of political economy rather than in that of nature. (These realms, not yet considered separate by the philosophers of

13. Bennett, *Formalism and Marxism*, pp. 120–21.

the Enlightenment, have become increasingly estranged over time as different technical modalities of knowledge, serving different functional ends.)

Before concluding this discussion of ideology, I should elaborate further the complex relationship between ideology and the novel. Far from offering a simple base-and-superstructure "reflection" of ideological concerns, the novel involves a problematic double movement that results in its inherent subversion of the very constructions of culture it ostensibly maintains. I work from four assumptions about this problematic relationship:

The first assumption is that all texts reveal evidence of working against their own apparent or stated intentions. This familiar tenet of deconstructive criticism is based in part on the familiar Freudian concept of parapraxis. Human intentionality is itself a complex of competing multiple motivations, and human subjectivity is circular, being both the combined discourses of multiple voices and that through which multiple discourses speak (Bakhtin, Foucault).

The second assumption is that texts are forms of discourse—here assumed to be written, though their relation to orality is a problematic one— deployed in support of particular ideologies. They thus function in the same way as do ideologies: as privileged points of view that attempt to establish themselves as credible and disestablish others as incredible—that is, attempt to create for themselves a position of hegemonic dominance. Since their audience invariably comprises holders of contending points of view who are attempting to accomplish the same project, texts disguise their fundamentally hegemonistic tendencies by thoroughly imitating their environment, becoming "nature," even as their undisguised (or deconstructed) meaning may in fact be subversive of it: hence the mimetic nature of bourgeois realism. Texts that lack mimetic disguise function as more or less overt propaganda, not as what we think of as "fiction."

The third assumption is that the novel (and fiction in general) naturalizes a particular ideology (itself already complex) by means of a mimetic technique that reflects the complex nature of human intentionality. The fact that ideology is fundamentally devious (Lukács, Barthes) and that the novel naturalizes (or cannot help naturalizing) itself by adopting at least the pretense of polyvocality (Bakhtin) means that the novel is inherently of a doubly complex nature which is deconstructive of the construction of reality in whose support it is ostensibly deployed.

The final assumption is that this double complexity is the very sign of the tensions characterizing bourgeois reality, which is founded on the myth (in Barthes's strong sense of the word) that its own privileged condition is natural and good, even as it depends on the oppression of others at home and abroad (slavery, colonialism, class exploitation, male dominance, and all other forms of hegemony) as well of itself (the brutalizing effects of narrow self-interest, bigotry, prejudice, intolerance, alienation, cynicism). The Marxist understanding of the deviousness of ideology is that the bourgeois subject is able to function only by concealing from itself and others the painful awareness of its own oppressive nature; similarly, the Freudian understanding is that the bourgeois subject is able to function only by concealing from consciousness the awareness of its own most horrific base drives.

In showing how particular novels serve this double function of ideology, I hope to suggest, here and in the Conclusion, how it might be possible to "read against" their claim to be "culture" itself. The following two chapters explore the particular ways in which ideology is articulated through the discourses of aesthetics and science. Yasunari Kawabata is best known for the way he transforms reality into an entirely aesthetic experience, one which, with its traditional aura of "profound mystery" (*yūgen*), is capable of blinding the reader to precisely the uncomfortable problem we prefer to experience only indirectly through the experience of art: who is exercising what kind of power, over whom, and by what sorts of culturally sanctioned arrangements? Kawabata's work treats this problem in terms the reader readily recognizes as belonging to that communal language through which art interacts with the realm of lived experience, at once concealing and exposing both the problem itself and the ways in which it is experienced and expressed.

Kōbō Abé, uninterested in equations of truth and beauty, prefers instead to challenge the idea that modern life can ever offer solid epistemological grounds for existence. What Kawabata achieves with mist and mirrors, Abé accomplishes, through his use of those (often parodic) explorations of the scientific method known as science fiction and mystery, by pulling the floor out from under the reader and turning on its head everything we thought we knew about the world we live in. He induces in the process not that pleasurable blindness of the aesthetic but rather the terrifying vertigo that characterizes the epistemological uncertainty of modern urban life.

Chapter 5

The Ideology of Aesthetics:
Yasunari Kawabata's *Thousand Cranes*
and *Snow Country*

Yes, you were born under my star! Tremble! for where that is the case with
mortals, the threads of their destinies are difficult to disentangle; knottings
and catchings occur—sudden breaks leave damage in the web.
—Charlotte Brontë, *Villette*

"To see my novel *Thousand Cranes* as an evocation of the formal and
spiritual beauty of the tea ceremony," declared Yasunari Kawabata, "is a
misreading. It is a negative work, an expression of doubt and a warning
against the vulgarity into which the tea ceremony has fallen."[1] Kawabata's
Thousand Cranes (*Senbazuru*, serialized 1949–54) could have been intended
as a casebook demonstration of the essential and complex relationship between ideology and aesthetics. So thoroughly are its characters absorbed into
the aesthetic construct of the tea ceremony, or *chanoyu*, that aesthetics seems
entirely to have replaced the realm of ideology.[2]

In Kawabata's novels, perhaps more palpably than in those of any other
modern Japanese writer, "art" becomes completely interchangeable with
"reality." It is through this art that ideology is articulated and made knowable, palpable, speakable. This chapter takes up the question of how Kawabata employs the aesthetic structure of chanoyu to imitate and naturalize
the ideological forces of dominant social relations and political structures, to

1. Kawabata, *Japan the Beautiful and Myself*, pp. 67–68. This text of Kawabata's Nobel Prize
acceptance speech rambles through nearly every cliché about Japanese aesthetics; its subtext
seems to be "Japan made mysterious for foreigners." This is one of the few remarks within it
that bear directly upon his own work.
2. The role of the tea ceremony in the novel is discussed by Yoshimura Teiji, "*Senbazuru*
ron," in *Kawabata Yasunari no ningen to geijutsu*, ed. Kawabata Bungaku Kenkyūkai (Tokyo:
Kyōiku Shuppan Sentaa, 1971), pp. 174–88, but his treatment offers little of interest.

reflect and buttress that reality at the same time that it challenges and subverts it.

> After drinking, Kikuji looked at the bowl. It was black Oribe, splashed with white on one side, and there decorated, also in black, with crook-shaped bracken shoots.
>
> "Do you remember it?" said Chikako from across the room.
>
> "Hmmm . . . ," Kikuji replied in an evasive answer and put the bowl down.
>
> "The ferns give it the feel of the mountains," said Chikako. "A fine bowl for early spring—your father often used it. To bring it out now is late for the season, but I thought it would be something you . . ."
>
> "It makes no difference to this bowl that my father owned it for a little while. It's four hundred years old, after all—its history goes back to Momoyama and Rikyū himself. Tea masters have carefully passed it down through the centuries—what difference can my father make?" So Kikuji tried to forget the associations the bowl called up.
>
> It had passed from Ota to his wife, from the wife to Kikuji's father, and from Kikuji's father to Chikako; and the two men, Ota and Kikuji's father, were dead, and here were the two women. There was something almost weird about the bowl's career. [24–25/62][3]

Chikako Kurimoto, the woman who has arranged for Kikuji to use the fateful tea-bowl, is a licensed teacher of the arts (*shishō*) in a school of chanoyu. Her professional affiliation corresponds to her social one: a middle-aged woman whose youth and talent have been absorbed into the power politics of a male world, she has deliberately traded away the privileges accruing to her sex (she is even specifically referred to by Kikuji as a "neuter" [*chūsei*; 15/58]) in return for a means of living and functioning within that world. In this sense she has simply chosen the only alternative to the two positions available to single women younger than herself in the traditional Japanese world: wife and mother, and professional entertainer—both of whom have essentially made much the same bargain in their respective realms.[4] The status of *shishō*, though not restricted to women, has traditionally been used to identify women of a certain age and class who never were (or no longer are) married or have no independent means of support.

3. References are, respectively, to Yasunari Kawabata, *Thousand Cranes*, trans. Edward G. Seidensticker (New York: Knopf, 1968). *Senbazuru*, in *Gendai Nihon Bungaku Taikei*, vol. 52, *Kawabata Yasunari Shū* (Tokyo: Chikuma Shobō, 1969).

4. Though tangential to the present discussion, the study of the specific conditions of the entertainer, whether traditional geisha, bargirl, or some other, provides the social underpinning for a real understanding of such strong, independent, and resourceful women as Kazu, the protagonist of Mishima's novel *After the Banquet* (*Utage no ato*, 1960). See the discussion of Komako of *Snow Country* later in this chapter.

She may be a spinster, or a woman whose husband has died or divorced her and left her without support, or an aging entertainer who has failed to attract a patron to set her up in a business of her own; or she may have chosen this profession of her own preference. In her younger years her training in the customary traditional arts (the tea ceremony, flower arranging, music, dance, and so on) was intended to attract a suitable husband; in her later years it serves to provide her with a socially acceptable modus vivendi. Her occupation is thus no less socially defined than that of the masseuse (*amma*), traditionally reserved for the blind—a similarly dependent class.[5]

The tea ceremony in *Thousand Cranes* functions in its contemporary form as a discourse of political power expressed in aesthetic terms—continues to function, that is, much as it did half a millennium ago in the time of its founder, Sen Rikyū. The characters in Kawabata's novel enter into relations with one another only through the structures provided for them by chanoyu, and those structures determine entirely the course and outcome of those relationships. To say that chanoyu functions as a primary articulation of power, even while in its ostensible quietism and unconcern for the world it appears to disregard that power entirely, is simply to say that the aesthetic realm functions to articulate the ideological, in the process both concealing the ideological entirely within itself and at the same time disguising the raw exercise of power.

While often remarking on the passivity of Kawabata's male characters commentators have rarely subjected the reasons for this passivity to more than superficial interrogation.[6] Whether the governing aesthetic structure of the story is articulated through the arts or, as in *Snow Country* (discussed below) through myth, the actions, affinities, and fates of Kawabata's characters are determined by forces so completely beyond their control that these characters typically appear to the Western reader almost pathologically passive and irresolute. To say this, however, is only to note the obvious fact that, by and large, there is not much room afforded in modern Japanese society—or, indeed, much need felt—for what we are accustomed to think of as an inherently human striving for individual self-determination. This does not mean that such characters as Kikuji and Shimamura in *Snow Country*, are therefore helplessly "passive"; rather, they simply accept and live within the

5. The *amma* is no more necessarily female than the *shishō*; perhaps the best known *amma* is the mythical blind swordsman Zatōichi, as popularly portrayed by the movie star Katsu Shintarō. As an ace swordsman he is able to use the pathos of his infirmity and resulting dependent position to turn the tables on his enemies. A woman in a similar position would have to resort to guile and cunning alone—except perhaps in pornographic films.

6. See, e.g., Hasegawa Izumi, "*Senbazuru to Yama no oto*" (1972), in *Kawabata Yasunari*, ed. Nihon Bungaku Kenkyū Shinkōkai (Tokyo: Yūseidō, 1973), p. 218.

reality that their lives are already determined largely, perhaps entirely, by forces beyond their control.

It is scarcely a condition unknown to us. Jane Austen's characters, for example, find their lives similarly constrained by a society that does not tolerate fidgety and flighty young females *or* males. It simply would not have occurred to either Austen or Kawabata that their characters might be sufficiently exercised by anything as inconsequential as sexual passion that they should hurl themselves headlong into the sorts of precipitous and disastrously destructive actions taken by an Anna Karenina, an Emma Bovary, or a Thérèse Raquin. In the end, Kikuji will remain broodingly aloof, and Mrs. Ota's suicide will seem somehow less than tragic; Shimamura will remain married, and Komako will be as happy or unhappy as her condition permits. These are simply the givens within which their lives are acted out.

We are not necessarily averse to the notion that characters' lives may be predetermined and sealed by a higher fate; it is rather that our own Romantic heritage even now leads us to expect them to hurl themselves against that fate and die. We tend not to think of the familiar and prosaic sense of quotidian *resignation* as anything worthy of reflection in fiction, as though, considering the essential desolation of the human condition, simple acceptance were not in fact already difficult and even heroic enough. From the standpoint of our particular understanding of narratives of individual self-determination, we are less inclined than others may be to recognize the degree to which our own lives are, like those of these characters, determined by conditions over which we have so little control. The narrative mythos of Romanticism is founded upon this very blindness, this willed refusal of creative genius to acknowledge the annihilating power of dumb fate in lives inevitably destined to be lived out and ended within the narrow compass of a few repetitive patterns.[7]

Our first reaction to such a proposition is that even if such fiction might seem closer to real life, it would scarcely make very good reading. Lucy Snowe, for example, the exasperating and agonizingly resigned narrator of Charlotte Brontë's *Villette*, is remarkable for her accurate and hardheaded calculations of just how little she is likely to attain for herself by way of happiness in this world, for her willingness to restrict her ambitions to that small pittance which she finds allotted to her. If we want for her the ambition of a happiness beyond her station, it may well be precisely because we

---

7. In this sense it is instructive to read the works of a writer such as the contemporary Egyptian author Naguib Mahfouz; most of the characters in his *Midaq Alley* live out their entire lives within their stereotyped roles of barber, waiter, matchmaker, without having once left the block on which they were born—or feeling in the least deprived because of that fact.

understand that it is beyond ours as well. The work somehow seems like an exercise in reader-baiting, and until its unexpected, powerfully halluci-nogenic climax straight out of Thomas De Quincey, we find it difficult to conceive of anything further from the stormy and fateful passions of Jane Eyre and Rochester.

This less romantic fiction unfolds like a symphony: we take pleasure in the fact that the themes are well known, and what captures and intrigues us are their development and variations, their twists and turns along the way, the unexpected harmonies and dissonances, the counterpoints against the un-derlying rhythms and melodies. Since we knew this all along, the charge of "passivity" is really as much a non-issue as it would be in a discussion of the characters of such a writer as Marguerite Duras. In the works of both Kawabata and Duras there is a similar sense of fated destinies, of dreamlike and inchoate realities, of lyrical resignation to some steadily encroaching fate in terms of which (rather than against which) life seems to take on its most important meaning.[8]

Thousand Cranes opens with a tea-ceremony gathering held by Chikako Kurimoto at a Zen temple in the ancient temple town of Kamakura just outside Tokyo, Kawabata's home and the setting for several of his works. Kurimoto, the abandoned and bitter mistress of Kikuji's deceased father, maintains a place for herself among her acquaintances by making herself indispensable to them. Her special expertise is the infinitely detailed ar-rangement of the people and utensils that must be brought together in the practice of chanoyu.

In Kurimoto's hands, however, everything about chanoyu becomes per-verted and grotesque. Far from a ritual acknowledgment of the illusion, transience, and insubstantiality of human existence, the tea ceremony has become for her a very substantial ritual of power and revenge. It provides her with a means of ensnaring others in the dark webs of intrigue she spins as she attempts to bring under her control relationships and objects that have eluded her in the past. She is as single-minded as any man in using every access to power available to her to forward what she understands to be in her own vital interests. If she possesses a man's straightforward desire for power and control, her only failing is precisely that she is *not* a man. Nor, except through the temporarily borrowed homes and families of people like Kikuji and his father before him, does she have access to the one realm, the domestic, in which women are conceded dominance.

Like most male Japanese authors, Kawabata simply cannot accept the idea of a woman with such "masculine" interests and the willingness and ability to

8. At the end of this chapter, however, I propose a further interrogation of this problem.

act on them; he can only make of her a kind of monster. It is therefore not even enough that she be aging, squat, ugly, and ungraceful; she must also be afflicted with a disfiguring hairy birthmark on her breast that becomes the object of Kawabata's most loathsome meditations. As a child, watching her trim the tough, black hairs that grew from it, "Kikuji was obsessed with the idea that a child who sucked at that breast, with its birthmark and its hair, must be a monster" (14/10). Kikuji has already spent a lifetime trying not to think of himself in this way.

Kawabata's women are invariably indispensable to their men, who are childish and undeveloped characters in both senses of that word. Men like Kikuji and Shimamura, or like Shingo in *The Sound of the Mountain*, seem completely incapable of getting along without their stronger female counterparts (Mrs. Ota, Komako, Kikuko), who yet have little life independent of the men. Few women in modern Japanese literature are allowed by their male *or* female authors sufficient space for a believable and independent existence of truly political dimension in what has until recently been entirely a man's world.[9]

When Kikuji's father asks Kurimoto, "Do you suppose I could have a cup of tea?" (11/57), it is scarcely the innocent request it appears either in Japanese or in English. To be sure, it is a man's offhand demand to be served, but it also marks the all-too-willing fly's fatal first move toward the spider's web. Unable to acquire power as a woman is meant to, through marriage and children of her own (a failure symbolized by Kikuji's revulsion at the idea of a child nursing at her disfigured breast), the childless Kurimoto maneuvers to obtain that power instead by possessing through the tea ceremony not only its objects but its actors. It is the only medium available to her by distinction of her condition and training as a woman. Indeed, precisely because these things are positively expected of her, they provide her

9. Again, especially in terms of the failure to understand how women's lives may be truly political, one thinks of Mishima's *After the Banquet*: The lively and able middle-aged Kazu, proprietress of a successful Tokyo restaurant catering to the political elite, trades her hard-won independence and financial ambitions for what she takes to be a woman's need for a home (a family tomb is what she actually wants) by marrying a dried-up, elderly former diplomat. When he decides to enter a political race, she abandons her former life to hurl herself energetically into the job of winning for him the election campaign that he himself has already foredoomed. After his inevitable defeat, unable to immur herself meekly in the coveted "family tomb" of her husband's living death, she returns to reclaim the vitality of her former existence. Far from a monster, Kazu is one of the most entirely sympathetic women in Japanese fiction; it is rather the man who is monstrous. While the work had a great success, one suspects that Kazu has the power to make modern middle-aged, male Japanese readers squirm with discomfort. Takako Doi, leader of the Socialist party until recently, is just such a capable woman, and the most vicious attacks the old-boy members of the entrenched Liberal Democratic party could think to level at her were couched precisely in terms of her monstrous lack of maternity: what can an unmarried, childless woman know of life, let alone politics?

with entirely plausible protective coloration for her actions, and she takes every advantage of the fact.

Kurimoto has invited the marriageable Kikuji (like Shimamura in *Snow Country* a young man of leisure with no visible means of support) to a tea gathering to which she has also invited one of her young female students, Yukiko Inamura. Kurimoto hopes to maneuver the two into an arranged marriage over which she, as matchmaker, will be able to exercise control. From the outset, however, Kikuji is dimly aware of the flawed nature of this arrangement and resists it. Although he is in fact attracted to Yukiko (he is immediately struck by her "cleanness," exactly as Shimamura is by Komako's), the mere fact of Kurimoto's intervention is enough to poison the relationship for him even before it has begun. Our only concrete image of the girl is the metonymic detail of the *furoshiki* or ritual cloth wrapper she carries to the gathering, with its "thousand crane" pattern—a symbol of hope for the future—printed in white against a pink background.[10] In one particularly telling passage, Yukiko, wearing an *obi* with a pattern of Siberian irises, runs into Kurimoto at Kikuji's house, where the older woman has just finished making a seasonal arrangement of Japanese irises in the alcove of the teahouse. "One sensed that [Kurimoto] had just arranged them," writes Kawabata, managing ambiguously to include in the verb's object both irises *and* young people (52/73). Having taken it upon herself to make other people's "arrangements" for them, Kurimoto proceeds to extend her arranging to every aspect of Kikuji's life.[11]

Fumiko Ota, another young woman, also arrives at the initial tea gathering in the company of her mother, called only "Mrs. Ota." The latter is another of Kikuji's father's former mistresses—the very one, in fact, for whom he had abandoned Kurimoto. Kurimoto reveals her intense aversion to Mrs. Ota by acknowledging her presence in the same casual terms she uses to refer to some Americans who had dropped in unannounced several days

10. The translator chooses pragmatically to render *furoshiki* as "kerchief," but the implication of something to be worn on the head, which it is not, misses entirely the ritual nature of the object as well as the significance of its pattern. A *furoshiki* (literally "bath-cloth") is generally used for the quotidian business of rendering objects socially acceptable for carrying around in public, but it has special overtones of those ceremonial occasions when gifts must be exchanged or ritual objects carried. The meaning of the "thousand crane" (*senbazuru*) pattern derives from the common practice of hanging colorful chains of one thousand tiny origami birds about Shinto shrines as a request to the gods for recovery from illness. Seidensticker's translation is generally serviceable, but another problem occurs here when Kurimoto reponds to Kikuji's awareness that Yukiko Inamura is "the one with the thousand-crane kerchief": "Kerchief," she replies, "what odd things you notice. *A person can't be too careful.* I thought you had come together. *I was delighted*" (17/59). The italicized sentences actually translate "Nothing escapes you, does it?" and "In spite of all my preparations, you still managed to surprise me."

11. Although the word for "arranging" flowers is *ikeru*, which means "bringing to life" and so does not not allow exactly the same pun as the English word, this passage is every bit as significantly ambiguous in Japanese as it is in English.

earlier. The images of Americans that crop up in Kawabata's work seem particularly freighted with malevolent otherness, as in the repugnant image in *Sound of the Mountain* of the large hairy foreigner on the train with his young Japanese boyfriend asleep at his side.[12] Like the jackbooted GI in Mishima's *Pavilion of the Golden Temple* who kicks his pregnant prostitute girlfriend in the belly, such minor figures encapsulate a wealth of barely repressed hostility toward the most visible feature of the postwar American occupation of Japan.[13]

Kikuji's father had been a business acquaintance of Mrs. Ota's husband, and when she was widowed, she had turned to him for help in disposing of her husband's valuable collection of tea bowls. "He had thus been drawn to the widow" (19/60), and it is through the development of their sexual alliance that the karma of the tea bowls is given added weight and passed along to Kikuji. At the tea gathering that opens the book, Kurimoto deliberately has the unsuspecting Yukiko Inamura prepare tea for Kikuji in a bowl that had once been given to his father by Mrs. Ota's husband. This is not merely an insult to Mrs. Ota; by this contrivance Kurimoto has found the perfect means of weaving together the destinies of the various actors, drawing into her web the generation of dead fathers, living (and dying) wives and mistresses, their marriageable children, and an innocent young bystander as well. In sharp contrast to the image of the thousand cranes rising from Yukiko's pink *furoshiki*, the reader's mental image of Kurimoto is inescapably that of a black widow spider sitting malevolently at the center of her web and poisoning her victims as they are drawn in and stuck fast. (The author's frequent mention of Kurimoto's "poison" or "venom," *doku*, is perhaps graphically if unconsciously associated in the mind of Japanese reader with the female rivals of her own generation by the fact that the main graphic element in the character for "poison" closely resembles that for "mother.")

The idea of "destiny" plays a crucial role in the development of the story. One of the words Kawabata uses for it, *innen*, is a common word for "kar-

12. Yasunari Kawabata, *Sound of the Mountain* (New York: Knopf, 1970), pp. 197–98: "The foreigner's arms, below the short sleeves, made one think of a shaggy red bear. Though the boy was not particularly small, he looked like a child beside the giant foreigner. The latter's arms were heavy, his neck thick. Perhaps because he found it too much trouble to turn his head, he appeared quite unaware of the boy clinging to him. He had a fierce countenance, and his florid robustness made the muddy quality of the boy's weary face stand out more. The ages of foreigners are not easy to guess. The large, bald head, the wrinkles at the throat, and the blotches on the bare arms, however, made Shingo suspect that the man's age was not too far from his own. That such a man should come from a foreign country and appropriate a boy for himself—Shingo suddenly felt as if he were faced with a monster."

13. Another member of the U.S. occupation forces is Jack, a quartermaster corps lieutenant who plays a minor role in Mishima's *Temple of the Dawn* as the ever resourceful Keiko's goods-dispensing boyfriend. Yet though he represents everything that is unpleasant about Americans—he is oversized, oversexed, and over here—Mishima portrays him less as an unsympathetic intruder than as some large, friendly, dog with access to precious goods.

ma."[14] Kikuji tells Kurimoto that his father's brief possession of a valuable four-hundred-year-old tea bowl is finally of very little significance in the greater scheme of things, "trying to dismiss the associations [*innen*] the bowl called up." But we know better than this: "It had passed from Ota to his wife, from the wife to Kikuji's father, from Kikuji's father to Chikako; and the two men, Ota and Kikuji's father, were dead, and here were the two women. There was something almost weird about the bowl's career [*unmei*, literally fate or destiny]" (25/62).

The concept of karma is at once so alien to Western thought and so familiar in its Western adaptations that one must make a conscious effort to understand how it is being used here. We might think of it as something akin to our notion of how qualities that cannot be entirely explained by genetic inheritance or environmental influences alone are yet thought to be somehow passed along from one generation to the next. Kikuji understands his "destiny" (*unmei*) to be in some terrible way linked to Kurimoto's ugly birthmark (14/58); the word is echoed when he senses "something weird in the bowl's career";[15] and commenting to Yukiko that it was Kurimoto who brought them together, Kikuji says, "I don't want that woman's destinies [*unmei*] to touch mine at any point" (56/75).

Through the dynamic of karmic action the bowls anchor and symbolize their owners' *zaigō* (138/108), a word somewhat misleadingly translated as "guilt." It means "sin, guilt, crime" but carries neither the Judeo-Christian nor secular legal implications of those words. Originally a Buddhist concept, *zaigō* comprehends the universal human failing of attachment to things and people which creates such powerful negative emotions as lust, greed, possessiveness, pride, avarice (a list not unlike that of the familiar Christian seven "deadly sins" except that, at least in theory, it includes all of 108). In Buddhist metaphysics, however, these passions take on the weight of the objects to which they are attached, and it is the accumulated weight of these objects that enables the passions to take on lives of their own, "weird careers" to which the human lives they come in contact with become subordinated. Characters in the Nō drama are thus rooted after death to scenes of overpowering passions during their lives and doomed to live out wretched existences there in a sort of limbo until freed by the prayers of a priest. Much the same mechanism of existences rooted to one place by the powerful passions evoked there in life can be found in the *genius loci* of Sophocles' *Oedipus at Colonus*, whose setting is the Grove of the Furies, where Oedipus believes he has committed his fateful "sins."

The climax of *Thousand Cranes* is a moment of violence of a sort rarely

14. *Inga, shukumei*, and *sukuse*, used in the novel in the same sense, have similar Buddhist overtones.
15. The same phrase is used in relation to still another tea bowl (107/96).

encountered in Kawabata's work: Fumiko Ota, finding herself prevented by her now dead mother's "curse" from making tea in the bowl that has taken on her mother's karma, hurls it to the ground and smashes it to pieces (140/109). (The pale white Shino bowl is stained at its rim with what appears to be lipstick, "the color of old, dry blood," the sign of the mother's "curse"; 93/90, 103–4/94.) The entire story might even have taken form around a single germinal image in an Edo-period poem:

Kure-en ni	On the veranda
gin kawarake o	[she] smashes to pieces
uchikudaki	a silver-glazed bowl.[16]

Kure-en, "curved veranda" or "Chinese veranda," is also a pun on a darkening "destiny" (*en*); and throughout the novel Kawabata employs a vocabulary of "bonds" (*en*) both "formed" (*en o musubu*) and "severed" (*en o kiru*), expressions commonly denoting marriage and divorce but applied here to every other sort of human relationship as well. Thus, when Kikuji speaks of "severing ties" or "cutting off his association" with chanoyu, he is speaking indirectly about releasing himself from all the problems he seems only dimly to recognize as involved in it. But Kurimoto understands better than Kikuji the implications of this sort of language: when he tells her that he "severed relations with tea long ago," she responds, "I suppose it's all right to sever old relations when you've struck up new ones" (109/96), aware that he thinks of his relationship with Fumiko as a way of freeing himself from her. It is that, to be sure, but like all struggles in the spider's web it is also a way of becoming trapped more deeply—here in the karmas of his father and their common mistress, Mrs. Ota. Indeed, at her first meeting with her dead lover's adult son, Mrs. Ota's response to Kikuji's professed lack of interest in chanoyu seems to doom him in advance: "Really?" she says. "But you have it in your blood" (22/61). Only leukemia could sound as fatal.

Having allowed himself to acquiesce in Kurimoto's "arrangements," there is nothing left for Kikuji in the end but to let her "dispose of" his father's collection of tea bowls, since in one way or another she has already managed to dispose of everything and everyone else. The blood and poison of human karma, like the tea that symbolizes and substitutes for them, have flowed systemically from bowl to bowl, from person to person, by the same channels and to exactly the same effect. The narrative strongly suggests that, like her mother, Fumiko Ota too has killed herself, the pair leaving behind them a Kikuji as cursed and venomous as Kurimoto, who has successfully managed,

16. By Ryūgen in *Izayoi*, cited in *Kyoraisho* (1699), ed. Tetsuya Ijichi et al., in *Nihon koten bungaku zenshū* (Tokyo: Shogakukan, 1953), 51:504. The poem leaves the sex of the actor ambiguous.

for all his dumb and half-comprehending resistance, to infect him with her poison. At the time this novel was published, Kawabata's own suicide was still more than two decades away, but the profound existential despair of the work already seems to offer an adequate explanation or at least a context for it.

"Since the end of the war," wrote Kawabata in 1953, "young girls seem to have taken up ballet and tea as fads."[17] He had apparently begun to sense, long before the event, the degeneration he would warn of in his 1968 Nobel Prize acceptance speech, when he expressed astonishment that people could possibly find in so thoroughly dark a work as *Thousand Cranes* "an evocation of the formal and spiritual beauty of the tea ceremony." The feckless Shimamura of *Snow Country* (*Yukiguni*, 1935–37, 1947) is an amateur of the postwar fad for Western ballet, and his character is often enough misread as an attack on dilettantism; but it would be just as mistaken to read *Snow Country* as an attack on the degeneracy of Japanese tastes or of ballet—or, for that matter, of the traditional Japanese dance that Shimamura so abruptly abandons for the novelty of the Western—as it would be to read *Thousand Cranes* as an attack on the tea ceremony.

Rather, *Snow Country* seems to remind us again that like the two young men Kikuji and Shimamura, and indeed like most of Kawabata's characters, we are ignorant of the ways in which our lives are already spoken for by forces whose relationships to ourselves we are at best only dimly aware of, and of how they are given expression and representation through complex social conventions within which what we take to be the self-willed actions of individuals come to assume the appearance of fixed dramatic roles. What is at stake in these works is precisely the ideological authority of such an idea, artfully concealed and made acceptable by articulation through the culturally potent and socially sanctioned discursive structures of myth.

The myth that provides the primary structure of *Snow Country* is known as the legend of Tanabata. Alluding to it in passing, Masao Miyoshi remarks in *Accomplices of Silence* only that "while *Snow Country* gives great prominence to the Tanabata legend, the scene of the starry heavens that concludes the novel is not clear enough in its significance to serve as a gloss on the work."[18] It is certainly true that no single interpretive scheme can ever suffice to explain a work entirely; the ideological implications of this particular construct, however, cannot be rendered visible until the elaborate homologies whereby it is articulated are at least given fuller delineation. As in the case of chanoyu in *Thousand Cranes*, what is articulated through the use of this construct is what it means to be, feel, and think as a Japanese. The question of precisely *how*

17. Quoted from *Hi mo tsuki mo* ("Day and Night") in Yoshimura, "*Senbazuru ron*," p. 178.
18. Masao Miyoshi, *Accomplices of Silence* (Berkeley: University of California Press, 1974), p. 109.

the story is developed in terms of this particular myth, then, warrants a closer analysis of its role in Kawabata's story.

Before we can begin to trace out its ideological implications, we first need to know something of the legend's background—that cultural backdrop against which all reading takes place. The Tanabata festival in Japan has its origins in ancient Chinese lore.[19] The five major Chinese festivals of the lunar calendar were early systematized in a series that followed the odd-numbered months of the lunar calendar, each paired with its corresponding day: 1/1, 3/3, 5/5, 7/7, and 9/9 (known in Japan as the *gosekku*; Tanabata falls on 7/7). Each festival embraces clusters of assorted mythic materials, often united only by accident of historical or geographical association, and the elements of the various mythic narratives contained in them were often still further confused and entangled during the absorption of these festivals into Japan.

The Tanabata legend, for example, unites in one story two entirely disparate elements. The first is the Chinese legend of "Seventh Night" *(ch'i-hsi)*: two lovers, the Herd Boy and the Weaver Girl *(kengyū* and *shokujō* in Japanese), are represented by a pair of stars in the constellations Altair and Vega, which are separated in heaven by the Milky Way (Japanese *ginga*, "Silver River" or *amanogawa*, "River of Heaven") and allowed to meet only once a year, on the seventh night of the seventh lunar month. The story of ill-fated astral lovers played out in the earthly realm is reminiscent both of Shakespeare's young "star-crossed lovers" in *Romeo and Juliet* and, much closer to Japan, of the equally tragic celestial fate of the lovers Baoyu and Daiyu in the late eighteenth-century Chinese novel *Hung lou meng* (Dream of the red chamber).

The second element of the Chinese legend is the customary request, known as "begging for skill" (ch'i-ch'iao), made to the gods by each young woman on this festival night for mastery in the female domestic skills of sewing and weaving, for good fortune in marriage, and for a glimpse in her dreams of her future husband. Tanabata in Japan today, rather like Halloween in the United States, has devolved into a costume festival for small children both male and female; they can often be seen decked out in pretty summer kimonos and installed along residential streets in crêches made of branches gaily decorated with small lanterns and colorful strips of paper inscribed with poems appropriate to the festival.

Kawabata's story is structured upon the interplay of elements of the myth associated with "stars" on the one hand and with "weaving" on the other, the two themes related and mediated through a complex synesthetic fire-and-ice imagery that centers on the story's famous opening episode, which has become known as "the night-mirror" (*yokagami*).

The theme of weaving is further compounded of two separate elements that meet in the making of silk, the material associated with the Chinese myth. The first of these is the two-part cycle of silkworm and moth, and the second is the finished woven material. In its juvenile phase the silkworm is inscribed with the attributes of youth, translucence, vitality, hunger, redness, smoothness, fineness, and reproductive immaturity; in its adult moth stage it is marked by maturity, opacity, dullness, lack of appetite, whiteness (from the powder that covers its wings), coarseness, reproduction, and death. In the normal rearing cycle, the voracious silkworm grows rapidly through successive larval stages until it finally abandons eating altogether to concentrate entirely on spinning its cocoon of silk fiber. The cocoons are boiled in the process of extracting the silk, both to degum the thread for reeling and to kill the moths inside before they emerge from the cocoon and so ruin the thread. Some of the moths, however, are allowed to hatch normally in order to produce future silkworms; they mate immediately after hatching and die soon after laying their eggs.

It should not require much effort to recognize in this biological schema the development of Komako, one of *Snow Country*'s two women. The lives of both Komako and Yōko, as implicated within this cycle, are intricately and ambiguously related to each other. Yōko first appears on the train that brings Shimamura back to the hot-spring resort in the dead of winter (the temporal scheme of the first section is so complex that a separate study would be required for its elucidation). Shimamura observes her reflection in the train window as, mysterious, beautiful, and remote, she tenders solicitous, maternal care to an invalid man. In the ensuing "night-mirror" passage a light from a fire or star somewhere outside the train appears to gleam through her eye and float in the space of the darkened train window, an event that establishes Yōko as the celestial half of the Yōko-Komako pair. She is nothing but cold, celestial light, as ethereal, mysterious, and aloof as the hot-blooded Komako is down-to-earth, gregarious, and prosaic. These women form the essential polar opposition around which the story is structured.

Beyond this clear opposition, Komako herself changes over the course of the story. Although she might appear to be one of the few women in Japanese fiction who really does develop over time, her development is in fact determined by the homology between her character and the myth. The vocabulary used to describe her existence is unavoidably feudal and technical. Born in this mountainous hot-spring "Snow Country" region, Komako (the name she adopts later as a geisha) as a young girl had been sent to Tokyo—sold, really—by her impoverished parents to work as a lowly *oshaku*, or geisha's assistant, helping to pour customers' drinks. Exactly as might have transpired in a story by the novelist Ihara Saikaku two centuries earlier, a wealthy patron eventually bought her contract from her employer, an expensive proposition that would doubtless include the exclusive right to her virginity. This patron was to have had her trained in the proper geisha arts and eventually set up as a teacher of dance (*shishō*), a profession in which—like Kurimoto, the teacher of tea in *Thousand Cranes*—she could have made an independent living. After only a year and a half, however, her would-be patron died, leaving her on her own. Still too young to make a living by teaching, she had no recourse but to return to her Snow Country home in order to find work.

The winter resort area of Echigo-Yūzawa, popular then as now among other things for its hot springs and skiing, is chronically short of geisha, whether the young and energetic apprentices known as *hangyoku* ("half-jewels") or the older full geisha known as *toshima* ("advanced in years"). Komako, who lives and studies with the local music teacher (also a *shishō*), is therefore in local demand to help out at parties. Given her situation and past experience, it is undoubtedly accepted that she will occasionally sleep with customers for money or favors, though in her ambiguous status as not-yet-quite-geisha there is no one either to require this of her or to take reponsibility if there are what she rather nonchalantly calls "complications." (Once she has placed herself under contract and become a professional geisha, however, her obligations and those of her master will become highly formalized in all details.)

The ambiguity of her situation is crucial. Shimamura plays on this ambiguity at their first meeting by asking her, half-jestingly and somewhat inappropriately, to call for a "real geisha" to spend the night with him. Later, when Komako has in fact become a real geisha, an unspoken tension in the professional nature of their encounters makes their relationship more complex: "Her being a geisha made it even more difficult for him to be free and open with her" (41/14).[20] Characters in Japanese fiction who have not yet fully settled into one of the established roles in life are especially "interesting" precisely because, like trickster figures, they are volatile, threatening, changeable; once they have fully adopted their formal roles, they become entirely predictable, and the provocative sense of female ambiguity, so obsessively explored by Tanizaki and Kawabata, seems to disappear into thin air. In *Some Prefer Nettles*, Tanizaki was interested in the more permanent sort of beauty that is found only in established roles; Kawabata, however, is interested in that more evanescent beauty found only *between* them.

It is Komako's ambiguity that so tantalizes Shimamura: he is attracted to her odd combination of childishness and maturity, passion and reserve, fire

20. Page numbers refer respectively to Yasunari Kawabata, *Snow Country*, trans. Edward G. Seidensticker (New York: Knopf, 1960); *Yukiguni*, in *Kawabata Yasunari shū* (Tokyo: Chikuma Shobō, 1969).

and ice. Throughout the work, his language toward her reveals a profound uncertainty—and therefore an equally profound excitement—over whether she should be regarded and treated as a girl or as a woman. Earlier in the story, when she is portrayed as an intellectually, socially, and sexually precocious girl, she lives in the music teacher's house in an attic room originally used for rearing silkworms; and Shimamura is "taken with the fancy that the light must pass through Komako, living in the silkworms' room, as it passed through the translucent silkworms" (50/18). During this period, moreover, she is most often described as "red," an attribute both of her youth and of the extreme cold of the Echigo-Yūzawa snow country: "Your cheeks are flaming [*makka*, bright red]," says Shimamura. "That's how cold it is" (45/16).

Later, however, when she has matured into a true geisha and moved into more appropriate lodgings provided by the man with whom she has contracted, Komako is described instead in terms of the "thick white powder" she wears, the customary makeup (*oshiroi*) of the mature geisha (82/30, 108/41). The first such description immediately follows a scene of moths beating white powder from their wings as they lay their eggs and die. Another reference to her white "geishalike skin" precedes the announcement that the now mature Komako no longer lives "in the silkworms' room" as before, but in "a real geisha house" (*okiya*; 86/32). The change in her status is further reflected in the already-noted ambiguity of Shimamura's continuing inability to determine whether she is girl or woman: at a crucial moment he tells her "You're a good girl" (*kimi wa ii ko da ne*), only to follow this a moment later by "You're a good woman" (*kimi wa ii onna da ·ne*; 120/47). The abrupt change only makes Komako furious: the romantic illusion of being desired with the innocence of young love is one thing, but the brutal reality of being desired because she is a woman who can be bought is suddenly something else entirely.

Yōko completes the mythical structure of the story from the other end: in contrast to Komako, who is in process both as silkworm and as moth, Yōko is characterized as finished material, a woman woven entirely of whole cloth, as it were. Indeed, the single detailed description of her in the work, aside from the completely etherealized image in the "night-mirror" passage, presents her entirely in textile terms: "The bold pattern of her *obi*, half visible over the [mountain-] trousers, made the rough russet and black stripes of the latter seem fresh and cheerful, and for the same reason the long sleeves of her woolen kimono took on a certain voluptuous charm. The trousers, split just below the knees, filled out toward the hips, and the heavy cotton, for all its natural stiffness, was somehow supple and gentle" (51–52/18). This presentation of character in terms of qualities of the local woven stuff and the clothing made from it only serves to render Yōko all the more abstract and, paradoxically, immaterial.

Although Komako is described just as sparely (we really are provided with almost no mental picture of her aside from the warm red or powdered white of her cheeks, the intense cold black of her hair, and the pervasive "cleanness"—"down to the hollows of her toes"—that seems such an obsession in Kawabata's writing), we have little trouble picturing her intense vitality, quick intelligence, and youthful beauty. The single lengthy description of her, though intensely physical (when not actually bizarre), succeeds in leaving her only slightly less an abstraction than Yōko:

> The high, thin nose was a little lonely, a little sad, but the bud of her lips opened and closed smoothly, like a beautiful little circle of leeches. Even when she was silent her lips seemed always to be moving. Had they had wrinkles or cracks, or had her color been less fresh, they would have struck one as unwholesome, but they were never anything but smooth and shining. The line of her eyelids neither rose nor fell. As if for some special reason, it drew its way straight across her face. There was something faintly comical about the effect, but the short, thick hair of her eyebrows sloped gently down to enfold the line discreetly. There was nothing remarkable about the outlines of her round, slightly aquiline face. With her skin like white porcelain coated over a faint pink, and her throat still girlish, not yet filled out, the impression she gave was above all one of cleanness, not quite one of real beauty. [33/11]

Where this portrait is not merely conventional or vague, it almost seems calculated to repel, its final appeal to "cleanness" not quite entirely canceling the effect of the writhing leeches, or the cumulative negative effect of lips that are *not* "cracked," color that is *not* "unwholesome" (*fuketsu*, unclean), a throat that is *not* "fleshy," and oddly straight eyes under strangely bushy eyebrows. Komako, as Shimamura observes, is certainly no "real beauty." And yet the drunken display that immediately follows this description reveals in her a manifest power that in the entirely ethereal Yōko is always only suggested, concealed and withdrawn under her reserve. The description of neither woman actually adds up to the picture of a real human being. The humanity of each emerges elsewhere: in Yōko's mysterious and tender solicitude for the music teacher's dying son, in Komako's sharp intelligence and intense sexual vitality. Otherwise, the one is embodied only as a lovely, pale, cool voice with a faraway light in her eyes, the other as a scrubbed red or white cleanness with a fiery temper.

The weaving metaphor is unpacked entirely in the long last section that ends in the fire at the cocoon warehouse *cum* movie theater (123/48ff.) and Yōko's ghastly and mystery-laden death there. This section begins with a description of *chijimi*, the silk crepe of the area, prized for a particular sheen widely held to be possible only in material that is spun, woven, finished, and bleached in the glare of sunlit snow. It is thought that local girls weave the best cloth when they are between the ages of fourteen and twenty-four—which is to say roughly between the ages of menarche and marriage, in folklore universally considered a dangerous and unsettled period for females precisely because they are still ambiguously indeterminate, half girls and half women requiring close supervision and expeditious marriage.

Even as Shimamura thinks of the *chijimi* as something entirely remote from Komako—"she hardly seemed the person to ask about the fate of an old folk art"—the very fact of its durability reminds him by contrast of the transience of their relationship. The discovery that the object of his attention, like his old *chijimi* kimonos, may once have been worn by someone else and may in the future be worn by another moves him to see her only in terms of her profession and to imagine her "as the mother of another man's children" (126/49). And it is when his musings have reached this significant point that the final rupture in their relationship occurs. After a hauntingly beautiful passage (deservedly noted in nearly every essay on the work) in which Shimamura's thoughts wander away from her in a long, complex, and typically Kawabata-like string of associations that start from the windlike sounds of a tea kettle, only to reemerge finally at Komako again, he realizes with a start that *everything* now makes him think of her. Alarmed by the recognition of his own obsession, he concludes that "the time ha[s] come to leave" (127/49). Departure now firmly in mind, he sets out through the sights of *chijimi* country on a trip that is intended to start him on his way back to Tokyo.

This section is preceded by an allusion to the chanting of Nō drama, and Shimamura's actions here seem to reflect and make explicit the often-mentioned Nō-like structure of this work,[21] though in its cataloguing of associations it also resembles the typical *michiyuki* scene of the Jōruri or Kabuki theater. Here too the remaining elements of the Tanabata myth are tied together in preparation for the dramatic ending. For the myth's tradi-

---

21. Though its chronological movement is infinitely more complex than that permitted by the drama, the story's organization does reflect the two-part division of Nō in Shimamura's first and second journeys (the Japanese text, however, indicates nothing of the clear division into "Part One" and "Part Two" of Seidensticker's translation). Shimamura can also be seen as the *waki*, typically a traveler who arrives at a spot filled with powerful dramatic meaning and elicits its tale; and Komako and Yōko, as *shite* and *tsure*, the primary actor and her companion, a modern-day Matsukaze and Murasame (from the play *Matsukaze*) sharing the memory of their mutual lover, who is similarly a visitor from the capital. Komako is both *maejite* and *atojite*, the main characters of Nō drama's first and second halves respectively, the second representing an earlier transformation of the first; and her drunk scene closely resembles the frenzied central dance of a typical "madwoman" play. The story, moving from quiet start to active development to urgent finale, has something of the traditional three-part developmental segmentation of Nō. Finally, the language of Kawabata's story has about it much of the heightened poetic quality of the Nō drama. J. Thomas Rimer, however, in *Modern Japanese Fiction and Its Traditions* (Princeton: Princeton University Press, 1978), pp. 172–75, sagely notes that no imposition of such structures on the work will ever be able to account for it entirely.

tional crows, which form a bridge across the "River of Heaven" over which the separated lovers cross for their once-a-year tryst (Komako twice calls Shimamura "the type who comes only once a year"; 82/30, 87/33), Kawabata substitutes a flock of Buddhist nuns crossing a bridge over a river: "On their way home from a service, they looked like crows hurrying home to their nests" (129/50).

Following his brief journey through the countryside, Shimamura finds himself drawn again to the resort, where the warehouse/theater fire occurs. The narrative immortalizes the actors at the very point of their inevitable separation by snatching them up to the heavenly plane and simultaneously bringing the heavens down to earth. In this powerful movement and interpenetration of images, the Milky Way, the "River of Heaven," flows down to earth to join the shower of sparks leaping upward from the fire, until in the confusion the union between the earthly and the heavenly realms is complete, the actions on one plane integrated fully with those on the other. In the acrid smoke of burning cocoons, the crowd watches in horror as Yōko falls from the balcony to the ground, though at the moment of falling she seems rather to float upward, having undergone in death a "metamorphosis" (*henkei*)—the biological term used to indicate the silkworm's passage from larva to moth. It is at this point that Shimamura recalls the reflection of Yōko's face in the "night-mirror" of the opening passage, which set up the initial mediation between the earthly and heavenly realms. It is clear that Yōko has returned to heaven to resume her eternal place there as a celestial body (it is literally accurate, if silly, to note that she has thereby become a star in the movies). The earthy Komako will remain rooted to her place in the Snow Country, to which the callow Shimamura will not return more than once a year.

Could Paul de Man's summary of Stendhal's *Charterhouse of Parma* suggest a basis in the universality of myth for a comparative understanding of Kawabata's novel?

> The novel tells the story of two lovers who, like Eros and Psyche, are never allowed to come into full contact with each other. When they can see each other, they are separated by an unbreachable distance; when they can touch, it has to be in a darkness imposed by a totally arbitrary and irrational decision, an act of the gods. The myth is that of the unovercomable distance which must always prevail between the selves.[22]

Such a reduction would entail certain problems. For one thing, even if both

22. De Man, "The Rhetoric of Temporality," in *Blindness and Insight*, p. 209.

stories are based on myths of separation, we are not dealing here with the arbitrary and irrational gods of Greek mythology and their peculiar relations with human men and women. Rather, the story is based on a very different sort of Chinese myth, long naturalized in Japan, whose theme is articulated through a modern social problematic and whose characters are assigned entirely Japanese meaning. Myth may indeed be universal, but the interpretations and functions assigned to it do not translate across culture, any more than does our history of readings of certain myths: the Oedipus story, as I have suggested, does not seem to survive importation across cultural borders as a way of explaining those phenomena we are accustomed to thinking of precisely in terms of such a myth.

It does not seem very difficult to allocate equitably between the two characters Komako and Yōko an erotic quality on the one hand and a spiritual quality on the other: certainly Komako is almost entirely physical and erotic, while Yōko is made to be immaterial (or perhaps more accurately "in material") and spiritual. This, however, is as far as Psyche and Eros can take us. The problem remains as to what quality we are to invest in Shimamura; and the answer proposes itself that it can be nothing else than a culturally constructed and culturally reinforced male demand for a female ambiguity that alternates between Mother and Whore, Heaven and Earth, Spirit and Flesh, Eros and Psyche—like the powerful and irrational desire of Kaname in *Some Prefer Nettles* to possess the two simultaneously, separate *and* united in the same person.

Like the mirror of the train window in the night, that "cinematic double-exposure" which superimposes inside and outside, Shimamura is in a sense ambiguity itself, a desire further constructed into the source of the tension between reality and fantasy. His almost perverse fascination with fantasy withdraws itself as soon as the unreal threatens actually to become real. A professional dilettante, he is what Sōseki once called a *himajin*, a "man of leisure"—by which he meant "someone who contributes nothing to the world," or precisely what the true artist is *not*.[23] Shimamura abandons his interest in the Japanese dance as soon as it threatens to become important to him, switching instead to the new, unfamiliar, and far less realizable abstraction of the Western ballet. Similarly drawn at first to Komako, who years before already knew more about the native performing arts than he does now, for all his "armchair scholarship," Shimamura shows signs of becoming alienated even further when the young woman, in her practical and down-to-earth way, proves to know entirely *too* much about these matters. His rationalization of her as someone interesting only because, like himself, she has been wasting her time on something so divorced from herself as to seem

23. *SZ*, 11:94–96.

unreal, is patently weak: "And something like that evening mirror was no doubt at work here too. He disliked the thought of drawn-out complications from an affair with a woman whose position was so ambiguous; but beyond that he saw her as somehow unreal, like the woman's face in that evening mirror. His taste for the occidental dance had the same air of unreality about it." (26/9). The "free, uncontrolled fantasy" of Shimamura's study of the ballet is compared to "being in love with someone he had never seen" (26/9). Only an essentially ambiguous Komako or Yōko can exert such a powerful attraction on this man-mirror situated in the space between reality and fantasy; a real and unambiguous woman cannot.

Ambiguity is the essence of the Nō drama. Based on the Buddhist premise that what we accept as reality is in fact illusion, Nō demonstrates that these are not polar opposites but realms that interpenetrate in complex ways. It is precisely this complex dimensionality, embodied in the "night-mirror" character of Shimamura, that permits the interpenetration in *Snow Country* of the carnal and the spiritual, purity and impurity, the mundane and the ethereal and that makes possible the meeting between worlds otherwise kept eternally apart. Viewed in this light, Shimamura is no longer merely the callow, vacillating figure he is most often taken to be. The ambiguity of his nature as it assumes the essential demand of *all* men for ambiguity, becomes the very condition under which the story can be narrated at all. It resembles the night-mirror of the train window moving through the darkness, that mirror which, as Foucault conceives of it in his study of *Las Meninas*, "by making invisible, beyond even the walls of the studio itself, what is happening in front of the picture, creates, in its saggital dimension, an oscillation between the interior and the exterior."[24] Shimamura functions as this Foucauldian mirror in providing the "central void" which, by means of its own effacement, permits representation to take place at all.

Much like *Thousand Cranes*, at the center of which loom absent but omnipotent fathers of whom Sen Rikyū is but the first, *Snow Country* represents and supports an ideology of male authority. It does so by depicting the fundamental role of such authority as the creation and occupation of that essential and seminal space which alone is able to unite the otherwise unbridgeable and oscillating polarities between the schizophrenically divided and eternally incomplete Whore/Mother and Heaven/Earth aspects of female nature. As I noted in discussing *Thousand Cranes*, Kawabata's males are far from being "merely" passive in a negative sense. So long as their mere presence permits continuity in the universe, men like Shimamura and Kikuji (as well as Shingo in *Sound of the Mountain*) *need* have no clear idea of where they came from or where they are going; they have, in fact, a culturally

24. Foucault, *The Order of Things*, pp. 11, 16.

sanctioned reason for simply existing. Like gods—or to make clearer the ideological nature of the problem, like the emperor himself—they need only exist to confer being and order upon an otherwise chaotically fragmented universe. And these male gods, potent precisely by virtue of their inaction (a remarkably secure way to assert potency), represent, like Foucault's crucial mirror, the centers of narrative galaxies around which starry females eternally revolve in fulfillment of their fated destinies. Threatened male authority is undoubtedly the dominant theme of Kawabata's novels, but that authority emerges remarkably unscathed, thanks to the active intervention of women—whose very existence, after all, depends entirely on keeping it propped up. Since aesthetics finally is, as Eagleton suggests, "born as a discourse of the body," it is both "the very secret prototype of human subjectivity in early capitalist society, and a vision of human energies as radical ends in themselves which is the implacable enemy of all dominative or instrumentalist thought. It signifies a creative turn to the sensuous body, as well as an inscribing of that body in a subtly oppressive law." And so, continues Eagleton as if in reference to Kawabata's work, "if it offers a generous utopian image of reconciliation between men and women at present divided from one another, it also blocks and mystifies the real political movement towards such historical community."[25]

25. Eagleton, *Ideology of the Aesthetic,* pp. 9, 13.

Chapter 6

The Ideology of Science:
Kōbō Abé's *Woman in the Dunes*

When people are placed under conditions which appeal to the brute only,
what remains to them but to rebel or to succumb to utter brutality?
—Friedrich Engels, *The Condition of the Working Class in England*

In exploring the ways in which ideology is articulated in fiction, we
have so far examined, in the work of Yasunari Kawabata, the relationship of
ideology to its expression in terms of aesthetics. I have attempted to show
that Kawabata's novels constitute deliberately aestheticized constructions
whose immediate artistic appeal is calculated to ensure the acceptance of a
particular dominant set of social relations. Thus, his positioning of actively
potent females in roles of active subordination around the centrality of inac-
tive, impotent, but dominant males clearly serves to buttress a cultural ideology of male domination. Kawabata further supports this ideological organization of gender prerogative by means of his frequently noted evocation of
the ancient aesthetic ideal of *yūgen*, or mysterious beauty, which offers a
powerful means of relegating all power relations to an always already accepted but essentially ineffable realm of aesthetics: everyone knows *yūgen*
when they see it, it seems, but no one can or needs to define it. Long
enthusiastically accepted by an acculturated public as a sign of its own cultural sensibilities, its greatest usefulness lies precisely in the fact that its assumptions need not—indeed, cannot—be discussed.

The central optimism of the scientific project is reflected most strongly in
its persistently positivist vision of the utopian society of ever increasing
amelioration. But its ideological nature is perhaps more clearly revealed by
society's even more familiar and chronic obsession with the *dystopian*, always
repressed to the periphery of the mainstream of both science and literature
in the form of science fiction, horror, spy and murder mystery novels. If from
the Freudian perspective displacement is particularly indicative of significance, the fact that literary dystopias so far outnumber utopias must no

doubt be understood as speaking to the repression and displacement away from the center of the fears they represent—and therefore of their inevitable and even more powerful subsequent return.

Never very interested in cheerful utopias, fiction (at least *capitalist* fiction) in the age of the post-ironic has for the most part turned its back on science and its promise of permanent material amelioration as difficult, horrid, Pollyannaish, irrelevant, and wrongheaded and has retreated instead to more genial performative games of language and gender.[1] As the humorous genre-capping works of such writers as Douglas Adams suggest, few "serious" novelists deal with science fiction any more, always excluding a few problematic writers like Doris Lessing and Kōbō Abé. This chapter considers the case of Abé, who has specialized in systematically subjecting to scrutiny the assumptions of rationality and logical deduction on which both science fiction and murder mystery are founded.

Abé's black humor, technological fantasies, and absurdist mentality all mark him as belonging to an already enshrined generation of writers whose time is past and whose visionary dystopic futures have, like George Orwell's in *1984*, already come and gone. The dominant absurdist element especially dates even as recent a work as *The Ark Sakura (Hakobune Sakura maru,* 1984), the absurd as a literary convention (persistent Czech affinities notwithstanding) being about as fashionable today as cubism in art. Since we pretty much know what to expect from Abé's work in advance, and since existential terror and absurdity have had their day, his work, as seen from a contemporary Western viewpoint, can seem mannered, repetitive, and ultimately boring.

What such a dismissal perhaps fails to account for, however, is the relevance, the persistent force, of a narrative of the repetitiveness, boredom, alienation, terror, and pervasive absurdity of everyday life in huge modern megalopolises from New York City to Bombay, which often seems to the outsider (and perhaps to the insider as well) to lie just this side of Pluto. In this context, Abé might be numbered among such cosmopolitan fantasists as Salman Rushdie, Gabriel García Márquez, and Thomas Pynchon. But not even Kafka—who has been amplified by Gulag narratives into a dystopic Eastern European alternative to socialist-realism modernity, a particularly Slavic version of reality, like a sort of sour, heavy black peasant bread leavened only by the biting irony of Kundera's sort of bleak urbane humor—can fully account for all the absurd qualities of modern Japanese life in such metropolises as Tokyo and Osaka. More unreal *topoi* would be hard to imagine, yet Abé has created a place for himself in fiction precisely by imagining them. Japan requires a Kafka all its own, and Abé has for decades

---

1. The important analysis is Lyotard's *Postmodern Condition.* For an argument of the role of scientific thought (though not of scientific thought as a *problem*) as the central paradigm of twentieth-century fiction, see N. Katherine Hayles, *The Cosmic Web: Scientific Field Models and Literary Strategies in the Twentieth Century* (Ithaca: Cornell University Press, 1984).

so firmly held that claim that studies of his work almost invariably include the obligatory comparison.

Over the years, Abé's master narrative, played out in several variations, has evolved along the lines of an absurdist detective story whose theme, Pirandello-like, is the narrator's carefully documented search for a missing person who turns out to be none other than himself. In *Woman in the Dunes* (*Suna no onna*, 1962), the theme of the hunter become the hunted lies, speaking strictly in terms of the narrative, just outside the framework of the work itself. To be sure, everyone knows the work is about an amateur entomologist trapped in a sort of killing-jar, but this subject is never explicitly stated either directly as a theme or indirectly by means of the narrative technique. Abé's *The Ruined Map* (*Moetsukita chizu*, 1967), however, makes the theme of the hunter turned prey progressively more evident by hints dropped at regular intervals, and it becomes explicit near the end when the reader realizes that the narrative is being repeated exactly, and in the same voice, but now from the point of view of the object of the narrator's investigation—a kind of self-consciousness which the narrator calls "a false sense of déjà-vu disguised as memory" (277/196).[2]

Both thematically and in terms of its narrative technique, *The Ruined Map* begins exactly where *Woman in the Dunes* ends: with the copy of an application form for the investigation of a missing person. But in *Secret Rendezvous* (*Mikkai*, 1977) the narrator abandons any pretense of objectivity toward this perverse business of intrusive self-consciousness and simply announces immediately after the now obligatory missing-person report that the person he is tracking is "none other than I myself." While admitting this to be as absurd as "a pickpocket filching his own wallet, or a detective slipping handcuffs on himself" (6/4), he proceeds—apparently, like anyone else, because there is nothing else to do—to get on with the job. Once the narrative plunges headlong into total absurdity ("Besides, the horse was in uncommonly good spirits this morning. He said. . . ."), we understand that we can only be in one of Abé's increasingly bizarre dystopias, and the hospital world in which the work is set does not disappoint.[3] It is generally the sort of world that figures in the work of the many popular writers who have followed in Abé's footsteps: for example, Takashi Atōda's lightly absurdist novel *Kuroi hako* (Black box, 1986).

The detective genre plays against conventional expectations of logic, sending readers up blind alleys and forcing them to come to the wrong conclusions about the facts.[4] Abé's works, as if set in a hall of mirrors,

2. Combined page references cite respectively Kōbō Abé, *The Ruined Map*, trans. E. Dale Saunders (Rutland, Vt.: Tuttle, 1969); and *Moetsukita chizu*, in *Abe Kōbō zensakuhin*, vol. 8 (Tokyo: Shinchōsha, 1972).

3. Kōbō Abé, *Secret Rendezvous* (Tokyo: Tuttle, 1981); *Mikkai* (Tokyo: Shinchōsha, 1977).

4. The importance of the technique of *peripeteia* or "reversal" in the detective story is the

subject the ostensibly deductive method of the detective genre (*tantei shōsetsu* or *suiri shōsetsu*) itself to a kind of infinite regression, investigating the idea of investigation by making problematic its conventions, its assumptions, its procedures, its quandaries. What is thus actually at stake in such works is the validity of deductive logic as a way of arriving at ultimate truth, and so of the very underpinning of the scientific method itself.

In Abé's hands, deductive logic becomes something truly terrifying. He is concerned especially with the violent collisions that occur when the awesome instrumental power of cold, self-contained rationality—generally the sole stock-in-trade of the otherwise entirely fallible detective—is trained on the patent absurdity of human life and, even worse, with how the results of such collisions haunt the menacing corridors of inhuman bureaucracies: the offices, penal institutions, and hospitals where criminals and victims, perpetrators and lawyers, doctors and patients, jailers and prisoners are no longer clearly distinguishable from one another.

Abé's labyrinthine underworld is a faithfully detailed mirror image, only turned upside down, of the world we take for granted. The world of Raymond Chandler's novels, by way of contrast, may sometimes become considerably absurd, but it never lapses into the truly Kafkaesque nightmare; and even when good guys and bad guys in Chandler's stories look very much alike, there is always a bottom line of decency that clearly separates them.[5] In Abé's stories, however, the all-too-human and the all-too-inhuman are not simply opposite sides of the same coin; after a while we realize that we have no idea which side of the coin we are seeing or, even worse, on which side our sympathies should lie.

The connective strand running through all of Abé's work is the idea that rationality, pursued logically to its logical endpoint, turns out to be insanely irrational. The most frightening thing about the world we live in is its power to rationalize itself to us as the only normality there is by its amazing trick of being able to account paranoically for everything down to the last tiny detail. And the name we give to the ability to perform this particular ideological accounting trick is "science." In Abé's hands, properly licensed and accredited scientific knowledge of the world proves not only as false as any other but even more so, and certainly more destructive in its consequences. And what is "logical" turns out to be the world we know turned on its head and made strange.

Jumpei Niki, the protagonist of *Woman in the Dunes*, is as ordinary a man as it is possible to be. Even the given name of this Japanese schoolteacher

subject of Dennis Porter's "Backward Construction and the Art of Suspense," in *The Pursuit of Crime*, ed. Dennis Porter (New Haven: Yale University Press, 1981).

5. For one interesting view of Chandler's work, see Fredric Jameson, "On Raymond Chandler," in *The Poetics of Murder: Detective Fiction and Literary Theory*, ed. Glenn W. Most and William W. Stowe (New York: Harcourt Brace Jovanovich, 1983), pp. 122–48.

and amateur scientist means "obedient and average," suggesting the dreary ordinariness of a man who has no use at all for the imagination. Though entirely plausible as a Japanese name, it has something of the ring of Meade E. Oaker to it, if not simply Everyman—and even this ordinary name is withheld from the reader until chapter 11, where it appears only as part of an imagined missing-person report. As in a Kafka tale, the protagonist Jumpei is known throughout simply as "the man" (*otoko*) or, more anonymously still, "he" (*kare*).

The narrative voice is deployed in the pseudo-objective tone of the official report which characterizes the detective genre and parodies the language of the police and bureaucracies everywhere.[6] Raymond Chandler has a way of beginning sentences in a flat narrative voice that suddenly breaks into bizarre simile, and his detective, Philip Marlowe, occasionally begins what was intended as a quiet chuckle but almost accidentally rises into an inappropriate cackle or guffaw. But Abé's narrative voice never loses its careful modulations even as it lapses smoothly into absurdity, and when his narrative veers off on bizarre tangents, they diverge from the ordinary so gently as to pass almost unnoticed:

> The theory had been advanced that the man, tired of life, had committed suicide. One of his colleagues, who was an amateur psychoanalyst, held to this view. He claimed that in a grown man enthusiasm for such a useless pastime as collecting insects was evidence enough of a mental quirk. Even in children, unusual preoccupation with insect collecting frequently indicates an Oedipus complex. In order to compensate for his unsatisfied desires, the child enjoys sticking pins into insects, which he need never fear will escape. And the fact that he does not leave off once he has grown up is quite definitely a sign that the condition has become worse. Thus it is far from accidental that entomologists frequently have an acute desire for acquisitions and that they are extremely reclusive, kleptomaniac, homosexual. [4–6/7–8][7]

This passage begins reasonably enough, and seems all the more reasonable in having been prepared for by the simple statement of the man's disappearance, his description, and speculation as to his possible motives. Yet, all the while continuing to deploy the same tone of detached objectivity, it drifts off unnoticed into absurdity. From the quite reasonable and accurate proposition that insect collecting is a common pastime among Japanese children, the logic simply marches inexorably onward, out of control: children who collect insects do so because they have Oedipus complexes and are insecure;

6. See below, Chapter 11, page 223.
7. Page references in the text are, respectively, to Kōbō Abé, *The Woman in the Dunes*, trans. E. Dale Saunders (New York: Knopf, 1964); and *Suna no onna* (1962), in *Abe Kōbō zensakuhin*, vol. 8 (Tokyo: Shinchōsha, 1972).

insect collecting continued into adulthood it is a sign of mental peculiarity; adult entomologists are notable for their deviant behavior; and these deviants end up more fascinated by the cyanide in their collecting bottles than in collecting and are thus likely to commit suicide. Even if it is not the sort of logic we are used to, by the end of this passage we find ourselves simply accepting the proposition that children who collect insects for a hobby become adult candidates for suicide. Such a proposition allows the world around the entirely unremarkable Jumpei to ignore his disappearance as just another unremarkable event.

In an essay on science fiction, Abé wrote that he first encountered this kind of logic in the work of Edgar Allan Poe. Tales such as "The Purloined Letter," "Descent into the Maelstrom," and "The Unparalleled Adventure of One Hans Pfaall," he wrote, are based on a logic of "bizarre reasoning that never leaves the realm of reason."[8] Quoting a passage from "Hans Pfaall" in illustration, Abé remarks on the balloonist's discovery of a phenomenon which, though contrary to all reason, can yet be reasonably explained: "What mainly fascinated me, in the appearance of things below, was the seeming *concavity* of the surface of the globe."[9] Poe's passage is worth quoting in full here, for it reveals the same logic that informs *Woman in the Dunes*:

> I had, thoughtlessly enough, expected to see its real *convexity* become evident as I ascended; but a very little reflection sufficed to explain the discrepancy. A line, dropped from my position perpendicularly to the earth, would have formed the perpendicular of a right-angled triangle, of which the base would have extended from the right-angle to the horizon, and the hypotenuse from the horizon to my position. But my height was little or nothing in comparison with my prospect. In other words, the base and the hypotenuse of the supposed triangle would, in my case, have been so long, when compared to the perpendicular, that the two former might have been regarded as nearly parallel. In this manner the horizon of the aëronaut appears always to be *upon a level* with the car. But as the point immediately beneath him seems, and is, at a great distance below him, it seems, of course, also at a great distance below the horizon. Hence the impression of concavity.[10]

"Rather than ask how this discovery holds up under the test of fact," Abé suggests, "we should ask how it elicits a feeling of surprise from the reader.

8. Kōbō Abé, "SF no ryūkō ni tsuite" (On the popularity of SF), in *Abe Kōbō zensakuhin*, vol. 15 (Tokyo: Shinchōsha, 1973), p. 112.

9. "The Unparalleled Adventures of One Hans Pfaall," in *The Works of Edgar Allan Poe*, ed. Edmund Clarence Stedman and George Edward Woodberry (New York: Scribner, 1894), 2:165. Abé quotes from a translation by Tanizaki Seiji.

10. Ibid.

The degree of proximity to the inner rules of the behavior we call 'discovery' is far more significant, in a literary sense, than any relationship to fact."[11] In the case of "Hans Pfaall," we need only accept that from the height of a balloon the base and hypotenuse of such a triangle would appear infinitely long; for all perceptual purposes, logic tells us that they would then for all intents and purposes be parallel, and the rest simply follows automatically.

Elsewhere in the same essay, Abé describes a novel by John W. Campbell, Jr., *The Moon Is Hell* (1951), as "a meticulously detailed depiction of a man who, having drifted to the moon, discovers a way of being able to live there and goes through the process of putting together a life."[12] This plot not only continues the story of "Hans Pfaall" but also sounds very much like a thumbnail sketch for *Woman in the Dunes*. Abé's theme in this essay is that science fiction, which he regards as the most strikingly imaginative of all fiction, has little to do with either science or ghost stories (a genre of the Edo period continued into modern times by the popular author whose pen name, Edogawa Rampō, puns on "Edgar Allan Poe"). Rather, he says, it occupies a world of "pseudo-science" (science, that is, in which all hypotheses are equally possible) and represents ghost stories (the popular genre, that is, which Poe intentionally satirized and parodied) "but without the ghosts."

The operation of the entire plot of *Woman in the Dunes* recapitulates the early passage I have quoted concerning insect collectors and their fate. Almost without noticing it, we are led by the incremental addition of bizarre descriptive detail, the logic of step-by-step deduction somehow gone a few degrees awry, to conclusions that turn common sense on its head. Central to this revolution in logic is Jumpei's normal human curiosity about how things work, his all-too-human egotistical desire for mastery, and even his absurd ambition in life (though he does not turn into a cockroach like Gregor Samsa, he does yearn to have a beetle named after him)—all qualities that resonate plausibly enough in ourselves. It is not long before the reader too, most likely for the first time in his life, finds himself thinking of sand as "a very interesting substance."

Beginning with a dry but somehow slightly implausible encyclopedia entry that reads like a passage from one of Borges's imaginary books ("Sand: an aggregate of rock fragments. Sometimes including loadstone, tinstone, and more rarely gold dust. Diameter: 2 to 1/16 mm"), the narrator informs us that sand is everywhere uniform ("The size of the grains shows very little variation and follows a Gaussian distribution curve with a true mean of 1/8 mm") and that it has much the same aerodynamic properties as a fluid (13/12). The narrator then turns to a consideration of sand's corrosive properties—"The sands never rested. Gently but surely they invaded and

11. Abé, "Sf no ryūkō ni tsuite," pp. 112–13.
12. Ibid., pp. 110–11.

destroyed the surface of the earth" (14/13)—carefully building up an equation between the flow of sand and entropy. This notion "excites" the man just as a new intellectual discovery excites us: sand is inhospitable not because it is dry (and here we simply accept its dryness as factual, although it is soon to be proved false) but rather because it is always in motion. Its entropic motion even affords the man a revelation of the truly moral life: "Didn't unpleasant competition arise precisely because one tried to cling to a fixed position? If one were to give up a fixed position and abandon oneself to the movement of the sands, competition would soon stop" (14–15/13). People fail because they cling together; sand succeeds because it does not. The idea sounds quite Buddhist, or perhaps Taoist, yet the logic appears at this point to lead as inexorably to the desolation of alienation as to the exhilaration of enlightened liberation.

Solitary, friendless, unmarried, a tiny cog in a huge bureaucracy, Jumpei is the very personification of the alienation of modern life. To this point in his very modern life he has managed to associate love only with sex (he scorns the emotion as "soap opera"), sex only with venereal disease ("the very opposite of soap opera"), and—since being trapped in his sandpit—venereal disease only with his new-found moral entropy, the measure of things running down over time: "Venereal disease [was] stealthily imported by Columbus in his tiny ships into tiny harbors [and] spread so diligently by everyone throughout the world. All men were equal before death and venereal disease" (134/83). In Jumpei's modern logic, love is equated with disease, disease with death, and death with sand.

This chain of associations does not end in the conclusion we are led to expect, however: in his new sandtrap world the sheer material fact of sand entirely preempts Jumpei's more usual neurotic obsession with venereal disease to become, as it were, a transcendent spiritual condition, the natural environment of life itself. For the first time in his life, he and "the woman" both covered with sand, Jumpei improbably finds real pleasure and fulfillment in sex (chapter 20) and, eventually, in love. His having been forced to live in nothing but sand, and thus fully in the flow of entropy, becomes for him the limiting condition within which human love becomes possible. We appear to be bordering here on the world of Mishima.

The world of the villagers who have trapped Jumpei and become his captors and tormentors, a world oddly normal *but entirely upside down*, is clearly a critique of the fate of the traditional rural village in modern, urban, capitalist Japan. These poor and remote farmers and fishermen have been abandoned by the state, which has given up on the impossible task of trying to prevent the constantly encroaching entropic sand from swallowing up their fields and homes (the story is set near the coastal city of Sakata, an area whose villagers' problems Abé became fascinated with after reading an arti-

cle about them in *Asahi Graph*). These peasants have therefore simply rein-
vented themselves in a new relationship to the state, surviving by selling their
problematic sand to be made into the equally problematic concrete used in
public highway and housing construction projects.

The woman and the others like her who live in these sandpits perform the
dual and necessary function of any underclass. By constantly digging
the ever flowing sand away from their homes only to find themselves at the
bottom of ever deeper holes (Abé's Sisyphian metaphor for the everyday life
of the proletariat), they serve as a front line of defense against the encroaching sand, which represents entropy, time, change, history. At the same time,
they provide raw labor and material for the state. The villagers are well aware
that their salt-laden sand is fatal to the structural integrity of any concrete in
which it is used, yet when Jumpei objects that bridges, buildings, and dams
made of such concrete will absorb too much water and eventually collapse,
he is shocked by the apparent callousness of the woman's reply: "Why should
we worry about what happens to others?" (223/134).

Her response is both an indictment of the heartlessness and inevitability of
the ruthless logic of capitalism and an accurate portrayal of the mentality of
peasants anywhere toward the larger world beyond their own limited horizons. By much the same Keynesian logic that can justify the notion of a well-
functioning economy, sadly though inevitably, leaving some of its members
out of work, the Japanese economy has found it expedient simply to ignore
these unfortunate but, in the end, expendable wretches. Their understandable response is that if, in order to survive, society can abandon them, they in
turn are justified in poisoning society for the same purpose. Along with the
generally suspicious nature of the villagers (who are at first certain that
Jumpei is some sort of official up to no good), nothing sums up this provincial mentality as pointedly as the woman's phrase *tanin no koto*: "what happens to others" is certainly none of *their* business.

The moment is pivotal for Jumpei. Until now he has naturally taken the
side of the "normal" outside world from which he came against these apparently demented brutes who have trapped him. Once he realizes the reason
for their hostility, however, their entire enterprise suddenly takes on a new
logic of its own: "It had never occurred to him to think of his relationship
with the village in that light. It was natural that they should be confused and
upset. But even if that were the case, and he conceded the point, it would be
like throwing away his own justification" (223/134). And then, recognizing
that he has in fact already thrown it away ("Yes, of course. It's true about
'other people's business'"), Jumpei makes an about-face and simply accepts
this new world and its logic built on shifting sand.

The idea that there is no such thing as an innocent victim pervades all of
Abé's work. His stories seem predicated on the urban myth that if one

repeatedly dials random phone numbers and yells, "Run, they're onto us," at least half of those who answer will flee town. Since *everyone* secretly feels guilty about *something*, what better premise with which to hook the reader? It is Abé's firm conviction that if you examine any life closely enough, you will find a crime—and from that starting point any good detective can reconstruct what will, inevitably, turn out all along to have been the criminal life.

The logic of Jumpei's insight is that of all accommodation in general: a logic of reversal, of the topsy-turvy. At first he is able to think of nothing but escape and spends all his time plotting it, only to fail at each more desperate attempt. The next stage occurs when, exhausted and ill from his efforts, he concludes that he must give at least the appearance of cooperating with his captors, both to lull their suspicions and to keep up his strength. In time, however, appearance inevitably becomes reality: needing something to do, like all men, he initiates little projects to keep himself busy. Among other projects, he fashions a trap from a wooden bucket sunk into the sand, hoping to catch a crow and tie a plea for help to its leg—even though he knows that the crows never fly farther than the nearby homes of the villagers who have trapped him. As he repeats this and other equally ludicrous quotidian tasks over and over, he comes to feel "a certain gentle contentment with the hand work which he performed daily and in the repeated battle with the sand" (215/129). Karma is the weight of these accumulated moments of a mindless, time-killing, hopeless repetition that eventually drowns each individual in the sea of time. Like all moderns, Abé's characters are in some way victims of it; it is only Mishima's quixotic heroes who can literally "kill time" by their fanatical determination to become the perpetrators of their own fate. Like the rest of humankind, Jumpei seems doomed to succumb to it.

Jumpei's epiphany occurs with his miraculous discovery that although his trap fails to catch crows, it succeeds in trapping something even better: fresh water. Sand is hygroscopic, attracts water, a fact he had noted long before, though in an entirely different context. That fog rose from the sand at night, or that the sides of the sandpit kept their shape best when damp from the morning dew, had impinged on his awareness only in terms of how these facts either contributed to or hindered his attempts at *escape*. The need for water from the village had been a major reason for continuing to cooperate in shoveling sand every day (though only one among many reasons connected with other basic human needs: to keep the sand out, to keep busy, to obtain sexual favors from the woman). Now, having discovered that a leaky wooden bucket sunk into the sand will trap fresh water, he suddenly realizes he is freed from any compulsion to cooperate: "If he were successful in this experiment he would no longer have to give in to the villagers if they cut off his water. But more important, he had found that the sand was an immense pump" (234/141).

"But more important" (*sore dokoro ka*): the sense of reversal in this conjunctive phrase is crucial, for it indicates that the logic of final accommodation has entirely replaced the earlier logic of escape. The sand, which he had thought to be destructive because it contained water that rotted everything it touched, now turns out *for exactly the same reason* to be constructive and so becomes the basis on which to construct a whole new world view and life: "The change in the sand corresponded to a change in himself. Perhaps, along with the water in the sand, he had found a new self" (236/142). His discovery has given him a purpose in life for the first time. When, soon afterward, the woman has a miscarriage, and the villagers, in their hurry to rush her to the hospital, leave a rope ladder dangling into his pit, he simply ignores the chance to escape and turns back instead to repair his water trap: "There was no particular need to hurry about escaping." He even hopes to impress the villagers with his new discovery; the logic of reversal is complete, his earlier ambition replaced with something resembling an ideal of communal endeavor. Gradually, step by step, we have been led to feel that the man trapped in this wretched topsy-turvy world is no longer alienated, anonymous, friendless, and without love. A much more content and fulfilled person than he was before he was trapped, he must acknowledge the truth that we are indeed our own jailers.

Exactly what is the logic of the world that Abé turns upside down? To begin with, it is a thoroughly modern urban world of identity papers, bureaucratic jobs, faceless institutions, and nameless people. It is the world of late capitalism as seen from a Marxist viewpoint (if only because late capitalism does not really see itself at all), but a hardboiled one, lacking any investment— romantic or otherwise—in the promises or lies of either the capitalist world or the Marxist teleology: the faith in the community of labor, the zeal for the class struggle. It is the bleak, sardonic, paranoid vision of Ridley Scott's films *Blade Runner* and *Black Rain* or Terry Gilliam's *Brazil*, portraying worlds in which a single individual is pitted against The System and, just by remaining alive for a time, manages a tiny but crucial affirmation of himself before being squashed for good.

It is the institutions that are evil, not the individuals. And since there are no bad guys, there are no evil geniuses, no Dr. No, not even a faceless SMERSH, if only because the State and its ubiquitous bureaucracies are quite malign enough as they actually are (the Orwellian critique that Ian Fleming's "Evil Empire" always seems to be expecting the reader to forget). The major class distinction for Abé is not between proletarian and bourgeois, not even between peasant and urbanite; it is between individual and system, ordinary citizen and bureaucrat. Abé's sympathies are entirely with the lower elements of society—a requirement of any hardboiled type, even

though his narrators, like Chandler's Marlowe, are always morally and intellectually just a cut above the sleazy types they move among; the reader would
be hardly be likely to identify with them otherwise.

In the infinite regression of Abé's investigation of investigation, the details
add up not to a whole rational picture but instead to a fragmented and
surrealistic atmosphere within which logical inference becomes impossible,
even irrelevant. As in any modernist detective story, absurd or otherwise,
"the facts" turn out to be nothing more than mismatched bits and pieces
entirely dependent on the game of interpretation for whatever sense they can
be made to yield up. The typical detective of the genre is a more or less
reliable interpreter who, like his narrator, may occasionally wander off on a
wrong track, get drunk and unpleasant, and even step over the edge of the
law but whose heart we trust to be, deep down, in the right place.

Abé's narrators, to the contrary, can never be trusted. If there are no
entirely innocent victims, neither are there any entirely guilty perpetrators;
worse yet, there are no entirely reliable detectives. The investigator's role, or
even the narrator's, is thus necessarily an ambiguous one. If he can (and will)
betray a trust, then by the same logic he and the reader can (and will) be
betrayed. In a world that refuses to draw anywhere the sort of moral bottom
line that Chandler does (so long as a client has not actually perpetrated a
felony, twenty-five dollars a day and expenses and the ability to arouse his
calloused sympathies buys Marlowe's absolute loyalty), betrayal is simply the
common currency. Marlowe may often have trouble staying just this side of
the law himself, but any case against him is only plausibly circumstantial and
always trumped up, nor are we ever given reason to doubt which side he is
really on. In the sort of world where human nature inevitably turns the
investigator into the investigated, however, there is not only no reliable interpreter; there is also no reliable narrator. Perhaps most unsettling of all, there
is certainly no such thing as a reliable reader. The narrator, who makes clear
how little he trusts the reader's intentions, seems always to be trying to throw
him off the track. In the semiotics of Abé's world everything is a sign, signs
point only to other signs, and all signs are essentially duplicitous. It is a
doubly and constantly shifting world of paranoia in which the person who is
out to get you is also the person you are out to get, and in such a world it is no
surprise when both turn out to be you, and you turn out to be not yourself
but someone else. In Chandler's stories we are made to feel the thrill of
walking near the fine line of what Foucault calls "the impossibility of thinking *that*"; but Abé has taken the line away altogether, and the ontological
abyss of his world—though often numbing, nauseating, and even terrifying—
is never thrilling.

Abé's work perhaps has its most significant dimension in its fuller realization of Natsumé Sōseki's adumbrations of an essentially immoral and even psychopathic modern Japanese "self." Sōseki carefully investigated that self in *Kokoro* (see Chapter 2), stripping it layer by accreted layer of its socially constructed sense of right and wrong only to find it nightmarishly hollow at the core. Abé's world, populated entirely by betrayed Senseis and their betraying uncles, is one in which the naive young narrator of *Kokoro* has grown up to become a down-at-the-heels two-bit private eye still doggedly on the trail of Truth in spite of having been warned off (like all detectives, Abé's receive unpleasant threats from time to time, perhaps only somewhat more cryptic and often from themselves). Even though his fusion of the detective story and the novel of the absurd is interesting, it is not in Western terms a new or original vision. It does resonate peculiarly, however, with the long Japanese history of mistrust of any appeal to reality as a permanent condition, as well as a perhaps concomitant mistrust and even fear of whatever it is modern man is supposed to possess by way of a soul. Mistrust and fear are the natural result of the sort of alien logical processes that can create so terrible a world and populate it with such frightening selves. This sort of logic poisons whatever value the very idea of knowledge might possess and calls into question the entire scientific project of epistemological certainty. It is on the firm basis of such a skepticism of modernity that the enthusiastic reception in Japan of Jean-François Lyotard's vision of a "postmodern condition" appears to have been predicated. Whatever "the modern" may have been, runs the suspicion, it was *certainly* nothing Japanese.

We must still account for the problem that the village setting of *Woman in the Dunes* begins as a terrifying dystopia but seems to end instead as an unexpected sort of utopia. It turns out, in spite of all its horrors, to be not only no worse than the world outside but in the end actually better. In the outer world Jumpei was alone, alienated, dissociated from other human lives; he knew sex but not love, colleagues but not friends, work but not fulfillment. His adventure in the sand dunes ends with his having become completely absorbed in meaningful work, enmeshed in new webs of social relations, and in love with a woman for the first time in his life. To dismiss this as nothing but the manipulated feelings of a prisoner for his captors is, I think, to have missed something more fundamentally problematic.

In his essay "The City," Abé has written of the missing person as a new kind of suicide.[13] The act of suicide cannot be dismissed as merely the product of a particular political system, he says, for "that music of unrest, that jazz of inquietude, [is] taken up as much by socialist youth as by capital-

13. What follows is either translated or summarized from "Toshi" (The city; undated), in *Abe Kōbō zensakuhin*, 15:117–20.

ist. Its uneasy rhythm, beckoning to death and escape, is no different in either case." From Rimbaud to the Beats, says Abé, the city has been pictured as a kind of hellish nightmare where every evil flowers:

> I think that the reason the city is associated with nightmare is that we have not yet found a way of adequately expressing the city, of putting it into words. This is because in our blood, contained at a pressure almost at the bursting point, there still breathes the language of the old collectivity [*kyōdōtai*]. When we speak of the city, we do so in this same communal language. And it is only natural that this old communal language, powerless to express something as antithetical to itself as the city, should produce only nightmares.

What is especially nightmarish about the city, continues Abé, is that in it the old satisfying village [*mura*] social relations between neighbors have become those between mere "others": "The city dweller has been liberated from the fixed values of the communal while his own have been magnified, thus giving him the possibility of free competition. . . . In this competition the winners are crowned with the laurels of social position, and with the exception of these fortunate few, the majority are crowned with thorns." Suicides, then, are the losers in the new competitive urban society. In the ancient communal ethos of the *kyōdōtai*, suicide was viewed by the authorities as a dangerous and impermissible form of social protest, and modern society follows in censuring it as the disgraceful and shameful recourse of the loser.

Here Abé seems caught in a dilemma of his own making. He tells us that people do not start killing themselves simply because social organization has changed from a satisfying communal relationship of neighbors to an alienated one of mere others; the real reason they kill themselves is that "the hell of competition" makes them cling to what he calls new "pseudo-collectivities": "those empty symbols of the nostalgia for a collectivity—family, religion, state—in which one could let down one's guard. . . . In phenomenological terms, the city proffers the spectacle of the pseudo-collectivity of the supermarket. . . . The city fosters not healthy human beings but candidates for suicide." His own task as a writer, he concludes, "is to find the city's own words in order to challenge the illusion of the city's disease of loneliness"; what is needed is not "a liberation *from* the city but precisely a liberation *toward* the city. Since suicides and missing persons are at the vanguard of that challenge, the protagonist of my novels is the private detective who stalks them."

The prewar language of the old village *kyōdōtai* is an atavism we might have expected from Mishima; resurrected by Abé it is somewhat disturbing. For Abé is apparently using the word here without irony, indeed with a sense of approbation for this not quite yet discredited essentialism, a nostalgia for a mythical village *Gemeinschaft* among neighbors as postulated against the alienated *Gesellschaft* of the demonic modern city. *Woman in the Dunes*, fraught with this same ambiguity, is also—in its depiction as a utopia of what we had been led to believe was a dystopia—clearly an exploration of the possibility of human existence made meaningful in these very terms.

At the time of *Woman in the Dunes* the detective-protagonist had not yet made his appearance in Abé's novels. And since the appealing notion of a uniquely Japanese form of communality most definitely does not reappear in his later writing, we can safely assume that the ambiguous results of the experiment led him in the direction of his conclusion in "The City": if on the one hand the older utopian social order does not exist except as a kind of nostalgia, and if on the other we are to avoid on principle characterizing the modern city as suffering from the "disease" of dystopic modern alienation, then all that remains to the author is the quest of the cynical but earnest investigator who, following his script of "liberation toward the city," endlessly pursues himself around that uncomfortable *topos* in the absurd attempt to find out why he has turned up missing there. Like my fantasy of the young narrator of Sōseki's *Kokoro* grown up to become a private eye (or more accurately a "private I"), he will spend his life trying to discover why his problematic "self" is missing and where it could have gone.[14] Abé's answer is that the village collectivity, no longer having any meaning, has disappeared, leaving nothing for the self to do but migrate to the city in search of work— and this, absurdly enough, is the sort of modern work it has found for itself.[15] It is the absurd logic of sand.

14. Discussing "the modernist obsessive explorations of the individual consciousness [the 'private eye']," Astradur Eysteinsson has written that "it is probably not too difficult to demonstrate how the modernist hero is frequently in the role of the detective who never solves the crime, for he is of course also the guilt-ridden criminal" (*The Concept of Modernism* [Ithaca: Cornell University Press, 1990], p. 120).

15. This hypothesis would seem to reflect the sort of socio-economic analysis, popular in the decade preceding Abé's novel, of works such as Okōchi Kazuo's influential *Reimeiki no Nihon rōdō undō*, (The dawn of the Japanese labor movement) (Tokyo: Iwanami, 1952), which analyze the movement from village to city in Japan and its effect on social values. Modernism and capitalism as destructive of the ancient *kyōdōtai* community is the thesis of Otsuka Hisao's *Kyōdōtai no kiso riron* (The community and its theoretical basis) (Tokyo: Iwanami, 1955); see Daikichi Irokawa, "The Survival Struggle of the Japanese Community," in J. Victor Koschmann, ed., *Authority and the Individual in Japan: Citizen Protest in Historical Perspective* (Tokyo: University of Tokyo Press, 1978), pp. 252–53; and Daikichi Irokawa, *The Culture of the Meiji Period*, trans. Marius B. Jansen (Princeton: Princeton University Press, 1985), pp. 273–80.

Part III

Narrative and the Novel

Chapter 7

A Narrative of Their Own:
Japan and the Novel

But the social order is a sacred right which serves as a foundation for all others. This right, however, does not come from nature. It is therefore based on convention—the question is to know what these conventions are.
　　　　　—Jean Jacques Rousseau, *The Social Contract*

Does the world, even the social world, ever really come to us already "speaking itself" from beyond the horizon of our capacity to make scientific sense of it? Or is the fiction of such a world, capable of speaking itself and of displaying itself as a form of a story, necessary for the establishment of that moral authority without which the notion of a specifically social reality would be unthinkable?
　　　　　—Hayden White, *The Content of the Form*

　　　The rise of the novel in the Third World, the striking appropriation by formerly colonized peoples of that quintessentially nineteenth- and twentieth-century European literary form, and its subsequent return from beyond the bounds of its earlier colonial contexts have had the effect of compelling a Euro-American audience to an increasing awareness and even acceptance of the possibility that other cultures' narratives need not— indeed, I suggest, *must* not—correspond exactly, or even very closely, to its own. We now regularly extend to the novel recognition as the major genre of fiction employed by authors who write in non-Western languages, as well as to works being written predominantly in French or English by the formerly colonized.[1] The Japanese novelists Yukio Mishima and Kenzaburō Ōe are

1. Of course, such works are not limited to these two languages. One example of the appropriation of the language of a colonizer for subversive purposes can be found in Anton Shammas's 1987 *Arabesques*. The scandalized reaction in Israel to a "Palestinian" novel written in Hebrew (and aimed specifically at one of Israel's best-known novelists) was every bit as gratifying as Shammas could have wished. See Hannan Hever, "Hebrew in an Israeli Arab Hand: Six Miniatures on Anton Shammas' *Arabesques*," *Cultural Critique*, Fall 1987, pp. 47–76.

instances of the former; the Nigerian novelist Chinua Achebe and the Malian author Yambo Ouologuem of the latter. V. S. Naipaul and Salman Rushdie, expatriate inheritors of different sets of "native" cultural circumstances expressed exclusively in the English of former colonizers, mark out some of the complex boundaries of the large and interesting area in between; they share much with novelists who are African-American and African-Anglo, Asian-American and Asian-Anglo, and so on.

Even as we celebrate the literary fruits of the disintegration of empires and the dispersal of an earlier colonialism, however, there inevitably lingers the older tendency to gauge all fiction, including the Japanese *shōsetsu* (which I shall continue to refer to qualifiedly if perhaps misleadingly by the term "novel"), by increasingly quaint Euro-American expectations of what properly constitutes the novel. Indeed, Fredric Jameson has even argued that in contrast to its role of politicizing the aesthetic in the Third World, the business of the novel in the postcolonial West is precisely the aestheticization of the political.[2] So anxious to avoid the overtly political that its obscured political contexts must now be read back into it, the mass-market novel in the West is increasingly restricted to the subgenres of spy, murder, horror, fantasy, and romance; truly political works such as Thomas Pynchon's 1990 *Vineland* and Nadine Gordimer's *The Conservationist* are few and far between. It is in the "symptomatic" sense of its ostensible lack of politics that the novel of aesthetic sensibility reveals its politics most clearly of all.

The other side of a seemingly inexhaustible demand for an unchallenging, old-fashioned, and thoroughly conventional mimesis in the popular subgenres of Western fiction is the concomitant expectation that the non-Western novel should be just that: truly *novel*. Westerners have learned to anticipate being entertained by the spectacle of an Africa of dark tribal potency, an Asia of malign and mysterious inscrutability, and more recently a Latin America of wonderfully magical realism—"novel" experiences to be shopped for, exactly as one might shop for spicy tandoori tonight and sushi tomorrow, as welcome changes from the fast-food varieties of quotidian prose. Writing and reading are, after all, from either the Marxist or the capitalist point of view, entirely a matter of production and consumption.

The mysteriously exotic need no longer be introduced only by way of the servants' entrance of the Victorian novel, through which it was forced to make its way back into the national psyche as the return of the repressed in such forms as that Caribbean madwoman in Rochester's attic or Henry James's weird little "Indian orphans." First it showed up in the window as the

2. Fredric Jameson, "Third-World Literature in the Era of Multinational Capitalism," *Social Text* 15 (Fall 1986). See also the response by Aijaz Ahmad, "Jameson's Rhetoric of Otherness and the 'National Allegory'" in the same issue.

exciting but dangerous Other in the works of Rudyard Kipling, Rider Haggard, and D. H. Lawrence; now it is invited straight in through the front door as a welcome guest of honor. Yukio Mishima understood and took full advantage of the fact that as a Japanese he was part of the West's returned repressed, newly acclaimed in the decades following World War II for its potent ability to stimulate new *frissons* in numbed moral and psychological receptors. As such, he was only too happy to accommodate the demand for novelty—though always at his own price. Kenzaburō Ōe (the only one still living of the authors examined in this book) also understands this demand, and he too, I shall suggest, has discovered ways to find advantage in it.

Like many others, Mishima found what he considered the Western novel's traditional method of the mimesis of reality to be anathema to a native sense of fiction. The convention of plots contructed according to a plausible Cartesian logic of cause and effect, consistent narrative point of view, lifelike characters, circumstantial detail, convincing dialogue—in short, all of the novel's technical ability to provide a particular sort of bourgeois credibility—are now, no less than constructions of the self, readily acknowledged to be far from universal and even peculiar to a particular time and place.

Even in the West, however, the terms of what is credible have changed or, rather, can be seen to have been changing all along. As Mishima was addressing the problem for Japan of what he considered the unitary "Western novel," its logic of cause and effect was already giving way to that of the random and aleatory; its characters were as likely to be *unheimlich* androids or aliens as merely human; and narrativity had fragmented into that shattered mirror of points of view and divergent spaces already pointed out by Erich Auerbach in his famous 1947 essay on Virginia Woolf.[3] And in Japan, as noted in the preceding chapter, writers such as Kōbō Abé were also at work helping to turn conventional expectations on their heads within a different context, forcing readers to ponder the possibility of an alternative—perhaps alternatively authentic Japanese—mode of absurd realism in a world obviously no longer able, for whatever reasons, to go on functioning as it once had.

Ever since Auerbach's trenchant analysis of the history of changing conventions in the novel's mimetic representation of social reality, one major strand of critical theory has continued to examine that problem, whether by focusing on the problem of "representation" in art and literature, on the construction of "social reality," or on a combination of the two. Roland Barthes and others have shown that the semiotics of a representation centered on an imitation of reality hinges on a simple deception whereby the

3. See Erich Auerbach, "The Brown Stocking," the last chapter of *Mimesis* (Princeton: Princeton University Press, 1974), p. 538.

created appears "natural," to have been always there all along, simply waiting for someone to transcribe it all faithfully. Semiotic theory has demonstrated that this sense of "naturalness" is achieved in large part by means of "transparent" signifiers, signs pointing to a "reality" beyond themselves even as they deflect attention from themselves entirely. Westerners have thus learned to expect to see *through* the surface medium of a painting, film, play, or novel to an underlying and exterior "reality," much as they expect to look through window glass at an exterior scene. The job of the medium (canvas, proscenium arch, screen, language) is to be transparent and not call undue attention to itself or intrude into the created illusion of a real world that exists "out there." This requirement can be understood as the technical concomitant of that Cartesian sense of self, discussed in Chapter 1, which demanded such a deception of perspective in order to maintain the illusion that subject and object were entirely separate and yet hierarchically related, that the creative and godlike author-subject remained in instrumental charge of his created object, to which—in obedience to the immutable laws of perspective—its author remained always potently central but remote and invisible.

To the extent that a medium calls attention to itself, then, it has traditionally been felt within the Western context to be somehow "foreign." Even the critical vocabulary adopted by English to speak about this sort of once shocking intrusion is tellingly alien: Bertolt Brecht's popular *Verfremdungseffekt*, (alienation effect), for example, or Viktor Shklovsky's *ostranenie* (defamiliarization). It seems in the very nature of the foreign to call attention to itself, after all. This is not true merely of the apparently deranged, arm-waving, and shaggy variety of the foreign, for even the most subtle of accents lends an air of unsurpassed authority and mystery to statements as simple as "Ve haff our vays," or "I vant to be alone."

It does not seem so very remarkable that dissimilar cultures should have arrived by dissimilar routes at the various forms of literacy involved first in the shift from oral storytelling to the appearance of written texts and later in the more advanced modern social technologies of storage and retrieval, dissemination and consumption. Even the ostensibly simple notion of "literacy," however, runs up against the fundamental problem of what such a word might denote in the cultures of China or Japan, where the semiotics of the social and psychological parameters of reading and writing diverge so widely from those in the West. Significant complexes of words—origin/originality, author/authority, creator/creativity, subject/subjectivity, and object/objectivity—have implications for fiction that we simply take for granted, yet such words point to fundamental cultural assumptions that ramify outward into literacy and the ways that it functions in our lives. Another culture, for example, may not necessarily confer upon its authors the same "authority," or consider what they do to be "creative" or even to entail "originality." Recall that until relatively recent times both in China and in Japan, the writing of fiction was circumscribed to a large degree by the fact that Confucius was considered to have limited the idea of authorship to editing for posterity, in specific opposition to "creating"—an idea long held as defining the proper attitude of the writer.

The writer was further defined by social vectors acting on literacy, such as the absolute and often even legally enforced distinction between history and poetry as "serious" forms of truth (being based in reality) and fiction as a "frivolous" form of untruth (being based in the unreal). As one result, fictional narrative in both cultures incorporated poetry and poetic techniques to create a very different sense of verisimilitude. For the same reason, Chinese fictional narratives were grounded in (and consciously played against) traditional modes of official historiography. Before the nineteenth century, and even after, a Chinese or Japanese writer who pursued the often lucrative but socially scurrilous career of popular fiction writing was likely to end up in trouble with the authorities and could at the very least be incarcerated for immoral and dissolute behavior; hence, any writer of fiction who had or hoped for an official career would certainly write under an assumed name. Such conditions were hardly congenial to the emergence of the modern idea of the author as a person respected for creativity and originality. This is certainly not to deny that fiction was written and read: it was, of course, and much of it continues to be read with great appreciation, in both the literary and the vernacular languages. But it was written within a general outlook, a social context, and personal circumstances so different from those we understand as to compel some understanding of how these differed from our own.

I have already noted that Western narrativity has until relatively recently been dominated by the aesthetic (and thus ideological) principle of what I have referred to as the "invisible" transparent signifier, a dominance that has contributed to that aestheticization of the political noted by Jameson. Even while acknowledging the little deception, we conspire with authors to ignore the pretense and even to enjoy the conspiracy, so long as they get on with their stories and intrude as little as possible into what Flaubert called le réel écrit, that unproblematic "transcription of reality" which sophisticated analysis of film has helped to reveal as being so problematic. There is of course an awkward parallel history of intentionally frustrated reading, running from *Tristram Shandy* through *Finnegans Wake* and *Gravity's Rainbow*. We allow ourselves be lulled by an occasional moment's peace in Laurence Sterne's jerky narrative, knowing all the while that the author is going to yank the narrative rug out from under us again at any moment. What Sterne precisely does *not* do is get on with his story.

Given our little fiction of unproblematic reading, then, it is a somewhat unpleasant discovery to find that neither artists nor authors ever do in fact quite manage to efface themselves entirely from their work. Before long, the reader of Rushdie's *Midnight's Children* tires of the narrator's constant whining about the difficulty of getting on with his story: "I am trying to stop being mystifying," "I must tell it all," and so forth. Even in the supremely realistic French painting of the eighteenth century, as Norman Bryson has shown, *l'effet du réel* owes as much to the cooperative way in which viewers go about their socially constructed task of interpreting the semiotics of what are in fact often no more than sketchy patches of light and dark, blurred focus, and illogical perspective and composition as it does to any masterful *trompe-l'oeil* technique that succeeds in appearing absolutely transparent.[4] Given half a chance, the eye and the mind, like miniature authors and readers, usually agree to connive at this sort of elision, carrying on their smoothly syntagmatic task of writing and reading, gliding together across the just-constructed and flimsy surfaces of "reality" as though there were no problematically paradigmatic gaps along the way.

In Chapter 4 I discussed the role of ideology in the construction of narratives that serve both to describe and to justify relations of power. Like "myth," this involves the stories we learn to tell ourselves to explain why things are the way they are and how they came to be that way: in other words, narratives that are not unlike "just-so stories." Like those of any other art, fictional narratives are to some degree self-referential; characterized by the foregrounding of the act of narrative itself, that is, they point to representation as a social act: I am telling, painting, acting, singing. Such narratives might thus be thought of as ritual presentations of the socially constructed act of representation. The novel, once the primary mode of modern, hegemonistic, high-bourgeois fiction, has now escaped from its earlier moorings to take the form, for example, of postmodern or mass-market fiction. I suggested in Chapter 1 that the Western novel served to gather and focus what we might call the scattered intersubjectivity of traditional Japanese narrative ("we are all speaking together") into a new mode of instrumental narrative focused on a single point of view ("I am telling all of you")—exactly as the scattered point of view of traditional art was collected and focused on a novel, singular, and all-authorizing if mysteriously vanishing point of awesome instrumental power.

Aesthetics in Japanese culture, rather than being implicated in a representational mimesis of content, has sometimes been interpreted as involved in a

4. Norman Bryson, *Word and Image: French Painting of the Ancien Régime* (Cambridge: Cambridge University Press, 1981), esp. pp. 8–28. The phrase *l'effet du réel* is from Roland Barthes, "The Reality Effect" (1968), in *The Rustle of Language* (New York: Hill & Wang, 1986), pp. 141–48; but see also Bryson's later critique of Barthes in *Vision and Painting*, pp. 61–62.

nonmimetic *presentation* of form. This involvement can perhaps be seen most clearly in the way signifiers are typically emphasized over signifieds in a production of meaning that more nearly resembles what we consider characteristic of ritual. In ritual, signifiers are intentionally rendered opaque for the purpose of heightening or dramatizing the production of the significant "mystery" it concerns, rather than rendered transparent in order to promote the apparent "naturalism" that characterizes the dominant mode of Western "realism."[5] In the mode of presentational realism, therefore, what is offered as the focus of attention is the significance of the creative act, *the production of meaning itself* (which we think of as the marker of ritual), rather than any particular by-product of the *reproduction* of that act (which we recognize to be the marker of mimesis). This technique of "significantly pointing to," central to Japanese Nō and Kabuki drama, tea ceremony, and cinema, among other arts, would seem central also to a Japanese sense of narrativity in general and to the novel in particular.

One theorist, Toshio Kawatake, thus differentiates the Japanese performing arts from the Western by distinguishing between the former's "tendency toward presentational form" and the latter's "tendency toward representational mimesis." He characterizes Japanese aesthetics as (1) concerned with form and semiosis rather than with reality and mimesis; (2) synthetic rather than analytic, insofar as the performing arts tend not to be differentiated into the separate media of gesture (mime/theater), rhythmic movement (dance/ballet), and music (voice/song); (3) implicit (that is, esoteric or concerned with mystery, the assumption that profound meaning remains occluded to the uninitiated) rather than explicit (exoteric, the assumption that all meaning is available to anyone); and (4) multilayered, in that past tradition is not discarded but accreted instead.[6] The emphasis on the esoteric seems especially central in any attempt to propose a semiotics of Japanese narrative, for it appears to confirm an emphasis on the *ideological* basis of sign function. In the case of Japan this ideology supports an aristocratic view of meaning as something always referred to a profoundly ingrained sense of hierarchical sociopolitical status; it can thus be contrasted with an American ideology (or "myth" in Barthes's strong sense) of meaning as something that is democrat-

---

5. See Ian Watt's discussion of formal or "presentational" realism in *The Rise of the Novel* (Berkeley: University of California Press, 1960), pp.30–34; Noel Burch, *To the Distant Observer: Form and Meaning in the Japanese Cinema* (London: Scholar Press, 1979), pp. 11–54; and David Pollack, "Action as Fitting Match to Knowledge: Language and Symbol in Mishima's *Kinkaku-ji*," *Monumenta Nipponica*, 40, no. 4 (1985): esp. 397–98.

6. Kawatake Toshio, "Nihon no geinō: Dentō geijutsu, koten geinō" in *Kōza Bigaku*, vol. 4, *Geijutsu no shosō*, ed. Imamichi Tomonobu (Tokyo: Tōkyō Daigaku Shuppanbu, 1984), pp. 192, 175–204. His notion of a "differentiation" of the various Western media, however, fails conspicuously to account for opera's obvious success in synthesizing the primary elements of song, dance, and drama.

ically available to all. Within its largest frame this hierarchy is used to discriminate that which is Japanese from all else.

A similar contrast could be maintained between the narrative strategies in European art and literature that evolved within the Roman Catholic ideology of ecclesiastical hierarchy, as opposed to those involved in the support of the less hierarchical and oppositional ideologies of an emerging Protestantism. Catholicism is "presentational" in its central concern with the performance of rituals such as the mass, dramatized mysteries (transubstantiation, for example) that may be carried out only by properly initiated celebrants. Every detail of Catholic ritual is coded as significant, and significance is reinforced by being rendered opaque, visible, meaningful. Protestantism, to the contrary, can be considered "representational" in its specific rejection of the ritual dramatization of mystery by the hierarchically superior celebrant and its call for a more egalitarian mimesis of "plain reality." Insofar as this reality is not "created" but simply "is," there must be no evidence of the machinery by which it was brought about. Such a proposition might further sustain a distinction between Christian allegory on the one hand and secular symbolism on the other, the first supporting a homology between scriptural story and human actions and the second sundering that homology. Such distinctions as these underlie Auerbach's notion of a complex "figural interpretation."[7]

Kawatake's inclusion of the accretion of artistic forms over time, long accepted in major Western studies of Japanese aesthetics, appears to follow as a corollary to this principle. If meaning is something created by esoteric reference to an established hierarchy of social classes, the historic rise of successive classes (which may themselves have ceased to exist) results over time in the accretion of successively superimposed layers of meaning. The emphasis on ritual and its production thus becomes a technical means of insisting on the priority of hierarchical privilege: since meaning is accessible only by social degree, emphasis on the proprietary nature of the means of its production deliberately renders these means opaque, which is to say both clearly visible and at the same time a kind of property inaccessible to the uninitiated.

The result of such a hierarchization of meaning is a cultural semiotics in which history is conceived in terms of a succession of "worlds" of meaning, each defined by the dominant ideology of its ruling class. We shall see in the following chapter how precisely such a concept serves to govern and unite the novels that constitute Mishima's *Sea of Fertility* tetralogy. Each of the four constitutes an entirely distinct ideological "world of meaning" which corre-

---

7. See Geoffrey Green, *Literary Criticism and the Structures of History: Erich Auerbach and Leo Spitzer* (Lincoln: University of Nebraska Press, 1982).

sponds to the dominant social class in each of four historical periods: the ancient court aristocracy (in contrast to the more recent Meiji aristocracy) in the first; the medieval warrior caste (as against the officer corps of the late nineteenth and early twentieth centuries) in the second; the modern pre– and post–World War II bourgeoisie in the fourth; and, interpolated in the third novel as a separate "modern" universe of meaning, the exotically foreign (as contrasted with the prosaically native). One effect of this progression of worlds of signification from the ancient (Heian), medieval (Kamakura-Muromachi-Sengoku), early modern (late Tokugawa–Meiji), and finally modern (here deliberately equated with the foreign) periods is an understanding of the foreign as something referring as much to the dimensional axis of time—that is, "the modern,"—as to any physical location outside Japan, such as Thailand, India, or the West. The foreign is only the most recent in a series of constructions of time, each of which contains its own esoteric meaning, its own internal "discourse." Time itself thus becomes a particular sort of interpretive structure, one that is constituted by the sequence of hermeneutic worlds of meaning.

Time might be thought in such a view to involve no particular end or *telos*, a notion that corresponds well with the last scene of the tetralogy in which time is finally denied any meaning. Mishima, however, establishes as the principle governing the telic interpretation of time in his work an interpretive project which follows that proposed in the "nativist" philosophical discourse of the Edo period. Thus, time in the tetralogy is that which first becomes historical within the religio-political ideology of the "feminine" courtly era and its concern with love; attains its zenith in the feudal mythos of a "masculine" warrior era that theoretically lived for combat—and, problematically, death; degenerates with the rise to social dominance (coeval with Japan's experience of the foreign) of a materialistic bourgeoisie whose sole interest is interest; and reaches its nadir and final extinction with Japan's pollution by foreignization—an awkward term but one that better exposes the tendentious nature of the popular word *kokusaika* than the usual inadequate gloss, "internationalization."

Time and history are the central elements that Mishima subjects to reinterpretation in his critique of the novel, and it is to a fuller exploration of this critique and its expression in *The Sea of Fertility* that the following chapter is devoted.

Chapter 8

The Critique of Everything:
Yukio Mishima's *The Sea of Fertility*

> But some say history moves in circles, and that may be very well argued; I
> have argued it myself. The fact is, human reason may carry you a little too
> far—over the hedge, in fact.
> —George Eliot, *Middlemarch*

> When a situation gets so bad that no solution seems possible there is left
> only murder or suicide. Or both. These failing, one becomes a buffoon.
> —Henry Miller, *Nexus*

For Yukio Mishima (1925–70) "the novel" itself was the central
problem of Japanese narrative. The Japanese had quickly realized that they
required this foreign Western technology no less than other technologies of
communication, such as the telephone, in order to be able to express themselves as other "modern" peoples were doing. Mishima understood, however, that using this indispensable alien technical device to express the native
story could only alienate the Japanese from their own narrative. The novel
required a use of language that Mishima considered entirely "foreign" to
Japanese. In his essay "What Is a 'Novel?'" he asserts that in contrast to the
language available to a Western writer such as Fyodor Dostoevsky or
Thomas Mann, in which abstract ideas could be expressed naturally, "Japanese lacks the traditions and background within which such abstract language developed."

> To the contrary, the overinflation of this abstract language in our dialogue, while
> indispensable to argumentation, gives an effect of satire even when one isn't
> being aimed for, and imparts to dialogue the image of some rootless, modern
> type of urban intellectual. As a consequence, it is nearly impossible to use
> dialogue involving abstract argumentation in one's work without unintentionally
> producing affected, limited images. In female characters especially, the lan-
> guage of abstract argumentation conjures up in the reader's mind the makeup,

hair style, clothing, and even facial features of a not very attractive type of woman. Of course this sort of thing is gradually changing as society changes. But the use of abstract language in dialogue with the intention of making a theme more universal has only succeeded in bringing the novel close to being a secondhand sketch of only one particular social group [i.e., the intelligentsia].[1]

To illustrate the failure of the vernacular to express abstract ideas, Mishima cites a line of dialogue from Riichi Yokomitsu's novel *Travel-Weariness* (*Ryoshū*): "So, which are you for, science or morality?" "It gives you the creeps," concludes Mishima.

Mishima's readers will readily agree with this evaluation. Although his can be a brilliant if often highly mannered prose, the result of his attempts to make vernacular speech communicate abstract thoughts is that his characters all too frequently deliver philosophical dissertations in language that seems unlikely ever to have actually been spoken by anyone. This same essay suggests, however, that he may have been deliberately experimenting with "unrealistic speech" in such writing, just as he experimented with every other aspect of the novel. In the face of language problems, he says, the Japanese novel has tended to play it safe by sticking to its traditional strengths, depictions of emotional and psychological states, and thus "exposing a continual fear of dialogue as eating away at the flesh of the novel":

> As the modern novel has progressed, the analytical, conceptual, and abstract nature of its narrative and descriptive language has accustomed the reader to going right up to the very limits of the Japanese language itself. *The unreasonable demand that dialogue be realistic, concrete, and functional tolerates not even the tiniest unnaturalism.* The modern novelist's métier has thus nearly become that of a swindler who develops his subject even as he soothes the reader's sense of being tricked. [P. 257; emphasis added]

Mishima ascribes to a culturally problematic orality what he sees as the inherent "frivolity" of dialogue—as opposed to the "seriousness" of descriptive narrative, of which he is an acknowledged master—yet he understands that the novel cannot do without it: "I have grudgingly resigned myself to thinking of dialogue in the novel as a sort of necessary evil" (p. 258). That he sometimes "failed" to write convincingly naturalistic dialogue may in fact be attributed to his willingness to experiment with it as part of a critique of all that the novel stood for, since he often does succeed brilliantly with vernacular speech.[2]

1. Yukio Mishima, "Shôsetsu towa nanika" (What is 'the novel'? 1968), *MZ*, 33:256–57.
2. Mishima is complaining about the difficulty of expressing complex ideas in dialogue, not of reproducing natural spoken language. An example of his ability in the latter is his reproduction in "What Is 'the Novel'?" (pp. 265–66) of the musings of a bored judge reading through a

In a 1969 essay concerning the overall structure of the tetralogy he was then in the midst of writing, Mishima notes that he had long sought an alternative to what he considered the unsatisfactory European idea of the novel. From jottings he turned up in 1951, he realized that ever since he was twenty-five years old he had wanted to write "a really long novel," something that could accommodate the very largest themes: "the human lifespan, heredity, generational change, history, epic, war—time magnified."[3] Achieving this, he knew, required a reconsideration of the very nature of time itself; in his impressionistic and fragmentary notes he imagines time as entailing "a long, helix-like revolution throughout eternity, transmigration, the anti-historicality of the novel, reincarnation." His long novel would be substantively different from its alien progenitor, the nineteenth-century European triple decker in which time figures simply as a linear chronological trellis along which character and action are plotted. "Completely fed up with such works," Mishima had been searching for a new form that demanded "a kind of narrative in which particular sorts of time have their own narrative structure": time "that makes a complete circle," time that could "make leaps."[4]

He had found a vehicle for some of these notions, Mishima continues, in the appearance in 1964 of a modern edition of a Heian-period romance. He describes *The Tale of the Hamamatsu Middle Counselor* (*Hamamatsu Chūnagon monogatari*)[5] as "a love-story . . . whose plot is carried forward by the devices of dream and reincarnation." These sketchy ideas mark another step in the direction of the envisaged "long work," although the scheme of *Hamamatsu* would provide only the barest of logistical and metaphysical underpinnings for what was eventually to become his final opus, the *Sea of Fertility* tetralogy.

To judge from this and other essays, Mishima apparently embarked on the work with only a few schematic notions in mind. As he conceived of it, and in keeping with his overall conception of time, the first volume was to take the form of an aristocratic love story, written in an ornate, courtly style appropriate to its subject (already one sees that dialogue would be problematic). Its

---

pile of manuscripts nominated for a major literary prize: "Aha! A woman. . . . Sounds kind of affected. . . . Doesn't seem to matter what awful things she says, though, the guy still falls for her. . . . Still, the author's got to be a mere kid to let her get away with this sort of thing. . . . Do guys really talk to women like this? . . . We could have never have imagined such a thing in my time."

3. This and the following quotations are from Yukio Mishima, "Hōjō no umi" ni tsuite" (On *The Sea of Fertility*), *MZ*, 34:26–29.

4. Although undoubtedly familiar with works such as Thomas Mann's *Magic Mountain* which are self-referentially "about" the nature of time itself, Mishima did not write of them as such in relation to his own experiments.

5. See Thomas H. Rohlich's translation in his study *A Tale of Eleventh-Century Japan: Hamamatsu Chūnagon monogatari* (Princeton: Princeton University Press, 1983).

aesthetic center was to be the ancient courtly ideal of *tawayameburi* or "feminine beauty," and the story would be presided over by the Shinto "mild deity," or *nigimitama*, which rules over such aspects of life as love, growth, procreation, and generation. The second book would exalt the medieval ideal of manly valor or *masuraoburi*, "masculine beauty," in a "suitably vigorous" style and would be ruled by the Shinto "rough deity," or *aramitama*, who presides over blood, war, revenge, and death. The third book would be "an exotic psychological novel," written in a "colorful style," and would come under the aegis of the Shinto "mysterious deity," or *kushimitama*, who is concerned with states of transformation.

So far, so good; up to this point Mishima seems to be giving an accurate outline of the work in progress. The final volume, however, he describes only as an "investigative" (*tsuikyū*, that is, suspense) novel that would "profusely incorporate details of the time in which it is set" and over which would reign the deity of happiness or good fortune, the *sakimitama*, who governs the native concept of festival or carnival known as *matsuri*.

It is particularly interesting that at the time of writing of this short essay, Mishima, always so firmly in control of his work and only a year and a half from the spectacular suicide he planned and carried out at the projected completion of the *Sea of Fertility* (November 25, 1970), seems as yet unable even to begin to provide an adequate account of the final volume. He arranged for this essay to appear on February 26, a potent date in his personal calendar of saints: the anniversary of the short-lived army revolt of 1936 that forms the setting for his notorious story and film *Yūkoku* (Patriotism). All that Mishima can accurately report at this late date is that he is as yet only a third of the way through the third volume and still has not even as much as a title for the fourth. Unless he was being deliberately deceptive (which in Mishima's case is always a possibility), it would appear that he had no clear idea as to what the fourth volume would contain. "Happiness" or "good fortune" are so much the very last words one would choose to describe this numbingly depressing work that one instinctively feels he is being deceptive or ironic in his choice of a presiding deity. And one suspects that even Mishima might have had a hard time explaining the rest of the description. If everything goes according to plan, he writes, he expects the work to be completed by the end of 1970. Yet in retrospect, a sense of misgiving is apparent: "The novel has become my life," he writes, adding with ominous ambiguity, "and I am afraid of the way it is going to end."[6]

The long essay "What Is 'the Novel?'" (serialized from 1968 to his death)

6. Mishima always appeared concerned to keep ambiguous the relationship between his art and his life, and actively sought to keep the public guessing. See my "Action as Fitting Match to Knowledge," pp. 397–98.

contains much the same ominous sense of what Mishima himself calls "premonition." Having just finished the third volume, he writes, he has no idea what the future may bring but realizes that whatever is to come is present in embryonic form in what has already been written. Fiction and reality are "non-Euclidean worlds in which parallel lines may in fact intersect," but "the end of the fictional world and the end of the real world do not correspond completely. . . . after all, things don't really happen as they do in Poe's 'Oval Portrait.'"[7] Authors live, and often die, struggling to keep the worlds of life and art apart, Mishima continues, recalling the story that on his deathbed Balzac called for a doctor he had created in one of his own novels: "But it is essential to my own methodology that I never confuse these two worlds. There are authors who get their inspiration from intentionally confusing the two, but my writing consists precisely in the struggle to keep them firmly apart—and the strain of keeping them apart has grown unbearable during the writing of this long novel."[8]

The fact that he has just completed the penultimate novel of his tetralogy seems to disturb Mishima most. In exercising the life-giving act of free choice, he says, he inevitably has to choose just one of an infinity of "free-floating" fictional possibilities, and each choice inevitably curtails further the freedom to choose between the two worlds of reality and fiction, those parallel worlds which in "the non-Euclidean geometry" of his life seem fated to intersect. Once such choices are made, he says, they are permanent, leaving "one world discarded, the other locked away inside the novel."[9] He knows, in other words, that he is writing himself as a character into his own work; and he sees, only dimly at first but ever more clearly, that his fate in the end can only be death. There is no place after "The End" for a still living author; as Henry Miller wrote (see the epigraph to this chapter), there is only murder or suicide—or buffoonery.

Near the end of this essay Mishima quotes one of his political heroes, Yoshida Shōin (a radical imperialist executed in 1859 for plotting against the government): "There are men whose bodies have perished but whose spirits live on. When the heart has died, there is nothing to be gained by remaining

---

7. "The Oval Portrait" is Edgar Allan Poe's story of a great artist who paints a portrait of his beautiful young wife. As he works, she grows steadily weaker: "And when many weeks had passed, and but little remained to do, save one brush upon the mouth and one tint upon the eye, the spirit of the lady again flickered up as the flame within the socket of the lamp. And then the brush was given, and then the tint was placed; and, for one moment, the painter stood entranced before the work which he had wrought; but in the next, while he yet gazed, he grew tremulous and very pallid, and aghast, and crying with a loud voice, 'This is indeed Life itself!' turned suddenly to regard his beloved:—*She was dead!*" (*The Works of Edgar Allan Poe*, 1:60). We have seen how influential Poe's work, so popular in Japan, was on Kōbō Abé.

8. This and what follows is from Mishima, "Shōsetsu towa nanika," 269–75 (pt. 11).

9. This idea should be contrasted with Kenzaburō Ōe's notion of "pluralistic universes" (see Chapter 10).

alive; but if the spirit lives on, there is nothing to be lost by dying." What clearer notice could he have given? But, he notes, the skeptical reader will have been sighing to himself all this time, "What a lot of nonsense! You're a novelist; your books sell, and you make a good living from them. Act your age and write your novels. We'll read them, and when we're tired of them we'll sell them to the used-book stores and you'll be forgotten. Isn't that what a novelist's life is all about?" Thanks for the advice, responds Mishima, but no thanks: I refuse to go quietly.

Perhaps the strangest sentence in this whole essay is this: "Unless the real world beyond the work forcibly drags me back (*although thorough preparations have been made for that*), I will probably fall into a deep despair" (p. 273; emphasis added). The grammar is the oddest thing about the sentence, with its concessive "although" couched inside a phrase that already begins with a concessive "unless." The grammar also deliberately obfuscates just who may have been making these only vaguely intimated "preparations" (*junbi ga shite aru noni*) which the mood of the verb "drag" (*ratchi shite kurenai kagiri*) insists are being made for his own good. What he seems to be saying through the oddly ambiguous grammar is exactly what I have noted above: the real world may do everything in its power to drag the author back into it again—contracts, talk shows, travel, fame, fortune—but Mishima refuses to go along. No buffoon, and certainly no murderer, he intends to die in order to guarantee life to his work—a position which, if inhuman, is at least logical.

As I elaborate below, it was impossible for Mishima to conceive of a universe, like those in Salman Rushdie's works, in which one choice does not necessarily and automatically close off all other possibilities, in which even death itself is not permanent, and in which the death of the author and the end of his work are not necessarily the same thing (it is the *narrator*, not the author, who ends in the final cataclysm of *Midnight's Children*, though Rushdie may seem to have written his own demise into his later work). In an interview with the critic Takashi Furubayashi one week before his death, thoughtfully tape-recorded for posterity, Mishima speaks extremely lucidly and powerfully of his "complete exhaustion" in the face of "The End"—the end of the novel, everyone assumed, though some friends undoubtedly knew better.[10]

Mishima also hinted at what was to come in his 1970 essay "The Spinning Top."[11] He tells of a young student who determinedly stations himself night and day in front of the author's residence until granted an interview (traditionally the way one would approach a Zen master). When finally told to state

10. Furubayashi Takashi, *Taidan: Mishima Yukio—saigo no kotoba* (Tokyo: Shinchô Kasetto, 1989).
11. Yukio Mishima, "Koma" (The spinning top), *MZ*, 34:483–87.

his business, the student blurts a single question to the author, the very one he had been dreading: "Sensei, when are you going to die?" Mishima likens youth to a top, "terribly precise and wonderfully beautiful," that "careens along without any concern for where it is going" until that inevitable moment when it begins to slow down and is suddenly in danger of ungracefully toppling over. He makes it clear that he knows his own career of beautiful careening is almost at an end; unless something is done, he too, like the slowing top, will no longer epitomize "transparent beauty" but soon "just lie there clumsily."

On the last day of his life, Mishima handed in the final chapters of the tetralogy to his editor, then went on, accompanied by his own little paramilitary band, to his spectacular *harakiri* at the Ichigaya Self-Defense Forces Headquarters in Tokyo—the two acts constituting the final installment of an almost insane discipline that perhaps only an editor could truly appreciate.

A major facet of Mishima's experimentation with the novel is his construction of the four volumes of *The Sea of Fertility* around a variety of seminal texts. The most obvious (and irritating) of these are the long, undigested helpings of Indian, Chinese, and Japanese Buddhist and Western philosophical speculation which provide the complex metaphysical underpinning for the overall scheme of the tetralogy. These include the tedious and archaic political hagiographies of the "League of the Divine Wind" (a xenophobic group that led an uprising in 1876), copied verbatim into the second volume, which to many Western readers and, I suspect, not a few Japanese must seem rather a large price to pay for whatever enjoyment the rest of the novel may afford. These intrusions, certainly not what we expect from a novel, have the effect of bringing the author's superb talent for vivid description and action to a screeching halt. (Perhaps this is what V. S. Naipaul had in mind when he wrote rather mysteriously of Mishima's "curious literalness which adds up to a detachment formidable enough to make the writing seem pointless.")[12]

To the extent that the embedded religious and philosophical texts appear to lack any organic integration into the story, they might be understood—like the similarly intrusive tracts in *The Brothers Karamazov*, or even the long narrative soliloquies of the more Modernist *Magic Mountain*—to represent a different tradition of narrative expectations. Mishima may not, like Dostoevsky, Charles Dickens, George Eliot, and other nineteenth-century authors, blatantly resort to addressing his readers directly. But he does work within a literary environment in which he can still feel free to incorporate verbatim into fictional narrative a substantial amount of what might be called "documentary" material—tracts on popular philosophy, accounts of court-

12. Naipaul, *An Area of Darkness*, p. 227.

room proceedings, hagiographical works, and the like—which constitute the circumstantial evidence of a reality familiar to a particular class of readers from materials they could expect to encounter in everyday life. "There is no one privileged 'language of fiction,'" Patricia Waugh writes of the Bakhtinian concept of the dialogical text. "There are the languages of memoirs, journals, diaries, histories, conversational registers, legal records, journalism, documentary. These languages compete for privilege."[13]

Mishima's work makes ample use of all of these "languages." Its extraordinary range of competing textual voices, in fact, makes the tetralogy appear to be one of Japan's most truly dialogical texts. Despite the wide range of voices introduced, however, the superordinate ironic consciousness of the narrator in the end succeeds in eliminating all but one—that of the author himself; for all the rest exist only to enhance his own. It is impossible to believe that Mishima, who single-mindedly insisted on total control over every aspect of his life and work, could ever have permitted unauthorized voices to run amok in his text.

Unlike a nineteenth-century (or pre-Modernist) audience, we are, perhaps unfortunately, no longer part of a society in which our lives—like those of Dickens's and Dostoevsky's clerks and landlords, Balzac's and Zola's petites bourgeoises and rentiers, or Mishima's Meiji-period ex-samurai and rationalist lawyers—are intricately enmeshed in the particular web of literacy that organized the reality common to minor bureaucratic functionaries, who could be expected to possess a familiarity with literary and semiliterary documents in a wide variety of formal epistolary, documentary, and other rhetorical styles. Ours might rather be characterized as embedded in the alphabet-soup acronymics of the Tom Clancy novel, the sort of illiteracy best described as a variety of the scribal literacy or technical literacy of record keepers, number crunchers and word processors.[14]

To think of literacy in this way is to suggest a central facet of the problem: we are part of a social milieu in which a line of poetry or an allusion to a poet can less and less plausibly be expected to release an economically encapsulated wealth of shared human experience and achieve a sense of group closure. Along with the idea of the "public man" (brought down perhaps by the sheer absurdity of juxtaposition with the connotation of the "public woman") has disappeared any notion of a proper distinction between the public and the private.[15] With the death of the public mode, poetry has become so private that the poet is in the odd position of sharing almost

---

13. Patricia Waugh, *Metafiction: The Theory and Practice of Self-conscious Fiction* (New York: Methuen, 1984), p. 5.
14. On various aspects of literacy, see Walter Ong, *Orality and Literacy: The Technologizing of the Word* (New York: Methuen, 1983), pp. 93–101.
15. See Richard Sennett, *The Fall of Public Man* (New York: Knopf, 1977).

entirely with her- or himself the emotional state of the isolated and usually alienated individual. Song may still serve much of the former communal function of poetry, but this is seldom a *literary* experience as such, and the audience for what remains of "traditional" elite communal literary experience seems to grow smaller every day. Opera (even with the help of supertitles) and art song scarcely achieve this function for a dwindling Western social elite today. Similarly, in spite of the large numbers of Japanese still able to recite by heart from the major Nō repertory, Mishima fretted in 1970 that within another decade there would be no one left in Japan able to understand the archaic language and emotions of the characters in a work such as his *Spring Snow*, to which the Nō drama is so very central.

It is useful to consider Mishima's intrusive narratives as part of his plan to problematize the novel's linear structure. Each of the brief and intense narratives of the tetralogy's sequential incarnations—Kiyoaki, Isao, Ying Chan, Tōru—commands our attention in part because of the way it cuts across the longer, duller, and intentionally low-keyed chronology of the ubiquitous observer, Honda. The other treatises likewise serve to break up expectations of linear narrative by interrupting each of these stories in turn with exegeses of Buddhism, Hinduism, Christianity, Greek philosophy, medieval alchemy, hagiography, and so on. All these interruptions have the effect of frustrating the reader's hope of a "good read," of becoming woven into the story's context. In his taped interview with Furubayashi, Mishima states that he packed even more of this intrusive philosophizing than usual into the third volume of the tetralogy precisely so that he could keep it out of the fourth, which he perhaps intended to leave as a reward to the patient reader. There is of course also the possibility that the fourth volume is devoid of such texts precisely because its theme is the death of philosophy—a condition in which there are no texts left to cite.

Beyond his blatant reproduction of disruptive religious, philosophical, and political tracts, however, we find a second mode of textual allusion in Mishima's tetralogy: the highly conscious and creative embedding within each novel of literary works that create, in rather more traditionally acceptable and organic fashion, versatile intellectual centers for their larger literary environments.

The most obvious of these works are the Nō plays *Matsukaze* (The wind in the pines) in *Runaway Horses*, the second book of the series; and *Hagoromo* (The feather robe) in the fourth, *Decay of the Angel*.[16] The theme of

---

16. On Mishima's sophisticated and complex use of this sort of embedded textual reference, see David Pollack, "Wang Wei in Kamakura: A Consideration of the Structural Poetics of Mishima's *Spring Snow*," *Harvard Journal of Asiatic Studies* 48, no. 2 (1988): 383–402. The seminal text in this instance is a poem by the famous T'ang dynasty Chinese poet Wang Wei, which would likely have been recognized by any educated Japanese reader of Mishima's generation and around which he structures much of the novel.

Hagoromo, the decay of a beautiful heavenly being who has been trapped on earth, is both embodied and parodied in the character of the beautiful but empty and degenerate Tōru. Mishima found fertile use for the dominant moon imagery of the play *Matsukaze*; it first appears in *Spring Snow* in a divination ritual (*otachimachi*) involving a wooden basin filled with water to reflect the moon (S31–32/H46–47)[17] and becomes explicit in the image of the moon reflected in the water pails of the characters Matsukaze and Murasame, where it connotes at once duality and nonduality, separation and union, delusion and reality. Mishima exploits the internal dynamics of a rich system of conventional imagery to suggest that the ostensibly separate lives of Kiyoaki and Isao, and of the two Thai princesses, are in fact different aspects of a single, more profound unity. Just as the moons in the separate water pails are merely different manifestations of the same greater reality, so the myriad moons reflected in the rice paddies of Southeast Asia become one when the monsoon rains arrive to flood the man-made boundaries between the fields:

> With every rainy season, the rivers in Bankok overflowed, the divisions between road and river, river and rice-paddies immediately vanished. . . . the isolated phenomena of this world, like islands dotting the vast stretch of water clearly reflecting the moon after the rains, might be the more difficult of the two to believe. The embankments had been broken down and all divisions had disappeared. [T110/A131]

In chapter 20 of *Runaway Horses*, however, Mishima, as he so often does, parodies the high seriousness of *Matsukaze* by transforming the Nō play's elegant poetic moon imagery into an entirely comic vision: reflections of the sky, alternately unbroken and shattered, mirrored in a wooden tub (*tarai*, which echoes the *otachimachi* ritual) as the fat and imperturbable Sawa ceaselessly launders his clothing so that he can die for the emperor in clean underwear whenever the opportunity presents itself (R220–21/H612–13). The imagery of rice paddies also seems to govern the Buddhist maxim that the purest lotus, as Isao discovers in this chapter, always grows from the foulest muck.

It is not difficult to see that *The Sea of Fertility* is organized throughout on the structural principles of the Nō drama (I have already remarked in Chapter 5 on Kawabata's use of this governing structure in *Snow Country*). Each novel is centered on a protagonist (*shite*) whose life and actions are the focus of the story and whose Dionysian existence is unburdened (and unre-

17. Page numbers refer to English and Japanese editions respectively: Yukio Mishima, *The Sea of Fertility*, 4 vols. (New York: Pocket Books, 1975); *Hōjō no Umi*, in *MZ*, vols. 18–19 (Tokyo: Shinchōsha, 1973). Abbreviations identify each of the four pairs of novels: S/H = *Spring Snow*, *Haru no yuki*; R/H = *Runaway Horses*, *Homba*; T/A = *The Temple of the Dawn*, *Akatsuki no tera*; D/T = *Decay of the Angel*, *Tennin no gosui*.

deemed) by reflection. As in the Nō drama, too, this protagonist changes from one form to another—from Kiyoaki to Isao to Ying Chan to Tōru—in accordance with Buddhist laws of karma and transmigration. Only the Apollonian deuteragonist (*waki*) Honda remains the same—always older, of course, but otherwise entirely unchanged—throughout the sixty-year span of the four books as he travels, inquires, seeks, observes, and records. Honda's role of crucial but ultimately impotent observer climaxes in the cruel but intensely accurate irony of the arrest of this once upright pillar of the legal community as a common Peeping Tom.

The logic of the tetralogy is Buddhist as well, but here the analogy with the Nō drama ends, for it involves the older version of the aristocratic Hossō sect of Nara-period (645–794 A.D.) Buddhism, which does not permit the later medieval Nō drama's more accessible sense of universal salvation. Karma still breeds suffering as always, but enlightenment, salvation, and the release of final transcendence do not automatically follow, as they inevitably do in the Nō drama. Because in Mishima's scheme there is to be no final enlightenment in the novel (the false moonlight reflected from the "Sea of Fertility" stands for delusion rather than enlightenment), there can be in the end no transcendence. This subtheme is symbolized throughout the work by the opposition of the true light of the sun, the traditional symbol of Japan's native Shinto vision of the world, to what Mishima saw as the false and deluding illumination of Buddhism, reflected in a moon that, by ironic synecdoche, lends its name to the title *The Sea of Fertility*. In the arid— lunatic?—light of Honda's scholastic and ultimately barren Western knowledge (he has failed even to produce any biological offspring), the world is revealed to be doomed to the finality of the *mappō*, that "final stage of the Buddhist Law" marked by utter degeneracy and depravity.

Mishima elaborates a complex Buddhist metaphysics as the basis of his tetralogy, only to reveal it in the end (not a little frustratingly, considering how much effort it costs the reader) to be irredeemably bankrupt. At the root of this philosophical insolvency is the problem that the sort of time which figures in Buddhist metaphysics, and so governs the novels, is entirely antithetical to Mishima's own vision of what time in fact means. If man is to attain immortality, Mishima requires that time's eternal downward spiral into decay be halted, something that can be achieved only by the sort of act of pure will carried out by Isao, Mishima's version of the Nietzschean Superman. In their failure arbitrarily to stop time, Honda and his ilk grow ever more grotesquely old and feeble, suffering the horrors of mortality that Kiyoaki, Isao, Ying Chan (and of course Mishima himself) succeed in escaping through death.

If *The Temple of the Dawn*, the third book, at first appears to be an exception to Mishima's practice of locating at the center of each work a heuristic literary text—one that serves as a fertile and ramifying source of diction, imagery, and structure—it is because one of this volume's major themes is the barrenness and sterility of art itself. Mishima's attacks here on pompous, self-proclaimed "artists"—the glib corporate flack Hishikawa (T26–27/A38–39), the vulturine poetess Kito (T152/A178), and the impotent literary critic Imanishi (T156/A182)—are every bit as vicious and brilliant as his attacks, here and elsewhere, on Japan's new upstart aristocracy.

What takes the place of a "real" embedded literary text in *Temple of the Dawn* is Imanishi's always unwritten masterpiece, which he has provisionally entitled "The Millennium of Sex" (*sei no mireniumu*): Mishima's brutal satire of Japan (*zakuro no kuni*, "The Land of the Pomegranate") as a nation of unproductive aesthetes who, claiming to live to cultivate beauty, succeed only in tormenting and destroying it. Even as this nonexistent text provides the author with a parody of a degenerate society which cannibalizes its own young, it also allows him to burlesque the debilitated exertions of the infertile "artistic" mind, cruelly lampooned in his description of the geriatric love-making of the aging Imanishi and Kito. *The Temple of the Dawn* embraces both extremes of Mishima's eccentric blend of talents, containing on the one hand some of the most idiosyncratic and ill-integrated religious and philosophical tracts since *The Brothers Karamazov*, and on the other some of Mishima's best descriptive writing as he forays into the lush beauty and horrifying brutality of the landscape and religious life of Southeast Asia and India.

The metaphysics of Mishima's tetralogy begins with the Buddhist principle that karma, not unlike Western cause and effect, operates mechanically and inevitably. We have seen that in Kawabata's *Thousand Cranes* the operation of karma is that of history itself, intricately linking a multitude of disparate, long-forgotten, apparently insignificant events and conditions submerged below the level of human awareness into the web of relationships that we take to constitute our world. The mechanism of karma might be imagined as a delicately balanced wheel on a stand, ready to revolve at the slightest impulse, and what provides the impulse is always human passion—the one thing, as I noted in Chapter 1, that the Confucian construction of the self cannot account for.

The karmic mechanism of the tetralogy is set in motion by several of the most primitive and powerful of human passions: lust, pride, humiliation, revenge. In a frantically modernizing Japan, Count Ayakura is a descendant of the elegantly declining, impoverished, and entirely irrelevant ancient court nobility. Marquis Matsugae—one of the nouveaux riches of the upstart capitalist aristocracy recently created along European lines—boasts to his niece, Ayakura's thirteen-year-old daughter Satoko, in front of her father, that thanks to the Matsugae wealth and influence she will not have to cause her impecunious father anxiety when it comes time for her to marry (S294/H316). Utterly humiliated by Matsugae's boorishness, the proud Ayakura plots revenge. He orders Tadeshina, an old family retainer and Satoko's nurse and governess, to arrange matters so that the girl will not be a virgin when the time comes for her to marry the man Matsugae selects to be her husband.

The nobleman Ayakura's revenge is appropriately described entirely in terms of the ancient courtly art of incense connoisseurship. Together with the equally ancient court ballgame of *kemari* (a uniquely Japanese group effort to keep a ball in the air), incense connoisseurship is Mishima's primary metaphor for the deepest meaning that life holds for this antiquated class:

> Wasn't there a revenge proper to court nobles, one that would match the way in which they perfumed the long sleeves of their robes with incense? Incense was hidden in the flowing sleeves of a court robe and burned slowly to a fine ash, showing scarcely a trace of flame. But, once it had burned out, the incense would leave behind a subtle, fragrant poison that would remain undiminished down the years to permeate the material. [S295/H317][18]

Not only is the image of incense indelibly perfuming a robe entirely appropriate to the court world of the noble Ayakura family; it is also an important metaphor in the Hossō Buddhist metaphysics that lies at the heart of the novel. The incense metaphor is used to illustrate the action of what is called "*alaya* consciousness," the central tenet of this aristocratic sect's metaphysics of "consciousness only" (*yuishiki*, often called "mere ideation"), which Mishima adapts as the metaphysical underpinning of the tetralogy. Mishima's dry and technical exposition of these matters in *Temple of the Dawn*, though always tedious, bears rehearsing in part:

> Now *alaya* consciousness is implanted by all seeds of all results. Not only the results of the seven senses we have already spoken of and their activity during life, not only the results of the mental activities, but also the seeds of physical phenomena that are the objects of such mental activities are implanted in it. Implanting the seeds into the consciousness is called "*perfuming,*" *in a manner similar to the way incense permeates clothing.*" [T112/A133; emphasis added][19]

The seeds of the phenomenal world, contained in the *alaya* or "storehouse" consciousness, exist before birth in a primal state independent of either

---

18. This passage is slightly retranslated to permit the idea to emerge more clearly.

19. For a concise discussion of the Hossō sect's philosophy of "consciousness only," see Junjiro Takakusu, *The Essentials of Buddhist Philosophy* (Honolulu: University of Hawaii Press, 1947), pp. 80–95; on the technical concept of "perfuming," see pp. 90–91.

human experience or consciousness. Mind is active, however, as it moves first outward to create, then inward to store, then outward to encounter again the phenomenal world it has created. During this complex process, mind stores the sensations impressed on it by the world that mind has already created. Thus impressed or "perfumed," the seeds of the phenomenal world are implanted in the mind, which again moves outward in reponse to their change. Subtly contaminated by the process of creating a world and then being recreated by the world they have created, the seeds "cause the world of illusion to materialize after being perfumed by the *alaya* consciousness" (T114/A134–35).[20]

This process, which may appear incomprehensibly self-contradictory, is fundamentally not so different from that by which a crop is grown. A stock of seed is required, containing the genetic material for the crop that is to be raised. But that seed is itself the product of a still earlier crop and bears its genetic imprint, which it will pass along to the next generation, together with any genetic evolutionary adaptations to a changing environment *which it itself has contributed to changing*. This process is karma, both creating and being perpetuated by human activity over time.

When one reads the tetralogy, it helps to know that Mishima does not indulge in this sort of abstract theorizing without providing at least one concrete demonstration of it in practice and often two, the first serious and the second in the form of a parody (as in the case of the moon imagery). Count Ayakura's revenge provides the demonstration of this theory in practice. With the ostensible intention of distracting her master Ayakura, who she sees has been badly put out by Matsugae's intolerable insult to his pride, Tadeshina suggests that he visit the somewhat disreputable inn of an acquaintance named Kitazaki, where he will be able to view an erotic scroll that Kitazaki has recently acquired. Though the scroll's message is didactic and solidly Buddhist, it also graphically illustrates a pornographic tale of fornicating monks and nuns; like Mishima's own work, it combines both moralizing sermon and travesty. In it, after explicit scenes of sexual debauchery and depravity, the ghosts of nuns who have died of excessive fornication, their faces now turned to vulvas, return in a bloody series of scenes to rip out the penises of the monks who debauched them. The scroll leaves the count

20. Cf. ibid., p. 90: "The old seeds latent in the [*alaya*] store-consciousness exist from time immemorial. These are called the original seeds. The new seeds are perfumed afresh from time to time. These are called the newly perfumed seeds. The old and new seeds together produce all manifestations of an error-stricken existence of life." Hegel uses a similar metaphor in discussing the relationship between object, consciousness, and self-consciousness: "The communication of pure insight is comparable to a silent expansion or *to the diffusion, say, of a perfume* in the unresisting atmosphere. It is a penetrating infection which does not make itself noticeable beforehand as something opposed to the indifferent element into which it insinuates itself, and therefore cannot be warded off" (*Hegel's Phenomenology of Spirit*, trans. A. V. Miller [Oxford: Oxford University Press, 1977], p. 331 (emphasis added).

both spiritually enervated and sexually excited. In this state of mind, which is further aggravated by the hot, humid weather of the rainy season, he turns for sexual relief to Tadeshina, on whom he had once deigned to vent his sexual urges many years earlier when his wife was pregnant with Satoko.

That single episode of lust years before is the cause of Tadeshina's own desire for revenge for what she feels has been his abuse and abandonment of her ever since, despite her unflagging and selfless devotion to his service. While she follows her master's instructions to the letter, therefore, she does so in a way calculated to bring him to devastating ruin. Knowing full well that Matsugae has arranged for the betrothal of Satoko to an imperial prince—an arrangement the impoverished Ayakuras see as their economic and social salvation—she has allowed her young ward to fall in love with Matsugae's own son Kiyoaki, and she sees to it personally that the young lovers have their first sexual tryst at that fateful spot, Kitazaki's inn (S173–185/H191–203).[21] The count's subtle revenge is thus very short-lived, for Tadeshina will have her even more viciously satisfying one: Satoko, whom Matsugae has engaged to be married to an imperial prince, becomes visibly pregnant with the Marquis's own grandchild.

Kitazaki's inn, which borders the parade grounds of the Azabu Third Regiment (now occupied, significantly enough, by the large Self-Defense Forces compound in Azabu near the shrine to General Nogi), figures as a powerful locus of karmic activity throughout the tetralogy. It appeared to Kiyoaki in a dream at the start of *Spring Snow*, blurred together with his childhood memory of a photograph of the memorial cenotaph to the war dead that opens the work. In this inn Ayakura viewed the erotic scroll, made love to Tadeshina, and plotted his revenge on Matsugae (and Tadeshina plotted hers on Ayakura). In *Runaway Horses*, it is where the dashing but faithless Lieutenant Hori is quartered, where Isao and the other young conspirators of his Shōwa League of the Divine Wind gather with Hori to plot sedition and assassination, and where they are finally arrested. In a brilliant later scene Kitazaki himself, now old and senile, is brought before the court as a prosecution witness at Isao's trial (R373/H764). Staring straight at Isao, the old man sees only the dead Kiyoaki, who had so often met Satoko at the inn twenty years earlier, just as Isao, upon first seeing Kitazaki's inn, was troubled by a powerful sense of *déjà-vu* (R122/H514). The photograph of the memorial to the war dead makes its last appearance in *The Temple of the Dawn*, floating up in Honda's memory when he hears the announcement that Japan is at war with the United States.

---

21. The Japanese character for "inn" is read *shuku* or *yado*. As an intransitive verb, *yadoru*, it means "to dwell temporarily" (or, read as *tomaru*, "to stay overnight"); as a transitive verb, *yadosu*, it means "to be made pregnant." The character is further used as part of such words as *shukuse* (or *sukuse*), "karma," and *shukumei*, "fate" or "destiny." The etymological complex indicated by these signifiers seems too significant to be dismissed as mere coincidence.

Tadeshina, in her final appearance in *Temple of the Dawn*, is discovered by Honda near the end of the war, now a wrinkled old hag squatting forlornly in the ashes of the bombed-out ruins of what had been the impressive Matsugae estate. Happening to have some eggs on hand, Honda presents them to her, and the starving old crone horribly devours one raw on the spot. In exchange, she gives Honda a copy of a Buddhist sutra, ironically one considered particularly efficacious in warding off snakes, which are an important symbol of young death and reincarnation throughout the tetralogy. Her appearance here also signals the complete reversal, wrought on Japan by the war, of the metaphor of the burning incense: the subtle perfume of revenge has vanished entirely, and nothing now remains of that world but its burnt-out ashes, everything "commingling indiscriminately" with everything else: "There were ashes caught in the breeze rising everywhere. There were white ashes and black ashes. Some floating ash adhered to a crumbling wall and rested there. Ashes of straw, ashes of books, ashes from a secondhand bookstall, ashes from a quilt maker's shop, floating about individually, commingling indiscriminately, moving, shifting over the face of the devastation" (T123/A144).

One of the great puzzles to readers of the tetralogy is that at its end, having chronicled the passage of some sixty years in great and portentous detail, Mishima seems to suggest that this lengthy and obviously significant passage of time has never meant anything at all. The problem is that this is to state the matter the wrong way: if the passage of time as *either* linear or cyclical chronology has meant nothing, that is precisely the final point of the tetralogy. At Honda's final interview with Satoko, now the elderly abbess of the Gesshūji temple in Nara, she even asserts that there has never been such a person as Kiyoaki Matsugae. When the bewildered Honda, vividly recalling his trip to see her with the dying Kiyoaki sixty years before, protests this chilling claim, Satoko replies,

> "Memory is like a phantom mirror. It sometimes shows things too distant to be seen, and sometimes it shows them as if they were here."
> "But if there was no Kiyoaki from the beginning—" Honda was groping through a fog. His meeting here with the Abbess seemed half a dream. He spoke loudly, as if to revive the self that receded like traces of breath vanishing from a lacquer tray. "If there was no Kiyoaki, then there was no Isao. There was no Ying Chan, and who knows, perhaps there has been no I."
> For the first time there was strength in her eyes.
> "That too is as it is in each heart." [D246/T646]

Considering the emphasis given the Buddhist concept of time throughout the novel, the ending might well be taken to indicate that Honda has reached a state of Buddhist enlightenment, of Nirvana, of absolute emptiness, one perhaps symbolized by the brilliantly sunlit temple garden in which he and Satoko confront one another at the end. Or again, it might be taken to be a particularly brutal and cynical denial of everything that has taken place. For Mishima, however, time is essentially cyclical, something that simply recurs meaninglessly over and over again, acquiring meaning *only* when its pointless cyclical repetition is halted by an act of will—as it is by Kiyoaki and Isao and even Ying Chan. For Honda, however, who does not stop it, time can mean nothing but the living death of old age and decay. "Why had he not stopped time?" the decrepit Honda asks himself, and understands (in one of the funnier images of the entire work) that the destiny of immortality entailed in such a dramatic act was not for such as he: "It would not have become me to raise my hand in farewell to those who were below, where time still ran on. Had I raised my hand in sudden farewell at a street crossing, I would only have stopped a cab" (D112/T486). Time for Honda, as for most of us, is of the sort that George Eliot wrote of so perceptively in *Middlemarch* in recounting how poor, ineffectual Mr. Vincey, who really has the best intentions of taking action to stop his daughter from rashly marrying young Dr. Lydgate, is too doting a father actually to *do* anything about it: "And in the meanwhile the hours were each leaving their little deposit and gradually forming the final reason for inaction, that action was too late."[22]

Mishima's view of time here is embodied in the Sino-Japanese concept of *kanreki*, "the return of the calendar" to its cyclical starting point in the sixty-year cycle (*kanshi*) of the Chinese system adopted during Japan's earliest contacts with China. At the end of the work Honda is seventy-six years old and Satoko seventy-eight—or, as Honda notes, exactly sixty years older than they were at the start. Although the tetralogy's frame of reference extends back somewhat before this point, for Honda and Satoko, the only survivors from the beginning, time has actually returned to its starting point, to zero. Two years older than Honda, Satako has already begun her new cycle, in her new karma recapitulating the career of her great-aunt, the former abbess of the Gesshūji temple, who makes a brief appearance early in *Spring Snow*.

Women, whose lives are bound up in cyclicality, pose the inevitable problem for Mishima, as they did for Tanizaki, of an entirely different phenomenology of time. As always in Mishima's novels, women's fatal biology determines their duplicitous destiny as they repeat themselves endlessly in a cycle keyed to the moon—for Mishima, the arid female symbol of Buddhism representing an inferior truth subordinate to that of the sun, male symbol of Shinto and Japan. It is duplicitous because woman stands halfway between the natural world and the human, just as man (or rather, men) stands halfway

22. George Eliot, *Middlemarch* (1872; Harmondsworth: Penguin Books, 1974), p. 336.

between the human world and the divine. When they do not actively aspire upward, women inevitably devolve downward. Women mimic the heroic man's shedding of blood, though for entirely the wrong reason, more travesty than parody; and Mishima's view of their bloody and therefore innately defiled nature is that of Shinto. Though the two may dwell in the same physical body, the passionate young woman and the enlightened old Abbess are two entirely different people. The Thai princess Ying Chan is even literally duplicitous, for she turns out to have been not one person but one of a pair of identical twins. The one who arrives in Japan as an exchange student bearing the unmistakable signs of the true incarnation, the three moles under her arm, is exotically beautiful, powerfully physical, and sexually ambiguous. After returning to Thailand, however, she dies of a snake bite at the age of twenty, thereby proving herself the "true" reincarnation in the line of the original Chantrapa, Chao P.'s betrothed after whom he names his daughter. (The little princess who claims she is Japanese when Honda visits her during a trip to Thailand, in *Temple of the Dawn*, is *not* the true incarnation but her twin.)

If the bisexual Ying Chan is duplicitous in physical love, Mishima permits the reader to believe that Makiko Kito in *Runaway Horses* is, even more dangerously, *spiritually* duplicitous: neither Isao nor the reader is allowed to understand until very near the end of the book that it was not in fact she but Isao's own father who betrayed him to the police. His father betrays him for much the same reason that Makiko willingly risks perjuring herself at Isao's trial, out of the human passions of love and venality. Although Makiko does not betray Isao directly, she reveals the weakness of a woman's unspiritual love by lying at the trial in order to save him—and to be saved is the very last thing Isao wants. Far from being pleased at what she believes she has done *for* him, the ever-pure Isao is horrified at what her weak woman's love has made her do *to* him:

> Makiko's only conceivable motive was love, a love that dared to face danger in full view of the public. Such a love! For this love Makiko did not hesitate to besmirch that which was most precious to him. Moreover, what was bitterest of all, he had to make a response to her love. He could not make a perjurer of her. On the other hand, no one but he knew the circumstances of that night, and so there was no one in the world but Isao who could call her testimony a lie. And Makiko was well aware of this. She testified as she did precisely because she was aware of it. The trap she had set for him was that he had no choice but to save himself if he was to save her, however repugnant the means. [R381–82/H778]

Though his reasons are very different, Mishima's perverse view of love here coincides with the Buddhist one. In the Buddhist view, there is no emotion as powerful and therefore as destructive as love, whether between parent and child or between man and woman; no attachment as sure to lead one away from enlightenment into the morass of illusion. It is for his illusions that Isao is to be reborn as a woman: "Maybe I ought to be reborn as a woman," he muses near the end. "If I were a woman, I could live without chasing after illusions" (R409/H803). He is reborn as Chao P.'s daughter, the little Thai princess, the one who does *not* bear the telltale sign of the true reincarnation—one of the difficulties (along with the problem of Tōru's birthdate) that signal the decay and point toward a final breakdown of the karmic mechanism.

The only significant woman in the tetralogy who does not seem duplicitous is Keiko—and she is simply a pragmatically cynical modern woman who, like a man, does without deviousness whatever she has to do to get what she wants. She and Honda end up a fitting spiritual match for one another, "an old voyeur and an old lesbian," as Keiko humorously but accurately calls them (D217/T612).

For Mishima, the central meaning of time as both primary indicator and agent of degeneracy in the world is best illustrated by the operation of modern capitalism. Throughout the tetralogy, capitalism is understood to be the very logic of the West and its proprietary concept of "the modern." Having been imported into Japan, it now stands for everything that is eating away at Japan's very heart and soul. As recounted in *Runaway Horses*, the nineteenth-century members of the patriotic and xenophobic League of the Divine Wind (on which Isao models his own group) so detested Western paper currency that they handled it only with chopsticks in order to avoid being polluted (for the same reason, they held an open umbrella over their heads whenever they had to walk under telegraph wires). Money is the basis of the detested new aristocracy, among whose members is Baron Shinkawa, head of the Shinkawa financial group (*zaibatsu*). But worst of all is the archcapitalist Busuké Kurahara, who, while outwardly even more of a clown than Shinkawa and Ayakura, is not a member of the capitalist aristocracy at all but rather one of Japan's new political oligarchy, the elite who run the economy from behind a "black curtain" (*kuromaku*), to use the modern term.

Kurahara piously and sincerely believes that a stable currency represents the ultimate Truth of life, and he is willing to sacrifice anything to that sacred goal, even the farmers who in Isao's fascist view of things have always stood for the traditional Japanese way of life. Kurahara represents a class of wealthy investors who have already profited from runaway inflation, getting richer while the farmers are forced off their land. He callously regards these improvident farmers as "a race that, when inflation strikes, lacks even the wisdom to turn its money into property to protect itself" (R168/H560)— which to Isao's ears is tantamount to saying that if the poor are starving, let them eat real estate. Kurahara now advocates a policy of resistance to any attempt to "reflate" the economy and of strict adherence to the gold standard—a policy clearly designed, of course, to secure the advantages the rich have already acquired at the farmers' expense. While others of his class, less firm in principle and frightened by the increasing social unrest among the dispossessed farmers and unemployed workers, expect reflation to ameliorate the situation, Kurahara pins his hopes instead on the rapid, military-led expansion of Japan's colonial empire in Manchuria, Korea, and Taiwan to save the situation by creating new wealth and jobs. The military and the colonies are the only institutions capable of absorbing the now impoverished farming population and providing them with jobs.

In the end, however, it scarcely matters what Kurahara thinks about the economy. Isao discovers that the main reason his father reported the assassination plot to the police was to protect the life of Kurahara, a friend of Baron Shinkawa who is the primary backer of the father's nativist institute. Kurahara's comical clumsiness does not help matters: a bear of a man, he has a bad habit of sitting on things—his glasses, his hat, his cigarettes. At a ceremony carried out at the Great Shrine of Isé, where the Sun Goddess is enshrined, Kurahara—having already committed the unspeakable sacrilege of stuffing himself with beef beforehand—proceeds absentmindedly to sit on a branch of the leaves sacred to the goddess. This alone is enough to doom him in Isao's eyes.

The novel ends as Isao assassinates Kurahara and then commits suicide while the morning sun rises over Japan (the fact that clouds have entirely obscured the sun is not ironic—it is the act itself that causes the sun to appear to him in a blinding flash). But part of the meaning of the spiritual degeneration of time for Mishima is that in Japan's modern postwar age a vigorous and lively politics of assassination, impractical as it may have been, is no longer possible. The truly "Japanese" destinies, embodied in the ancient "feminine" beauty of Kiyoaki, the feudal "masculine" warrior beauty of Isao, even the vital and exotic foreign beauty of the Thai princess Ying Chan—all are irretrievably gone. In the end, nothing remains for Japan but the empty physical and spiritual beauty of Tōru, fallen angel and modern antihero, emblem of the end of Japan's time in the trash heap of the West.

Meanwhile, as past and future both recede, Honda through little effort of his own has become a rich man. Shortly after the end of the war, when there was precious little wealth in Japan, Honda received as attorney his share of a settlement from an old court battle over the disposition of state lands, enough to make him a millionaire. He divided his fee of thirty-three million yen into three parts allocated to stocks, real estate, and savings, and now "the portion in real estate had increased tenfold, the stocks threefold, and the savings had diminished" (D107/T480). Time, a negative quantity that eats away at everything, especially the heart and soul of Japan, reveals an odd property when associated with capital: it makes money grow by means of interest.

Indeed, for Mishima, interest itself is the emblem of the passage of time. And since for him time equals decay, interest is the sign and agent of decay, with all the properties of a parasitic mold or fungus:

> People thought at any rate that their holdings increased. If they kept ahead of interest they did increase. But something that increased by laws fundamentally in opposition to those of life could exist only by eating away at what stood on the side of life. Growing profits were the incursions of the termites of time.[23] A slight increase here and there brought the gentle, steady gnawing. And then one became aware of the fact that time bearing profits and time for life were of a different nature. [D109/T483]

The metaphor of the termites eating away at life is strengthened in Japanese by the expression Mishima uses in the immediately preceding passage for "as time passes": *toki o kizamu*, literally "carving away at time." Interest, which increases automatically as time passes (elsewhere, Mishima writes that "interest accrues like moss over a great plain of time"; D110/T484), can also be thought of as a measure of time, and both time and interest are measures of entropy: the rate at which the universe is running down.

Youth's lack of self-consciousness turns in middle age to a painful awareness of self and in old age to an even more painful awareness of time. It is only the hypertrophied awareness of old age that can hear the sound of the termites gnawing away:

> As he grew older, awareness of self became awareness of time. He gradually came to make out the sound of the termites gnawing bones away. Moment by moment, second by second, with what a shallow awareness men slipped through time that would not return! Only with age did one know that there was a richness, an intoxication even, in each drop. The drops of beautiful time, like the drops of a rich, rare wine. Time dripped away like blood and was gone. Old men withered, dried up, and died. In payment for having neglected to stop time at the glorious moment when the rich blood, unbeknownst to the owner himself, was bringing rich drunkenness. [D110/T484; translation slightly amended]

Tōru is self-awareness reified. An employee of a shipping company when we first meet him, his life consists of eternally watching the sea from a tower,

---

23. *Shiroari* can mean either "white ants" or "termites." I have amended the former of the English translation to the latter as the more universally recognizable term for the insect that destroys material by eating it away.

reporting in minute detail everything he observes, and understanding nothing. The ships that loom on and off his mindless horizon represent the final decay of "mind only" Buddhism's elaborate metaphysics of reality: indistinguishable in fact from the products of his own mind, these ships merely come into and pass from existence; once accounted for they have no further reality or significance. This condition might be taken for enlightenment; for Mishima, it is simply mindlessness.

Such a condition is intolerable to Mishima, whether in the young or the old, as sufficient a warrant for suicide as the certain knowledge that one can either die an awful and undignified death from cancer or take one's own life with dignity. Honda, however, though in fact dying of cancer, is long past the point of being able to kill himself; and Tōru, now literally blind, his only mirror on the world his demented girlfriend Kinué, lacks the insight. Each of them epitomizes in a different way the famous principle of the Chinese philosopher Wang Yang-ming of which Mishima was so fond: "Those who are supposed to know and do not act simply do not know."[24]

Did Mishima succeed in *The Sea of Fertility*, as he hoped, in creating a genuinely Japanese literary form? No more, I suspect, than Salman Rushdie in *Midnight's Children* can be said to have succeeded in creating a genuinely Indian novel. Where Rushdie's work positively extends the boundaries of a sensibility common to postcolonial literatures around the globe, however, Mishima's sets itself the negative task of establishing a restrictive difference which mocks the idea that anything else could be as meaningful. His critique of Western models and of Japan's response to them insists on exclusiveness, not on universality. Mishima's Japan refuses to look beyond itself to the totality of those differences which constitute the common lot of mankind. Instead, he goes to the trouble of carefully replacing each minutely analyzed foreign proposition with a construction that turns out to be not only unique to Japan but unique to Mishima as well. *The Sea of Fertility* thus proposes a one-time solution to a universal set of problems, a solution that is clearly Mishima's alone, whether in his writing, his life, or his death.

It is worth noting that the few foreigners who figure in the tetralogy soon go home, for foreigners and foreign ideas are if anything even more unwelcome in Mishima's fictional Japan than in the real one. The two Thai princes and the dangerously beautiful Thai princess Ying Chan come as exchange students, which is the primary (perhaps the only) category in which the Japanese have traditionally been willing to include others or, conversely, in which they have been willing to go abroad.

24. In Wang Yang-ming, *Ch'uan-hsi lu* (Instructions for practical living), cited in Chan, *Source Book*, p. 667.

Shūsaku Endō's novel *Foreign Studies* insists, however, that Japanese who go abroad to study and allow themselves to experience fully the shock of another culture can only sicken and die as a result. Japanese, like some rare bloom, are incapable of being transplanted. Only the strong—those who carefully maintain close ties with their primary networks at home and take care to associate only with Japanese when abroad—are able to survive the profoundly alienating experience of even temporary expatriation. Takeshi Kaikō writes of Japanese touring Paris, and Kenzaburō Ōe shows them in Harlem, riding in tour buses from which they never emerge, like people in a bathysphere five hundred feet below water, from which escape could only be fatal. Going abroad for "foreign study," in Endō's writing, turns out to be a form of inoculation against foreignness. But anything as drastic as an exchange of bodily fluids would inevitably be fatal: "We cannot receive blood from those of a different blood group," laments Endō's wretched protagonist Tanaka. "That is what I thought about on those lonely winter evenings in Paris."[25]

Just as a dying Ayatollah tried to make his death sentence the ultimate interpretive noose around Rushdie's work and neck, so Mishima tried to make his suicide the ultimate scaffold upon which any interpretation of his own work could be executed. He clearly hoped by welding his life irretrievably to his work to enforce a permanent end to interpretation by others. It was in the all-important act of stopping time that Mishima hoped to stop interpretation; but when, like his character Honda, he raised his hand in farewell to stop time, he was able to accomplish only something ludicrous. His last diatribe, delivered from his chosen interpretive scaffold, the balcony of the Ichigaya Self-Defense Forces headquarters in Tokyo, was greeted by the hastily assembled troops below with hoots and jeers (though Japan as a whole has perhaps had occasion to think long and hard about his message). Like Honda, he had, in effect, managed only to "stop a taxi," certainly in the eyes of the rest of the world, who could have been expected to see his final act only as some proof of Japanese alienness.

At first reading, Mishima's often lively text seems full of something like polyvocality and openness and intertextuality. By the end of the work, however, there is really only one voice, the one that has pronounced a death sentence on itself and that hopes by that pronouncement to bring an end to interpretation for all time. In Rushdie's case there is always the possibility of reopening the text, of allowing a new discussion (if only, as now, the endless debates over Muslim/Koranic versus Christian/New Testament—not to mention Old Testament—sensibilities). The demand of the Other to be

25. Shūsaku Endō, *Foreign Studies* (*Ryūgaku*, 1965), trans. Mark Williams (Tokyo: Tuttle, 1989), p. 225.

heard, paid attention to, and respected on its own terms is a valid one; but if it is only a demand to establish yet another single authoritarian Voice to replace that of the Western Satan, then again—as I indicated in discussing the critical stance of Edward Said—there is only the monologic of authority and submission to which the free play of the open text is anathema. Much better the multilingual and multicultural cacophony of voices in a work such as Anton Shammas's *Arabesques* than the hegemonic claim of any single Voice.

Though Mishima offers us a multitude of voices, then, some of which he allows briefly to compete for their hearing, in the end he succeeds in stifling each in one way or another. This, among other reasons, is why Kawabata was by far the better choice for the Nobel Prize in Literature. For all the younger author's *gemütlich* displays of antiforeignism, which he took on a sort of around-the-world campaign tour for the prize to London, New York, Paris, Hamburg, and finally Stockholm in 1965, the committee selected Kawabata. In an essay of congratulation, Mishima notes that the older writer's work "has inherited the most fragile and the most profoundly mysterious traditions of Japanese literature," and that in his work "a modern despair has always blended into the quietude of classical beauty."[26] For all his ideological resistance and obstreperous thrashing about, Mishima never did succeed in replacing the Western novel with anything "authentically" Japanese— whereas Kawabata in spite of being almost pathologically shy, may have succeeded through the almost postmodern formlessness of his best work in achieving something very like that.

Given all this, it comes as something of a surprise to find that Mishima managed to critique, along with nearly everything Western, the very Japanese right-wing and militarist ideas with which he is most often associated. Militarism is portrayed in the tetralogy as having failed Japan, just as Buddhism, colonialism, international belligerence, Western ideas, modernism, and even capitalism have all failed it. Perhaps most surprising of all, even the chauvinistic cult of a nationalist State Shinto has failed it. The aged nativist fanatic Masugi Kaidō, who in *Runaway Horses* runs a Shinto training camp in the mountains for young believers, is simply an old fool who at the slightest provocation buttonholes complete strangers and harangues them about the duplicity of Buddha: "I realize we have only just met," he rants, "but, really, that fellow Buddha was a fraud. I suspect he's the devilish rascal that robbed the Japanese of their Yamato Spirit and their Manly Soul" (R243/H634). Mishima quite accurately portrays the extreme right wing in Japan as being

26. Mishima Yukio, "Chōju no geijutsu no hana o: Kawabatashi no jōshō ni yosete," *MZ*, 33:461. The title might be interpreted as a sardonic poke at the reason Kawabata was chosen over Mishima: it can be translated as "The fruits of a long life of writing: Kawabata receives the Nobel Prize."

in cahoots with gangsters. Isao's father's nativist academy is built on hush money extorted from politicians and their wealthy backers. It is only Isao who is able to cut through the systematized dishonesty of such organizations as those of Masugi and his father by the "pure" and simple (if politically senseless and ineffectual) acts of assassination and suicide.

Though he probably would have been appalled at their expropriation of it, Mishima's version of a final solution appeals to only one group today: the extreme right-wing goons of the sort that shot and almost killed the mayor of Nagasaki when he proposed, following the death of Hirohito, that the late emperor should have taken more responsibility for Japan's role in World War II. But if appeal it does (and there is every evidence that it does indeed), Mishima must answer for it in some final judgment.

Unfortunately, as I have noted before, there is no fixed and easy correlation between political stance and artistic worth. Mishima's work is generally insightful, often humorous, occasionally lyrical, and frequently brilliant. His prose style—the despair of translation—is uniquely his own, and so is his wit, which happily fares somewhat better in translation. The best scenes in the tetralogy are those that give the fullest scope to his particular talents—and, significantly, these are the scenes that also best confine his particular faults, especially his penchant for wretchedly excessive diatribe. For sheer fun there is little in Japanese literature to match Mishima's penetrating character sketches of the members of the decadent aristocracy. His shrewd insight into the smallest details of exactly how class (in both senses of the word) will out inevitably recalls George Eliot's beautiful handling of Grandcourt in *Daniel Deronda*: it is because he is the very model of his class that one does not know whether to laugh at him in derision or recoil from him in horror.

Consider for example the following snatch of fatuous conversation between Mishima's Baron Shinkawa and Count Ayakura during a lawn party at which they are competing to see which of the two can be the more dazzlingly and vacantly "British":

> "As to animals," said the Count unexpectedly, "whatever one says, I maintain that the rodent family has a certain charm about it."
> "The rodent family . . . ?" replied the Baron, not getting the drift at all.
> "Rabbits, marmots, squirrels, and the like."
> "You have pets of that sort, sir?"
> "No, sir, not at all. Too much of an odor. It would be all over the house."
> [S124/H140–41]

What could more closely resemble such stunning inanity than this conversation in *Middlemarch* between the enthusiastically foolish Mr. Brooke and the foolishly profound Mr. Casaubon?

"But now, how do you arrange your documents?"

"In pigeonholes, partly," said Mr. Casaubon with rather a startled air of effort.

"Ah, pigeonholes will not do. I have tried pigeonholes, but everything gets mixed in pigeonholes. I never know whether a paper is in A or Z." [P. 21]

The characters Mishima does best with—the decadent and pretentious aristocrats, the pompous and cowardly military men, the dry-as-dust and self-centered officials, the strutting and ridiculous artists—are precisely those, one senses, with whom he felt some foiled affinity—as if, but for the intervention of an importunate and superior destiny, he might even have enjoyed their recognizing him as one of their own. Perhaps it is this ironic sense of misrecognition, then, that gives to all his humor and wit, to all his perceptiveness and insight, its bitter and sardonic cutting edge. One always senses Eliot's desire to make us aware of her own keen, ironic intelligence at work behind her characters, and the same is true of Mishima; but one can never keep from suspecting that just beneath the laugh that begins to break into a cackle there lurks the madman in his military zoot suit. Fortunately, we have the testimonial of a lifetime of brilliant writing and eminently sensible essays and interviews to reassure us that if he *was* mad, he was mad as a fox and sane enough to know how to joke about it.

Sadly, the cult of Mishima appeals to those, Japanese or otherwise, who have an investment in the idea of the man and his work alike as fascinatingly and uniquely Japanese. One can only hope that both will eventually come to be seen, as I suspect they are seen already, as brilliant but inevitably failed attempts to close off interpretation. They fail because, although Mishima provides all the voices necessary for dialogue, in the end there is no voice but his own, as unwelcome as that of a conductor who forgets himself and outsings the voices in the opera. His world turns out to be much like Swiss conceptual artist Jean Tinguely's clever onetime installations whose real message was their own glorious destruction. It is amusing to watch Mishima self-destruct, certainly, but only because his world is advertised as a funhouse; when we see that it has no exit, it stops being fun. We can only watch from outside while Mishima is left trapped within, ranting and slashing away at the Other, like the movie actor Tatsuya Nakadai slashing the *shōji* paper screens at the end of *Sword of Doom*. Since his funhouse is a hall of mirrors, however, what Mishima sees is only himself, posing narcissistically, as in the famous publicity stills he had taken of himself dressed only in brief homoerotic loincloth, muscles flexed, rose in teeth, sword in hand. And, not surprisingly, the image at which he is slashing turns out, as in some story by Poe, to be himself.

Part IV
The Problem of Culture

Chapter 9

Culture:
Reading in the Hall of Mirrors

The exotic charm of another system of thought is the limitation of our own,
the stark impossibility of thinking *that*.
— Michel Foucault, *The Order of Things*

"Culture," the totality of the stories that groups of people tell themselves about how they have come to live the way they do, can be understood
as a kind of myth. Taken together, these stories constitute that group narrative of "the imaginary" of ideology, defined by Louis Althusser as "the
imaginary relationship of individuals to their real conditions of existence."[1]
As the totality of the stories each dominant imaginary tells about itself,
culture not only defines the spaces within which we live but, in doing so, also
creates the darker shadows of those spaces, the marginal areas in and beyond
which exist our Others. Describing both a positive and a negative space, the
idea of culture delimits and confines our existence even as it structures it.
While it is the overall purpose of this book to examine the constructive and
inclusive as well as the destructive and exclusive aspects of the idea of
culture, the chapters that follow will more directly engage the problematic
nature of that concept itself.

The idea of culture as myth is useful in emphasizing the "imaginary"
nature of ideology. In the Introduction I proposed that Yasunari Kawabata's
1968 Nobel Prize acceptance speech could itself be seen as an expression of
the cultural myth of *yūgen* or "profound mystery" which is so fundamental to
his work in general. As a cultural myth, this concept serves automatically to
include all Japanese within a restricted seminal space while simultaneously
excluding to a barren one all foreigners, who, as the result of this deploy-

---

1. Althusser, "Ideology and Ideological State Apparatuses," p. 153.

ment, are left marveling at the mysterious Orientalness of it all. The myth is thus immediately recognizable from either side of the cultural divide as not merely representing Japan but representing it to some invidious purpose: in this instance, helping to distinguish what Japanese are and what others are not.

On their own side of that divide, of course, Americans tell themselves their own mythical stories: about lone cowboys against hordes of Indians, rugged individualists against the herd; about how power is accessible to those with brains and ambition "regardless of color, religion, ethnicity, or place of national origin" (a formulation that seems to exclude from neutrality such categories as gender, age, and social class); about what used to be called the great melting pot and more recently the rainbow patchwork quilt. While such stories inevitably contain the usual historical kernels of truth, in practice their mythical nature becomes all too evident. For in practice, as I have pointed out, the rugged individualist is more commonly known as the loose cannon who fails to be a team player, and brains and ambition alone fail conspicuously to guarantee the same access to power and privilege as those things that have always guaranteed it: power and privilege. The ideological investment in our myths prevents us from seeing such problems, even as we live and feel at home with them. The primary vehicles of ideological dissemination, media and textbooks, are full of phrases about open doors and level playing fields, free trade and equal opportunity. Our ideological commitments, however, might just as plausibly be understood as commitments to the benefits of unfettered consumption, the morality of the marketplace, and the unique ability of "enlightened self-interest" (formerly known as greed) to create the best of all possible worlds. Democrats and Republicans, liberals and conservatives, are in contention precisely over the issue of who is to define the essential American mythology—whose "imaginary," that is, is to describe the American way of life.

Liberal humanism as an ideological force endorses altruistic efforts within the academic and arts communities to "understand others," efforts facilitated by and directed through such official and unofficial agencies as the National Endowments or the Fulbright Commission. In recent years, however, this benevolent enterprise has been challenged as in reality working to diminish the potential threat of anarchic disruption and to ensure instead a tidy, sanitized unity. The unspoken agenda of "understanding others," as illustrated in such authorized explanations of other cultures as Ruth Benedict's *Chrysanthemum and the Sword* or Bernard Lewis's *Political Language of Islam*, seems in fact to be one of understanding others before they understand us. If there is money and fame to be made in the instrumental application of ostensibly "neutral" knowledge, it is only because knowledge turns out never to have been neutral at all, not even in the humanities.

As the totality of those articulations of ideology which add up to an explanation of why we submit to the relations of power in which we are embedded, "culture" is what we cannot see, precisely because, like the mirror, it is that which allows us to see ourselves. The idea of culture as that which is always unnoticed is an especially important one, for it is only in the unacceptable things *others* do that culture becomes noticeable.

For example, Westerners have frequently commented on the apparent fondness of Japanese men for urinating together in public, a custom known in Japanese as *tachishōben*. Almost a national communal male practice, it became the object of a self-conscious nationwide public relations campaign during the Tokyo Olympics in 1964, much as during the Seoul Olympics in 1988 the Korean government felt it necessary to shut down the popular dog-meat restaurants in the capital. The novelist Takeshi Kaikō, however, writing in Paris, is fascinated by the fondness the *French* show for urinating in public, "right out in the Bois de Boulogne and on the banks of the Seine, too—even old ladies."[2] And V. S. Naipaul describes as "invisible" those myriads of Indians whom he, a conflicted Trinidad-born British tourist of Indian descent, cannot help but see publicly defecating on the beaches, the promenades, the railroad tracks, in any open space:

> These squatting figures—to the visitor, after a time, as eternal and emblematic as Rodin's Thinker—are never spoken of; they are never written about; they are not mentioned in novels or stories; they do not appear in feature films or documentaries. This might be regarded as part of a permissible prettifying intention. But the truth is that *Indians do not see these squatters* and might even, with complete sincerity, deny that they exist: a collective blindness arising out of the Indian fear of pollution and the resulting conviction that Indians are the cleanest people in the world.[3]

"To observe the squatters," Naipaul continues, "is therefore distorting; it is to fail to *see through to the truth*." In much the same way, denizens of crowded Tokyo whose apartment windows open directly onto each other may truthfully be said not to see their neighbors, ostensibly "visible" though they may be: they "see through" one another in the interests of living out a higher cultural myth, which Mishima saw as the public life of an older Japan. In this formulation what is highly public becomes invisible, while the private becomes all too visible. The myth of culture might therefore even be defined as the totality of those agreements by which we make such practices invisible.

---

2. Takeshi Kaikō, "Ojisama no tanoshimi" (The pleasures of being an older guy), in *Kaikō Ichiban* (Tokyo: Shinchōsha, 1984), p. 69.

3. Naipaul, *An Area of Darkness*, p. 74.

This invisibility is necessary if we are both to live within our own culture and to accept others'. Yet even while I understand and appreciate the convention of invisibility, I cannot pretend not to see these things (although I do recognize the necessary difference between not seeing and pretending not to see). This book is automatically limited by its inevitable failure to achieve that collective blindness which allows the insider not to "see" but rather to "see through to the truth" of culture. What I am condemned to see of culture instead are the myths, the smoke and mirrors, the mist of cherry blossoms, so seductive and helpful in creating its mystery—and so impossible for the cultural outsider to see *through*.

To the extent that it is complex, culture can usefully be likened not just to a mirror but to the hall of mirrors in a funhouse. A space entirely sealed off from the world outside, the hall of mirrors makes itself into an exclusively *interior* space, endlessly reflecting only itself and refusing to admit the existence of any "outside" at all—which is why it is both fun and frightening. The metaphor of culture as a hall of mirrors has the advantage of comprehending both the elusiveness of the concept itself and its essentially tautological nature. Unlike the genetically imprinted knowledge of the spider's web, the funhouse creates an entirely virtual *imaginary* space, a socially constructed site in which the mirrors can be arranged and rearranged in an infinite variety of ways, though always to the same design of catching, surrounding, and trapping its inhabitants in endless reflections of themselves. In surrounding us by reflections of ourselves, it is at once comforting and disturbing, and thus shares in the Freudian sense of "the uncanny": "on the one hand, that which is familiar and congenial, and on the other, that which is concealed and kept out of sight."[4]

It seems especially important for nearly all the authors treated here to take as an article of faith that what is special about their particular cultural funhouse is that nothing from outside can ever be permitted within the self-reflecting mirrors of that culture. Often, however, those mirrors have aged, and their ancient silvering has so eroded that confused and fragmented glimpses of an outside world have inevitably begun to leak into the interior. Kawabata's cinematically inspired image of the "night-mirror" (*yokagami*) in *Snow Country* provides a useful analogy. The darkened window of a train whose interior, as the train passes through the night, is only dimly lit becomes an imaginary surface on which inside and outside blur and fuse to create the hallucinatory effect of a new virtual reality that is in fact pure myth—or, in the case of *Snow Country*, to permit the worlds of myth and reality to interpenetrate and become indistinguishable. We have seen how

4. Sigmund Freud, "The Uncanny," in Sigmund Freud: Collected Papers, ed. Ernest Jones, trans. Joan Rivière (London: Hogarth, 1956), p. 435.

well Kawabata succeeds in recuperating this fascinatingly disturbing pal-
impsest within a national narrative comprising a thousand years and more of
aesthetic discourse of culture. "Yume ka utsutsu ka?" (Is this dream or is it
reality?), the author asks, together with the myriad Japanese poets of centuries past, thereby setting into play a well-worn conventional construction of
"reality" that began when the ancient Chinese philosopher Chuang Tzu
awoke from sleep to ponder a riveting dilemma: either he had just been
dreaming he was a butterfly, or else he was now a butterfly dreaming it was
Chuang Tzu.[5] Either way, even the proposition reality : dream :: earth :
heaven, with its rigidly fixed sets of alternating spaces, significantly leaves no
room for other possibilities. Kawabata's true achievement was to have described this carefully modulated oscillation in terms of the more confused
condition of synesthesia and blurring that is the way we ordinarily experience
life. And what permits that condition is only the mirror, busily at work
creating its seminally confined space of culture.

Or it may be that the funhouse mirrors of culture have crazed or bent,
calling our attention to themselves by the wildly distorted versions of reality
they create and reflect. This is of course the condition governing how *others*
look—surely *we* are not that monstrous. In Japan such problems were also
once automatically referred to the comforting context of an all-embracing
Buddhism: our idea of reality is after all only an illusion, the all-too-human
distortion or perversion of a universal Truth. In later centuries more interested in the all-too-human than in abstract Truth, the very playfulness of
such a reponse could itself become a convincing basis of representation. The
denizens of eighteenth-century Edo (now Tokyo), for example, quite likely
conceived of their lives in terms of the elaborate and barely concealed stage
machinery of their beloved Kabuki theater. The revolving stage mechanism
called the *karakuri*, permitting one scene to disappear as the next rotates into
view, is a mechanical reproduction of the abstract motion of *samsara*, the
Buddhist wheel of karma: existences come around, disappear, come back
around again as something else, over and over again, each existence constituting one small part of the ongoing narrative of life. It is "revolution"

5. Cited in Chan, *Source Book*, p. 190. Cf. René Descartes, "First Meditation," in *Discourse
on Method and the Meditations*, trans. F. E. Sutcliffe (London: Penguin, 1968), pp. 96–97: "How
many times have I dreamt at night that I was in this place, dressed, by the fire, although I was
quite naked in my bed? It certainly seems to me at this moment that I am not looking at this
paper with my eyes closed; that this head that I shake is not asleep; that I hold out this hand
intentionally and deliberately; and that I am aware of it. What happens in sleep does not seem as
clear and distinct as all this. But in thinking about it carefully, I recall having often been deceived
in sleep by similar illusions, and, reflecting on this circumstance more closely, I see so clearly
that *there are no conclusive signs by means of which one can distinguish clearly between being awake and
being asleep*, that I am quite astonished by it; and my astonishment is such that it is almost
capable of persuading me that I am asleep now" (emphasis added).

literally transmogrified into the revolving stage of life: a worthy Brechtian parody of the Marxist vision! To get the truly subtle flavor of it, we have to imagine it as that long, mysterious flow that passes over Kawabata's darkened night-mirror—but, unlike the flow proposed by Heraclitus, one in which man is forever fated to step over and over again.

What is reflected in the complexities of the window of the train passing through the darkened countryside (or in those of the darkened Kabuki theater) is neither the profound *credo* of a medieval faith that would see in the problematic window an icon of belief, nor the radical *cogito* of an Enlightenment doubt that would see through the window as if it were not there at all. It resembles rather a parodic and perhaps even postmodern *ludo* or *res ludans*, "the thing at play," something simultaneously opaque and transparent. The special urgency in this playful proposition is the insistence that what lies on either side of the window is quite literally the annihilation of nothingness. There are elegant names for that condition in Japan, of course: that Zen "emptiness" to which Kawabata so frequently alludes in his Nobel Prize acceptance speech, for example; or again, the "place of emptiness" elaborated by the philosopher Kitarō Nishida, which that indigenous Hegel regarded as the site of "absolutely contradictory self-identity."[6]

But the bright Kabuki stage, which lacks the ontological frame of the proscenium arch, is framed only by the scarcely concealed secret of its mechanical fabulizing on one side and on the other the illusion of the perceiving consciousness that willingly endows it with phenomenological reality; beyond these, as Mishima proposes at the close of his tetralogy, is, literally, *nothing*—or, at any rate, if not his profoundly existential Nothing, then that more quotidian and ordinary nothing that seems to matter even more here and now. It is this nothing that lies beyond the mirrors of the funhouse, in the shadows beyond the lights of the theater, in the alien darkness of the unknown; and why would anyone want to hazard the nightmares of *that* abyss? For in a very real sense, to step into that abyss is to walk off the edge of the world of Japan itself. If we are to judge from Japan's choice early in the seventeenth century to seal itself off almost entirely from such terrifying nothingness for the next two hundred and fifty years, little indeed must have seemed as frightening as *that*; that choice has had, by all accounts, a heritage of considerable staying power.

Recent critical thought has been justifiably leery of claims of the entirely self-contained idea that attempts to set apart from consideration everything outside itself, and has become adept at catching out the shifty maneuvers of such attempts. Especially at issue are hegemonic endeavors to arrive at a

---

6. Akira Asada, "Infantile Capitalism and Japan's Postmodernism: A Fairy Tale," *South Atlantic Quarterly* 87, no. 3 (1989): 632–33.

uniquely privileged point from which to gain leverage on the rest of the world. The claim to hegemonic privilege is the characteristic gesture of the presumed Self or Center and implies all of the Center's doubtful assumptions about such aspects of power (and of narration) as origin and originality, author and authority, property and propriety, gender and engendering, subject(ivity) and object(ivity). And so one must at least agree to make such invidious discriminations provisional by bracketing them in quotes in order to suggest the more inclusive realm of greater validity beyond: as the deconstuctionist pun has it, there is literally an entire world of *différence* between claims of privilege and "claims of privilege." The response to the problem of whether in doing this one is not just playing with language—here as perhaps always, and certainly long ago in Japan—is that playing with language, celebrated in Jean-François Lyotard's notion of the performative language games of paralogism, may in fact be the very point. Still, we dwell within a delicate web of fragile human egos (or, if you prefer the other metaphor, spend a great deal of our time looking into mirrors, either examining those putative egos for signs of their reality or, conversely, frightening ourselves into forgetting their unreality), and our attitude toward this response seems inevitably to depend in large part on exactly who is playing with whose language. An important problem for this book, aspects of which I explored in the introductory Paradigm, is the extent to which one may legitimately play with another's language and still claim not to presume to be speaking for the Other.

It also seems something of a problem here that Japan may be neither part of the dead and oppressive objectivity claimed by some to characterize the First World, nor yet part of the concomitant vital but oppressed subjectivity of the Third. Some Japanese critics have even concluded that it is not so much that the Japanese have caught up with (or even surpassed) the West as that the West has only belatedly begun to deconstruct itself toward a condition that might be shown to have existed in Japan ever since the tenth century and perhaps earlier. From this point of view, Japan possesses the necessary qualifications to pronounce on such issues with authority (ironically, one hopes). These qualifications are both internal, in the notion of Japan as having existed in a postmodern condition (more accurately a condition of never having been "modern" in the first place) long before any such notion occurred to the West; and external, in the vision of a nation that is not only emerging from the shadow of American hegemony but even thinking of itself—whether ludicrously or seriously—as showing others the way out.[7] Surely the exit sign showing the way out of the hall of mirrors of culture is

7. See David Pollack, "Modernism Minceur; or, Is Japan Postmodern?" *Monumenta Nipponica* 44, no. 1 (1989): 75–97.

not written in Japanese alone; but, just as surely, *one* of the many languages that sign is written in is Japanese. It is important that we not limit ourselves to the condescending admiration of the pretty characters (in all senses of the word) in Japanese novels as somehow evincing a superior aesthetic taste, and equally important that we not dismiss altogether the attempt to read them as being impossibly exotic, or devoid of (or, with Roland Barthes, liberated from) significance. If we are searching for exits, however, we do want to be sure we are not just walking into yet another mirror.

Fredric Jameson has written of the novel as "a hegemonic work whose formal categories as well as its content secure the legitimation of this or that form of class domination."[8] In at least one of its forms from the nineteenth century on, the novel does reveal the logic of the modern bourgeois nation-state concerning itself and its others—those other races, peoples, and classes whom colonizing empires had learned to rationalize as inferior and strange and therefore deserving of missionary conversion, anthropological classification, colonial exploitation, imperialist ambition, and capitalist expropriation, not to mention simple slavery, murder, rape, and pillage (and whose "return" as repressed otherness was therefore guaranteed to play such an important role in the novel of the period). Those on the wrong end of such projects have had their own opinions on inherent moral superiority, noblesse oblige, fair play, just war, religious tolerance, human rights—and, along with all these, the purposes and functions of literature as it inevitably represents (or misrepresents) such notions.

For all or any one of these reasons, the novel has been justifiably held to be fundamentally incapable of representing the voice of the Other, having already appropriated that voice for purposes that amount to an ideological rationale of exploitation. Having foisted upon the Third World the hegemonic claim that its own particular mode of mimetic realism is universal, the novel has ended by dictating to others the very terms in which they and their concerns are to be represented. From this point of view, good intentions aside (and good intentions are, like those of Kurtz, all the more suspicious), when one speaks *about* others, one is inevitably presuming to speak *for* them and so by extension *against* them. There is that chilling suspicion, amounting to a certainty, of Kurtz's *real* intentions in having gone into the jungle, pious professions of high purpose on behalf of native souls notwithstanding.

The problem of the native voice marginalized by imperialistic expropriation is a complex one. Its difficulties are embodied in someone like V. S. Naipaul, who has made such a successful career of being a permanent ex-colonial, what the French call an *apatride*, or we a man without a country.

---

8. Jameson, *The Political Unconscious*, p. 288.

Intent on making capital of his wounds even as he parades his losses, like one of his Indian beggars showing their awful and often self-imposed sores, his own irony often seems blind to that of speaking in the voice of his own oppressor.[9] Should he protest if, like his picturesque and finally unwanted Indian beggar, he now "finds, unfairly, that he provokes annoyance rather than awe"?[10] It seems entirely improbable that Naipaul's rustic Wiltshire neighbors in *The Enigma of Arrival* should be so blind as to fail to notice, especially in that traditionally conservative farming district, that the man living just across the garden fence is what any of them would recognize immediately as another of England's problematic teeming "Asians." Certainly the neighbors in Haneif Kureishi's cinematic versions of East End London never decline an opportunity to take violent notice of racial difference. But then, to be fair, Naipaul's metaphor is not the Sodomic city but the Edenic garden; and the garden is precisely that idyllic space where, permanently for some, difference does not exist—at least not yet.

The choice of Kawabata to receive the Nobel Prize can logically and with justification be ascribed to the Western judges' discovery of a new kind of writing that seemed particularly delicate, lyrical, and suggestive enough to warrant its author that special recognition. But it also seems the sort of recognition one extends to a foreigner's interesting if naturally inadequate command of the language: it is, above all, captivatingly *quaint*.[11] Much the

9. This is the critical view of Naipaul adopted by Rob Nixon in "London Calling: V. S. Naipaul and the License of Exile," *South Atlantic Quarterly* 87, no. 1 (1988): 1–37. Nixon's unflattering assessment of Naipaul ends with the ironic picture of a man "secure, esteemed, and integrated into the high culture of metropolitan England, asserting his homelessness, while considerable numbers of genuinely disowned people struggle to be acknowledged as legitimate members of the society he is at liberty to reject rhetorically although he depends on it in every way" (p. 32). This seems ungenerous, not unlike accusing Hemingway of a life misspent in writing stylishly about bullfighting instead of working to protect the poor animals from such wanton brutality. Naipaul at least has the ability to distinguish the death of an ordinary ox, which, being of concern to no one, may be put quickly out of its agony, from that of a sacred cow, which must be solicitously guarded so that it can die its agonizing death without any interference.

10. V. S. Naipaul, *India: A Wounded Civilization* (New York: Vintage Books, 1976), p. 57.

11. The political dimensions of the award make it clear that what it recognized was actually the success of the English translations (done for the most part by Edward G. Seidensticker) rather than of the original Japanese, which was of course impenetrable to the judges—a point raised by the Japanese press at the time. Critics were acutely aware that the voice the Westerners were honoring was that not so much of Kawabata as of a not always reliable but capable and particularly consistent translator—one whose uncanny ability to make narrative voices as disparate as those of Murasaki Shikibu, Nagai Kafū, Tanizaki, Kawabata, and Mishima sound exactly the same has undoubtedly influenced the way that Westerners have come to think about Japanese literature. (Similarly, the work of Haruki Murakami is more recently becoming known to English-language readers through translations which, excellent though they may be, were originally intended to provide Japanese students of English with a kind of idiomatic English slang that does violence to the unrelieved flatness of Murakami's postmodern language.) The "Special Nobel Prize Commemorative Edition" of the literary journal *Gakutō* (December 1968)

same could be said of the cute Anglo-Indian, of the "Wah, wah, sir! Absolutely master shot!" variety, often used by Naipaul's friend Salman Rushdie. Besides the fact that Rushdie is *intentionally* writing this sort of English, however, there is beneath the playful quaintness of *his* language the awesome power to bring down on his head the wrath of all Islam.

Like so many Japanese authors, Kawabata had to kill himself, even though, as Masao Miyoshi has suggested, in betraying the "community of silence" he was like all other Japanese authors in a sense *already* dead, having alienated himself from the community of believers no less thoroughly than did Rushdie: "Silence powerfully invites the Japanese," writes Miyoshi, "but for the writer, accepting the invitation is always fatal."[12] As we are all too well aware, the once gregarious Rushdie is in fact also already dead, at least in the sense that he has been shut away in a sort of living death of the spirit whose merely physical endpoint, whether at the hand of some eventual zealot or his own, or even through natural causes, is no longer relevant—except, no doubt, to himself. It seems increasingly unlikely, however, that the present and future generations of writers in Japan—Haruki Murakami, Banana Yoshimoto, Yasuo Tanaka, and others—will follow past writers in finding that fatal invitation inevitable. Any "community of silence" that might once have existed, as Miyoshi has been quick to observe, seems today to have given way entirely to the reassuring, inane babble of the television talk show and the roundtable discussion.

It is not really surprising that Miyoshi should more recently have come to discover in the *shōsetsu*'s primary constituent elements (song, group creation, contextuality, non-linear plot) evidence of Japanese literature as the product of a Third World "oral" culture rather than of a First World "literate" one.[13]

---

features contrasting articles by Edward G. Seidensticker and Saitō Jōji on the particular difficulties of translating Kawabata; the nastiest jabs at the translator are the work of Itō Sei, the dean of the critical establishment. Kjell Espmark (*The Nobel Prize in Literature*, p. 142) reveals that Tanizaki, had he not had the misfortune to die on the eve of the Nobel Prize committee's decision to give the award to a Japanese, would most likely have been chosen, and that Mishima, who was nominated together with Kawabata by Donald Keene, was considered but judged to be too derivatively "European"—a common notion that would have galled Mishima.

12.. Miyoshi, *Accomplices of Silence*, p. 179. Even when Kawabata writes in *Japan the Beautiful and Myself* that "I neither admire nor am in sympathy with suicide," since it is "not a form of enlightenment," he has in fact brought himself right up to the brink of that abyss into which Japanese authors seem so often unable to resist peering, hypnotized, and into which he himself was to leap only four years later. Still, in the interests of fairness it would be comforting to see actual comparative ratios of Japanese and American novelists and poets who have one way or another done themselves in. It is even possible that there may be no significant difference at all.

13. Masao Miyoshi, "Against the Grain: The Japanese Novel and the Postmodern West," *South Atlantic Quarterly*, Summer 1989, p. 548. Miyoshi insists on the Chinese-derived term *shōsetsu* instead of "novel," which reveals the logic of imperialism, and for similar reasons objects to the words "modern" and even "Japanese." While acknowledging the validity of such arguments, I refrain from taking the principle quite so militantly to heart, noting only that if I do use these words it is with the ironic voice of Miyoshi's necessary caveats firmly in mind. See Pollack, "Modernism Minceur," pp. 88–90.

This attitude merely recapitulates the ethnologist Kunio Yanagita's early predilection for a primitive native orality over a modern foreign literacy. As Marilyn Ivy has noted, "Authentic Japanese culture resided, for Yanagita, in the spoken tradition, not the literate, urban culture; for Yanagita, 'rural' was almost synonymous with 'oral,' 'urban' with 'literate.'"[14] A case *can* be made that the traditional *kōdan* genre of oral storytelling for a mass audience, which persisted into the modern Shōwa era (in *Runaway Horses* Mishima depicts Isao's companion Sawa reading the popular magazine *Kōdan Kurabu* or "Storytelling Club"), was regarded by the authorities as inherently safe because, in spite of inclinations toward the pornographic, it otherwise upheld fundamental traditional values and was read solely as entertainment. The new novels, on the other hand, intended to be *read silently by the individual*, were, as Jay Rubin has observed, regarded by the authorities as "subversive agents threatening communal solidarity [i.e., the *kokutai*] not with obscenity but with something far more insidious: privacy."[15]

Wishing not to promote Western essentialisms about Japan, Miyoshi generously extends the privilege of Third World orality to other Asian literatures as well, although he does not specify which ones, or why. This suggestion amounts to elevating a primordial "Asian" orality to the status of something morally superior to a fallen "Western" literacy, which is thus revealed as the technical precondition of a malign Western hegemony over Asia. We do not have to look very hard to see in this Kenzaburō Ōe's alarming suggestion that Japan is somehow the natural ally, perhaps even the natural leader, of an Asian Third World attempting to liberate itself from the oppressive yoke of Western hegemony, whose "Coca-colonization" has proved an attractive and more effective alternative to the clumsier and more intrusive earlier gunboat version. One can only wonder just what Ōe might have meant when at the 1986 "Challenge of Third World Culture" conference at Duke University he declared Japan's solidarity with "other" Third World writers and suggested "an idea of Japanese culture that could perhaps play a unique role among the cultures of the Third World."[16] Since Japan has never been one of the

14. Ivy, "Discourses of the Vanishing in Contemporary Japan," p. 98; see pp. 105ff., however, for Yanagita's later turn to a valorization of writing over speech in his own literary creation *Tales of Tōno* (*Tōno monogatari*, 1909).

15. Rubin, *Injurious to Public Morals*, p. 94. Rubin wonders (p. 95) whether it was more significant that heretofore tolerated pornographic literature was beginning to appear on the Police Bureau censorship lists, or that what had long been regarded as merely harmless erotica was becoming identified with the novel. The same ambivalence can still be seen today in the government's strict censorship of all foreign materials simply depicting sexual acts, even as it takes a relaxed attitude toward the more sadomasochistic and violent depictions favored by native genres. The one seems to be regarded as dangerous simply because it is foreign, the other as unthreatening to the social order solely by virtue of being native.

16. Kenzaburō Ōe, "Japan's Dual Identity: A Writer's Dilemma," *World Literature Today* 62 (Summer 1988): 360; reprinted in Masao Miyoshi and Harry Harootunian, eds., *Postmodernism and Japan* (Durham, N.C.: Duke University Press, 1989), p. 191.

nonaligned nations, and Ōe was clearly not proposing some version of a cold-war Marshall Plan of strategic financial or military aid, it can only be supposed that he had in mind some other "unique" literary "role" for Japan. The prewar vision of advanced Japan as the natural leader of Asia's backward masses is in the "post-postwar" setting at once potently practical and troubling. Japan is, and is likely to remain for the foreseeable future, the primary source of development capital in East Asia—if not in the world, as the United States once was—and it may well be no more reticent about wielding that immense power to further its own ideological interests than the United States has ever been.

Ōe has always vilified Yukio Mishima, but there is little in his own intense and overwrought language and imagery to match Mishima's powerfully spare indictment in *The Decay of the Angel* of a Japan whose ancient mythical sites are littered with Coke cans. It is only fair to ask what it means to want to sweep them away, get them out of sight—Naipaul's "prettifying intention." What, for example, are they to be replaced with? Takeshi Kaikō's ironic response is that Japan might get revenge of a sort by exporting its distinctively shaped Ramuné soft-drink bottles back to the French, from whom their design was borrowed. Even though Japan has so long been sufficiently littered with purely native trash that it need no longer fret over that of foreign origin, the problem of "trash" itself will always somehow be identified as a foreign one, as we have seen in Mishima's blithe identification of the noisy transistor radio as just another demonic "Western" device.[17]

It does not help matters that Miyoshi apparently refuses to find any sort of epistemological break in the self-contained historical time of "Japan": he unproblematically locates the conditions of the *shōsetsu* lurking in what, in spite of his deconstructionist language, the reader is given to understand to be ten unbroken centuries of "Japanese literature." This idea seems not only no less mythic than but perhaps even coextensive with the unbroken continuity claimed in Japan for the imperial family. But there are too many problems with the funhouse mirrors, too many cracks and crazes and distortions, too many historical ruptures and fractures, to permit such blindness to its radical discontinuities. Perhaps more than anything else, such a claim only demonstrates the essential truth about the return of the repressed: the problems we think we have escaped, whether by psychoanalysis, Marxism, feminism, deconstruction, or any other critical attitude, have an uncanny way

17. Or (see note 15) as "pornography" is considered "foreign," in contrast to the more congenial native *ero* ("erotic"). The cultural formula *modern = foreign = pollution*, still functional today, appears to have been handed down intact from the Tokugawa nativist philosophers. Since it coexists with the opposing formulation *modern = foreign = stylish*, however, we might conclude that European style is attractive in part precisely because it affords the fetishistic excitement of a ritual pollution.

of showing again up at the back door to haunt those especially who have the most at stake in being rid of them.[18]

To be sure, as I suggested in Chapter 7, the late nineteenth- and early twentieth-century novel *is* predicated in part upon the experience of colonial empire with its shock, to all parties involved, of otherness and alienation. The modern Japanese *shōsetsu*, however, might be understood as predicated instead, if not on the *lack* of such experience (or at least the pretense of lack), on what the Japanese prefer to think of as a long experience of comforting cultural sameness and identity. Even at the start of its modernization during the Meiji period, that Japan was scarcely a Third World country was precisely the problem that so puzzled contemporary visitors such as Rudyard Kipling. Only relatively belatedly did Japan become modern enough briefly to possess a colonial empire of its own: Korea in 1910, then Taiwan, later Manchuria and Sakhalin, and during the Pacific War an appetite for China, the Philippines, and Southeast Asia. The same may be said of Japan's postwar experience as colonized (occupied) country and, in the view of many Japanese who still tend to think of themselves as having suffered a uniquely Japanese victimization, tragic casualty of Western technology.[19] This poses a quandary, one that perhaps lies at the heart of Ōe's vision of Japan as a Third World country: without the radical shock of otherness, after all, what is there against which to posit the idea of a self?

I once proposed that the otherness of China afforded the Japanese a dialectic of culture that would embody the terms in which Japan was to experience and express the modern intrusion of the alien West, and that the modern Japanese experience is perhaps best understood by seeing everything outside Japan itself—not merely the particular experience of colonization—as capable of providing that shock. This is to propose against Ōe's claim for a new Japan as a potential leader of the world's oppressed a sort of structural, consummately communal paranoia about what Japan is in the world. While the phenomenon of "Japan-bashing" is familiar enough in the United States, the Japanese press daily carries alarming articles whose burden is that "no one likes us because we're different," "everyone has joined against us because we're special," and so forth. It is little wonder that the major component of a rather halfhearted Japanese anti-Semitism (actually just one facet of a much broader xenophobia) is a backhanded sympathy for another group that is simultaneously acclaimed and persecuted for what

18. See Pollack, "Modernism Minceur," pp. 89–90.

19. There is an interesting view of Japan as having been victimized not by the West (or by the West alone) but (as well) by its own leaders, which seems akin to the disingenuous blindness of the postwar generation of Germans in dissociating themselves from their Nazi elders. See Makoto Oda, "The Ethics of Peace" in Koschmann, *Authority and the Individual in Japan*, pp. 154–70.

has often been described to me in Japan as "their unique talent for making money."

Each of the authors treated in this book has had to come to grips with this problem of what Japan is in the world in the context of his own time, and doing so does not appear to have been a very happy or rewarding experience for most of them. One is left with the strong impression that no one in Japan has ever again been quite as happy as Kita and Yaji, the comic stars of the picaresque Edo-period work *Shank's Mare* (*Tōkaidōchū hizakurige*, 1802–22), who clowned their way together down the road of life two centuries ago— unless perhaps we count the cheerful pornographers Subuyan and Banteki of Akiyuki Nosaka's equally picaresque modern novel *The Pornographers* (*Erogotoshitachi*, 1963) bumbling *their* way together through the dirty movie of Japan's postwar existence.

If there is such a thing as that "master narrative" proposed by Fredric Jameson of a "collective struggle to wrest a realm of Freedom from a realm of Necessity" (and I have no doubt that there are as many such narratives as there are different groups of people), then Japan's might even be quite the opposite, more resembling the Habermasian collective enterprise of binding the destructive force of the individual to the communal realm of social necessity. The answer appears to have been worked out so well in the two and a half centuries between 1600 and 1867, following the bitter experience of more than one hundred years of *ran* or civil chaos (a period which, oddly enough, now evokes a powerful Romantic nostalgia), that little since has seemed to offer as powerful a set of solutions. Individual longings for something as unsubstantial as "freedom" were referred and subordinated to a modified Confucian state ideology in the form of a hierarchy based on the ties of a pyramidal "family" (*ie*) that extends upward from the lowest commoner and downward from the gods, embodied and mediated in the person of the emperor himself (who is portrayed in Mishima's work as a pure white horse, in Ōe's as a Korean gangster, but significantly enough *never* as the emperor). Since early in the eighteenth century the great mythic precedent of this narrative has been enshrined in the forty-seven *rōnin* of the *Chūshingura* (Storehouse of loyal retainers) story, who enjoyed their just revenge but, like soldier bees, had to die for it.[20] Such a scheme responded to the notion of revolution by identifying it as exterior, alien, unnatural.[21] For better or for worse, a self-contained Japan has seen itself as thereby manag-

---

20. The seasonal locus (December 14) of this Japanese mythos of revenge as a reimposition of social order, falls roughly at that time of the year which is given over in much of the West to a mythos of sacrifice and the salvation of mankind.

21. In *The Fracture of Meaning* I analyze the exteriority of the idea of revolution: eighteenth-century nativist thinkers referred it to what they saw as the degenerate Chinese idea of a "mandate of heaven" that could permit such change, which they rejected as anathema to the Japanese experience of eternal continuity following the will of the gods.

ing so far to escape the calamity of either the radical republican or the communist solution, though it appears in the process to have remained obstinately unaware of the problems inherent in refusing the modernist one.[22]

It seems necessary, then, that we recognize this approbation of realm-wresting as a local and socially conditioned phenomenon, rather than a universal essence that can be applied everywhere (if anywhere) with felicitous results. Even Jameson is aware that the French mythos of "liberation" can plausibly be opposed to a German narrative archetype of "totality"—as if these two poles were able between them to summarize the experience of the world in all its particularity (though the Germans no doubt view the French as disorderly and the French find the Germans to be repressed).[23] In one sense, this distinction merely continues Descartes's earlier separation of the human into two camps, with the French and Germans now lumped together on one side and their common alien others, "Chinese and cannibals," on the other.[24] Only after the official euphoria of the bicentennial of the French Revolution had exhausted itself was it noticed that still to be accounted for (albeit without benefit of celebration) was the subsequent Reign of Terror, with its fearful suppression in the name of an ideological absolute of much that was good and decent. In Japan, too, authorities since the Tokugawa have been mindful of the power of the mob and the destructive consequences of its rule. This idea constitutes a powerful cultural essentialism which, lying at the very center of Ōe's novel *The Silent Cry*, generates its problematic resolution.

To one degree or another, as part of the social contract of any socially organized life form, the individual is finally subordinated to the welfare of the whole, but it is quite likely that the United States and Japan are even more distant on the spectrum of possible accommodations of the former to the latter than are France and Germany in Jameson's vision. It is even entirely conceivable that another culture should have raised a myth of dependence to the level that we have raised our myth of independence, and that it may prefer to comfort itself with narratives about its own utopia, based on the positive social virtues of communality, homogeneity, isolation, and hierarchical social relations; and to frighten itself with stories about another dystopic world, pulled to pieces by such negative and antisocial forces as license ("freedom"), mob rule ("democracy"), the breakdown of the social fabric ("ethnic and cultural diversity"), and alienation ("individualism"). We may have our own ideological reasons for disliking such stories, but one premise of this book is that—like it or not—others' ideologies, along with their manifestations in fiction, are not ours to will otherwise.

22. On refusing "modernity," however, see the Conclusion below.
23. See Jameson's foreword to Lyotard's *Postmodern Condition*, p. ix.
24. See the beginning of Chapter 1 above.

Chapter 10

The Archaeology of Difference:
Kenzaburō Ōe's *The Silent Cry*

The storehouse was in every station called the fetish, perhaps because of
the spirit of civilization it contained.
—Joseph Conrad, "An Outpost of Progress"

The concept of a "Pacific Rim" is perhaps more interesting for what
it conceals than for what it purports to reveal. Just beneath the exciting
images of new geographical communities bound by shared interests lurk all
the instabilities of the underlying geological structures known ominously as
the "ring of fire." We have invented a new metaphor for the encounter of
disparate cultures, one that uses the terms of the deep geology of plate
tectonics: as things heat up along the abrasive edges of these oddly shaped
pieces of the globe, unexpected instabilities and dimensionalities erupt that
are reflected in the coinage of tricky new terms like "drift" and "subduc-
tion." What appears to move one way on the surface may in fact be moving in
a very different direction deep below. The resulting earthquakes and vol-
canoes are only the external signs that, as Chinua Achebe has restated Yeats
in a new context, things continue to fall apart.

Since the discovery of the New World, the topography of the Western
imagination was last altered in a major way a century ago, with the populariz-
ation of Freud's theories of the psyche, which suggested that our separation
of a familiar and rational self from the bizarre irrationality of otherness was
scarcely constructed on the solid bedrock it had been imagined to be. Our
daytime mental world was instead complexly controlled by underlying night-
time forces, the two often incomprehensibly related. Freud's ideas reflected
Europe's deep involvement in the business of colonial empire and slavery,
enterprises repugnant enough to warrant their obliteration from the consciousness of people who had a stake in thinking of themselves, ambiguously,
as being more civilized "than that." In the topography of this new New World
of the mind, primal and potentially dangerous dark forces were subordinated

to more developed powers of light, inside and outside worlds constructed as mirror images of each other. The more developed powers found useful the rationalization that their mission was to rule benevolently over those primitive dark forces for their (again the ambiguity) own good. The uncharted new forces were relegated to a dark, hidden place, understood in metaphorical terms as the rank and teeming jungles of the unconscious mind. This repression was not the only price of sanity and civilization, however; the very fact of repression itself had to disappear from view, out of terror of what it told of the human condition.

Along the lines of the then fashionable axiom that ontogeny recapitulates phylogeny, the evolution of psychological self into social being provided Freud with a model for the evolution of the human species into civilization. Freud even framed his mistrust of the instinctual impulses in the common currency of the racial metaphor, couched in a revealingly aggressive language: "We may compare [the instinctual impulses] with those human half-breeds who, taken all round, resemble white men, but betray their colored descent by some striking feature or other, on account of which they are excluded from society and enjoy none of the privileges of white people."[1] The devious and treacherous lower elements, attempting to subvert the established social order, try to disguise themselves as us. Fortunately, however, they inevitably "betray" their real nature by some "striking" feature, allowing their "exclusion" from the "privileges" of their betters. Such a passage makes us marvel that Freud could, apparently without reflection, have made use of the very language then being directed in Vienna against his fellow Jews, whose assimilation into bourgeois society was increasingly the target of anti-Semitic investigations into such suspect stereotyped "striking features" as large noses, curly hair, and swarthy skin.[2]

Civilization could be seen, as Freud understood it in *Civilization and Its Discontents*, as comprising the totality of these necessary acts of repression and displacement of the primitive animal instincts, together with the acknowledged price inevitably to be paid for such an arrangement. The same argument has often been extended, by substituting Marxist terms for the Freudian, to an analogy between the conditions prevailing in the colonies and those among the working classes at home. The threatening and chaotic lower orders, wherever they existed, were to be kept in check at all costs.[3]

---

1. Sigmund Freud, "The Unconscious," quoted in *General Psychological Theory*, ed. Philip Reiff (New York: Macmillan, 1965), p. 138. I am indebted to Rajani Sudan for this citation.

2. See Carl Schorske, *Fin-de-Siècle Vienna: Politics and Culture* (New York: Vintage Books, 1981), pp. 185–88; for Schorske's discussion of Austria's two most important anti-Semites, Matthias von Schonerer and Karl Lueger, see pp. 120–46.

3. "The Growth of Empire was ideologically motivated, its major function being to intervene in what might otherwise have resulted in either a disastrous technological retardation or a violent confrontation at home" (Graham McMaster, "Henry James and India: A Historical Reading of *The Turn of the Screw*," *CLIO*, 18, no. 1 [1988]: 28).

It is no mere coincidence that Joseph Conrad's *Heart of Darkness* (1898–99) was written just when Freud was publishing his theories about the unconscious mind, its relation to the conscious and, even more problematically, to civilization. The world of Conrad's fiction is a complex two-dimensional flatland in which the fullness of white Europe is superimposed ironically over the emptiness of black Africa. The Thames, a mirror of the Congo, leads back into the thickening gloom of busy London exactly as the Congo leads into the darkest part of the "blank" Dark Continent. And Kurtz's chilling cry "The horror, the horror" is of course directed not at Africa at all but at the terrifying discovery of moral and social darkness at the very heart of the white man's lust for "Africa," at what Marlow calls "the fascination of the abomination." Conrad strips away pious European social and moral pretentions—discarded along the trail into the interior with equally irrelevant bits of ruined construction materials, useless clothing, and native carcasses—until nothing remains but ivory and greed and brutality and death. The psychological and moral depravity of slavery in the colonies cannot of course adequately be framed by recourse to a Freudian or Marxist analysis alone. Conrad's irony was aimed at the social Darwinism, in popular favor since the 1860s, which saw the idea of social evolution as justifying white European ascendancy over the benighted black races, as well as over its own working classes.[4]

In *Heart of Darkness*, the familiar and morally clear vertical dimensionality of Christian good and evil is replaced by an ambiguous contemporary horizontal juxtaposition setting an inner primitive darkness against an outer civilized light while ironically depicting these qualities, like the Congo and the Thames, as mirror images. The vilified and anonymous Company (which is "run for profit") is located in a "whited sepulcher of a city" understood to be Brussels; all that gleams in the dusky animation of King Leopold's Belgian Congo, however, is ivory and the whites of feverish native eyes. This ironic inversion is what distinguishes Conrad's technique of superimposition from the relatively straightforward correspondences of traditional allegory. Reflecting the increased effort required in an age of colonial empire and machine manufacture to sustain a gratifying distinction between good and evil, Conrad's irony marks in its dimensional complexity a further technical advance in the imitation of reality. The real triumph of European technology, both in science and in fiction, was its ability to miniaturize morality, just as it had such other indispensables of modern civilization as quinine tablets, Bibles, and weapons, to a size small enough to be carried about in the pocket for the more efficient management of its increasingly exploitative and profitable ventures abroad.[5]

4. See Patrick Brantlinger, "Victorians and Africans: The Genealogy of the Myth of the Dark Continent," *Critical Inquiry* 12 (Autumn 1985): 167–203.

5. Chinua Achebe takes quite another view of Conrad, who, he writes, "saw and condemned

Not long after the publication of *Heart of Darkness*, the Japanese writer
Natsumé Sōseki (who was studying in London at the time of its publication)
would write the story of his own horrified discovery of this same blank
emptiness in the human heart (*kokoro*) where there ought to have been
fullness, of benighted darkness where there was supposed to have been
enlightened illumination, of moral failure where there was presumed to have
been grace.[6] Sōseki's work is thematically similar to Conrad's, if rather more
schematic in its structure: the Japanese writer meticulously strips away, layer
by layer, the ancient Confucian social ethic, then in the process in Japan of
being repackaged to serve as the basis of a new ideology, to reveal the hollow
core at the center of the newly imported Japanese "self." That self appears to
echo Marlow's description of Kurtz who, for all his "magnificent eloquence,"
is "hollow at the core."

Conrad and Sōseki can both be thought of as having attempted a "novel"
archaeology of the human condition. What their respective excavations into
the soul's inner depths brought to light was the spiritual ruin, the fragmenta-
tion and degradation, attendant upon ambitions of empire. Conrad's work
was an autopsy performed on an England whose heart had been fatally
infected by its gangrenous extremities (or perhaps whose poisonous heart
had infected its extremities); Sōseki's was a prognosis of a Japan whose heart
had also recently become infected with this same Occidental fever for empire.

Archaeology, as one of the new sciences growing out of European colony
and empire, was employed (no less than missionary work) to rationalize and
even to front for them. Its purpose was the scientific excavation, classification, and analysis of the ruins of past civilizations in the search for the roots
of European greatness—and, by invidious extension, of others' failure to

---

the evil of imperial exploitation but was strangely unaware of the racism on which it sharpened
its iron tooth" ("An Image of Africa: Racism in Conrad's *Heart of Darkness*," in Achebe, *Hopes
and Impediments: Selected Essays* [New York: Anchor Books, 1988], p. 19). His criticism of
Conrad as racist is as true as it would be of any other writer of the time, but his attack on the
novelist for lacking the sort of modern morality unlikely to have been held by anyone circa 1900
seems misplaced. Although Conrad was as yet no more able than Europe in general to think
about the lives of real Africans, he *was* able to write about "Africa" not for the usual purpose of
revealing Europe's greatness but in order to expose instead Europe's moral depravity. The
difference is new and important. To the extent that the book never *could* have been the one that
Achebe has in mind (he evidently wants one more like his own narrative of Ibo life in *Things Fall
Apart*, written half a century after Conrad's book), it is unfair to belabor it for *not* being that
book. Achebe notes (p. 9) that the relationship between Europe and Africa in Conrad is an
ironic one, only to dismiss that irony as merely Conrad's way of "set[ting] up layers of insulation
between himself and the moral universe of his story." We must surely read Conrad's vision of
Africa as inevitably tainted by the larger racist and colonialist vision of his time, but we must just
as surely recognize that his novel advances beyond mere reflection of that racist and colonialist
vision, with consequences just as important for Nigerians who write novels in English as for
European writers.

6. See Chapter 2 above.

achieve greatness or, having achieved it, to hold on to it. To anthropology fell the task of classifying and analyzing the residue of contemporary human detritus left behind in the ruins of these past civilizations.

Sōseki's literary explorations share the ambiguity of this European attitude toward culture. As he unearthed the ruined past of Chinese civilization as a way of accounting for "modern" Japan—the task Japan would generally set itself in relation to China, one that continues to this day—his probing exposed the moral bankruptcy of the ideology of empire within which the archaeological method was itself embedded. If his archaeologizing was not yet motivated by a need to rationalize the exploitation and brutalization of others, it was only because Japan was not yet sufficiently advanced along the road to respectable colony and empire to require such technologically advanced and even novel fictional tools. If it is true, as Patrick Brantlinger has written, that one of the most common ways of rationalizing brutality is to create an other worthy of our brutalization, such remarks demonstrate that colonial and postcolonial Europe found itself in greater need of rationalizing its behavior with regard to China than to Japan.[7]

Kenzaburō Ōe (b. 1935), in *A Personal Matter* (1964), turns *Heart of Darkness* inward to articulate a vision of Japan as its own brutal "Africa." Surprisingly, however, Ōe has recently explained away as nothing more than "an image" his frequent early use of Africa—"a fantasized romantic haven from the real world rather than a place with ontological significance." As "an image," then, it is finally nothing much: "a lot of difficulties, full of sufferings, and yet romantic—that is Africa for me."[8]

For Bird, the protagonist of *A Personal Matter*, the map of Africa in a bookstore window cannot be brushed off so lightly: coveted with his whole being, it is a place every bit as morally blank as it had been for Marlow, a place of the same "unnatural death, raw and violent." Gazing at the map of Africa as a boy, Marlow had been fascinated by "a mighty big river that you could see on the map, resembling an immense snake uncoiled, with its head in the sea, its body at rest curving afar over a vast country, and its tail lost in

7. Brantlinger, "Victorious and Africans," p. 184. McMaster makes a provocative (if incidental) case for the nineteenth-century novel as the narrative of the problematics of imperialism and colonialism in writing of *The Turn of the Screw* as an example of the "Indian orphan" theme ("Henry James and India," p. 27): "If the tale [we can substitute "novel" in general] has at its secret center the protection of an imperial ideology, imperialism must have been capable of arousing anxieties urgent enough to warrant being assuaged." McMaster goes on to propose that even "the domestic novel must necessarily refer to the absent colonial system, at least implicitly: all novels between 1879 and about 1945 are, then, imperialist" (p. 29).

8. Sanroku Yoshida, "An interview with Kenzaburō Ōe," *World Literature Today* 62, no. 3 (1988): 372–73.

the depths of the land" (*Heart of Darkness*, p. 216); the map of it "fascinated me as a snake would a bird—a silly little bird."

Bird's very name suggests the debt Ōe's African imagery owes to *Heart of Darkness*. "Since I like Conrad," Ōe has allowed, "[Africa] is a Conradian image for me. . . . To me, Africa is what India or other Asian countries are to Western authors."[9] As "a Conradian image," Ōe's Africa certainly means more to his work than a mere "fantasized romantic haven from the real world." Bird's name is only one of many firm links that join Ōe's new cultural topography, haunted by "the fear that roots in the backlands of the subconscious" (6/209),[10] to the Conradian Africa he superimposes on Japan. The first chapter of *A Personal Matter* concludes with an episode of tribal warfare in downtown Tokyo: members of a street gang, "with the alertness of wild animals whose territory is being invaded" (12/213), turn on Bird, "in whom they had sighted an existence too feeble, and savage instincts had been aroused" (15/217). And this Africa/Japan double exposure is fixed indelibly in the episode's final image of a train which, passing overhead on a trestle, turns into "a colossal black rhinoceros galloping across an inky sky" (17/218).

Ōe quickly moves beyond Conradian double exposure, however, toward an even more modern technique of superimposed multiple exposure (also explored in "Aghwee the Sky Monster" ["Kaibutsu Aguii"], published the same year as *A Personal Matter*). It was in part this unusual use of imagery and language that would earn him a reputation as Japan's first "postmodern" author, although Erich Auerbach had shown twenty years earlier in *Mimesis* that such techniques as multiple consciousness and the complex stratification of time were by Virginia Woolf's day already established conventions of high modernism.

The technique of multiple exposure is introduced in *A Personal Matter* by Bird's girlfriend Himiko, who tells him about the "pluralistic universe" (*tagentekina uchū*) she ponders when she can't sleep at night:

> Every time you stand at a crossroads of life and death, you have two universes in front of you; one loses all relation to you because you die, the other maintains its

9. Ibid., p. 372. But what, one would like to know, about the "Africas" of Haggard and Hemingway? By specifying "India" rather than an undefined place of romantic qualities, Ōe seems to be unconsciously expressing a "Western" sense of loss of empire, a displaced nostalgia for a Raj of one's own. Yukio Mishima saw Ōe's "Africa" as merely the infatuation of a morally depraved Japan with "the primitive lifestyle of tropical third-world barbarians" and wondered idly why the subject should make him feel so angry ("Gendai bungaku no san hōkō," in *MZ*, 31:398). The answer is obvious: he saw in Ōe a whole Japan full of well-off spoiled brats who spent the 1960s rioting in the streets, and in Bird the passive victim of tragic circumstances who couldn't even rise to the level of a tragic victim of character—he hadn't any.

10. Page references in the text cite respectively Kenzaburō Ōe, *A Personal Matter*, trans. John Nathan (New York: Grove Press, 1969); and *Kojinteki na taiken*, in *Ōe Kenzaburō zensakuhin*, vol. 6 (Tokyo: Shinchōsha, 1966).

relation to you because you survive in it. Just as you would take off your clothes, you abandon the universe in which you only exist as a corpse and move on to the universe in which you are still alive. In other words, various universes emerge around each of us the way tree limbs and leaves branch away from the trunk. [58–59/250]

Himiko has arrived at a vision of herself at the center of exfoliating universes out of her profound need for solace. This philosophy allows her to believe that the husband who committed suicide in the universe they once shared continues to live on with her in another. As she explains it to Bird, however, it seems to amount to little more than a convenient moral expedient: in her view the deformed infant to which Bird's wife has just given birth can safely be left to die of starvation in the knowledge that in another universe the baby is well and thriving. Bird immediately sees that this glib rationalization is nothing but a "philosophical swindle"[11] she has invented "in order to rob death of its finality" (60/252), but he can no more muster the moral strength to resist its blandishments of cheap comfort than he can resist those of cheap whiskey.

If Bird's weakness in the face of ambiguity and arbitrariness is the very emblem of his modernity, his eventual discovery of moral strength seems too facile a way out of the modern dilemma. By the end of the novel Bird has narrowed the matter down to a clear existential choice: unable to let matters simply go on happening around him, he decides that he must assume personal responsibility and either kill the baby with his own hands or accept it and bring it up. Every reader must wish that Ōe had ended the novel when Bird makes his choice, abandoning Himiko to the easy solace of her "pluralistic universes," and rushes off in a taxi to rescue his baby from death. But the author went on instead to append a terrible resolution in which the baby undergoes successful surgery that may make it normal, and Bird, now a recovering alcoholic, decides to do penance by becoming a guide for foreign tourists—not in Africa but in Tokyo, which turns out to have been the real "Africa" all along. As in Ōe's later work, "Africa" turns out to have been in fact an empty "image" and never really a serious alternative—a problem to which I return at the conclusion of this chapter.

In *The Silent Cry* (1967), Ōe provides a more satisfying exploration of how his "pluralistic universe" might function beyond the limited roles, tentatively assigned to it in *A Personal Matter*, of solace or moral expedient for the weak. The work is set in a time full of resonances, exactly one century after the Meiji Restoration brought Japan into the "modern" world of the West with

11. Literally "psychological swindle" (*shinritekina sajutsu*).

its attendant crises of modernization. The story superimposes present and past in a series of worlds, each complexly related to the others. Thus, into the present 1967 narrative of the novel Ōe weaves stories of the violent student protests of the summer of 1960, a pitched battle between Korean and Japanese villagers in the summer of 1945, and two peasant uprisings: one violent and unsuccessful in 1860, another peaceful and successful in 1871. These events are connected through history and historiography, geography and topography, annual festivals and village rites, the psychopathology of family, myth and legend, letters and narrative—all joined through an act of narrative archaeology as the narrator/author literally digs into the earth to uncover layer after layer of narrative artifacts that demand to be reconstructed in some plausible relation. Only the narrative(s) resulting from such a reconstruction will make it possible to fabricate any meaning of the present.

The novel opens with the twenty-six-year-old narrator, Mitsusaburō (Mitsu) Nedokoro, emerging from his Tokyo home before dawn, adrift somewhere between memory and dream, to sit in the dark at the bottom of a muddy pit (excavated in his back yard for a septic tank) in order to sift through the personal and family ruins of his young life. The novel ends with the narrator sitting at the bottom of another pit, this one the recently discovered cellar of the ancient Nedokoro family home deep in the mountains of provincial Shikoku, pondering all that has transpired in between. The site of the novel's action is the rural village of Okubo ("Big Pit"), the family hometown to which Mitsu, his wife, his younger brother Takashi, and two of Takashi's young friends have returned in order to "begin a new life." The family name, Nedokoro, literally means "place of roots": "In America," says Takashi, "I often heard the word 'uprooted,' but now that I've come back to the valley in an attempt to make sure of my own roots, I find they've all been pulled up. I've begun to feel uprooted myself, so now I've got to put down new roots here" (59/64).[12] It is in the Nedokoro family home, "where the soul of the valley people has its roots" (132/143), that the narrator begins his proleptically anticipated archaeological dig into the crumbled and intermeshed layers of past memory in an attempt to excavate the "truth" of those roots.

What he discovers there, however, is no single Truth, but the multiple, competing "truths" of individual memories that constitute different possible worlds of interpretation. The narrative method is indeed "archaeological" in proposing to excavate this welter of mythologically rooted and historically conditioned worlds by digging down into the earth. While only one world can

---

12. Page references cite respectively Kenzaburō Ōe, *The Silent Cry*, trans. John Bester (New York: Kodansha International, 1974); and *Man'en gannen no futtobōru* (1967), in *Ōe Kenzaburō zensakuhin*, 2d. ser., vol. 1 (Tokyo: Shinchōsha, 1977).

be occupied at a time, each has been occupied in historical time, and historical time can be collapsed and unified through the ahistoricality of myth. This play of the diachronic dimension of history against the synchrony of myth accounts for much of the dynamic tension of the novel—but for inescapable problems as well; we shall have to ask ourselves whether Ōe adequately articulates and, finally, resolves them.

"Truth" exists as the property of individual characters in the form of unreliable memories, visionary dreams, and gradually uncovered private documents. It also exists, however, as communal property in the form of village lore, documents in the public domain, and ritually reenacted myth. To be sure, the line between the individual and the communal is a blurred and constantly negotiated one: recounted dreams become shared memories, shared memories become village lore, village lore becomes ritually reenacted myth, which after sufficient repetition achieves the status of history. Private documents also have a way of inevitably becoming public, though we find that even in the public domain they are no more reliable than any other private property. Nor is the narrator himself particularly trustworthy, since he has clearly abdicated any claim to absolute knowledge simply by permitting competing "truths" to contend side by side.

As in Ōe's earlier "Aghwee the Sky Monster," the narrator of *The Silent Cry* has one "good" eye, which can see only what passes for exterior reality, and one "bad" eye, which can look only inward on a more private and mysterious vision. He is thus both blessed and cursed with the unique ability to validate internal memory and dream against various competing external versions of "reality." To put the situation somewhat schematically: the transparent lens of the "good" eye engages in direct, analytical observation of external, public reality, the celebratory world of daytime activities staged by the Dionysian younger brother Takashi; the opaque lens of the "bad" eye speculates reflectively upon the Apollonian older brother Mitsu's own inner, anguished private world of dream.

This denial of binocular perspective has the effect of reducing the diachronic perspective of history to the flattened synchronic flatness of myth. Such an ecology of sight privileges the detached, contemplative subject,[13] alienating the subject who can only observe the action from the narcissistic object who can only be observed in action. The narrator/older brother thus distances himself from the younger, who acts out a scenario that could have come straight from one of Yukio Mishima's works. It seems no coincidence that Mishima was the person from whom Ōe has always been at greatest

13. See Martin Jay, "In the Empire of the Gaze: Foucault and the Denigration of Vision in Twentieth Century French Thought," in *A Foucault Reader*, ed. Paul Rabinow (New York: Pantheon Books, 1984), p. 179.

pains to dissociate himself. Nor is it entirely an accident, one imagines, that the elder brother Mitsu has set himself the task of translating the works of the zoologist Gerald Durrell, whose own younger brother was the far more Dionysian writer Lawrence.

As he sits in his muddy pit at the start of the novel, bad eye inwardly contemplating the thought of the inevitable decomposition of a friend who has committed suicide, the narrator considers two kinds of time: the "pure" linear time that forms the single arc of one human's birth, growth, decline, and death, and "that other kind of time, soft and warm as the top of an infant's head, that admits of repetition" (5/6). We saw in Chapter 8 that this same opposition of linear and cyclical time is a major theme of Mishima's tetralogy as well. Repetition here is not, however—as it was for Santayana, Marx, Freud, and very likely Mishima—merely evidence of man's failure to understand the significance of his own acts. For Ōe, as for so many Japanese authors, repetition appears to hold the central meaning of time itself.

The primary symbol of historical repetition in Ōe's novel is the peasant uprising (*ikki*), which he appears to treat as an authentically native consequence of Japan's particular form of traditional agrarian-based social structure. It is generally accepted that those uprisings followed a typical cyclical pattern. After legal appeals against unbearable conditions had been exhausted, no recourse remained to peasants other than violence. When violence finally exploded, the rigid feudal social structures that bound villagers and rulers together fractured and broke apart in the primal cataclysm of the peasant uprising, unleashing autochthonic forces from below to erupt violently against the confining structures that had given them coherence and social effectiveness. Loftier targets usually being inaccessible, it was the property of wealthy peasants, saké and soy brewers, and merchants—the nearest symbols of peasant frustration—that was usually destroyed in "smashings" (*uchikowashi*), riots of great destructiveness.[14]

The roots of Ōe's story are buried deep in the years immediately preceding the Meiji Restoration, when peasant uprisings were especially widespread but antiestablishment forces as yet too inchoate to offer a real challenge to the Tokugawa regime itself. Of the three major peaks of peasant uprisings during the 1780s, 1830s, and 1860s, the years 1860–67 saw by far the most violence. The Japanese title of Ōe's novel means literally "Rugby football in the first year of the Man'en reign period." As it turned out, the first year of that period, 1860, was its *only* year; the title of the reign period

14. See, e.g., Irwin Scheiner, "Benevolent Lords and Honorable Peasants," in *Japanese Thought in the Tokugawa Period, 1600–1868: Methods and Metaphors*, ed. Tetsuo Najita and Irwin Scheiner (Chicago: University of Chicago Press, 1978); and Herbert P. Bix, *Peasant Protest in Japan, 1590–1884* (New Haven: Yale University Press, 1986).

(see below) was changed the next year, undoubtedly because the outbreak of peasant uprisings had shown it to be an inauspicious name.

The chaotic state of the times can be gauged from one popular pocket history's abbreviated chronology of uprisings in the single year 1860:

Third month: 400 peasants riot against wealthy peasant leaders in Inaba.

Fourth month: 2,000 peasants in Tamba protest extortionate practices by saké brewers, moneylenders and landlords.

Eighth month: 18,000 peasants rise up against tyrannical government in Tamba in the Ichikawa Riots.

Ninth month: because of widespread crop failure, several hundred starving peasants roam the Uzen area pillaging for food.

Eleventh month: 2,000 peasants engage in "smashings" in the Tamba region to protest lowered rice prices paid by saké brewers.

Twelfth month: 500 peasants from twelve villages in Chikuzen Province riot against their local leaders.[15]

Though there were apparently few significant peasant uprisings that year in the area in which Ōe's novel is set (a tiny mountain village inland from the coastal city of Kōchi in the Tosa *han*, in what is now Tokushima Prefecture in Shikoku), it was rocked by nearly constant *ikki* in the years between 1865 and 1867. That such disturbances were a common fact of Tokugawa life is attested by the organizational scheme of the handy chronology from which the foregoing examples are cited: events before the Tokugawa period are listed under the heading "culture and personalities" and events after it under "culture and education"; during the Tokugawa period itself, however, the list is headed "culture, thought, and uprisings."

The internal dynamics of these uprisings has long attracted scholarly interest in Japan and elsewhere, among either those who would see them as somehow uniquely Japanese or, by contrast, those who see them as fitting a more universal (and generally Marxist) pattern.[16] A long-standing cultural mystique in Japan has imagined secret millenarian forces at work behind such uprisings, considering them "revolutions" (*yonaoshi*) in the most literal sense. One of the most widely read postwar works of Ōe's teenage years (mid-1950s to early 1960s), for example, was a comic book (*manga*) series by the popular cartoonist Shirato Sampei called "The Fighting Record of the

15. Tōkyō Gakugei Daigaku Nihonshi Kenkyūshitsu, ed., *Nihonshi nempyō* (Tokyo: Tokyōdō, 1984), p. 315.
16. These issues are summarized in a review article by Roger Bowen in *Journal of Asian Studies* 47, no. 4 (1988): 821–32.

Invisible Organizers," which portrays an unknown and unseen group operating throughout Japan's feudal period as the secret organizing force behind peasant discontent. As its anonymous members died, they were replaced by new ones; those whose names have been left to history were merely the apparent actors.[17] Writers of Ōe's generation were strongly influenced in their late teens and early twenties by such comics. This cultural phenomenon is reminiscent of the much older tradition in China celebrating the theme of righteous outlaws, most famously in the Ming novel *Shui-hu chuan* (translated into English successively as *All Men Are Brothers*, *Outlaws of the Marshes*, and *Water Margin*, and extremely popular in Japan after its translation into Japanese in the seventeenth century) and persisting in millenarian groups such as the Taiping "Boxers" of the late Ch'ing period.

For Ōe, what is especially important in the mystique of the *ikki* is its archetypal cycle of terrifying and chaotic excess followed by repentant expiation and the reimposition of order. The usually short-lived but intense violence, only rarely successfully directed against the authorities themselves, more often turned its fury upon the social fabric of village life itself, which then had somehow to be knit back together. As in Ōe's novel, these local events often pitted elder brother against younger, creating bad blood between relatives and neighbors which required some form of atonement or expiation. Instigators and leaders were almost invariably put to death by the authorities as a condition of the normalization of life for the rest of the community. If they did not do the honorable thing and give themselves up or commit suicide, they would most likely be yielded up by their own relatives and fellow villagers as martyrs to the necessity of communal harmony. Each turn of events in the novel proposes a different end for the younger Nedokoro brother, who led an uprising in 1860, subsequent theories holding that he was killed in the riot, allowed himself to be sacrificed afterward, committed suicide, escaped to foreign lands to write letters back home, or spent the rest of his life hiding in the cellar of his own house in the village and sending letters to his family purportedly from abroad. The ambiguity of his story blurs with that of Mitsu and Takashi's dead older brother, who died earlier as either the bold hero, the tragic victim, or the pathetic scapegoat of a pitched battle with the village's Korean settlement.

Ōe's novel is articulated around yet a further cultural essentialism: the belief that communal ritual, by drawing violent events into local lore and neutralizing them through their reenactment in village festivals, has the power to reestablish social order. The chief mediating ritual in *The Silent Cry* is the Nembutsu dance, which is performed each year as part of the traditional Bon celebration in mid-August. This dance, arranged and coordi-

17. Shunsuke Tsurumi, *A Cultural History of Postwar Japan* (1984; London: KPI, 1987), p. 34.

nated by the village tatami-maker and resident expert in matters of ritual protocol, is performed by masked and costumed dancers who assume the roles of the spirits of the dead to be reincorporated into the life of the community. Many of these spirits hail from so far back in the village's past that the present villagers can no longer recognize them. There is, for example, the spirit of the "Chosokabé," originally merely the name of the samurai clan that had for centuries held control in the area but now regarded as a kind of bogeyman useful for frightening children: "If you don't behave, the Chosokabé will get you." Other spirits include villagers who led violent lives or died violent deaths, such as those who died in the typhus epidemic that swept the area near the end of World War II. After Japan's defeat in 1945 the dance included figures in military uniform to represent villagers who died in the war, those who died like the eldest Nedokoro brother in a battle between the Japanese and the "Korean" villagers, and even one young villager who was killed by the atomic bomb in Hiroshima, "his whole body blackened like a lump of used charcoal" (125/125).

The Nembutsu dance is thus capable of absorbing and reenacting as legend *any* violence threatening the fabric of communal life. In its largest sense, the festival also structures Ōe's own narrative, since its final function in the novel is to absorb the terrible violence wrought by the story's own characters and reintegrate them into the larger community. This last function serves also to integrate the reader, horrified and alienated by the book's violence, back into the storytelling community (as we shall see, this becomes a problem when the community thus restored is understood to be Japan alone in the face of international threat; there is no ritual capable of absorbing the rest of the world "back" into Japan). The tatami-maker, who is forced to abandon the village after the new "Korean" supermarket's cheap modern floor coverings render his most traditional of trades superfluous, returns at the end to resume his old occupation of tatami-making and to represent the new "spirit" of the story's main sacrificial victim, the dead younger brother Takashi, in the annual village festival. It is in this nostalgic return to an idealized past that the story reveals its profoundly mythical nature, and in which lies its greatest problem.

On the cycle of excess and expiation of the peasant uprisings of 1860 and 1871 Ōe superimposes the extraordinary violence of the 1960 student uprisings in Tokyo against the Japan-U.S. Mutual Security Treaty:

> Takashi had originally gone to America as a member of a student theater group. Their leader was a Diet member, a woman from the right wing of one of the progressive political parties. The troupe consisted entirely of students who had taken part in the political riots of June, 1960, but had since thought better of it. Their play was a penitential piece entitled *Ours Was the Shame*, and was followed

by an apology to the citizens of America, on behalf of repentant members of the student movement, for having obstructed their President's visit to Japan. [12/18]

Once back in his native village, however, Takashi organizes among the village youths the rugby football team that furnishes the Japanese title of the novel. His ultimate aim in doing so is to prepare the players for an uprising against a Korean local known as "the Emperor of the Supermarkets," whose modern entrepreneurial activities Takashi sees, Mishima-like, as destroying the traditional life of the village. This man has bought up all the rice the villagers can produce, so that they are forced to buy their traditional holiday rice cakes from him at exorbitant prices. This grotesque parody of the Japanese emperor (along with the equally grotesque parody of a compulsively consuming modern Japan, represented by the enormously fat woman Jin, who gorges herself to death) is compatible with Ōe's own conception of a new postwar vision of Japan: "I have trod a path leading to the 'relativization' of an emperor-centered culture," he has said, noting emphatically that such a path is "exactly the opposite of that taken by Yukio Mishima."[18] The Korean has also made plans to buy the Nedokoro family home, the most important and imposing in the village, in order to dismantle it and rebuild it in Tokyo as a nouveau-rustic restaurant (the nostalgia of myth here seems tempered somewhat by an acute sense of irony). When this ruthlessly capitalistic "Emperor" and his goon squad finally begin to tear down the ancient house, however, they reveal a hidden cellar containing evidence of a "final" truth about the uprisings of 1860 and 1871. By the end of the novel even the "Emperor" has been absorbed into the Nembutsu dance and thereby reintegrated as a functioning member of the village community.

The plot of the novel is far too complex, and the structures that sustain it too closely interwoven, to permit more than this cursory adumbration. At this point I want to turn instead to the problem of how we might begin to understand Ōe's attempt at a new sort of archaeology of the past. We should first acknowledge that, unlike earlier writers such as Sōseki, Ōe is clearly intending to unearth not "origins" (whether empty or otherwise) but rather the more relativized modern concept of genealogical *relationship*. As he delves through the layers of the past, no single "truth" is finally turned up; instead, he inventively juxtaposes the various layers that are brought to light, each containing its own lode of possible "truth," to suggest a number of possible interpretive worlds able to accommodate the "facts" that have surfaced in the process.

18. Ōe, "Japan's Dual Identity," p. 368.

Ōe has recently written about "postmodernism" in Japan, which, he says, poses much the same problem there as does any *other* "ism":

> Young Japanese intellectuals [have] conjectured optimistically that, insofar as some cultural theory was in existence, a new one would follow if they simply added the prefix *post-* to the existing one. I am sure that there were not a few young intellectuals who were stricken by . . . self-destructive impulses when they learned that the concept of "post-such-and-such" was in fact insubstantial and when, in turn, they learned that the "such-and-such" thoughts themselves meant very little, if anything at all.[19]

While apparently continuing to essentialize Japan as a culture with a "remarkable [capacity] for absorbing new cultural theories," Ōe does worry that "almost no effort [has been] made to interpret them meticulously in view of specific situations in which Japan found has itself." One idea after another, he frets, is imported, translated, and discarded in the rush to the next, implying that this peculiar sort of frantic acceleration has itself been mistaken for a "postmodern condition." Ōe is especially concerned about what he calls "the absence of any and all effort to accept a variety of cultural thought synchronically," to allow for "the synchronic existence of two opposing new schools of thought—for example structuralism and deconstructionism—and the resulting combination of antagonism and complementarity, which can lead, in turn, to a mutual deepening of the two schools."

I propose that *The Silent Cry*, written twenty years before Ōe advanced to this concept of a vital juxtaposition of contradictory critical ideas (dialogism, we might want to call it today), can be read quite literally as just such an attempt to confront structuralism with deconstructionism. This incipient movement toward a deconstruction of the fullness of truth and presence and the search for origins, however, is almost entirely abandoned by the end of the novel in favor of the single overarching structuralist, socially saturated "truth" of a Japanese myth of "mediation" (*wa*), with its overtones of the "holonic society" discourse of contemporary social theorists Shumpei Kumon and Esyun Hamaguchi.[20] After initially distinguishing between two contrasting sorts of time, Ōe seems content in the end to allow the problematic nature of history, memory, and narrative to be entirely subordinated to the invocation of myth-ritual grounded in an autochthonous and unassailable sense of closed community. The narrator concludes that he can get on with his life (and once again face the existential choice, increasingly schematic and meaningless, between "Japan" and "Africa") only after the communal myth has successfully reintegrated the broken shards of violent events and

19. Ibid., p. 365.
20. See Chapter 1, notes 2 and 3.

shattered lives, and the uncomfortable multiplicity of the potential worlds they represent has been reduced to the unity of that shared myth's single world.

This problem is already concealed in the date indicated by the novel's Japanese title, literally in "The reign period 'Ten Thousand Years Prolonged,' year 1." Although this odd way of designating time—an auspicious-sounding name followed by the number of years it has been in use—goes back to the dawn of Chinese and Japanese historiography, it is only in Japan that it is still in use today. Every Japanese newspaper and magazine contains on its masthead two kinds of information: for example, that today is July 4, 1992, *and* that it is the fourth day of the seventh moon of the fourth year of the "Pacification Accomplished" (Heisei) reign era.[21] The Western notion of linear chronology, dating from a mythical if widely accepted conventional zero-point marking the birth of Christ, was not in common use in Japan until well into the twentieth century, and for strictly internal purposes it is still largely ignored. It means little to Japanese that I was born in 1942, for example, but everything that I was born in the seventeenth year of Shōwa. That information immediately identifies me not only as part of a certain generation but even as a type: everyone knows that Shōwa 17 is the Year of the Horse, which classifies me as a personality even more certainly than being born in late December makes me a Capricorn. The way one is thought of and treated by others is, for many social purposes, inscribed in the sign of one's birth (which is thus literally part of one's "character," for names are still often assigned in reference to the almanac).

From the point of view that time is something moving in this essentially cyclical fashion (the concept of *kanreki*, or cyclical time, is discussed in Chapter 8 above), the idea of a linear sequence of numbers stretching endlessly into the future (and negatively into the past) from some arbitrary reference point can only seem bizarre. For one thing it requires the odd notion of an origin, and for another it implies an end; and the idea that time should have a single beginning and end is ridiculous on the face of it. The idea of cyclical time avoids the problem, for in this kind of time Japan and its culture always has been and always will be, even as the teleological arc of the West "rises and falls" (many Japanese today have come to think of the popular Toynbean phrase as pretty well summing up the historical fate of the West).[22] What linear chronology fails to account for, what it is perhaps

---

21. "Heisei" is the title selected in 1989 by the Imperial Household Agency (*kunaichō*) for the present emperor's reign; my translation offers one significant alternative to the official version of these two characters: "Peaceful Accomplishments."

22. The words also resonate with the expression *seisui* ("flourish and decline") in the grand opening invocation of the great medieval romance *The Tale of the Heike* (*Heike monogatari*), the epic narrative of the Taira clan's rise and fall.

even meant to obscure, is precisely cyclicality, the most important quality of time as it is experienced by humans. The dominance of a concept of linear extension and mensuration began only with the introduction of the Western project of modernity. To imagine time as stretching endlessly is merely to render it meaningless and—even worse, as Mishima understood it—to imply the inevitable degeneration of some seminal impulse that cannot be renewed.

Ōe's choice of the year 1860 has its own problems: this "first year of Man'en," as I have pointed out, was the *only* year of that era and is thus an anomaly, a discrete point crying out for continuity in the succession of points that Ōe has provided to explore this phenomenon. Since the novel's temporal scheme makes it clear that no sense will emerge from linear chronological history, however it is excavated and reconstructed, meaning can finally emerge only from the cyclical sort of mythical time ("soft and warm as the top of an infant's head") contained in the novel's title. At the same time, however, we are confronted with the obvious irony that Man'en, whose name means "Ten Thousand Years Prolonged," endured even less than one full year (March 18, 1860–February 19, 1861). In the end, it seems, even this aborted scheme of cyclicality fails adequately to contain myth. Ōe would resolve this problem in his later work *Dōjidai geimu* (Simultaneous games, 1979) by frankly treating time as essentially arbitrary: because all events can be conceived of as taking place simultaneously (remember Ōe's earlier "pluralistic universe"), "one can choose a single reality quite arbitrarily, as if playing a game, and rearrange the history of mankind as one wishes it to be."[23] Ōe recognizes that the problem of arbitrariness, in other words, can finally only be resolved only arbitrarily.

The problem remains, we realize, that history cannot simply be rewritten "as one wishes it to be." Having accepted this rationale for arbitrary closure, Ōe abandons his archaeological methodology, sealing off its problematically ambiguous multiple possibilities. Unable to reduce competing realities to the truly aleatory, however, *The Silent Cry* finally takes refuge in notions of blood roots springing from the soil, the unique discourse of race, and a mythology of communal mediation of conflict. Although he seems to be speaking against such essentializations of culture, Ōe seems trapped by the sorts of essentialist reactions to the problems of modernity which have become the subject of recent Western criticism. Far from any "postmodern" resolution of the boundaries constituting the problem, this criticism observes instead a stubborn tendency in Japanese thought, postwar as well as prewar, to reject

23. Kenzaburō Ōe, *Dōjidai geimu* (Simultaneous games) (Shinchōsha, 1979), p. 491; cited in Sanroku Yoshida, "Kenzaburo Ōe: A New World of Imagination," *Comparative Literature Studies*, 22, no. 1 (1985): 94. See also the analysis of Michiko N. Wilson, *The Marginal World of Ōe Kenzaburō: A Study in Themes and Techniques* (Armonk, New York: M. E. Sharpe, 1986).

the very idea of "modernity" itself as something originating in (and plaguing) the West and therefore essentially alien. Rather than exbibiting evidence of what Lyotard has called a "postmodern condition," in other words, Japanese thought tends instead to return to an imaginary "premodernity" centering on a recuperated discourse of self-identity.[24] And while *The Silent Cry* has begun to entertain the possibility of an archaeology of real difference, it too finally falls back on the myth of an inescapably different and unique body politic through which such a discourse flows. In attempting to move in the opposite direction from Mishima, Ōe seems to have backed his way into his own trap of culture. If we compare *The Silent Cry* with the works of authors most often thought of as postmodern and postcolonialist in outlook and technique—Italo Calvino, Anton Shammas, Salman Rushdie, Gabriel García Márquez—Ōe's has the look of precisely the sort of gesture of self-stabilization which such authors rigorously resist.

With this problem in mind, we might reconsider Ōe's declaration of Japan's solidarity with "other" Third World writers and his idea that Japanese culture "could perhaps play a unique role among the cultures of the Third World."[25] Having often publicly emphasized the significance of Japan's own marginalized populations of ethnic Koreans and Okinawans, Ōe is clearly aware of the ambiguity of his position here. Even so, he seems to be entertaining the possibility that the domestic Japanese myth of *wa* or consensual mediation as a means of deterring chaos might prove suitable for export to that quarrelsome international community which has paid it so much attention of late. The mythic proportions of such a notion are evident in the persistence with which the author sees with the "bad" eye that reflects upon an imaginary interior world where problems are always successfully mediated, rather than with the "good" one that observes a stubbornly irksome and problematic exterior world which lends itself far less satisfactorily to such simplistic solutions. It is not merely that time as viewed through that bad eye is always "the first year of Man'en" rather than 1860; it is also, perhaps most significantly of all, *never* the present.

It is not only Ōe's agonized narrators who, maimed and passive, failing to find their way out of the endless two-dimensional surface of a self-contained, Klein-bottle idea of culture, vacillate endlessly between unacceptable alternatives: "Europe"? "Africa"? "Japan"? One thinks, for example, of the infantile wretches of Osamu Dazai's works or, more recently, of the Oblomov-like expatriate protagonist of Takeshi Kaikō's *Darkness in Summer*, who is if anything even more passive and inert in the face of the call to be "interna-

---

24. For criticisms of Japan's reaction to the idea of modernity, see Miyoshi and Harootunian, *Japan and the Postmodern*, and my response in "Modernism Minceur."
25. Ōe, "Japan's Dual Identity," p. 360.

tional," supine and paralyzed in the face of his impossibly deracinated existence, for all the world like a large beached jellyfish (see Chapter 11). It is a
posture reminiscent of the one that Edward Said claims to be characteristic
of not only past and present imperialism but of the postmodern condition as
a whole.[26] In response to the increasingly clamorous demands of others to be
treated seriously as equals, others who can no longer be dismissed with
either customary hierarchical condescension or dismissive idolization, these
characters are frozen into what Said (echoing Lukács) calls "paralyzed gestures of aestheticized powerlessness" and "self-conscious contemplative passivity."[27] Kaikō's character, however, is paralyzed precisely because he is
caught *outside* Japan; Ōe's, because he cannot move beyond that imaginary
line marking Japan as only one small part of a larger world in which Africa
actually exists as a nonrecuperable entity *outside* Japan, not merely as a
"romantic" metaphor for its own internal problems.

If Japan is to be neither "Europe" nor "Africa," exactly what it *is* to be
clearly will not be decided by someone cowering at the bottom of a hole in
the ground or in the gigantic self-contained nuclear bomb shelter of Ōe's
1973 novel, *The Flood Reaches unto My Soul*. Perhaps even Ōe, regarded both
at home and abroad as one of Japan's chief spokesmen for nuclear victimization, realizes that a post-postwar Japan cannot go on eternally reopening this
wound for the purpose of gaining public sympathy. The narrator who finds
himself in the bottom of the pit at the start of *The Silent Cry* is not even sure
whether to try to dig his way out and get on with his story or to claw the walls
down and bury himself inside, effectively putting an end to his difficult story
forever. What is certain is that by the end of the work he has succeeded in
digging himself even deeper into his own cultural predicament and, although
the terms are different, that it is still the same old predicament. It is not likely
to be Ōe's generation that will manage to dig its way to the place outside of
culture where, as Foucault writes, one must finally "think *that*." Ōe has given
Japan a new and more complex sense of the problems involved in the topography of its own internal depths, but the other side of that cramped world
is still a sort of mythical "China": a children's fairytale land of exotic impossibility on the other side of the world, where people walk about on their
heads.

26. Said, "Representing the Colonized," pp. 222–23.
27. Georg Lukács, "Reification and the Consciousness of the Proletariat," in *History and
Class Consciousness: Studies in Marxist Dialectics*, trans. Rodney Livingstone (1922; Cambridge,
Mass.: MIT Press, 1986), pp. 83–222. See also Jameson's development of this idea in *Marxism
and Form*, pp. 202–3, 386–87.

Chapter 11

The Escape from Culture:
Takeshi Kaikō's *Into a Black Sun*

> One of my major karmic missions this time around is to get outside of
> Japanese insular craziness, be international *assukikkaa, ne?*
> —Thomas Pynchon, *Vineland*

Takeshi Kaikō, who died in November 1989 at the age of fifty-nine,
will be remembered in Japan for two very different reasons. Some may recall
the gripping reportage, stories, and novels he wrote as a journalist in Vietnam
during the 1960s. But many more will remember him the way he undoubtedly hoped to be remembered: as a bon vivant who thought of himself as
Japan's—perhaps the world's—premier contemporary fisherman. Kaikō
covered the entire globe in his search for the perfect platonic form of Fish,
devoting stories, articles ("Fish On!"), books, documentaries, and TV appearances to reporting on his endless fishing (and gargantuan eating and
drinking) journeys to Thailand, Poland, Nigeria, Vietnam, Alaska, Israel,
Inner Mongolia—anywhere there were fish to be caught. Like riding the
world's railways for Paul Theroux, fishing was for Kaikō the perfect excuse
for adventure, always able to provide sufficient matter for writing. It was Life
Itself, and, miraculously, some editor was always willing to pick up the tab to
permit him to go "Further!" or "Deeper!" (the titles of two of his books on
fishing) in search of the Ultimate Fishing Experience. And, in his writing,
just as in *The Old Man and the Sea* or *Moby-Dick*, the primal struggle between
man and sea creature becomes a primary metaphor for life itself.

Two episodes involving fish in Kaikō's work, one set in Vietnam in 1964,
the other in the Bavarian Alps a few years later, seem to offer a summary
definition of humanity and delimit its place among the various forces at work
in the cosmos.

The first of these episodes, which appears in *Into a Black Sun* (1968), takes place outside the hamlet of Fai Fo near Danang in South Vietnam (10–20/109–17).[1] The unnamed narrator, who is covering the war for a magazine in Japan (we may as well call him Kaikō), encounters a platoon of South Vietnamese soldiers and their American "advisor," Captain Wain,[2] shooting up a large pond in the middle of the rice paddies while a group of reverent and alarmed villagers watches nearby. Wain explains to Kaikō that this is "Magic Fish Water" (the phrase is written in characters that read *mahō no sakana no mizu* but are glossed in the script used to transliterate foreign words to indicate the pronunciation *majikku fuishu uōtaa*), which the soldiers are busily "pacifying" with hand grenades and machine guns. A persistent rumor that the pond contains a magic fish capable of performing miracles of healing has led to such a crush of pilgrims—poor peasants and rich cityfolk alike—that the government, always fearful of enthusiastic outbreaks of popular superstition, has ordered the army to "pacify" the fish and display its body to the populace. (This tragicomic operation is appropriately a joint effort of the Ministry of Culture and the Ministry of Psychological Warfare.) But the magic fish, with its mysterious ability to migrate from one pond to another, cannot be found, to the disappointment and puzzlement of the soberly earnest Wain. "The strange thing," Wain laments, "is that whenever I turn up, the fish disappears. It's really weird. The VC cadres even brainwash fish" (16/114).

The attack on the Magic Fish is only one of several metaphors the novel deploys for the war in Vietnam. The South Vietnamese government, fearful of popular belief, can respond only by trying to annihilate it with the help of their American allies. The ridiculous act of blowing up fish ponds manages only to destroy precious resources and lives, yet for all their massive firepower the troops still cannot eradicate this powerful autochthonous force buried deep in the spirit of the countryside. For Captain Wain there is no great moral dilemma at work here; a soldier carries out his mission without asking questions and moves on to the next. But for Kaikō, for whom the act of fishing encompasses the most profound meaning of human life, nothing more powerfully demonstrates the senseless brutality and moral and spiritual depravity of the war than the sight of soldiers machine-gunning and hand-grenading fish.

1. Page numbers cite respectively Takeshi Kaikō, *Into a Black Sun*, trans. Cecelia Segawa Seigle (New York: Kodansha International, 1980); and *Kagayakeru yami*, in *Kaikō Takeshi zensakuhin*, vol. 8 (Tokyo: Shinchōsha, 1968). I have slightly modified some of Seigle's excellent translations for the sake of literal accuracy.

2. "Wain" is the translator's romanization of the Japanese transliteration *uein*, though for Kaikō's American army captain—rough-and-ready but fair, bourbon-swilling but tender, simple but earnest—"Wayne" might better capture the resonances of the popular 1968 film *The Green Berets* starring John Wayne.

The event recalls to Kaikō his own mother's powerful belief during World
War II in a popular ouija-board-like divination called *kokkuri*:

> While B-29s rained oil-and-sulphur incendiary bombs and "Molotov Bread
> Baskets" all about them, Japanese women would be busy seeking "Kokkuri's"
> forecast for tomorrow. When would the divine wind [*kamikaze*] blow? Where
> could they buy potatoes? Would there be air raids in the next place they were
> evacuated to? . . . A high-school boy in despair, I used to tear up the news-
> paper chart and throw it away whenever I found it. [15/112–13]

The "magic fish water" episode offers an example of what is unique in
Kaikō's work. He is either blessed or cursed with the ability to see everything
from a double point of view, but without being blind in one eye like Ōe's
narrator. His is a confusing binocular perspective that few Euro-Americans
in Vietnam would be able to lay claim to—or, even more important, would
want or have to claim. For like modern Japan itself he is obliged to see
simultaneously from two perspectives, that of the Westerner and that of the
Asian. Kaikō's greatest dilemma, and so Japan's, is to have to decide which of
the two perspectives represents his own, and the answer to this dilemma—
both and neither—is no easier to live with than the problem. His most
formative and traumatic memories are those of a fourteen-year-old growing
up in Japan during the terrible last months of World War II, when American
aircraft bombed and strafed Japan's cities at will, raining death and destruction everywhere. The most telling passage in the novel comes much later,
when Kaikō describes the horrors of those early days, which have left him
with paralyzing bouts of depression and anomie. Yet as an adult in the 1960s,
although he understands the complexities of his situation and is keenly aware
of its ironies, he has unaccountably come to be an ally of another generation
of those same Americans—aided quietly (if unenthusiastically) by his own
government—as they try to annihilate yet another Asian people.

Into a Black Sun ends with a terrifying account of a fire fight into which the
narrator stumbles during a news-gathering visit to the front. Living in and
reporting from Saigon, his old paralyzing depression stealing over him, he
feels compelled to go to the front in order to subject himself again to the
soul-defining black-and-white terrors of kill-or-be-killed warfare. In the
final scene, the platoon he is on patrol with finds itself caught in a withering
Vietcong crossfire. Stumbling over and shoving aside bodies alive and dead
in the common blind rush to escape the carnage, Kaikō finally reexperiences
the stark terror of his childhood—he and a friend were strafed in a field; he
lived, the friend died—that was to leave him as an adult paralyzed by simultaneous and contradictory messages of life and death. At the end of the work
nothing is left but the calm of the silent forest, the absolute experience of

that which simply *is*. Again the dead are all around him, and again he is still alive. Japan has survived and prospered, parading its nuclear victimization; America, striving for national amnesia, has shut down memory; Kaikō alone seems willing to suffer, together with Vietnam, the horrors and memories of the survivor. The horrors may be similar to those that will haunt Vietnam's American survivors, but the memories are a world apart.

The second of the two fishing episodes, which forms the climax of *Darkness in Summer* (1971), finds the narrator on a fishing trip to a lake somewhere in northern Europe (further detailed as a "highland lake in the Bavarian Alps" in Kaikō's 1979 story "Monster and Toothpick"). Having recently left Vietnam to live in Paris, the narrator has met a former Japanese lover there and returned with her to the German university where she is pursuing a doctorate. He leads an indolent existence of food, drink, and sex, but beginning again to suffer the familiar, ever-worsening bouts of debilitating depression that threaten to overwhelm him with complete paralysis, he hits upon the idea of a fishing expedition as a means of restoring his equilibrium. And indeed, for a while the trip works its anticipated miracle of recovery: for Kaikō, the mere act of fishing is itself enough to restore the short-circuited current of life. When he succeeds in catching an enormous and wily old pike, a sort of *genius loci* of the lake with mysterious life-giving powers reminiscent of those of the Magic Fish, life reaches one of its rare and transcendent epiphanies, not unlike the earlier calm of the jungle after the fire fight or, even earlier, of the boyhood meadow after the strafing: "We had been sitting for hours lashed by the icy rain, and my bones creaked all over when I rose. But it was all right now. I felt confident; I was reborn. Simple, completely fulfilled, and solid" (143/175).[3] Lovemaking follows, right there on the ground in the cold rain, and food and drink and talk—all the simple, elemental pleasures of life.

But then the couple returns to town: pre-unification Berlin, known only in the novel as "this side of the other side," a place epitomized in the experience of the sealed train in which one rides round and round seeing only the station signs of "this side" and "the other side." There, where the endless, indecisive oscillation between "East" and "West" is surely significant, Kaikō's depression begins insidiously to return. Discerning from sketchy news accounts the beginnings of the military buildup in Vietnam that will eventually terminate in the notorious bloody Tet Offensive, he decides that he can free himself of his debilitating anomie only by returning once again to

3. Page numbers cite respectively Takeshi Kaikō, *Darkness in Summer*, trans. Cecilia Segawa Seigle (New York: Knopf, 1973); and *Natsu no yami*, in *Kaikō Takeshi zensakuhin*, vol. 9 (Tokyo: Shinchōsha, 1971).

face the terrifying primal scene of combat between Asians and Americans. Everything else, including his frequent excesses of food, alcohol, drugs, sex, sleep, and even fishing, has ultimately failed to do more than forestall the existential agony for a little while. But Vietnam will oblige him to experience again the single emotion that has the power to tell him he is alive: the terror of death in war that he first learned as a child. "If you are not in the situation of killing or being killed," the narrator of *Darkness in Summer* tells his lover, "you can talk or argue about anything" (191/209–10).

For Kaikō, the war in Vietnam represents an extremely complex set of images: it is not merely personal but speaks to the dilemma of his very identity as a Japanese. Born in 1930, growing up during Japan's war years, and coming to maturity in the 1960s and 1970s, he and his generation are caught between cultures: they are both Asian and Western, yet neither quite Asian nor quite Western. As a sort of honorary white man in this American war in Asia against Asians (and he does not forget that it has also been a Chinese war, a Japanese war, a French war), Kaikō finds himself sharing many of the tastes of the American soldiers: their steak and bourbon, their stimulants and sins, their books and movies. Certainly his own life as a Japanese writer and journalist is closer to the urban and metropolitan experience of Europe and the United States than to that of the rural peasantry of a Third World country such as Vietnam. His is a life of brand-name consumption, of simulacra, of the technologically induced sensation of the virtual. Kaikō is certainly no rice farmer—even the Japanese rice farmer is no rice farmer, he notes, in the "Asian" sense of a lifetime of bare subsistence farming carried on from behind a water buffalo. In *Darkness in Summer* Kaikō mercilessly skewers (among others) the Japanese farmer who sits on his wealth of underutilized, overpriced, government-subsidized farmland and travels with groups to Paris in order to buy famous brand names at the headwaters.

Yet however Western he may be, Kaikō also demonstrates an ability to think, feel, and act as an Asian which sets him entirely apart from the Americans. During the Magic Fish episode, for example, he finds a Vietnamese Buddhist monk who speaks no English, but because the canon of Buddhist texts is written everywhere in East Asia in the same literary Chinese, Kaikō finds it possible to communicate with the monk in a shared *lingua sinica*, which he would have studied as a schoolboy in Japan:

In the shade of a pine tree, I spotted a yellow-robed monk praying. He was covered with sweat and dirt, and was obviously a mendicant. Most middle-aged monks here had some knowledge of Chinese Buddhist literature and were capable of communicating in written Chinese. I had often stopped at temples and conducted written dialogues with the priests.[4] My Chinese is neither literary nor conversational, just a random arrangement of characters, but somehow no priest had ever failed to understand my atrocious sentences; they always came up with answers. [This monk's] sentences were far better than mine, correct and refined, and his handwriting was superb. [*Black Sun*, 13/111]

Kaikō not only can communicate with the monk in a makeshift literary Chinese but also knows enough to recognize the important nuances of the man's literary style and handwriting. Although he reproduces their exchange in Japanese, we can get a feel for it from the terse closing salutation to the monk that is left in Chinese: *Shengan. Duoxie. Wo renshile duoshi* ("I'm deeply grateful and moved. I've learned a great deal"; 16/113). While the first phrase has a somewhat literary feel, the rest reproduces a quite colloquial and even idiomatic modern spoken Chinese. (The effect is a bit as if Hemingway had tried communicating with Italians in Latin, though in practical terms it more resembles a conversation between Hemingway and a Cuban in a Spanish that could never be mistaken on the part of either for Castilian.)

In this way Kaikō shares a dimension with certain Vietnamese (though not all by any means—only Buddhist priests, the many Vietnamese of Chinese ancestry, or those who for any reason have had occasion to learn Chinese) which is shared by no Westerner and which he shares with no Westerner. At another point in *Black Sun*, Kaikō as a Japanese novelist is invited to attend an underground meeting of a group of Vietnamese intellectuals—among them novelists, playwrights, and critics who work in Vietnamese, Chinese, French, even English—who gather secretly in Saigon and have produced an open letter to André Malraux (whose powerful novel of the Chinese revolution, *La Condition Humaine*, they would of course know) for internal discussion. They have written similar "open letters" to such figures as René Char, Henry Miller (whose work long after World War II was still forbidden in the United States and available only in France), and Martin Luther King; they have read Sartre, Camus, and Simone Weil together. I have never seen the existence of this important class of Vietnamese intellectuals so much as hinted at in any American work, fiction or nonfiction, perhaps because Americans no longer understand the idea of the committed intellectual. And it is doubtful that American novelists writing about the war in Vietnam would refer to the works or authors listed here, if only because they are so heavily colored by the French colonial literary experience. Besides Malraux, the

4. "Written dialogues" renders the word *hitsudan*, "brush-talk," an ancient term denoting the mode of communication first used when Japanese and Chinese monks traveled to each other's countries beginning in the sixth century A.D. The limitation is significant, however: only the "middle-aged" can communicate in this common language the young no longer learn.

parallel that comes most readily to mind is works of Marguerite Duras such as *The Lover* or *The Sea Wall*.

These people, who call themselves *évolués* ("evolved ones"), a colonial elite educated in France and returned to Vietnam, serve Kaikō as a mirror in which he sees himself unflatteringly reflected, together with the Japan he so frequently and openly scorns. These dedicated "writers, poets, and journalists disappeared, died suddenly, died mysteriously, committed suicide," he writes, whereas modern "Japanese intellectuals are a cautious and sensitive breed, veering constantly, reacting like statoscopes [*bikiatsukei*; we might have said barometers] to shifts in the political climate; for me, the Vietnamese who made their suicidal protests in that hermetically sealed political atmosphere shone through like beacons in a thick fog" (99/182).

Kaikō is constantly aware of the contrast between these people—who, epitomizing Malraux's ideal of *l'homme engagé*, live and die for their convictions—and their Japanese counterparts, who appear to waver with every change in the breeze (his most blistering attack on Japanese intellectuals appears in *Darkness in Summer*, 115–20/154–58). The West may think of Japan as Asian, but to Kaikō it does not qualify even as that:

> Abundant and poor, grand and ugly, frivolous and energetic, Tokyo was two thousand five hundred miles away. It was a tiring and relentless city. It was the only capital in Asia where none of the many protests and demonstrations of the past twenty years had ever resulted in martial law. Its crises never developed into an armed silence after 11 p.m., either in the streets or in the minds of its inhabitants. Set against the standards of Saigon, where curfew had become a ritual as familiar as breathing, *it was questionable whether Tokyo was really part of Asia at all.* [*Black Sun*, 148–49/218; emphasis added]

Perhaps it is possible in some sense to understand this feeling of civilized constraint, this un-Asian acquiescence to authority, as somehow "Western" in contrast to a First World view (Kaikō's adopted perspective) of the Third World as unruly and chaotic—though we need only recall the Tokyo student riots of the 1960s to refute such a notion. Nor need we mention that from a slightly broader world perspective the most purportedly "civilized" Western nations have scarcely behaved like angels.

Kaikō's vision of a seething, roiling Asia teeming with life lacks only the supremely transcendental holiness of the filthy and disease-ridden Calcutta and Benares of Mishima's *Temple of the Dawn* (the third volume of *The Sea of Fertility*). But the vitality of his Asia is, like Mishima's, foregrounded and heightened by the stench of decay and death in every imaginable form, and Kaikō clearly understands their inseparability. In one scene in *Black Sun*, for example, he has just witnessed the blood-drenched execution in Saigon of a nineteen-year-old Vietcong guerilla:

> Small black holes bored through his chest, his stomach, and thighs. From each hole, fresh red blood slowly welled out, and branching rivulets soon soaked his trousers and spilled onto the paving. The boy's head, hanging, swung slowly to the right, then left. An officer approached and, pulling out a pistol, shot him in the temple. Blood spurted and the body sagged, hanging away from the stake but held by the rope, immobile. His cheeks and neck were drenched with blood. Blood dripped from his nose like a lead sinker at the end of a long light line. [134/207]

In the next scene, seated at a French restaurant later the same day, Kaikō joins a colleague in a blood-rare Chateaubriand steak washed down by rich Algerian red wine:

> When I first drew my knife across the rare meat, fragrant with garlic, a puddle of pale red blood oozed out. I put my fork down and stared at the red liquid spreading over the white plate. A pink cross-section with its blackish crust was exactly like a wound—a wound where flies would swarm, sucking, feasting, fucking on some peasant's body found abandoned in high grass. I speared a piece of meat and chewed it slowly. It was succulent, delicious. There was no physical revulsion. No resistance on the way down. [136/209]

When he hankers for Western food, or when he is in the company of Westerners, Kaikō heads automatically for the Tour d'Argent, a tony Saigon hangout for journalists. But when alone or with Vietnamese, he gravitates by instinct to the back alleys of Cholon, the Chinese quarter of Saigon, where he can indulge a taste for the homely familiarity of rich, greasy, flyblown Chinese food and drink. In his 1978 story "Building a Shell Mound," Kaikō recounts a fishing expedition with "a bigwig among the Chinese in Cholon," a man who, like Kaikō, lives to fish. Before this Chinese-Vietnamese will accept the Japanese writer, however, he first probes his credibility as an Asian in a very Chinese way, quoting from well-known Chinese literary texts that Kaikō is expected to recognize as a sort of common cultural password. And even after Kaikō passes this test, there are always more to come: Can he recognize an allusion to a poem about a perch by the Sung poet Su Tung-p'o? The well-known passage by the philosopher Chuang Tzu about the butterfly? The famous T'ang poem by Chang Chi about sleeping at night on a boat moored on the river . . . ? Kaikō recognizes them all, and the man is satisfied; they are after all fellow Asians who share a common culture, and that—in the spirit of Confucius's words "all men are brothers"—is all the man need know about him. To the extent that they share that culture, the Chinese-Vietnamese and the Japanese are brother Asians under the skin. But this culture represents only half of Kaikō's heritage. For all his familiarity with China's greatest philosophers, poets, and novelists, for all his ability to quote from such disparate sources as Lu Xun and Wang Wei, *Water Margin* and *The Analects of Confucius*, Kaikō also finds important resonances in *Gulliver's Travels* and *A Connecticut Yankee in King Arthur's Court*—works he probably knew in common with fewer Westerners in Vietnam than he appears to realize. He mentions Dostoevsky's *The Idiot* once, but it is not essential, and in the heat of battle he tosses the book away. Like Malraux's *La Condition Humaine* for the French in Asia, however, Mark Twain's *Connecticut Yankee* seems to him especially applicable to the American experience in Vietnam (one wonders if Kaikō had read *Innocents Abroad*): "It was first published in 1889, but there were so many parallels to the situation in Vietnam that one couldn't simply shrug them off as coincidences" (43/137). His summary description of the work ends with the sorcerer Merlin's cackling imprecation "Ye were conquerors; ye are conquered! These others are perishing—you also!" before he too falls dead (45/140).[5] "The similarities overwhelmed me," writes Kaikō:

> Americans, English, French, Japanese, the Left, the unaligned, and Right: from almost every conceivable angle, people had written about the United States, its foreign policy in Asia, its military policy, and I had read many of them and been impressed. Yet none had the devastating reach of Twain's fantasy.
>
> I found all my answers in his amazing book. The Americans were spending astronomical amounts of money here, perhaps as much as six million dollars daily; and yet we'd known the outcome all along, from a novel written seventy-five years ago [that cost less than two dollars]. The war—its beginning and its end, its details and essentials, its accidents and its inevitable course—was all there, encompassed in this tale that combined Don Quixote and Gulliver. [46/140]

Twain, Kaikō thinks, seems to have foreseen everything, including losing the war in Vietnam: "Good will, he showed us, couldn't forestall *it*. The Caucasian fraternity couldn't prevent *it*. Anglo-Saxon kinship couldn't stop *it*. The absence of Communism couldn't hinder *it*. And King Arthur died, Sir Launcelot died, the Knights of the Round Table died, Merlin died. And the American died. The war died seventy-five years ago" (48/142).

5. Although the translator appropriately works from the original English here, Kaikō's text is clearly taken from a Japanese translation: "You may have won the wrestling [sumo] bout but you have lost the match! [Omaetachi wa sumō ni katte shōbu ni maketa no da!]." See Mark Twain, *A Connecticut Yankee in King Arthur's Court* (1889; London: Penguin Classics, 1986), p. 407.

During one of several talks with Captain Wain in *Black Sun*, Kaikō explains that, according to Japanese opinion polls reported in the press, 70 percent of the Japanese people are against the war in Vietnam. "There was a time when they believed that American democracy was based on fair play, but this war's terribly unfair. So America has betrayed democracy—that's how they look at it" (77/164). When Wain offers the usual rote responses of the well-intentioned American—we are fighting to prevent the spread of Communism, protecting Asia and Japan as well, it's they who are attacking us, and so on—Kaikō responds: "The point is that it's an uneven contest [elsewhere *anfeya purei*, "unfair play"] and ideology doesn't come into the picture. Charlie Cong is small, poor, and barefoot, and Uncle Sam is huge, strong, and rich. And you drop napalm and kill innocent women and children. You're a Goliath, so you should let David alone and stop killing the children" (77/165).[6]

But in spite of his personal sentiment against the war, Kaikō has adopted the attitude of professional journalistic neutrality, which allows him to evade the crucial moral issues involved in taking sides. Is he going to side with the goal of "Western democracy" to bring some sort of recognizable order to this chaotic Asiatic land even if it means Lyndon Johnson's vision of killing everything and everyone in it, all these fellow Asian men and their astonishing energies? Kaikō, after all, *is* one of those he despises: the Japanese intellectuals, "veering constantly," who congregate each day at the same cafe with the other journalists in Saigon to try to make sense of the war, for all the world "like a school of feeding fish":

> No outsider could hope to understand this war or have it well conveyed to him. Yet all these journalists used to fret that the odor of a red clay trench at night was hopelessly, irretrievably fading in the chilled air and coffee fumes; and, eyes glinting, in hushed tones, they'd rummage in their little bags of words and strain to give some tangible meaning to their experiences, though they knew it couldn't be done. And in the end, invariably, they'd draw a snap conclusion; and when the verdict was out, their look said somehow they'd betrayed themselves, lost face; but they couldn't resist the urge. [155/223]

When Kaikō writes again and again of his position in terms of "uninvolvement," "neutrality," and even "voyeurism" (71/159), we understand that he is speaking not just about himself personally but about Japan's postwar attitude of an expedient neutrality in world politics, which he sees as a purely

6. For all that it is appropriate here, there is nothing in the Japanese text about David and Goliath: "Whatever your ideology [*ideorogii*, ideologically motivated self-rationalization], as a great nation America should yield and put an end to this murder of children."

intellectual and situational commitment that runs counter to human emotions and moral values. Accompanying a platoon on a dangerous search-and-destroy mission, Kaikō refuses, as the code of the journalist demands, the captain's offer of a rifle "for self-defense," and then agonizes over this necessary decision precisely because of his own personal past *and Japan's*: "I sneered at myself for clinging to a precious neutrality, trying to keep my hands and nose clean even out here—allowing the curse of elitism, of pallid intellectualism, to follow me even this far. . . . For whose benefit was I trying to prove my innocence—hoarding a conscience that had grown rusty with disuse?" (35/130). Even though he cannot allow himself to act on the impulse to shoot back, which Wain justifies in the best American tradition as mere self-defense, he is still compelled to submit himself to the painfully remembered primal trauma of being shot at, and in so doing finds himself drawn into in a sort of willing complicity with this war on Asians. In the last analysis, he and Japan seem to need the war for their own reasons as much as the Americans do for theirs. It is perhaps a way of trying to recreate the trauma of defeat and at the same time identify with the victors; the trouble is that if America is not winning this war, then neither is Japan.

The uniqueness of Kaikō's observation of Vietnam derives in part from his ability to identify with the South Vietnamese, soldiers and civilians alike. Kaikō's descriptions of the American GIs are couched in a lexicon of large hairy bodies, steak and bourbon, fries and Coke, and the infinite technical details of warfare. Having established, in a brief conversation with Wain that opens the book, the exterior "American" frame of reference for his presence in Vietnam, he engages with Wain's Vietnamese counterpart, Lieutenant Binh, in the context of the game of Asian chess (*shōgi*) shared by Chinese, Japanese, and Vietnamese alike. Binh is a simple but wily man who wins nearly every game, letting Kaikō win occasionally only to permit him to save face—an Asian sensitivity to an Asian need that is of course little known among the Americans.

Kaikō emphasizes, however, that the Vietnamese and Chinese version of the game differs significantly from the Japanese in that "captured pieces can't be used against one's opponent; the enemy can't change his colors, and once captured he's dead" (5/105). Reflecting on the significance of this simple but important distinction, Kaikō writes: "I thought about Japanese chess as I made a move. I wondered who could have devised the Japanese rule, so subtle and vigorous, that turns an enemy into an instant ally, where a piece captured from an opponent can be dropped straight back into the enemy base, a private being promoted to a general. What war experiences in Japanese history could have inspired this stroke of genius?" (6/105). Heavily ironic here, Kaikō realizes that the single virtue the Japanese game glorifies is in fact treachery. In spite of the claims of the medieval warrior code of

bushidō as portrayed in famous fictional romances such as *Tales of the Heike*, it
was common in Japanese warfare for the cornered warrior to turn coat and
take his subordinates with him. For all that Kaikō would like to sneer at the
Vietnamese game as crude and simplistic, however, Binh defeats him consis-
tently: "Even with the simplest of rules, this chess had its own range and
depth, its own unique gambits. With no knowledge of them, I recklessly
challenged Binh with a game of different rules, and naturally got slaughtered
every time" (6/105).

This, of course, is precisely the Americans' problem in Vietnam. As Kaikō
puts it elsewhere, reporting a conversation among a group of correspon-
dents, the Americans are fighting like gentlemen according to Marquis of
Queensbury rules, while the Vietnamese are using the anything-goes style of
Thai kick-boxing. Wain echoes the common American complaint of an enemy that holds life cheaply: the Vietnamese are so poor, he grumbles, that
"they don't even have lives to lose" (19/117). (In a similar hyperbolic vein, he
says Vietnam is so humid that "everything [gets] damp in this country, even
the water.")

For all his intimacy with Jack Daniels, *Lolita*, and corn on the cob, Kaikō
writes of Vietnam in scene after scene with the sort of Asian recognition that
must necessarily remain permanently inaccessible to an American. He understands why Colonel Kiem should be called neither Buddhist nor Christian but rather Confucian; he likes to guzzle putrid gizzard gruel salted with
smelly *nuoc mam* bought in back-alley stalls; he appreciates the brushwork of
an decrepit but proud old master calligrapher who writes squatting on a
sidewalk without even deigning to look at the money his customers leave; and
he can read in the headlines of a discarded Chinese newspaper blowing
down the street that a French stripper is in town ("Thrills!" it screams:
"French Body Bomb Arrives!" [51/143]). His very language recognizes an
identity with the truly Asian beauty of this tropical land that we cannot know
(along with the miseries of the godforsaken war, American writers would
have to make do with the sunrises and sunsets, the jungles and the beaches,
the dope, the booze, and the women).

His descriptions of the life of the common people are earthy, redolent,
richly beautiful:

> On a dark corner, a storyteller strumming on a coconut viol wailed a forlorn tale
> about the rise and fall of some ancient dynasty. On roadside stands, Dunhill
> lighters were being sold along with condoms. There were shamans hawking
> tiger claws and elephant's hair. Perched on the shoulders of a man selling pets, a
> monkey and a parrot stared around with goggle eyes. The motor of a juicer
> whirred, squeezing sugarcane. In Cholon, the din of gongs mingled with the
> voices of young women moaning to the night sky, *"Aiya . . . ho!"* [54/147]

For the governments of *either* side, however, Kaikō reserves another, more brutal sort of language:

> An unqualified, uninformed, and unprincipled bunch they were; and their citizens were probed, examined, spied on, commanded, legislated, ruled, classified, educated, lectured, judged, reprimanded, and convicted. At every business transaction and fluctuation of the price index, they were registered, written up, investigated, fined, stamped, measured, appraised, taxed, exempted, confirmed, permitted, addendumed, admonished, interrupted, reformed, re-oriented, and rehabilitated. [101/183]

This is the common jargon of East Asian bureaucratese, recognizable immediately by its very appearance on the written page as the sort of lumpy, undigestible mass of Chinese characters that clogs official reports and newspaper articles and seems to serve only to grind the incomprehensibly variegated miscellaneousness of delicate human lives into the homogeneous stuff of official record-keeping. In either case, Kaikō's use of language seems inspired by the Rabelaisian excesses of Henry Miller, to whom he alludes frequently (certainly his specification in *Darkness in Summer* [39/98] that really good *rognons de veau* must retain a tang of urine is taken straight from such a work as *Sexus*).

With his instinctual recognition of the Vietnamese as people with whom he shares important if half-understood bits and pieces of a common culture, Kaikō is sensitive to elements in the relationship between the Vietnamese and their American "advisors" that the latter are rarely able to perceive and that very few American novels about the war seem able to pick up on. In one telling scene Kaikō describes a young Vietnamese soldier who has taken his machine gun outside on a beautiful sunny day to strip, clean, and oil it. While he is cheerfully and dexterously engaged in this handiwork, an American soldier happens by and begins to lecture him on how he *should* be doing the job. The transformation is immediate and complete: the Vietnamese soldier goes limp, his face turns vacant, and after a short while he simply gets up and walks away, to the consternation of the well-intentioned American:

> There are insects and animals that suddenly turn over and feign death when chased into a corner by a stronger enemy. It may not be a pretense, however, but something that physically happens to their body mechanism. The insect's nervous system may cause its legs to freeze in a conditioned reflex faster than its consciousness. In other words, it may actually be dead at that instant, the body's shutter closing automatically.
>
> The soldier's face had shown no resentment, hatred, scorn, or rebellion; that is, no indication of conscious resentment on his part; but suddenly he shut off, though his hands and legs still moved. [61/152]

There are in fact several different Kaikōs: the observer and the participant, the writer and the adventurer, the neutral and the engaged, the Japanese, the Asian, the Westerner. And even if they are generally at odds with one another, they are all still parts of the single Kaikō that narrates. In his work, unlike Mishima's, no single voice rises inevitably to silence all the others; indeed, as he self-consciously tries to explain to Wain, it is impossible to narrate in Japanese without taking into account the several sorts of "I" that constitute the individual—an idea that is of course incomprehensible to the American: "Unlike English, where 'I' takes care of all kinds of first person singular, there are numerous personal pronouns; so the choice of the 'I' form can determine the tone of the work. This is a difficult point, one that no other country's writers have to contend with. There is even a style in which you don't have to use a single 'I'" (75/163). As Kaikō warms up to his explanation, he notices that Wain's eyes are beginning to glaze over; how, after all, can this American—his sturdy Western "self" as firmly and uncompromisingly in place as his pistol in its holster—be expected to understand such nuances? There may be a dozen different problematic Kaikōs, but there is only one unproblematic Wain. It is a little like a Hindu trying to explain to a Christian, Muslim, or Jew about yet another deity that requires worshipping.[7]

Kaikō's lecture to the Westerner on the complexities of written Japanese recalls Masao Miyoshi's discussion of "its tendency to omit the subject, especially the first-person pronominal subject, in its sentences," and "its writing medium whose ideograms resist being spoken aloud."[8] But it also smacks of the American's lecture to the perfectly contented Vietnamese soldier on cleaning his machine gun—and elicits exactly the same glazed reaction from Wain. True, if Japanese literature can be said to differ from that of other cultures, then these are precisely the sorts of grounds on which those differences must be established. But Kaikō's urge to rehearse these matters to Wain—and at just the point when the Japanese has managed to work up a fine anger toward the entire self-righteous Western project of saving Asia from itself—can also be understood as prompted by the ever-present modern discourse of *nihonjinron*: that almost automatic impulse to "explain" Japan, both to oneself and to others, in terms of a cultural uniqueness behind which the Japanese retreats in order to seal off his problematic identity from the presence of an alien otherness. It is rather like the squid fleeing behind its portable cloud of ink from whatever it perceives as a threat.

7. Mishima, comparing Ōe's prose style with Kōbō Abé's ("Gendai bungaku no san hōkō," p. 397), offers an observation in somewhat similar terms: Abé's prose, he says, is "forbiddingly monotheistic" as it "gazes coldly across the world of his work," whereas Ōe's barrage of metaphors with its "verbal eros" is "seductively polytheistic."

8. Miyoshi, *Accomplices of Silence*, p. 179.

This is not to belabor either Kaikō or Miyoshi but to point out that just as the Americans in Kaikō's book seem childishly to expect everyone to love them for their eager sincerity, their self-righteous assurance, their material abundance, their technical gadgetry (indeed, their sheer physical size), the Japanese writer seems to hope that by perfecting a studied, chameleonlike camouflage, a mysterious insubstantiality of character,—a lack of pronominal referentiality—he will be able to trick everyone else into failing to notice that he is there at all. Having too many *I*'s can perhaps be a convenient excuse for refusing to have one at all at crucial times.

In what must seem to Wain an ultimate demonstration of some sort of Oriental mysteriousness, Kaikō asserts that the essence of his Vietnam can be reduced to the insubstantiality of its *smells*; in an equally definitive gesture of American pragmatism and missionary zeal, Wain speaks of a "*mission* in life"—which, perversely, seems even more unsubstantial to the Japanese. Wain says:

"I mean it's up to you, but if it was me, I'd be writing about my purpose in life. Smells disappear, but one's mission doesn't."

"It doesn't?"

"Of course not."

"But the interpretation of man's purpose changes with time. Smells don't. Sweat smells of sweat, and papaya of papaya. I know papaya doesn't smell of anything much, but its odor doesn't die out, and it doesn't change. I want to write about smells that don't fade."

Teeth clenched on a cigarette, leaning back behind the hibiscus, I was thinking that novels begin to rot from their adjectives, just as corpses begin to rot from the most delectable parts: the eyes and intestines. The captain might just be right. If missions were bones, they would last, be exposed after everything else dissolved; but what bones remained after a smell had gone? [76/163]

Not only has Kaikō reached a complete impasse with the American here; he has managed to reach one with himself as well: he is no longer certain what is right or wrong. What is clear, however, is that the American will never change his mind about such matters (to be fair, Kaikō's novel also features in a cameo role an elderly Quaker whose conscience has brought him to Vietnam to save lives rather than take them as everyone else is doing). At this point, feeling compelled to retaliate somehow, Kaikō tells Wain that according to one survey seven out of ten Japanese think the United States is in the wrong in Vietnam, and has the satisfaction of watching him react to this unpleasant news like a man who has just been kicked below the belt. It may be out of some sort of need to atone for this bad behavior that in the next chapter Kaikō viciously skewers the Japanese community in Saigon as they observe their most significant holiday, New Year's Day (which significantly corresponds to that of the solar Julian calendar used in the West rather than the lunar calendar used in China and Vietnam). The ludicrous scene in which the people gathered for the festivities at the Japanese Embassy suddenly panic at the mention of leprosy, quickly remove all their clothing, and spread it with their money in the sun to be disinfected is one of the nastier bits of self-satire in Japanese literature.

If Kaikō believes in anything at all, it appears to be the humanity one discovers in doing simple, harmless things. He has an almost Taoist faith in the lowly and even the useless, and a Taoist's profound distrust of great ideas and elaborate technology (a feeling shared by many Americans who sought answers to the debacles of the era in various back-to-the-land movements). "I've been in countless workshops and come to know the gentleness of things," Kaikō writes:

> Useless objects, the kind that clutter vacant lots, and tools like lathes—there's no real difference, each is pure and vigorous, yet complete within itself. Stoking ovens or kneading dough, my old attacks [of anomie] would often reappear and lay their stifling hands on me; but standing at a lathe in the corner of some small plant where the smell of hot metal and oil hung round me like the soft sunlight from a window overhead, I found an inner peace and joy. The sight of a delicate yet powerful bit, without fuss or hesitation, cutting into the body of a metal cast was almost sexual. I could keep going all day on just a pack of cigarettes. My mind was blocked and rusty, doubting everything, but in my hand I held an absolute conviction that shaped and moved things and created value. I knew no doctrine I could kneel before, but worshipped things. [176/240]

The work of the great Chinese Taoist philosopher Chuang Tzu in passage after passage makes this same point that man's greatest happiness lies in the skillful use of simple tools and the avoidance of doctrines one might kneel before.

At one point in *Darkness in Summer* Kaikō and his girlfriend in Paris stroll to a nearby park where two local characters in particular have caught his fancy, simply two of the many "eccentric" (*kawatta*) sorts that haunt the neighborhood. One is an old man who has the knack of throwing five cardboard disks into a small circle chalked on the pavement in such a way as to make them touch without overlapping. It looks easy, but no one else ever seems able to manage the feat. When Kaikō's girlfriend fails to do it and complains that she feels somehow cheated, Kaikō responds that such is "the art of a great master" (*kyoshi no shigei*).

The other eccentric is the "Frog Man," who collects money by assembling a crowd to watch him calmly swallow a frog and then, after a short interval, belch it back up unharmed. The man and his frog have been earning a living this way since Kaikō first encountered them three years earlier. "Lao-tzu would have been delighted to see him," says Kaikō. "Sloth is the True Way" (35/96).[9] He is one of Chuang Tzu's large cast of skilled master craftsmen content to spend their lives performing their humble trade perfectly over and over. The girlfriend tries to argue that the ridiculous frog act would appeal more to an absurdist, Ionesco or Beckett, but Kaikō demurs: "No, Lao-tzu. Look at him. He has no air of tragedy. He's content. The theater of the absurd has none of his style. The laughter of the absurd is sophisticated but it's convulsive. There's no abandonment. It is a sudden attack. I'd rather take this man, if I had my way. As a matter of fact, I've been thinking he might be used in something, a novel or a play" (36/96). And while they talk, the Frog Man, perfectly aware that no one is watching him any longer, swallows and belches out his frog one last time just for the joy of it, then carefully washes the creature off and slowly walks out of the park into the Paris evening.

Even as Ōe struggles frantically to dig himself out of Japan only to find himself mired ever more deeply, Kaikō has written himself around the world and back a dozen times. He has what Ōe has lacked since *A Personal Matter*: that lightness of being which signals the ability to hold multiple points of view simultaneously, to be inside oneself and outside at the same time. And this, we recall, is also what characterizes Kipling's vision of Japan and is lacking in Barthes's: the ability of the deracinated colonial to understand the essential difference between himself and those others among whom he lives, a difference that remains a purely hypothetical construct in the hands of the comfortably French semiotician. It is the vision of the North African *pied-noir* rather than of the Parisian, the old India hand rather than the bureaucrat in Whitehall. What saves Kaikō is his fishing, for it is probably as difficult to become sententiously theoretical about fishing as it is about frog swallowing.

Ōe has suffered the sad but understandable fate of becoming canonized in the Japanese school curriculum much as J. D. Salinger was in the American, selected for the edification of the young by teachers to whose generation his work once spoke directly. Haruki Murakami, a middle-aged icon of the young whose style is obviously influenced by Ōe's work, refers to him in his novels as an already canonized Great Writer. In *Norwegian Wood* (*Norueii no mori*, 1987), for example, Murakami's young protagonist Tōru Watanabe—a sort of cross between Ōe's Bird and Salinger's Holden Caulfield—finds in a small neighborhood bookstore only cheap mysteries, historical novels, popu-

9. Kaikō uses a Chinese expression of three characters intended to parody the look of Taoist writing; however, no such dictum as "Sloth is the True Way" (*lai shih chen*, perhaps to be read in Japanese as *monoui kore wa makoto*) appears in any canonical Chinese text.

lar romances, and the usual gamut of how-to books: "That's it," he says. "No *War and Peace*, no Kenzaburo Ōe's *Homo Sexualis*, no *Catcher in the Rye*."[10] Elsewhere, listing the sorts of writers he likes, Murakami mentions popular writers—Truman Capote, Scott Fitzgerald, Raymond Chandler—but not, he says, the "greats" such as Ōe and Mishima that everyone else in the college dorms is reading. Ōe must understand the irony of being read by a younger generation for whom he has become an assignment on a course syllabus rather than a necessity of life—not to mention the terrible historical fate of being lumped together in the same sentence with Mishima![11]

Murakami's students resemble the Bird of *A Personal Matter* before he has made his rather wretched peace with life; but now—alienated, cool, free-floating, affectless, watchful ciphers who, obsessed with death and suicide, numb themselves with booze, drugs, sex, music, and pinball—they resemble Fitzgerald's characters more than they do the bizarre and driven Bird, and it is little wonder that the book Tōru mentions most frequently is *The Great Gatsby*. Even the title of Murakami's 1980 work *Pinball, 1973* (*1973-nen no pinbōru*) is clearly a parody of Ōe's "Football, 1860" (*Man'en gannen no futtobōru*, translated into English as *The Silent Cry*). Murakami's characters are as incapable of perceiving their lives in terms of myth or history as Ōe's would be of seeing theirs in terms of rock-and-roll or pinball. The difference in generations seems as absolute as a wall.

Kaikō has successfully staked out the vital space between the safe shallows occupied by Murakami—whose characters seem all talk and no action—and the horrifying and dangerous depths inhabited by Mishima, for whom action alone is enshrined as the final and absolute imperative. Like Mishima, he recognizes the fatal ineffectiveness of introspection ("Talk is syphilis, self-knowledge is syphilis. To me, peace is syphilis" [*Darkness in Summer*, 199/215]), but unlike Mishima, he also recognizes the impossibility of an outdated and romantic ideology of action, the futility of taking up the gun for the purpose of affirming one's own existence, whether through murder or self-murder. In the end, it seems, there is only fishing, and somehow Kaikō manages to convince us that nothing else could be as important, nothing as significant—unless, perhaps, it is the pragmatic, unmysterious, and un-Oriental art of frog swallowing.

---

10. Haruki Murakami, *Norwegian Wood*, trans. Alfred Birnbaum (Tokyo: Kodansha International, 1989), 1:119; *Noruuei no mori* (Tokyo: Kodansha, 1987), p. 78. The work by Ōe referred to is the as yet untranslated 1963 *Seiteki ningen* (Sexual man, sometimes referred to in English by the title "The Perverts").

11. The young Honda in Mishima's *Spring Snow* similarly shudders to think how future generations will inevitably lump him and Kiyoaki into a homogeneous group with their witless, sports-loving school chums (S91/H108).

Conclusion
Narrative and Ideology:
Toward a Practice of Reading

> It is time for us to turn our attention to the nature of this civilization on
> whose value as a means of happiness doubts have been thrown.
> —Sigmund Freud, *Civilization and Its Discontents*

As my contrasting paradigmatic examples of Rudyard Kipling and
Roland Barthes suggest, Japan has exercised a powerful and various fascination on the Western imagination. Viewed from the outside, Japan appears an
endlessly intriguing culture, and to live there—as countless writers from
Lafcadio Hearn to the most recent resident foreign correspondent attest—is
to have a sense of peeling away at an enormous onion, layer after layer, with
no expectation (or indeed worry) of ever getting to the core. Rather, the very
essence of "Japaneseness" itself comes to seem to have something to do with
this act of peeling.

The Western resident in Japan sets to work at a chosen part of the onion,
be it martial arts, Nō drama, Zen, flower arranging, tea ceremony, language,
literature, politics, or business (the increasing numbers of non-Western resident aliens, often illegal, have little leisure from their menial *gastarbeiter* jobs
for such cultural diversions). After years of growing mastery, outsiders who
have slowly begun to think of themselves as Japanese may even begin to be
accepted by country village or city ward and allowed to participate in local
festivals, helping in the sanctioned role of "strange foreigner" (*henna gaijin*)
to carry the portable shrine from which the local deities survey the boundaries of their ever stranger domains. Some foreigners stay on forever, happy
as clams in seawater.

For most, however, there inevitably comes a rude moment of awakening, or perhaps a crescendo of increasingly rude moments. Perhaps one has spent years mastering a traditional art, being told encouragingly that "you understand us even better than we do ourselves," only finally to be told that "foreigners can never really understand us Japanese" and that at best one will only be able to teach to or perform with other foreigners. Or one has married a Japanese, only to find one's children officially and unofficially denied acceptance as Japanese citizens. Or one discovers that businesses prefer to buy at almost any price from fellow Japanese than at a lower price from foreigners, "in order not to disrupt traditional arrangements." Perhaps after many years, then, one returns for good past the ALIENS sign that welcomes foreign travelers at Narita airport immigration control, going back to the "home" to which one had been expected to return all along, with a bitter sense of having been forced to leave home instead.

After my own first stay of three years, I left Japan with ambivalent feelings of regret and relief, resigned to living the rest of my life as an American—*not* because I felt that it was necessarily better to be one or that America was inherently a better place, but because I knew I would never be simply accepted in Japan. And I did not intend to live my life as a gaijin—not merely, like the expatriate, someone by definition permanently out of place but someone unwanted as well. To have lived in Japan is, inevitably, to have been caught up as a foreign body in the endless self-enclosed discourse of Japanese identity and to have finally been ejected from that discourse rather the worse for wear.

That it is not only foreigners who find Japan endlessly fascinating is evidenced by the very existence of the popular "discourse on Japanese identity," *nihonjinron*, that occupies so much of the nation's collective time and energy. Long accepted in the West as offering unique insider (in social science jargon, *emic*) views of the mysterious onion, this entire discourse has recently come under increasing attack from outside Japan precisely for its central role in manufacturing both mystery and metaphors such as that of the onion (there are also a green tea theory of Japaneseness, a tofu theory, a rice theory . . .). During the 1960s and 1970s, Western observers were fascinated with works by Japanese authors proposing the Japanese to be a unique race possessing a unique sense of language (Susumu Ono, Shōichi Watanabe, Takao Suzuki), philosophy (Tetsurō Watsuji, Kitarō Nishida, Daisetsu Suzuki), psychology (Shōma Morita, Takeo Doi), social structure (Chie Nakane, Shumpei Kumon, Esyun Hamaguchi), and even brain function (Tadanobu Tsunoda), to list only some better-known examples. This reception has more recently turned to disenchantment with such ideas as just plain silly, empirically wrong, or, perhaps most damaging, intimately linked not only to the sort of aggressive "Japan, Inc." world view and behavior that have so frequently irritated Western observers but to the very heart of Japan's pre-World War II fascist state ideology.[1]

Peter N. Dale's study *The Myth of Japanese Uniqueness*, offering a thoroughgoing if somewhat eccentric and always highly tendentious analysis of *nihonjinron* ideas, illustrates the recent trend toward disenchantment.[2] Dale is bothered by those "works of cultural nationalism" which are "concerned with the ostensible 'uniqueness' of Japan in any aspect," and "hostile to both individual experience and the notion of internal socio-historical diversity."[3] The first part of Dale's objection shares much with most recent Western writing concerning *nihonjinron* claims to Japanese uniqueness in the world. The issues raised in the second half, however, offering Dale's particular reasons for finding *nihonjinron* ideas objectionable, are both less commonly raised and more central to my own project of reading. Among the major postindustrial powers, Dale argues, the Japanese alone have failed to become modern in a world in which all the other major players have succeeded in doing so (though such a claim might be construed as offering still further evidence of Japanese uniqueness). Instead, he says, the Japanese—like the prewar Germans from whom they adopted so much of their common social currency about racial homogeneity and cultural uniqueness—have fallen back on an outmoded fascist ideology that refuses to admit the growth of a healthy individualism and insists instead on an exclusive sense of social homogeneity. His argument thus relies on at least three assumptions which my own study treats as problematic at best: that modernism is inherently good; that individualism is inherently healthy; and that social homogeneity in a Japanese sense is somehow more pernicious than its manifestations elsewhere in an increasingly fractious and discordant post-Cold War world.

Dale traces the origins of what he perceives as this Japanese ideological

1. It is worth noting that a great deal of postwar *nihonjinron* writing was stimulated by Ruth Benedict, *The Chrysanthemum and the Sword: Patterns of Japanese Culture* (Boston: Houghton Mifflin, 1946). This study, commissioned during the war, was the first to propose that "the Japanese" should be understood as a race motivated by a comprehensive set of concepts setting them apart as universally different from Westerners.

2. Peter N. Dale, *The Myth of Japanese Uniqueness* (Kent: Croom Helm, 1986). A recent study framed in social science format and complete with statistics is Ross E. Mouer and Yoshio Sugimoto, *Images of Japanese Society: A Study in the Social Construction of Reality* (London: Kegan Paul International, 1990); although expressing a need to supplant *nihonjinron* with more acceptably "scientific" studies, it does not argue, with Dale, that the genre itself demonstrates a profound failure of social discourse. Among the earliest and most forceful *nihonjinron* debunkers has been linguist Roy Andrew Miller, see esp. in *The Japanese Language in Contemporary Japan: Some Sociolinguistic Observations* (Washington, D.C.: American Enterprise Institute for Public Policy Research, 1977); and *Japan's Modern Myth: The Language and Beyond* (New York: Weatherhill, 1982).

3. Dale, *The Myth of Japanese Uniqueness*, [p. i].

failure to the last years of the Meiji period, especially the crucial years 1906–11 when, having emerged after military victories over China in 1895 and Russia in 1905 as the only modern Asian power, Japan turned its attention inward to the creation and enforcement of an official ideology of homogeneity in an attempt to protect what it perceived to be its fragile "national polity" (the infamous *kokutai*) against the destructive influences of the Western world. Rather than contend for a modern identity with the West, Dale argues, a profoundly reactionary Japanese ruling elite, in firm control of the media and with the collusion of the intellectuals, crushed the budding diversity of voices within and invented in place of a real discourse of mutual human relationships a paranoid and monovocal one of the uniqueness of the Japanese and their desperate place in a world of hostile others.

What gives Dale's analysis a certain strength, apart from its inclusiveness, is his willingness "to treat this mythological ensemble [*nihonjinron*] as a social ideology," rather than as merely a loose collection of more or less silly studies by variously respectable or disreputable Japanese academics. In doing so he moves beyond recent single-issue studies, including those tracing *nihonjinron* ideas back to the Tokugawa nativist thought fostered during the period of the insular mentality of the exclusion edicts. As an analysis of social ideology, Dale's work is modeled on Tatsuo Arima's earlier thesis of a "failure of freedom" during the experiment in democracy of the Taishō period (1912–26), focusing on the ideological issues involved in what Dale sees as the critical failure of the attempted modernization of the preceding Meiji years.[4]

Because a "reductive unmasking of this ideological facade in terms of economic interests and social control appear[s] insufficient" to Dale, however, he goes even further and places place his Japanese subject on the couch of Western psychoanalysis. This is unfortunate, for the result is his discovery in *nihonjinron* ideology not merely of the underpinnings and the sign of fascism but, in an attempt at a sweeping psychobiography of national character, of an entire nation characterized by a fundamentally perverse infantilism that stubbornly refuses to grow up and become modern like everyone else (though we certainly saw something like this in Tanizaki).

In constructing a mythology of culture which denies the existential distinction between "I" and "Thou," and in supplanting that original and ineluctable

4. Ibid., [p. iv]. While acknowledging that there were some intellectuals "whose lives and works were committed to the preservation and promotion of constitutional government," Tatsuo Arima, *The Failure of Freedom: A Portrait of Modern Japanese Intellectuals* (Cambridge, Mass.: Harvard University Press, 1969), p. vii, argues that "the Taishō intellectuals on the whole failed to support these thinkers in their efforts to perpetuate that form of government, known as 'Taishō democracy,' which might have guaranteed their intellectual freedom." Arima's concluding text (p. 215) is from Sōseki, who wrote in his novel *Passers-by* (*Kōjin*), "I have no other course for my future but to become insane, to die, or to embrace religion."

estrangement between self and other with the cosy affirmation of the identity of subject and object as an ethnic ontology, the mandarinate legitimates a world in which neither the individual nor the group may obtain a pregnantly dialectical relationship of enhancing exchange. . . . In such a world of contrived discourse, one is permitted no ripe articulation and reciprocal expression of instructive difference, but only a fallow and banal silence, a dumb solidarity of the unknown self with an unknown world.

This is Dale's conclusion, which begs a question central to my own study: why should that "ineluctable estrangement between self and other" be so desirable (or for that matter ineluctable), that "cosy affirmation of the identity of subject and object" so objectionable, from any other than the purely Eurocentric modernization-theory point of view whose necessity and superiority Dale takes for granted?[5]

Dale's is the vision of Karel van Wolferen in *The Enigma of Japan*, which portrays Japan as an oppressive state whose power—occulted through an ideologically watertight construction of a homogeneous culture defined entirely by a rigid inclusion of all those within the group and an enforced exclusion of all others—fails with fiendish cleverness to be traceable to anyone who can be blamed for what the author perceives to be its terrible effects on an unwittingly oppressed citizenry. For all that the Japanese are evidently willing to complain about the same sorts of things as people in any other country (high prices, despoliation of the environment, erosion of traditional values, foreigners), such criticism cannot but seem inappropriate applied to a Japan where the benefits of remarkable economic success, the world's lowest crime and highest savings rates, superior medical and educational systems, and a larger proportion of the populace enjoying the comforts (and curses) of a middle-class lifestyle than almost anywhere else on earth have combined to persuade the inhabitants that a certain amount of spiritual discontent may indeed be the necessary concomitant of civilization. (Dale also seems unaware of the possibility that, for all its problems, general affluence may more quickly than anything else produce the sort of change he apparently favors. If it is taken for granted that *we* always have good intentions, however, then the problem clearly must lie with the bad intentions of others.

5. Dale, *The Myth of Japanese Uniqueness*, pp. [iv], 223, 116–72 (esp. the concluding passage). In his first chapter, "The Otherness of the Other," Dale dismisses the kinds of questions I have asked in this book as a Western "failure of nerve," characteristic of the "cultural relativism" of those who have performed "critical self-lobotomisation" upon themselves. While we seem to agree that Roland Barthes's *Empire of Signs* reveals much more about Barthes's inability to get beyond the fascinating interior of his own mind than it does about Japan (p. 4), Dale's view of Barthes (and of Edward Said as well) is perhaps even more disenchanted than either my own or Philip Thody's (see the Paradigm above).

Dale's argument for what he sees as Japan's failure to come to terms with modernization centers on an analysis of the period of social ferment following the end of the Russo-Japanese War (1904–5), a period marked by unprecedented migration from the "traditional" countryside to the problematic modern city and its concomitant social unrest. In 1906 the prewar Japan Socialist party was created (only to be outlawed by the government the next year), and the first thesis of a national socialist philosophy of state was put forth by Ikki Kita in *The National Polity and Pure Socialism* (his more comprehensive *Outline Plan for the Reorganization of the Nation*, 1919, would become a guiding light of later right-wing zealots such as Mishima).[6] By 1911 the state had made clear its intolerance of left-wing political dissent in the infamous trial and execution of Kōtoku Shūsui and eleven other socialists on charges of treason against the emperor; the case tied together what the state had come to regard as "the twin subversive elements of socialism and individualism."[7] A famous passage from Nagai Kafū's essay "Fireworks" (1919) is usually read as pointing to the shameful silence of writers at the time: "Of all I had experienced in the world to this point, it was this incident which filled me with the most inexpressible loathing. As a literary man, I ought not to have remained silent about this problem. Didn't Zola cry out for justice in the Dreyfus affair and as a result have to flee France to live abroad in exile? But, along with all the other literary men, I said nothing."[8]

In his overview of the intellectual contexts of the development of *nihonjinron* ideology during this period of intense national political turmoil and state reaction, Dale properly cites (among others) the folklorist Kunio Yanagita's "discovery" of an "authentic" native Japanese folk (*minzoku*) in *Tōno monogatari* (Tales of Tōno, 1910); the philosopher Kitarō Nishida's idea of a uniquely native dissolution of the alienation between subject and object in *Zen no kenkyū* (A study of good, 1910); Shōma Morita's development around 1909 of a theory of a uniquely Japanese sort of neurosis brought about by contact with a West that thinks too much; Tsunetsugu Muraoka's revitalization of Tokugawa nativist thought in his monumental study of its primary exponent Motoori Norinaga (*Motoori Norinaga*, 1911); and Hajime

6. See Takehiko Noguchi, "Mishima Yukio and Kita Ikki: The Aesthetics and Politics of Ultranationalism in Japan," *Journal of Japanese Studies* 10, no. 2 (1984), 437–54.

7. Rubin, *Injurious to Public Morals*, p. 8.

8. Nagai Kafū, "Hanabi," in *Kafū zenshū* (Tokyo: Iwanami Shoten, 1962), 15:12 (my translation); see the full translation in Edward Seidensticker, *Kafū the Scribbler* (Stanford, Calif.: Stanford University Press, 1965), p. 46. Kafū's cynical conclusion is that writers have no business with politics, and he declares his intention to live out the rest of his life recreating for himself as writer the humiliating and dissipated lifestyle and art of a long-vanished Edo period. See Arima, *The Failure of Freedom*, p. 52, and Rubin, *Injurious to Public Morals*, pp. 192–93. Kafū's withdrawal from the world of politics may perhaps more usefully be interpreted as the traditional posture of the disaffected *bunjin*, or literary man, so often adopted over the centuries both in China and Japan in the face of a dangerously destructive state authority.

Kawakami's opposition of a unique Japanese sense of "nationality" (*kok-kakushugi*) to a Western "personality" (*jinkakushugi*) in *Nihon dokutoku no kokkashugi* (Japan's special nationalism, 1911). Dale is certainly correct in observing that these few years saw the creation of a telling mass of significant texts making the case for a uniquely Japanese national character.

Though claiming not to wish to tar all Japanese with the brush of ultranationalist thought, Dale does find in "the Japanese" a "stubborn, parochial tendency to regress from the modern" which permits little hope of the possibility of independent thought. Even "if the mere complexity of socio-economic life in Japan should suffice to expose the presumptuousness of a style of pseudo-intellectual chat about 'us Japanese,'" he writes, "powerful institutional forces and interests still aspire to sustain the fictions of socio-psychological and racial homogeneity"—an accurate conclusion similar to Harry Harootunian's far less cautious assertion that the "Japanese will never be able to break away from nativism."[9] If the latter is indeed the case, then the prospect for mutual understanding seems gloomy, if not entirely hopeless.

It would be instructive to test the texts examined in this book against the vision of an apparently incorrigible Japan to see whether, as Dale argues, a profoundly paranoid and reactionary Japanese ideology of culture has indeed rendered hopeless all possibility of polyvocality, of tolerance for diversity, whether from within or without. If so, then my intial plea for "heterogeneity" can only amount to what Dale anathematizes as a weak-kneed endorsement of a pernicious insistence on an exclusive and racist sense of homogeneity—though even if this were the case, it would be more useful to think of it as a problem the West also confronts in itself, as well as in resurgent fundamentalist and nationalist movements around the globe, rather than in a somehow uniquely intransigent Japan alone. Although I have clearly moved in this direction when I find in Mishima, for example, this sort of intransigent monovocality, I have emphasized as well the impossibility of such a project.

Indeed, I would propose that a self-contained discourse of identity has not eliminated all possibility of polyvocality if only because it *cannot*. First, the claim of any near-totalitarian flattening of the cultural landscape—at either extreme of the political spectrum—does not take into account the problem-

9. Dale, *The Myth of Japanese Uniqueness*, p. 10; Hartoonian, *Things Seen and Unseen*, p. 437. Harootunian has more recently suggested, however, that even "nativism" is not a monological discourse, seeing in the work of Yanagita and other folklorists an effort to create an ideology of an "authentic folk" that could compete with the modernizing urban state ideology (denied as inauthentic) and the socialists (as foreign and left-wing), as well as the *kokugakusha* nativists themselves (as un- or prescientific). See his "Disciplinizing Native Knowledge and Producing Place: Yanagita Kunio, Origuchi Shinobu, Takata Yasuma," in *Japanese Intellectuals during the Interwar Years*, ed. J. Thomas Rimer (Princeton: Princeton University Press, 1990), pp. 99–127.

atic nature of the novel which, in any but the most ruthlessly totalitarian environment (a description that may have described Japan in the fascist 1930s and 1940s but not in the Meiji and Taishō or postwar years) tends to be inherently intolerant and even subversive of official ideologies and cultural norms. What has been called the "naturalist" novel of the late Meiji period had as its goal the description of *the world as it really was;* it emerged specifically in relation to that other major opposing fiction, the state ideology of *the world as it should be*—which is to say the antique vision of a traditional community ruled by an idealized Confucian social morality and entirely unconcerned with the messy problems of human life as it is actually lived.

Even the aspirations of naturalism cannot entirely explain the inherently subversive nature of the novel, however, for all novels can be found to conceal agendas running counter not only to the intentions of the state but even to those of their authors.[10] One need not even agree with the full agenda of deconstructionist thought in order to make such an assertion. The history of Western hermeneutics, after all, has its origins in centuries of frustrated attempts to corral vagrant interpretations of holy writ into unified orthodoxy; and more recently, Freud's principles of parapraxis, displacement, and projection, as well as Marxist and semiotic investigations into the function of narrative, have confirmed that any assumption of fiction's unitary nature and simple innocence is extremely problematic.

A strong case can and has been made in support of those writers whom Dale's study either dismisses as a class of collaborators or ignores altogether.[11] In tracing the history of government censorship during the Meiji years, for example, Jay Rubin has found that novelists and critics, if scarcely uniformly libertarian, in fact often displayed the courage of their personal political convictions: "In relations between writers . . . and the Meiji state, we encounter the familiar Japanese pattern of avoiding confrontation, but this is by no means the dominant pattern. While outright bans were often faced with silence or resigned hopes for ultimate vindication by the historical process, there were also organized protests, bursts of outrage, and long and impassioned arguments for artistic freedom."[12]

But even this merely confirms that, short of massively thorough totalitarian measures, it is more difficult to cow writers into silence than either the Meiji state had imagined it could do or than Dale seems to believe it actually did. In contrast to Dale's assertion of a "fallow and banal silence,"

10. This point is examined at some length at the end of Chapter 4 above.

11. Dale does examine Tanizaki's work, but his analysis is forced into the service of demonstrating that the author was deeply implicated in *nihonjinron* essentialisms—which is to demonstrate very little, since it is equally true of every Japanese author of the time. I have tried to show that, more important, their work can be seen as simultaneously resisting these same cultural essentialisms by subverting them *even as they work within them.*

12. Rubin, *Injurious to Public Morals*, p. xiv.

Masao Miyoshi argues that modern Japanese authors have constituted a unique community of "accomplices" to a unique "silence" broken only by acts of exclusion and suicide. By remaining entirely within text and biography, however, Miyoshi's assertion ignores not only the political dimensions of the problem explored by Rubin but, perhaps even more significantly, ignores the ways in which the inherently subversive nature of the novel inevitably works against such a claim.

Within a political context, this subversive function seems less some mysterious property of texts themselves than what might even be considered a natural economy of art: as in the parable of the rivalry between the sun and the wind to see which could make a man remove his coat, the state probably more effectively stifles dissent (always short of the sort of brutality the "enlightened" and "liberal democratic" Meiji state could scarcely afford) by co-opting artists with money (and not merely honors), thus blunting their cutting edge, than by attempting to proscribe their work, which only sharpens it. Much of what Dale refers to as the "coziness" of the modern *nihonjinron* discourse can be traced to the specific mechanism of the Meiji censorship system, especially the government's refusal to engage in censorship prior to publication or even to spell out clearly the limits of the unacceptable. Instead, as an extension of the old Tokugawa laws enforcing "mutual responsibility," the government specified that publishers were to incur the entire cost of printing a run *before* turning a novel over to the censor for review, leaving them liable to large financial losses or even prosecution and imprisonment should the work then be found by the state to be (as the code ambiguously put it) "injurious to public morals." Authors also suffered directly from this practice: if their work was banned, they were customarily expected to return any advances against royalties they had received from the publisher. Nagai Kafū's *Furansu monogatari* (French stories, 1909), for example, was banned the same day it was sent to the censor; although Kafū professed himself unconcerned (as he saw it, writers and censors were not even the same species of animal), he was outraged at his publisher's demand that he make good the entire anticipated royalties on the first edition.[13]

Government policy did not merely threaten publishers and authors with fines and incarceration, however; it also encouraged them to engage in informal "private consultation" (*naietsu*) with the police and the censors beforehand to determine whether a given book might later be found problematic.[14] Once such a self-policing mentality was successfully fostered among publishers, there was little need for direct suppression except to set the occasional example. It is clear that part of the "coziness" of relations

13. Ibid., pp. 5, 117.
14. This seems quite similar to the so-called *shidō*, or informal "guidance," which industry is encouraged to seek from appropriate government agencies today.

between the government and the press can be attributed to the ruinous consequences of overstepping carefully undefined limits, together with the favorable results of preemptive negotiations.

A point of no return in the formation of novelistic careers was reached with the flowering of the "naturalist" movement after 1908, when authors began to think of themselves as no longer merely socially despised purveyors of vulgar entertainment (as they had been considered the Edo period) but as a group of serious and socially involved activists on the side of modernism and change, in opposition to government attempts to stifle change and uphold the dead hand of tradition.[15] It seems ironic if inevitable that the more actively the state tried to stifle or co-opt these increasingly self-conscious authors, the more rapidly they moved in the direction of principled opposition.

Japan is a modern postindustrial society as well as an (ever less) picturesque place of rice paddies, shrines, and temples. But even in its modern condition, to those outsiders who have come within its sphere as well as to insiders, Japanese culture still retains an intensely complete and seamless feel—the feel of a premodern, tradition-oriented culture with that "thickness" of Clifford Geertz's Bali about it which is perhaps only another way of suggesting the "thinness" of modern Western cultures. To propose to "read against" such a powerfully close-knit construct amounts, from within, to an act of betrayal and, from without, to the sort of gratuitous belligerence invariably referred to by the Japanese media as "Japan-bashing."

To say this is not to make yet another claim for "uniqueness" but rather to acknowledge that a high degree of ideological manipulation is indeed required to fuse such disparate quantities as export conglomerates and flower arranging in a society in which major Japanese corporations, for example, provide and encourage training in the traditional arts for their employees. The mechanisms by which the Japanese "culture" funhouse is created and maintained are exactly those of any other; there are merely more mirrors, arranged more densely and reflecting one another more intricately, resulting in that feeling of whole-cloth seamlessness. The assembly line worker is given instruction in the tea ceremony, the office worker is sent to a Zen monastery for training in meditation, the retired worker joins a haiku poetry club: from cradle to grave, it seems an unusually full-participation society.

America, to the contrary, is typically experienced by Japanese visitors as unconnected, sparse and lonely, alienating, terrifying in its empty vastnesses and its inability to provide that sorely missed sensation of snug coziness which Americans misinterpret as overcrowding, that *gemütlich* feeling of

15. Rubin, *Injurious to Public Morals*, p. 83.

"being packed together like sardines" (*sushizume*).[16] A visit to the Grand Canyon, much like a trip to the moon, offers the Japanese tourist an experience of peering into the terrifyingly empty abyss of un-Japaneseness. The "thickness" of American culture is paradoxically perceived less from inside than from outside, in the waning cultural hegemony that has been the subject of passionate imitation around the world, a hegemony fabricated increasingly of images more than of substance: in the Hollywood movies that were already a cultural ideal for Tanizaki in the 1920s, the TV shows, the advertising, popular music, and fashions. To understand that these images are part and parcel of the fascination with and justification of the exercise of power is to begin to "read against culture" in both senses of that phrase.

In the last analysis, however, "reading against culture" is not something done by the critic, the reader, or even the author. It is, as I proposed at the end of Chapter 4, *an activity of the novel itself* as it perversely undoes the very real seams of that ostensibly seamless cultural fabric which it appears to be industriously engaged in stitching together.

In such an analysis, Sōseki's *Kokoro*, read today as a coming-of-age novel, becomes instead a potent attempt to dismantle the central ideological tenet of the Meiji emperor's Imperial Rescript on Education—the state's official rationale, promulgated twenty years before the novel was written, of an ideal of cultural continuity as modeled on the homology of the family-state. This official document upheld the validity of the received Mencian Confucian orthodoxy of human nature as essentially social and good, as opposed to Hsün Tzu's heterodox belief that it is essentially brute, antisocial, and evil. In theory, such an orthodoxy should render laws, punishments, and even education unnecessary, for it regards men as inherently amenable to social ideals and able to form themselves into an ideal social collective without need of compulsion. The more realistic if heterodox view of man's evil nature emphasized the central role of the teacher (*sensei*) in a process of socialization exterior to man himself: systems of education, of laws, of rewards and punishments. The possibility, given the imported Western idea of a modern individual self characterized by a frightening technological instrumentality and unencumbered by traditional social restraints, that Hsün Tzu's might have proved the more accurate vision of modern man drove the state to resist its devastating implications for the received sense of an ideal of "traditional" Japanese culture. (And here we understand that that received sense, to which we give the name "tradition," is always constructed, never simply "real.") In the face of a threat to social cohesion that was always identified as external,

16. This word has been used in a positive sense to describe to me the pleasant sensations stimulated by the crowded trains most Westerners find so trying. It might not be easy to find another culture that exalts the experience of sleeping in a single room of an inn together with as many skiers as can be squeezed through the door (the infamous *sukiiyazu beddo* or "skier's bed").

the state simply took the view that *Japanese* man was by nature inherently good and therefore by nature socially orthodox; it was only the corrupting nature of *foreign* man which, inherently evil, was dangerous heterodoxy and needed to be countered by the prophylaxis of education.

For Sōseki, the comforting sense of culture as a sort of communal public bath of shared norms had forever lost its old attraction, and no amount of official propaganda would be able to warm it up again: hence his intense irritation with the officially orchestrated patriotic exercises at the funeral of General Nogi. Rubin emphasizes also Sōseki's angry reaction to the attempt of the Ministry of Education to confer upon him a Doctor of Letters degree in 1911, rejecting it in a public act that "treated the Katsura government to a shock it was not prepared to handle."[17] *Kokoro* must thus be read as Sōseki's explanation of why he would not let the state reward him for being what he considered that impossible if necessary creature, a *sensei*; in his view the true function of the teacher is to reveal to humankind the horrifying nature of its own contemporary condition and the hypocritical nature of the state, not to serve the interests of that state in its old exercise of "rewarding virtue and punishing vice": that is, cynically filling its citizens full of pious propaganda (officially sanctioned education) about their inherently good nature while responding to their actual but unacknowledged evil with brutal laws.

Sōseki was far from the only writer to take such an alienated modern view. The tension between an official state ideology of culture and its subversion by contestatory voices and texts was at issue in his time and would remain so right up to the temporary setback of more harshly enforced censorship during World War II and the postwar occupation (when many simply stopped writing rather than knuckle under); and it resumed as soon as those restrictions were lifted. The murder of the proletarian writer Takeji Kobayashi by the police in 1933 was just one of those little demonstrations the state found it effective to stage from time to time; the state was greeted only with scorn, however, in its notorious 1972 attempt to prosecute the novelist Akiyuki Nosaka and a literary magazine that published his modern translation of a short erotic tale by Nagai Kafū. That reaction seems to reflect the traditional attitude that pornography was something that could be tolerated as the safer alternative to sedition.

This book, then, has called attention to the ways in which the writing of various authors, even as it unavoidably works within and contributes to an apparently seamless construction of culture, can be seen as simultaneously working against such a construction. Tanizaki's dark sexual perversions, for

---

17. Rubin, *Injurious to Public Morals*, p. 195. Rubin notes that the only mention of the Kōtoku Shūsui incident in Sōseki's writings is his inclusion in *And Then* (*Sore kara*, 1909) of the socialist in "a catalog of recent foolishness that includes the government's comical fear of Kōtoku, to spy on whom the Shinjuku police alone were spending over one hundred yen per month."

example, while clearly rooted in a profound psychological desire for infantil-
ization, just as clearly remain at least one step beyond the boundary of any
accepted sense of a "traditional" social order; I have shown how they subvert
even his own nostalgic recreation of tradition, "the folk," and a natural
cultural ecology of blood and soil. In Tanizaki's *Some Prefer Nettles*, the ideal
of a blissful dissolution of the self in the folk begins to come apart precisely
over the issue of the somewhat less than gladly "traditional" O-hisa's revulsion at the folk's lack of "sanitary facilities." (For all his famous prose about
Japan's "traditional" interior architectural aesthetic of darkness and
obscurity, in his essay *In Praise of Shadows*, Tanizaki had to confess that
where his own convenience and comfort—notably modern concepts—were
concerned, he personally preferred modern plumbing to the murky fra-
grance of the traditional outhouse.)[18] And it continues to come apart when a
hankering for the impurity of Western sexuality asserts itself as the necessary
complement of Kanamé's indulgence in an orgy of Japanese purity. The
tension at work as modernity inevitably erodes the credibility of constructions of "traditional" culture is especially conspicuous in the images of
Mishima, that zealous fanatic of Japaneseness (or perhaps more accurately,
of the Japanesque), muscularly lounging about his rococo fantasy of a Medi-
terranean villa, complete with Greek statuary and swimming pool, in Tokyo.

Again, Kawabata's attempt to recuperate male privilege in the face of the
(still) growing challenge to received gender norms posed by the situations of
modern women clearly reflects the force of the stormy social problematic,
even as it tries to overlay it (in the function of the night-mirror) with myth,
aestheticism, and the recreation of culture as nature itself. Though neither
the reader nor Kawabata ever seems quite so happy as when the author is
blinding us with blizzards of cherry blossoms, it is impossible not to notice,
even through the aesthetically pleasurable atmospherics, that his males
amount to little more than pale shadows projected by real and vital women.
His work is an excellent example of how an ideological problematic, having
taken refuge in the camouflage of culture as nature because of the danger of
appearing in the open, will inevitably irrupt from that artificial setting, like a
live animal from a museum diorama, in all its living force.

In the cases of Kōbō Abé and Kenzaburō Ōe, whose works have typically
been treated in Japan as inherently antagonistic to a received sense of culture, it has been my concern to show how, to the contrary, the alleged "un-
Japaneseness" of their work conceals fundamental problems of cultural
essentialism—especially ideas of the communal *Gemeinschaft* group
(*kyōdōtai*) and the folk cycle of group violence and individual expiation
(*ikki*)—which have remained unresolved in the general rush to read their

18. Tanizaki, *In Praise of Shadows*, p. 48.

thought and work as absurdist, surrealist, modernist and even postmodern, always "Western" in orientation: that is, as anything but Japanese. In much the same way, though in the opposite sense, I have endeavored to show how Mishima, portrayed to the West as either buffoon or saint, quite accurately perceives and analyzes the constituent elements of real cultural difference, even as he strives to close off all interpretation from other voices, whether from within or from without. These contradictions are reminiscent of Georg Lukács's well-known observation that it was precisely *because* of Balzac's staunch royalism that he proved to be a better observer than Zola, the archnaturalist. As Frederic Jameson has noted, "The great realists, Lukács tells us, are those who somehow fully participated in the life of their times, who were not mere observers, but actors also, 'engaged' in a far less limited and more political sense than in Sartre's familiar usage."[19] That Mishima was indeed an engaged actor, participating fully in the life of his times, there can be no argument; and we have seen in the life and fate of his character Honda what he thought of the "mere observer," that ideal of detachment celebrated by the earlier naturalist school.

In the last analysis, it may even be possible to regard Mishima's tetralogy as the death knell of an impossibly quixotic ultranationalism, and his own suicide as its grave monument. It may well be that in his work, as well as in his life and death, he managed to demonstrate, better than any liberal or left-wing writer could have done, the futility of an atavistic and reactionary politics of assassination. Mishima has perhaps ironically made it more diffi-cult for the ultranationalist right wing to be taken seriously as it tries to compensate for its growing irrelevance to Japan's modern condition by the insane volume of its ubiquitous loudspeaker trucks. Ultranationalist acts of assassination and suicide may no longer call to mind the historical heroism of Mishima's idol Heihachirō Oshio (who in 1837 led, and died in, a local uprising) or even of his mythical warrior Isao, as much as they will the desperate fantasies of the narcissist in paramilitary drag.

Finally, if Takeshi Kaikō returned to Japan from the torment of the 1960s to fish, eat and drink well, appear as a popular guest on TV shows, and smoke himself to death in the congenial company of that same coterie of paralyzed intellectuals he (and Mishima) once railed so bitterly against, he did so because, not being a social revolutionary, he had managed (as nearly everyone finally does) to make that separate peace with his own culture which seems almost to define middle age. His work is remarkably uninterested in participating in the construction of a cozy cultural context for itself, and he remained to the end as fond of poking fun at his beloved Japanese culture as at that of foreigners. Toward the end of his life he wrote of the weary traveler

19. Jameson, *Marxism and Form*, pp. 202–4.

to foreign lands who returns home to sigh with relief, "Ah, isn't Japan wonderful!"—only to observe all the more keenly the next day, with eyes renewed by travel, the filth, overcrowding, exorbitant prices, and exclusivism. Why do I write of such things? Kaikō asks, and answers in the words of the great Chinese patriot and revolutionary Lu Xun: "The more a man loves his country, the more he is willing to speak ill of it."[20] It is a motto that might serve anyone well.

Kaikō's position may recall to the reader our initial goal of "heterogeneity," Catharine Stimpson's appeal for "living generously with all but homicidal difference."[21] For even if we are intellectually disposed to accept a principle of generosity, of inclusivity, of difference, we are still confronted in the real world, at home as well as abroad, not only with our own manifest failures to have achieved this goal but also with belligerent and even homicidal assertions of exclusivity, sameness, and identity. Stimpson's principle has emerged from the many overlapping projects of women's studies, and "women"—even granting that their interests are not unitary enough to identify them as a homogeneous group—have been unlikely to find as much ground for antagonism toward one another or toward men as have historically rival and even murderous racial, ethnic, religious, and national groupings. Intolerance anywhere continually erodes the possibility of heterogeneity, as does state sponsorship of terrorism, political exclusion, or the marginalization of dissenting voices.

Even though we are not talking here about anything as tangible as international trade, budget deficits, or global military, political, and economic strategy, in the area of the complex and difficult issues of representation and ideology we *are* talking nonetheless about national territories, if virtual ones, marked by their own territorial claims, border defenses, and immigration policies. The West has for a long time prevailed in a now declining world hegemony over important areas of cultural representation, and that decline reopens the inevitability of contention. As only one part of the greater cultural intercourse, enormous amounts of Western fiction have been translated and purchased each year in Japan ever since the opening to the West, and there has been a regular, if much smaller Western commerce in Japanese literature. Indeed, this book is predicated on the existence in the United States of a recognized corpus of modern Japanese novels available in English translation and increasingly taught in classes not necessarily specializing in Japanese literature, in literature, or even in Japan (though the number of

20. Kaikō Takeshi, "Subete wa 'Yamata no Orochi,'" in *Kaiko ichiban* (Tokyo: Shinchō Bunkō, 1984), p. 169. This title means something like "Japan is all a myth": Yamata no Orochi is the fearsome mythical serpent that was beheaded by the culture hero Susanoō and whose many tails became the rivers of Japan.
21. Stimpson, "Woolf's Room," p. 143.

Japanese novels regularly available in English appears if anything to have decreased since the early 1980s. The American public may have had its problems with the idea of "selling off America" to the Japanese (though apparently not to the English, French, Dutch, or Australians), but it was only when giant entertainment and media conglomerates went on the block—the very institutions of U.S. cultural hegemony itself—that howls of outrage were heard (by the media): were Americans now going to have to make their movies and songs conform to Japanese tastes? The Japanese purchasers have had to reassure the American public that they are happy enough with the profitmaking power of such industries as they are—a situation which, however, is bound to change as cultural hegemony changes hands.

What is at stake here, then, is an attempt to evolve a practice of reading the cultural artifacts that are vying for representational hegemony. This is a practice, as I wrote in the Introduction, which consciously recognizes, seeks out, and tries to take account of difference in the belief that if what I have called deterritorialization is desirable, it will become possible only by means of a difficult dialectical accounting of the particular ways that power has been articulated through various particular cultural constructions in the creation and maintenance of our own and others' territories. Those territories may be virtual, but their reality is attested by the way they are overtly or covertly contested and defined in and by novels, which assert a very material reality both in the economic terms of monetary exchange and in the representational terms of their power to speak for, claim, and maintain in the face of others' claims particular privileged points of view. As primary forms of representation, novels at once gratifyingly reflect our cultural attitudes back to us and, equally gratifyingly, project them outward toward others for the purpose of asserting and confirming our own positions, creating the cultural terms within which we expect to be read. It remains unclear whether they can do this without simultaneously denying to others the right to confirmation of their own.

As we have seen, however, novels are always subversive of our most determined efforts to confine their representation to the sorts of gratifying manifestations of communal social myths to which we might all happily subscribe, like contented children in one big happy family before the sandman comes. Even those genres most obviously invested in confirming this mythical entity and displacing otherness elsewhere—that is, the ever popular spy, murder, romance, and horror stories—if read beyond their usual summery intentions of amusement and self-gratification, possess (in what Freud called "the uncanny," now recognized as a central feature of fairytales before they were pabulumized) an inherent boreal power to make us distrust the desire they exert for yet more *jouissance*, by which I mean not liberation but compulsive, mindless, and repetitive excitement and release. Real liberation will be found only in the less immediately gratifying, more complex, difficult, but invigorating and, I hope, ultimately revitalizing act that I have called "reading against culture."

Bibliography

Abé, Kōbō. *Mikkai*. In *Abe Kōbō zensakuhin*, n.s. vol. 10. Tokyo: Shinchōsha. 1979.
———. *Moetsukita chizu*. In *Abe Kōbō zensakuhin*, vol. 8. Tokyo: Shinchōsha, 1972.
———. *The Ruined Map*. Trans. E. Dale Saunders. Rutland, Vt.: Tuttle, 1969.
———. *Secret Rendezvous*. Tokyo: Tuttle, 1981.
———. "SF no ryūkō ni tsuite" (On the popularity of SF). In *Abe Kōbō zensakuhin*, vol. 15. Tokyo: Shinchōsha, 1973.
———. *Suna no onna*. In *Abe Kōbō zensakuhin*, vol. 8. Tokyo: Shinchōsha, 1970.
———. "Toshi" (The city). In *Abe Kōbō zensakuhin*, vol. 15. Tokyo: Shinchōsha, 1973.
———. *The Woman in the Dunes*. Trans. E. Dale Saunders. New York: Knopf, 1964.
Achebe, Chinua. *Hopes and Impediments: Selected Essays*. New York: Doubleday, 1989.
Adorno, T. W. *Aesthetic Theory*. Trans. C. Lenhardt. London: Routledge & Kegan Paul, 1984.
Ahmed, Aijaz. "Jameson's Rhetoric of Otherness and the 'National Allegory.'" *Social Text* 15 (Fall 1986): 3–27.
Althusser, Louis. "Ideology and Ideological State Apparatuses." In *Lenin and Philosophy, and Other Essays*. London: New Left Books, 1971.
Arima, Tatsuo. *The Failure of Freedom: A Portrait of Modern Japanese Intellectuals*. Cambridge, Mass.: Harvard University Press, 1969.
Asada, Akira. "Infantile Capitalism and Japan's Postmodernism: A Fairy Tale." *South Atlantic Quarterly* 87, no. 3 (1989): 629–34.
Atōda, Takashi. *Kuroi hako* (Black box). Tokyo: Shinchōsha, 1986.
Auerbach, Erich. *Mimesis*. Princeton: Princeton University Press, 1974.
Barthes, Roland. *The Empire of Signs*. Trans. Richard Howard. New York: Hill & Wang, 1982.
———. *Mythologies*. Trans. Annette Lavers. New York: Hill & Wang, 1972.
———. *The Rustle of Language*. Trans. Richard Howard. New York: Hill & Wang, 1986.
Basic Writings of Mo Tzu, Hsün Tzu, and Han Fei Tzu. Trans. Burton Watson. New York: Columbia University Press, 1967.
Benedict, Ruth. *The Chrysanthemum and the Sword: Patterns of Japanese Culture*. Boston: Houghton Mifflin, 1946.
Bennett, Tony. *Formalism and Marxism*. New York: Methuen, 1979.
Bhabha, Homi, ed. *Nation and Narrative*. London: Routledge, 1990.
Biggers, Earl Derr. *The House without a Key*. New York: Grosset & Dunlap, 1925.

Bix, Herbert P. *Peasant Protest in Japan, 1590–1884.* New Haven: Yale University Press, 1986.

Blacker, Carmen. *The Japanese Enlightenment: A Study of the Writings of Fukuzawa Yukichi.* Cambridge: Cambridge University Press, 1964.

Bowen, Roger. Review article. *Journal of Asian Studies* 47, no. 4 (1988): 821–32.

Boyle, T. Coraghessan. *East Is East.* New York: Viking, 1990.

Brantlinger, Patrick. "Victorians and Africans: the Genealogy of the Myth of the Dark Continent." *Critical Inquiry* 12 (Autumn 1985): 167–203.

Bryson, Norman. *Vision and Painting: The Logic of the Gaze.* New Haven: Yale University Press, 1983.

――――. *Word and Image: French Painting of the Ancien Régime.* Cambridge: Cambridge University Press, 1981.

Burch, Noel. *To the Distant Observer: Form and Meaning in the Japanese Cinema.* London: Scholar Press, 1979.

Caudill, William, and David W. Plath. "Who Sleeps by Whom? Parent-Child Involvement in Urban Japanese Families." In *Japanese Culture and Behavior,* ed. Takie Sugiyama Lebra and William Lebra. Honolulu: University of Hawaii Press, 1974.

Chan, Wing-tsit. *A Source Book in Chinese Philosophy.* Princeton: Princeton University Press, 1963.

Chikamatsu, Monzaemon. *The Love Suicides at Amijima.* Trans. Donald Keene. In *Four Major Plays of Chikamatsu.* New York: Columbia University Press, 1964.

Clifford, James. "On Ethnographic Allegory." In *Writing Culture: The Poetics and Politics of Ethnography,* ed. James Clifford and George E. Marcus. Berkeley: University of Calif. Press, 1986.

――――. "On Orientalism." In *The Predicament of Culture: Twentieth-Century Ethnography, Literature, and Art.* Cambridge, Mass.: Harvard University Press, 1988.

Conrad, Joseph. *Heart of Darkness.* In *Great Short Works of Joseph Conrad,* ed. Jerry Allen. New York: Harper & Row, 1967.

Crapanzano, Vincent. "Hermes' Dilemma: The Masking of Subversion in Ethnographic Description." In *Writing Culture: The Poetics and Politics of Ethnography,* ed. James E. Clifford and George E. Marcus. Berkeley: University of California Press, 1986.

Culler, Jonathan. "Comparative Literature and the Pieties." *MLA Profession 86,* pp. 30–32.

Dale, Peter N. *The Myth of Japanese Uniqueness.* Kent: Croom Helm, 1986.

De Man, Paul. *Blindness and Insight: Essays in the Rhetoric of Contemporary Criticism.* Minneapolis: University of Minnesota Press, 1983.

Derrida, Jacques. *Of Grammatology.* Trans. Gayatri Chakrovorty Spivak. Baltimore: Johns Hopkins University Press, 1976.

――――. "Structure, Sign, and Play in the Discourse of the Human Sciences." In *Writing and Difference,* trans. Alan Bass. Chicago: University of Chicago Press, 1978.

Descartes, René. *Discourse on Method and the Meditations.* Trans. F. E. Sutcliffe. London: Penguin, 1968.

DeVos, George, and Hiroshi Wagatsuma. "Alienation and the Author: A Triptych on Social Conformity and Deviancy in Japanese Intellectuals." In *Socialization for Achievement,* ed. George DeVos. Berkeley: University of California Press, 1973.

Doi, Takeo. *Amae no kōzō*. Tokyo: Kōbundō, 1971.
———. *The Anatomy of Dependence*. Trans. John Bester. New York: Kodansha International, 1973.
Eagleton, Terry. *Criticism and Ideology*. London: New Left Books, 1985.
———. *Ideology: an Introduction*. London: Verso, 1991.
———. *The Ideology of the Aesthetic*. London: Blackwell, 1990.
———. *Literary Theory: an Introduction*. Minneapolis: University of Minnesota Press, 1983.
Eberhard, Wolfram, ed. *Folktales of China*. Chicago: Chicago University Press, 1965.
Eliot, George. *Middlemarch*. 1872; Harmondsworth: Penguin Books, 1974.
Endō, Shūsaku. *Foreign Studies* (Ryūgaku). Trans. Mark Williams. Tokyo: Tuttle, 1989.
Espmark, Kjell. *The Nobel Prize in Literature: A Study of the Criteria behind the Choices*. Boston: G. K. Hall, 1986.
Eysteinsson, Astradur. *The Concept of Modernism*. Ithaca: Cornell University Press, 1990.
Foucault, Michel. *The Order of Things*. New York: Vintage Books, 1973.
Fowler, Edward. *The Rhetoric of Confession: Shishōsetsu in Early Twentieth-Century Japanese Fiction*. Berkeley: University of California Press, 1988.
Frankel, Hans. "T'ang Literati: A Composite Biography." In *Confucianism and Chinese Civilization*, ed. Arthur F. Wright. New York: Atheneum, 1959.
Freud, Sigmund. "The Uncanny." In *Sigmund Freud: Collected Papers*, ed. Ernest Jones, trans. Joan Rivière. London: Hogarth, 1956.
Fukuzawa, Yukichi. *Fuku Yukichi's "An Encouragement of Learning."* Trans. and ed. David A. Dilworth and Umeyo Hirano (Tokyo: Sophia University Press, 1969.
———. *Gakumon no susume*. In *Fukuzawa Yukichi zenshū*, vol. 3. Tokyo: Iwanami Shoten, 1960.
Furubayashi, Takashi. *Taidan: Mishima Yukio—saigo no kotoba* (Interview: Yukio Mishima—his last words). Tokyo: Shinchō Kasetto, 1989. Sound recording.
Geertz, Clifford. *The Interpretation of Cultures*. New York: Basic Books, 1973.
Gluck, Carol. *Japan's Modern Myths: Ideology in the Late Meiji Period*. Princeton: Princeton University Press, 1985.
Graves, Robert. *The Greek Myths*. Baltimore: Pelican Books, 1966.
Green, Geoffrey. *Literary Criticism and the Structures of History: Erich Auerbach and Leo Spitzer*. Lincoln, University of Nebraska Press, 1982.
Hamaguchi, Esyun. "A Contextual Model of the Japanese: Toward a Methodological Innovation in Japan Studies." *Journal of Japanese Studies* 11, no. 2 (1985): 289–321.
Hamaguchi, Esyun, and Kumon Shumpei, eds. *Nihonteki shūdan-shugi* (Japanese Collectivism). Tokyo: Yūhikaku, 1982.
Harootunian, H. D. "Between Politics and Culture: Authority and the Ambiguities of Intellectual Life in Imperial Japan." In *Japan in Crisis: Essays on Taishō Democracy*, ed. Bernard S. Silverman and H. D. Harootunian. Princeton: Princeton University Press, 1974.
———. "Disciplinizing Native Knowledge and Producing Place: Yanagita Kunio, Origuchi Shinobu, Takata Yasuma." In *Japanese Intellectuals during the Interwar Years*, ed. J. Thomas Rimer. Princeton: Princeton University Press, 1990.

_____. *Things Seen and Unseen: Discourse and Ideology in Tokugawa Nativism*. Chicago: University of Chicago Press, 1988.

Hasegawa, Izumi. "*Senbazuru* to *Yama no oto*" (1972). In *Kawabata Yasunari*, ed. Nihon Bungaku Kenkyū Shinkōkai. Tokyo: Yūseidō, 1973.

Hayles, N. Katherine. *The Cosmic Web: Scientific Field Models and Literary Strategies in the Twentieth Century*. Ithaca: Cornell University Press, 1984.

Hegel, G. W. F. *Hegel's Phenomenology of Spirit*. Trans. A. V. Miller. Oxford: Oxford University Press, 1977.

Hever, Hannan. "Hebrew in an Israeli Arab Hand: Six Miniatures on Anton Shammas' *Arabesques*." *Cultural Critique*, Fall 1987, pp. 47–76.

Hsu, Francis L. K. *Iemoto: The Heart of Japan*. New York: Wiley, 1975.

Irokawa, Daikichi. *The Culture of the Meiji Period*. Trans. Marius B. Jansen. Princeton: Princeton University Press, 1985.

_____. "The Survival Struggle of the Japanese Community." In *Authority and the Individual in Japan: Citizen Protest in Historical Perspective*, ed. J. Victor Koschmann. Tokyo: University of Tokyo Press, 1978.

Ivy, Marilyn. "Discourses of the Vanishing in Contemporary Japan." Ph.D. diss., Cornell University, 1988.

Iwamoto, Yoshio. "The Nobel Prize in Literature, 1967–87: A Japanese View." *World Literature Today*, special issue: (Spring 1988), "The Nobel Prizes in Literature, 1967–87: A Symposium."

Jameson, Fredric. *Marxism and Form: Twentieth-Century Dialectical Theories of Literature*. Princeton: Princeton University Press, 1971.

_____. "On Raymond Chandler." In *The Poetics of Murder: Detective Fiction and Literary Theory*, ed. Glenn W. Most and William W. Stowe. New York: Harcourt Brace Jovanovich, 1983.

_____. *The Political Unconscious: Narrative as a Socially Symbolic Act*. Ithaca: Cornell University Press, 1979.

_____. "Third-World Literature in the Era of Multinational Capitalism." *Social Text* 15 (Fall 1986): 65–88.

Jay, Martin. "In the Empire of the Gaze: Foucault and the Denigration of Vision in Twentieth Century French Thought." In *A Foucault Reader*, ed. Paul Rabinow. New York: Pantheon Books, 1984.

Johnson, Chalmers. *MITI and the Japanese Miracle*. Stanford, Calif.: Stanford University Press, 1982.

Kafū, Nagai. "Hanabi" (Fireworks). in *Kafū zenshū*, vol. 15. Tokyo: Iwanami Shoten, 1962.

Kaikō, Takeshi. *Darkness in Summer*. Trans. Cecilia Segawa Seigle. New York: Knopf, 1973.

_____. *Into a Black Sun*. Trans. Cecilia Segawa Seigle. New York: Kodansha International, 1980.

_____. *Kagayakeru yami*. In *Kaikō Takeshi zensakuhin*, vol. 8. Tokyo: Shinchōsha, 1968.

_____. *Natsu no yami*. In *Kaikō Takeshi zensakuhin*, vol. 9. Tokyo: Shinchōsha, 1971.

_____. "Ojisama no tanoshimi" (The Pleasures of being an older guy). In *Kaiko Ichiban*. Tokyo: Shinchō Bunkō, 1984.

_____. "Subete wa 'Yamata no Orochi.'" In *Kaiko Ichiban*. Tokyo: Shinchō Bunkō, 1984.

Kawabata, Yasunari. *Senbazuru*. In *Gendai Nihon Bungaku Taikei*, vol. 52, *Kawabata Yasunari shū*. Tokyo: Chikuma Shobō, 1969.
———. *Snow Country*. Trans. Edward G. Seidensticker. New York: Knopf, 1969.
———. *Thousand Cranes*. Trans. Edward G. Seidensticker. New York: Knopf, 1968.
———. *Utsukushii Nihon no watakushi; Japan the Beautiful and Myself*. Bilingual ed. Trans. Edward G. Seidensticker. Tokyo: Kodansha International, 1969.
———. *Yama no oto*. In *Kawabata Yasunari zenshū*, vol. 8. Tokyo: Shinchōsha, 1959.
———. *Yukiguni*. In *Gendai Nihon Bungaku Taikei*, vol. 52, *Kawabata Yasunari shū*. Tokyo: Chikuma Shobō, 1969.
Kawatake, Toshio. "Nihon no geinō: Dentō geijutsu, koten geinō" (Japanese performing arts: Traditional arts, classical performing arts). In *Kōza Bigaku*, vol. 4, *Geijutsu no shosō*, ed. Imamichi Tomonobu. Tokyo: Tōkyō Daigaku Shuppanbu, 1984.
Keene, Donald. "Japanese Writers and the Greater East Asia War." In *Appreciations of Japanese Culture*. Tokyo: Kodansha International, 1981.
Kipling, Rudyard. *Kipling's Japan: Collected Writings*. Ed. Hugh Cortazzi and George Webb. London: Athlone Press, 1988.
Kristeva, Julia. *About Chinese Women*. Trans. Anita Barrows. London: Marian Boyars, 1977.
Kumon, Shumpei. "Some Principles Governing the Thought and Behavior of Japanists (Contextualists)." *Journal of Japanese Studies* 8, no. 1 (1982): 5–28.
Kyoraisho. ed. Ijichi Tetsuya et al. In *Nihon Koten Bungaku zenshū*, vol. 51. Tokyo: Shogakukan, 1973.
Lacan, Jacques. "The Mirror Stage as Formative of the Function of the I" (1949). In *Ecrits: A Selection*, trans. Alan Sheridan. New York: Norton, 1977.
———. "The Signification of the Phallus." In *Ecrits: A Selection*, trans. Alan Sheridan. New York: Norton, 1977.
LaCapra, Dominick. *Soundings in Critical Theory*. Ithaca: Cornell University Press, 1989.
Lau, D. C. *Mencius*. London: Penguin Books, 1970.
Lévi-Strauss, Claude. *Tristes Tropiques*. Trans. John and Doreen Weightman. New York: Pocket Books, 1977.
Lukács, Georg. "Reification and the Consciousness of the Proletariat." In *History and Class Consciousness: Studies in Marxist Dialectics*, trans. Rodney Livingstone. Cambridge, Mass.: MIT Press, 1986.
Lyotard, Jean-François. *The Postmodern Condition: A Report on Knowledge*. Trans. Geoff Bennington and Brian Massumi. Foreword Fredric Jameson. Minneapolis: University of Minnesota Press, 1984.
McMaster, Graham. "Henry James and India: A Historical Reading of *The Turn of the Screw*." *CLIO* 18. no. 1 (1988): 23–40.
Miller, Christopher L. *Blank Darkness: Africanist Discourse in French*. Chicago: University of Chicago Press, 1985.
———. "Theories of Africans: The Question of Literary Anthropology." *Critical Inquiry* 13 (Autumn 1986): 120–39.
Miller, Roy Andrew. *The Japanese Language in Contemporary Japan: Some Sociolinguistic Observations*. Washington, D.C.: American Enterprise Institute for Public Policy Research, 1977.

_____. *Japan's Modern Myth: The Language and Beyond*. New York: Weatherhill, 1982.
Miner, Earl. *Japanese Poetic Diaries*. Berkeley: University of California Press, 1976.
Mishima, Yukio. "Bunka bōei ron" (On the defense of culture). In *Mishima Yukio zenshū*, vol. 33. Tokyo: Shinchōsha, 1976.
_____. "Chōju no geijutsu no hana o: Kawabatashi no jūshō ni yosete." *Mishima Yukio zenshū*, vol. 33. Tokyo: Shinchōsha, 1976.
_____. "Gendai bungaku no san hōkō" (Three directions in modern literature). In *Mishima Yukio zenshū*, vol. 31. Tokyo: Shinchōsha, 1975.
_____. *Hōjō no Umi*. In *Mishima Yukio zenshū*, vol. 18 (*Haru no yuki*, and *Homba*); vol. 19 (*Akatsuki no tera*, and *Tennin no gosui*). Tokyo: Shinchōsha, 1973.
_____. "*Hōjō no Umi* ni tsuite" (On *The Sea of Fertility*). In *Mishima Yukio zenshū*, vol. 34. Tokyo: Shinchōsha, 1976.
_____. "Koma" (The spinning top). In *Mishima Yukio zenshū*, vol. 34. Tokyo: Shinchōsha, 1976.
_____. "Puraibashii" (Privacy). In *Mishima Yukio zenshū*, vol. 30. Tokyo: Shinchōsha, 1975.
_____. *The Sea of Fertility*. 4 vols.: *Spring Snow*, trans. Michael Gallagher; *Runaway Horses*, trans. Michael Gallagher; *The Temple of the Dawn*, trans. E. Dale Saunders and Cecilia Segawa Seigle; *Decay of the Angel*, trans. Edward G. Seidensticker. New York: Pocket Books, 1978.
_____. "Shōsetsu towa nanika" (What is 'the novel'?). In *Mishima Yukio zenshū*, vol. 33. Tokyo: Shinchōsha, 1976.
Miyoshi, Masao. *Accomplices of Silence*. Berkeley: University of California Press, 1974.
_____. "Against the Grain: The Japanese Novel and the 'Postmodern' West." *South Atlantic Quarterly* 87, no. 3 (1989): 525–50.
Miyoshi, Masao, and Harry Harootunian, eds. *Postmodernism and Japan*. Durham, N.C.: Duke University Press, 1989.
Mouer, Ross E., and Yoshio Sugimoto. *Images of Japanese Society: A Study in the Social Construction of Reality*. London: Kegan Paul International, 1990.
Murakami, Haruki. *Noruuei no mori*. Tokyo: Kodansha, 1987.
_____. *Norwegian Wood*. 2 vols. Trans. Alfred Birnbaum. Tokyo: Kodansha International, 1989.
Naipaul, V. S. *An Area of Darkness*. New York: Vintage Books, 1964.
_____. *India: A Wounded Civilization*. New York: Vintage Books, 1976.
Nerval, Gérard de. *Journey to the Orient*. London: Michael Haag, 1984.
Nixon, Rob. "London Calling: V. S. Naipaul and the License of Exile." *South Atlantic Quarterly* 87, no. 1 (1988): 1–37.
Noguchi, Takehiko. "Mishima Yukio and Kita Ikki: The Aesthetics and Politics of Ultranationalism in Japan." *Journal of Japanese Studies* 10, no. 2 (1984): 437–54.
Nosaka, Akiyuki. "American Hijiki" (*Amerika hijiki*). Trans. Jay Rubin. In *Contemporary Japanese Literature*, ed. Howard Hibbett. New York: Knopf, 1977.
Oda, Makoto. "The Ethics of Peace." In *Authority and the Individual in Japan: Citizen Protest in Historical Perspective*, ed. J. Victor Koschmann. Tokyo: University of Tokyo Press, 1978.
Ōe, Kenzaburō. "Japan's Dual Identity: A Writer's Dilemma." *World Literature Today* 62, no. 3 (1988): 359–69.

_____. *Kojinteki na taiken*. In *Ōe Kenzaburō zensakuhin*, vol. 6. Tokyo: Shinchōsha, 1966.

_____. *Man'en gannen no futtobōru*. In *Ōe Kenzaburō zensakuhin*, 2d ser., vol. 1. Tokyo: Shinchōsha, 1977.

_____. "Nijusseiki e mukete: Sakka no yakuwari" (Toward the twentieth century: The role of the writer). *Kokusai kōryū* 14, no. 1 (1990): 100–109.

_____. *A Personal Matter*. Trans. John Nathan. New York: Grove Press, 1969.

_____. *The Silent Cry*. Trans. John Bester. New York: Kodansha International, 1974.

Okōchi, Kazuo. *Reimeiki no Nihon rōdō undō* (The dawn of the Japanese labor movement). Tokyo: Iwanami Shinsho, 1952.

Ong, Walter. *Orality and Literacy: The Technologizing of the Word*. London: Methuen, 1983.

Otsuka, Hisao. *Kyōdōtai no kiso riron* (The community and its theoretical basis). Tokyo: Iwanami, 1955.

Passin, Herbert. *Society and Education in Japan*. New York: Teachers College, Columbia University, East Asia Institute, 1965.

Plaks, Andrew. *Archetype and Allegory in the Dream of the Red Chamber*. Princeton: Princeton University Press, 1979.

Poe, Edgar Allan. *The Works of Edgar Allan Poe*. Vols. 1–2. Ed. Edmund Clarence Stedman and George Edward Woodberry. New York: Scribner, 1894.

Pollack, David. "Action as Fitting Match to Knowledge: Language and Symbol in Mishima's *Kinkakuji*." *Monumenta Nipponica* 40, no. 4 (1985): 387–98.

_____. *The Fracture of Meaning: Japan's Synthesis of China from the Eighth through the Eighteenth Centuries*. Princeton: Princeton University Press, 1986.

_____. "Modernism Minceur; or, Is Japan Postmodern?" *Monumenta Nipponica* 44, no. 1 (1989): 75–97.

_____. "Wang Wei in Kamakura: A Consideration of the Structural Poetics of Mishima's *Spring Snow*." *Harvard Journal of Asiatic Studies* 48, no. 2 (1988): 383–402.

Porter, Dennis. "Backward Construction and the Art of Suspense." In *The Pursuit of Crime*, ed. Dennis Porter. New Haven: Yale University Press, 1981.

Pyle, Kenneth. *The New Generation in Meiji Japan: Problems of Cultural Identity, 1885–1895*. Palo Alto, Calif.: Stanford University Press, 1965.

Reiff, Philip, ed. *General Psychological Theory*. New York: Macmillan, 1965.

Rimer, J. Thomas. *Modern Japanese Fiction and Its Traditions*. Princeton: Princeton University Press, 1978.

Rohlich, Thomas H. *A Tale of Eleventh-Century Japan: Hamamatsu Chūnagon monogatari*. Princeton: Princeton University Press, 1983.

Roth, Philip. *The Professor of Desire*. New York: Farrar, Straus & Giroux, 1977.

Rubin, Jay. "The Evil and the Ordinary in Sōseki's Fiction." *Harvard Journal of Asiatic Studies* 46, no. 2 (1986): 333–52.

_____. *Injurious to Public Morals: Writers and the Meiji State*. Seattle: University of Washington Press, 1984.

_____. "Sōseki on individualism: *Watakushi no kojinshugi*." *Monumenta Nipponica* 34, no. 1 (1979): 21–48.

Said, Edward W. *Orientalism*. New York: Vintage Books, 1978.

_____. "Orientalism Reconsidered." *Cultural Critique* 1 (Fall 1985): 89–107.

———. "Representing the Colonized: Anthropology's Interlocutors." *Critical Inquiry* 15 (Winter 1989): 205–25.

———. *The World, the Text, and the Critic.* Cambridge, Mass.: Harvard University Press, 1983.

Scheiner, Irwin. "Benevolent Lords and Honorable Peasants." In *Japanese Thought in the Tokugawa Period, 1600–1868: Methods and Metaphors*, ed. Tetsuo Najita and Irwin Scheiner. Chicago: University of Chicago Press, 1978.

Schorske, Carl. *Fin-de-Sìecle Vienna: Politics and Culture.* New York: Vintage Books, 1981.

Seidensticker, Edward G. *Kafū the Scribbler.* Palo Alto, Calif.: Stanford University Press, 1965.

Sennett, Richard. *The Fall of Public Man.* New York: Knopf, 1977.

Shively, Donald. "Bakufu *vs* Kabuki." In *Studies in the Institutional History of Early Modern Japan*, ed. Robert Hall and Marius Jansen. Princeton: Princeton University Press, 1968.

Silverman, Kaja. *The Subject of Semiotics.* Oxford: Oxford University Press, 1983.

Sollers, Philippe. "On n'a encore rien vu." *Tel Quel* 85 (1988).

Sōseki, Natsumé. *Kokoro.* Trans. Edwin McClellan. Chicago: Henry Regnery, 1957.

———. *Kokoro* (Heart). In *Sōseki zenshū*, vol. 9. Tokyo: Iwanami Shoten, 1928–29.

———. *Sōseki bungaku senshū.* ed. Ara Masatō. 11 vols. Tokyo: Shūeisha, 1974.

———. *Sōseki zenshū.* 20 vols. Tokyo: Iwanami Shoten, 1928–29.

Spivak, Gayatri Chakravorty. *In Other Worlds: Essays in Cultural Politics.* New York: Methuen, 1987.

Stimpson, Catharine R. "Woolf's Room, Our Project: The Building of Feminist Criticism." In *The Future of Literary Theory*, ed. Ralph Cohen. New York: Routledge, 1990.

Takakusu, Junjiro. *The Essentials of Buddhist Philosophy.* Honolulu: University of Hawaii Press, 1947.

Tanizaki, Jun'ichirō. *Chijin no ai.* In *Tanizaki Jun'ichirō zenshū*, vol. 10. Tokyo: Chūōkōronsha, 1961.

———. *Diary of a Mad Old Man.* Trans. Howard Hibbett. New York: Knopf, 1965.

———. "Haha o kouru ki." In *Tanizaki Jun'ichirō zenshū*, vol. 7. Tokyo: Chūōkōronsha, 1958.

———. *In Praise of Shadows (In'ei raisan).* Trans. T. J. Harper and E. G. Seidensticker. New Haven, Conn.: Leete's Island Books, 1977.

———. "Longing for Mother." Trans. Edward Fowler. *Monumenta Nipponica* 35, no. 4 (1980): 467–84.

———. *Naomi.* Trans. Anthony Chambers. New York: Knopf, 1985.

———. *Some Prefer Nettles.* Trans. Edward Seidensticker. New York: Knopf, 1955.

———. *Tade kuu mushi.* In *Tanizaki Jun'ichirō zenshū*, vol. 12. Tokyo: Chūōkōronsha, 1973.

———. *Tanizaki Jun'ichirō zenshū.* 15 vols. Tokyo: Chūōkōronsha, 1958–73.

Theroux, Paul. *The Mosquito Coast.* Boston: Houghton Mifflin, 1982.

Thody, Philip. *Roland Barthes: A Conservative Estimate.* London: Macmillan, 1977.

Tōkyō Gakugei Daigaku Nihonshi Kenkyūshitsu, ed. *Nihonshi nempyō* (A chronology of Japanese history). Tokyo: Tokyōdō, 1984.

Tsurumi, Shunsuke. *A Cultural History of Postwar Japan*. London: KPI, 1987.

Tu, Wei-ming. *Centrality and Commonality: An Essay on Confucian Religiousness*. Albany: State University of New York Press, 1989.

Twain, Mark. *A Connecticut Yankee in King Arthur's Court*. London: Penguin Classics, 1986.

Two Zen Classics: "Mumonkan" and "Hekiganroku." Ed. and trans. Katsuki Sekida. New York: Weatherhill, 1977.

Ungar, Steven. *Roland Barthes: The Professor of Desire*. Lincoln: University of Nebraska Press, 1983.

Walker, Janet A. *The Japanese Novel of the Meiji Period and the Ideal of Individualism*. Princeton: Princeton University Press, 1979.

Watt, Ian. *The Rise of the Novel*. Berkeley: University of California Press, 1960.

Waugh, Patricia. *Metafiction: The Theory and Practice of Self-Conscious Fiction*. New York: Methuen, 1984.

Wilde, Oscar. "The Decay of Lying." *Nineteenth Century*, January 1889. In *The Complete Works of Oscar Wilde*. London: Collins, 1966.

Wilson, Michiko N. *The Marginal World of Ōe Kenzaburō: A Study in Themes and Techniques*. Armonk, N.Y.: M. E. Sharpe, 1986.

Wolferen, Karel van. *The Enigma of Japanese Power: People and Politics in a Stateless Nation*. London: Macmillan, 1989.

Yoshida, Sanroku. "An Interview with Kenzaburo Ōe." *World Literature Today* 62, no. 3 (1988): 369–374.

———. "Kenzaburo Ōe: A New World of Imagination." *Comparative Literature Studies* 22, no. 1 (1985): 80–96.

Yoshimura, Teiji, "*Senbazuru* ron." In *Kawabata Yasunari no ningen to geijutsu*, ed. Kawabata Bungaku Kenkyūkai. Tokyo: Kyōiku Shuppan Sentaa, 1971.

Yu, Beongcheon. *Natsume Sōseki*. New York: Twayne, 1969.

Zola, Emile. *Thérèse Raquin*. New York: Penguin, 1986.

Index

Library of Congress Cataloging-in-Publication Data

Pollack, David.
  Reading against culture : ideology and narrative in the Japanese novel / David
Pollack.
    p. cm.
  Includes bibliographical references and index.
  ISBN 0-8014-2752-5 (cloth). — ISBN 0-8014-8035-3 (pbk.)
   1. Japanese fiction—20th century—History and criticism.
2. Culture in literature. 3. Ideology and literature. 4. Japan—
Civilization—Philosophy. I. Title.
PL747.65.P65   1992
895.6'34409—dc20

                                 92-52769